"This is the Christian's answer to Bennett's *Book of Virtues*, compiled by one of the best-read and best-informed personalities on the intellectual circuit."

—LARRY WOIWODE
Best-selling Author, The Neumiller Stories *and* Acts

"*The Christian Treasury* is full of surprises . . . some will delight, encourage and edify; others will provoke . . . all are worth reading."

—MARVIN OLASKY
Acclaimed Author, The Tragedy of American Compassion

"What a surprising diversity of voices Lissa Roche has assembled in this Christian treasury—each witnessing in his or her unique way to the extraordinary power and lovability of the Christian message. Here indeed is God's plenty."

—PAUL MARIANI
Poet; Author, Prime Mover *and* Salvage Operations;
Professor of English, University of Massachusetts

"Lissa Roche's anthology is the right book at the right time, and grateful parents will thank her for its outstanding selections."

—JOHN FUND
Editorial Writer, Wall Street Journal

The Christian's Treasury

*of Stories and Songs, Prayers and Poems,
and Much More for Young and Old*

Edited and compiled by
Lissa Roche

CROSSWAY BOOKS • WHEATON, ILLINOIS
A DIVISION OF GOOD NEWS PUBLISHERS

The Christian's Treasury of Stories and Songs,
Prayers and Poems, and Much More for Young and Old

Copyright © 1995 by Lissa Roche

Published by Crossway Books
        a division of Good News Publishers
        1300 Crescent Street
        Wheaton, Illinois 60187

Manuscript editor: Steven Hawkins

Cover illustration: Jim McGinness

Cover design: Cindy Kiple

Book design: Mark Schramm

First printing, 1995

Printed in the United States of America

Library of Congress Cataloging-in-Publication Data
The Christian's treasury of stories and songs, prayers and poems, and
    much more for young and old / edited and compiled by Lissa Roche.
      p.   cm.
    1. Christianity—Miscellanea. 2. Christian life—Miscellanea.
I. Roche, Lissa.
BR123.C576 1995   242—dc20   95-15100
ISBN 0-89107-857-6

03	02	01	00	99	98	97	96	95
15	14	13	12	11	10	9	8	7	6	5	4	3	2	1

To my son, George V

Contents

Introduction   **xxi**

MEDITATIONS

Prayer   **25**

Alexis Carrel
St. Augustine
Corrie ten Boom
Søren Kierkegaard
Fyodor Dostoevsky
Samuel Taylor Coleridge
Mother Teresa
Abraham Lincoln
Robert E. Lee
Martin Luther
William Cowper

Christian Witness   **27**

Elizabeth I
Benjamin Franklin
Helen Keller
John Calvin

Christianity   **29**

B. C. Forbes
Henry Wadsworth Longfellow
Flannery O'Connor
Calvin Coolidge

Dwight L. Moody
Fulton Sheen
Blaise Pascal
Andrew Lytle
D. James Kennedy
Frederick Douglass
C. S. Lewis
George Washington
C. S. Lewis
G. K. Chesterton
Malcolm Muggeridge
Frederick Douglass
Sir Francis Bacon
Benjamin Franklin
Thomas Jefferson
Samuel Johnson
Ambrose Bierce

God's World   **35**

Robert Browning
Larry Woiwode
George Washington Carver
Nicolaus Copernicus
Johann Wolfgang von Goethe
Martin Luther
Charles Williams
Thomas à Kempis

John Burroughs
Elizabeth Barrett Browning

Sacrifice, Obedience, and Duty   37

James Gibbons
John Ruskin
Florence Nightingale
Grover Cleveland
John Keble
William Wordsworth

Thankfulness   39

George Washington
Elizabeth Barrett Browning
Robert Louis Stevenson
George Washington Carver
William Shakespeare

Faith and Reason   40

St. Augustine
Alfred, Lord Tennyson
Harriet Tubman
Thomas J. Watson
Jeremy Taylor
James Russell Lowell
Ralph Waldo Emerson
Larry Woiwode
Søren Kierkegaard
George VI
C. S. Lewis
Ralph Waldo Emerson
Edna St. Vincent Millay
Dwight D. Eisenhower
Thomas Carlyle
Norman Vincent Peale
Blaise Pascal
St. Thomas Aquinas
St. Thomas More

John Greenleaf Whittier
Jean-Pierre de Caussade
Thomas Jefferson
Alexander Pope
Leo Tolstoy
John Greenleaf Whittier
Sir Francis Bacon
Walker Percy
William Blake
George Roche
Robert Browning
Samuel Taylor Coleridge
George MacDonald
John Milton
Paul Johnson

Virtue   48

Blaise Pascal
Lyman Abbott
John Milton
Dante Alighieri
Samuel Johnson
William Shakespeare
John Wesley
John Quincy Adams
Maltbie D. Babcock
Joseph P. Thompson
Thomas Jefferson
William Makepeace Thackeray
Sir James M. Barrie
Michelangelo
Fulton Sheen
Michael Bauman
Robert Schuller
Anne Morrow Lindbergh
Russell Kirk
Arthur Compton
Jane Austen

Fyodor Dostoevsky
Benjamin Franklin
Simone Weil

Love   54

Mother Teresa
Dame Agatha Christie
Robert James McCracken
Nathaniel Hawthorne
Russell Kirk
Henry Ward Beecher
Louis O. Williams
Fyodor Dostoevsky
Russell Kirk
Michael Novak
Arthur S. Maxwell

Truth and Understanding   58

St. Thomas More
St. Thomas Aquinas
Geoffrey Chaucer
Ben Jonson
John Milton
Henry Ward Beecher
John Wesley
Charles Colson
St. Augustine
Ralph Waldo Emerson
Leonardo da Vinci
Karl Barth
John Woolman

Man   61

Robert Louis Stevenson
Blaise Pascal
Thomas Merton
William Faulkner
Annie Dillard

James Fenimore Cooper
John Henry Newman
Michel de Montaigne

Freedom   63

Thomas Jefferson
John Witherspoon
William Penn
Joseph Story
John Knox
Samuel Rutherford
Daniel Webster
Benjamin Franklin
Douglas MacArthur
Abraham Lincoln
Alexis de Tocqueville
St. Thomas Aquinas
James Madison
Herbert Hoover
Lady Margaret Thatcher
Alexis de Tocqueville
M. Stanton Evans
Miguel de Cervantes
Alphonse de Lamartine
Pat Robertson
Arthur James Balfour
Alexander Hamilton
G. K. Chesterton

Overcoming Adversity   70

Robert Pierce
William Penn
Martin Luther King, Jr.
Robert Cromie
Theodore L. Cuyler
Lyman Beecher
Michel de Montaigne
Fulton Sheen

Edmund Burke
Ralph W. Stockman
Robert Schuller
Fulton Sheen
George Chapman
C. S. Lewis
Malcolm Muggeridge
John Skelton
William Shakespeare
Noah Webster
Aleksandr Solzhenitsyn

Sin and Redemption   75

Fulton Sheen
Robert Browning
Lew Wallace
John Fletcher
Benjamin Franklin
St. Augustine
Geoffrey Chaucer
Miguel de Cervantes
John Bunyan
Elbert Hubbard
John Milton
Sir John Dawson
Albert Camus
Leo Tolstoy
Whittaker Chambers
Peter Marshall, Sr.
Larry Woiwode
Oliver Wendell Holmes
Jonathan Edwards
Aleksandr Solzhenitsyn
Blaise Pascal
Norman Vincent Peale
Aleksandr Solzhenitsyn
Robert Bolt

G.K. Chesterton
Jonathan Edwards
John Calvin
St. Augustine
Jean-Pierre de Caussade
G.K. Chesterton
Adelaide Anne Procter
William Shakespeare
Sigrid Undset

Death and Eternal Life   82

John Henry Newman
Peter Abelard
John Bunyan
Joaquin Miller
Thomas Parnell
William Penn
James Aldrich
Malcolm Muggeridge
C. S. Lewis

God   85

Sir Francis Bacon
St. John of Damascus
St. Anselm
Robert Browning
Francis Joseph Spellman
John Ruskin
Pat Robertson
Gerhart Niemeyer
St. Thomas Aquinas
Fyodor Dostoevsky
C. S. Lewis
Jonathan Edwards
St. Augustine
Alexis de Tocqueville
Simone Weil
St. Thomas Aquinas

Martin Luther King, Jr.
Honoré de Balzac
Elizabeth Barrett Browning
William Shakespeare
Bret Harte
John Milton
Miguel de Cervantes
Ralph Waldo Emerson
George Herbert
George MacDonald
Walt Whitman
Thomas à Kempis
Robert Browning
Robert W. Service
Thomas Ken
Henry Wadsworth Longfellow
William Cowper

Jesus 92

Blaise Pascal
Harry Emerson Fosdick
Matthew Arnold
Fulton Sheen
Unknown
George Eliot
Ralph Waldo Emerson
J. C. and A. W. Hare
Richard Moreland
Thomas à Kempis
Unknown
C. S. Lewis
Blaise Pascal
William Shakespeare
C. S. Lewis
Erasmus
Dorothy Sayers
Albert Schweitzer
Madeleine L'Engle

John Henry Newman

POEMS, SONGS, AND BALLADS
Percy Bysshe Shelley

Prayers 103

A Child's Evening Prayer
Samuel Taylor Coleridge
Good Night
Victor Hugo
The Knight's Prayer
Unknown
The Prayers I Make†
Michelangelo
Lord, Make Me an Instrument
of Your Peace†
Saint Francis of Assisi
A Prayer of Thanksgiving
Robert Louis Stevenson
We Thank Thee
Ralph Waldo Emerson
Prayer for Gentleness to
All God's Creatures
John Galsworthy
Prayer for Generosity
St. Ignatius of Loyola
Prayer for Serenity
Reinhold Niebuhr
Grace and Thanksgiving
Elizabeth Gould
The Blessing of Light
Unknown
Lead Back Thy Old Soul†
George MacDonald
A Last Prayer
Helen Hunt Jackson
Others
Charles D. Meigs
The Day Is Done
Unknown

A Better Resurrection
  Christina Rossetti
The Universal Prayer
  Alexander Pope

Family, Friends, Church, and Community   113

To My Mother
  Edgar Allan Poe
A Mother's Birthday
  Henry Van Dyke
The Hand That Rocks the Cradle
  Willliam Ross Wallace
The Watcher
  Margaret Widdemer
My Mother
  Francis Ledwidge
A Prayer for Fathers
  Marjorie Holmes
A Thank You for Friends
  Rodney Bennett
What Life Have You?†
  T.S. Eliot
The Church Walking with the World
  Matilda C. Edwards

God's World   123

Pippa's Song
  Robert Browning
Nature's Creed
  Unknown
The Summer Sea
  Charles Kingsley
The Robin's Song
  Unknown
Arbor Day Song
  Mary A. Heermans
A Passing Glimpse
  Robert Frost

I Love All Beauteous Things†
  Robert Bridges
High Flight
  John Gillespie Magee, Jr.
Is There Care in Heaven?†
  Edmund Spenser
Like an Angel†
  Thomas Traherne
The Evening Clouds†
  Sir Walter Scott
God's World
  Edna St. Vincent Millay
April and May
  Ralph Waldo Emerson
Miracles
  Walt Whitman
All Things Bright and Beautiful
  Cecil Frances Alexander
i thank You God for most this amazing
  e.e. cummings
The Lamb
  William Blake
God's Grandeur
  Gerard Manley Hopkins
Robin's Song
  Rodney Bennett

Work   135

Envoy to the Toiling of Felix
  Henry Van Dyke
Work
  Angela Morgan
Work
  Henry Van Dyke
Song of Work
  Mary Blake
The Glory of the Garden
  Rudyard Kipling
Inspiration
  Henry David Thoreau

Providence and Purpose   139

Under the Leaves
Albert Laighton

Sometime
May Riley Smith

This World Is Not Conclusion†
Emily Dickinson

Providence
Reginald Heber

The Hidden Line, or
The Destiny of Men
J. Addison Alexander

Thankfulness   144

On Jordan's Bank
Charles Coffin

All Good Things†
Leonardo da Vinci

Thanksgiving for the Earth
Elizabeth Goudge

This Day
William Dean Howells

A Hundred Prayers of Praise†
Annie Dillard

Time   147

A Name in the Sand
Hannah Flagg Gould

Timeless Halls†
J.R.R. Tolkien

The Water Mill
Sarah Doudney

Divine Delight
Walter de la Mare

God's Time†
Robert Browning

Faith and Reason   151

Faith of Our Fathers
Frederick W. Faber

Faith Came Singing†
Elizabeth Cheney

Rock of Ages
Augustus M. Toplady

Chartless
Emily Dickinson

Whoever Plants a Seed†
Elizabeth York Case

Faith and Reason†
John Dryden

Shall We Gather at the River?
Robert Lowry

The Agnostic
Edna St. Vincent Millay

The Convert
G.K. Chesterton

The Pilgrim
John Bunyan

By Faith Alone†
Michelangelo

O World
George Santayana

Virtue   158

On Virtue
Phillis Wheatley

It's In Your Face
Unknown

The Divine Image
William Blake

Life Sculpture
William Croswell Deane

Love   161

The Day with a White Mark
C. S. Lewis

From All That Dwell
Below the Skies
  Isaac Watts

How Do I Love Thee?†
  Elizabeth Barrett Browning

Who Adores the Maker†
  Michelangelo

Truth and Understanding   163

In His Name†
  Johann Wolfgang von Goethe

God Our Refuge
  Richard Chevenix Trench

"I Am the Way"
  Alice Meynell

I Believe in Him†
  Johann Wolfgang von Goethe

Truth†
  James Russell Lowell

As Spring the Winter
  Anne Bradstreet

See in Me†
  George Macdonald

Man   167

Mortals†
  Michelangelo

To Cry to Thee†
  George Herbert

On Being Human
  C.S. Lewis

The Wants of Man
  John Quincy Adams

Young and Old
  Charles Kingsley

Legends and Heroes   172

The Late Passenger
  C. S. Lewis

Provençal Legend
  Willa Cather

George Washington
  John Hall Ingham

Good King Wenceslas
  Unknown

Columbus
  Edward Everett Hale

The Pilgrim Fathers
  Felicia Hemans

Washington, the Brave,
the Wise, the Good†
  Unknown

Abraham Lincoln
  Samuel Valentine Cole

The Ballad of John Henry
  Unknown

Johnny Appleseed
  Reeve Lindbergh

King Robert of Sicily
  Henry Wadsworth Longfellow

Freedom   193

America
  Samuel Francis Smith

The Star-Spangled Banner
  Francis Scott Key

America the Beautiful
  Katherine Lee Bates

Battle Hymn of the Republic
  Julia Ward Howe

Go Down, Moses
  Unknown

Free at Last
  Unknown

Onward, Christian Soldiers
  Sabine Baring-Gould

Creed
  Edgar A. Guest

Our Nation Forever
  Wallace Bruce

Land of Our Birth
Rudyard Kipling

Overcoming Adversity   202

The Shepherd Boy's Song
John Bunyan

He Knows He Has Wings!†
Victor Hugo

On My Blindness†
John Milton

Jesus to His Disciples
Edna St. Vincent Millay

The Old Rugged Cross
George Bennard

Nearer to Thee
Sarah Flower Adams

"My Peace I Give Unto You"
G. A. Studdert Kennedy

A Mighty Fortress Is Our God
Martin Luther

Griefs
Emily Dickinson

What the Chimney Sang
Bret Harte

Victory in Defeat
Edwin Markham

The Cross Hath Lifted†
Jacopone Da Todi

A Psalm of Life
Henry Wadsworth Longfellow

Up-Hill
Christina Rossetti

Sin and Redemption   212

Amazing Grace
John Newton

A Hymn to God the Father
John Donne

Hear Me, O God!†
Ben Jonson

The First Psalm

Robert Burns

The Character of a Happy Life
Henry Wotton

Recessional
Rudyard Kipling

The Fool's Prayer
Edward Rowland Sill

Death and   219
Eternal Life

On Death
Johann Wolfgang von Goethe

Afraid?
Emily Dickinson

Wayfaring Stranger
Unknown

Swing Low, Sweet Chariot
Unknown

As from the Darkening Gloom
John Keats

Bound for the Promised Land
Unknown

Broad Is the Road†
Isaac Watts

Triumph O'er Death†
Michelangelo

A Sonnet
William Shakespeare

The Dying Christian to His Soul
Alexander Pope

The End of the Play
William Makepeace Thackeray

Crossing the Bar
Alfred, Lord Tennyson

The Last Invocation
Walt Whitman

The Passionate Man's Pilgrimage
Sir Walter Raleigh

Prospice
Robert Browning

L'Envoi
Rudyard Kipling

Then Sings My Soul
Paul Mariani

Joy, Shipmate, Joy!
Walt Whitman

Peace
Rupert Brooke

The Christian's "Good-Night"
Sarah Doudney

Last Lines
Emily Brontë

Death, Be Not Proud
John Donne

Jesus   237

O Simplicitas
Madeleine L'Engle

Jesus, He Loves One and All
Charles Kingsley

That Holy Thing
George Macdonald

Little Jesus
Francis Thompson

Guiltless Blood†
Robert Burns

Unto Us a Son Is Given
Alice Meynell

A Legend
Tchaikovsky

At the Manger Mary Sings
W.H. Auden

Thanksgiving Day   244

The First Thansgiving
Jack Pretlusky

The Beautiful World
W. L. Childress

The First Thanksgiving Day
John Greenleaf Whittier

Thanksgiving Day
J. J. Montague

Christmas   248

The Shepherd Who Stayed
Theodosia Garrison

Everywhere, Everywhere
Christmas Tonight
Phillips Brooks

A Child of the Snows
G. K. Chesterton

The House of Christmas
G. K. Chesterton

The Oxen
Thomas Hardy

An Offertory
Mary Mapes Dodge

Easter   253

Most Glorious Lord of Life
Edmund Spenser

Nature's Easter Music
Lucy Larcom

Easter Week
Charles Kingsley

At Easter Time
Laura E. Richards

Seven Stanzas at Easter
John Updike

Easter Night
Alice Meynell

When Mary Thro' the
Garden Went
Mary E. Coleridge

STORIES FOR YOUNGER READERS

Providence and Purpose   263

A Handful of Clay
Henry Van Dyke

Thankfulness   266

The Ears of Wheat
The Brothers Grimm

The Master of the Harvest
Mrs. Alfred Gatty

Homesick at Home
G.K. Chesterton

Faith and Reason   275

A Lesson of Faith
Mrs. Alfred Gatty

Love   279

The Loveliest Rose in the World
Hans Christian Andersen

In the Beginning
Max Lucado

Legends and Heroes   285

The Legend of the Stranger Child
Count Franz Pocci

The Wonder Tree
Friedrich Adolph Krummacher

They Heard the Angels Sing
Arthur S. Maxwell

Columbus at La Rabida
Washington Irving

Salvaging Scrap
*Shirley Graham and
George D. Lipscomb*

Overcoming Adversity   305

The Four Days' Blizzard
Laura Ingalls Wilder

Death and Eternal Life   311

The Angel
Hans Christian Andersen

A Child's Dream of a Star
Charles Dickens

Thanksgiving Day   317

The First Thanksgiving
Lena Barksdale

Christmas   322

The Wooden Shoes of Little Wolff
François Coppée

Baboushka and the Three Kings
Ruth Robbins

The Legend of the First
Christmas Tree
Elizabeth Goudge

Playing Pilgrims†
Louisa May Alcott

Easter   343

The Beauty of the Lily
Frances Jenkins Olcott

The Apple Tree
Margery Williams Bianco

STORIES FOR OLDER READERS

Sacrifice, Obedience, and Duty   357

Unzen
Shusako Endō

Faith and Reason 370

The Blue Cross
G.K. Chesterton

The Hint of an Explanation
Graham Greene

Love 399

The Other Wise Man
Henry Van Dyke

Give What You Are Given†
Jan de Hartog

Truth and Understanding 429

The Three Hermits
Leo Tolstoy

The Fire Balloons
Ray Bradbury

Legends and Heroes 454

The Death of King Arthur†
Donna Fletcher Crow

Joan Meets the King†
Mark Twain

Sin and Redemption 476

The Slough of Despond and
The Interpreter's House
John Bunyan

Brother Orchid
Richard Connell

Jesus 503

The Crucifier Becomes a
Christian†
Lloyd C. Douglas

The Bread of Heaven
Dorothy Sayers

Christmas 535

The Greatest Gift
Philip Van Doren Stern

Easter 545

Maundy Thursday
Walter Wangerin, Jr.

Acknowledgments 553

Guide to Abbreviations and Symbols

b.   date of birth
c.   circa or about
fl.   year(s) in which the author flourished
d.   date of death

The ✳ symbol that appears before some selections indicates suitability for younger readers.

The † symbol indicates that an untitled work has been given a title.

Introduction

Stories lie at the very heart of the two-thousand-year-old Christian tradition. The master of parables Jesus of Nazareth relied on storytelling not only because it is a highly effective tool of communication but because it is undoubtedly the best way of interpreting and explaining all human existence.

Moreover, as one modern educational psychologist has observed, "People have a need for stories. Without stories, they become less human." We live in an age when that need is greater than ever before. Stories told from a spiritual perspective can help us resist the temptations of the increasingly secular, "value-free" attitudes that have taken hold in our schools, in our communities, and in our culture. Parents eagerly look for tales that will teach their children "moral literacy"—that is, to cherish the right beliefs and attitudes and to make the right decisions. But they are not the only ones engaged in this search. None of us ever outgrows the need for stories, especially stories that are informed by a Christian outlook and that offer vital guidance on how we should "write" the story of our own lives.

There is an old expression, "Tell me what you read, and I will tell you what you are." What we read *does* have a profound impact on our moral character. We should seek, therefore, those stories that champion Christian conceptions of right over wrong, virtue over vice, and responsibility over license. But a casual glance at what fills literature shelves today reveals that there has been far too much emphasis on just the opposite. Traditional religious values are often denigrated or attacked. Conventional anthologies are overwhelmingly secular. Anti-heroic, angst-ridden stories—laced with heavy doses of moral relativism, pessimism, fatalism, and pointless tragedy—have become the staples of much of the "serious fiction" that has acquired a permanent place on required reading lists in English departments around the country. It is no wonder that record numbers of students are dropping out of literature courses; they have been fed a steady diet of this kind of thing, and it is hardly palatable.

A Christian Treasury reminds us that although man is a fallen creature, he is also touched by the grace of God and that Christianity is, above all, a doctrine of light, not darkness. It helps us appreciate the marvelous mystery, diversity, and sanctity of life, the simultaneous frailty and strength of human nature, and the image of God in the world, which, although seen only dimly, is staggering in its beauty and power. There are virtually hundreds of selections by authors who will sometimes surprise you, since they are not generally acknowledged as Christian writers. Some of the most famous and best-loved stories by the likes of C. S. Lewis, George MacDonald, Kenneth Grahame, and others have been omitted to make room for less well-known ones, but even the most discerning reader will agree that the quality and scope of what is included is impressive.

Although not all of the selections were written by Christians, all of the selections included in the book reflect Christian principles and are of enduring value for all to read. Similarly, the selections written by non-Christian authors help us see how deeply Christian thinking has influenced our literature, as is evident in the writing of those non-Christian authors who have been included here. Lastly, I did not include the many wonderful Bible stories that could have been added, since the Bible is readily available for all to read. Indeed, I would encourage everyone to read the Bible often and in depth. At the same time, timeless stories and poems such as those that comprise this book can often help us understand Christian truth and principles in a fresh and deeper way.

LISSA ROCHE
Hillsdale, Michigan, July 1995

ONE

Meditations

❧ PRAYER ❧

Prayer is a force as real as terrestrial gravity. As a physician, I have seen men, after all other therapy had failed, lifted out of disease and melancholy by the serene effort of prayer. Only in prayer do we achieve that complete and harmonious assembly of body, mind and spirit which gives the frail human reed its unshakable strength.

> —ALEXIS CARREL (1873-1944)
> French surgeon, biologist, and Nobel laureate

Do what you can do, and pray for what you cannot do.

> —ST. AUGUSTINE (354-430)
> Roman Catholic bishop of Hippo, North Africa
> Author, *Confessions* and *City of God*

Any concern too small to be turned into a prayer is too small to be made into a burden.

> —CORRIE TEN BOOM (1892-1983)
> Dutch evangelist and writer*

Prayer does not change God, but changes him who prays.

> —SØREN KIERKEGAARD (1813-1855)
> Danish philosopher

---

*Corrie ten Boom and her family were Christians who hid 700 Jews from the Nazis during World War II.

Be not forgetful of prayer. Every time you pray, if your prayer is sincere, there will be a new feeling and a new meaning in it, which will give you fresh courage, and you will understand that prayer is an education.

—FYODOR DOSTOEVSKY (1821-1881)
Russian novelist
From *The Brothers Karamazov*

He prayeth well, who loveth well
*   Both man and bird and beast,*
He prayeth best, who lovest best,
*   All things both great and small;*
For the dear God who loveth us,
*   He made and loveth all.*

—SAMUEL TAYLOR COLERIDGE (1772-1834)
English Romantic poet
From "The Rime of the Ancient Mariner"

We must bring [the] presence of God into our families. How do we do that? By praying.

—MOTHER TERESA (1910—)
Yugoslavian-born nun and Nobel laureate

I have been driven many times upon my knees by the overwhelming conviction that I had nowhere else to go. My own wisdom, and that of all about me, seemed insufficient for that day.

—ABRAHAM LINCOLN (1809-1865)
Sixteenth president of the United States

Knowing that intercessory prayer is our mightiest weapon and supreme call for Christians today, I pleadingly urge our people everywhere to pray. . . . Let there be prayer at sun-up, at noon day, at sundown, at midnight, all through the day. Let us all pray for our children, our youth, our aged, our pastors, our homes. Let us pray for our churches.

Let us pray for ourselves, that we may not lose the word "concern" out of our Christian vocabulary. Let us pray for our nation. Let us pray for those who have never known Jesus Christ and redeeming love, for moral forces everywhere, for our national leaders.

Let prayer be our passion. Let prayer be our practice.

—ROBERT E. LEE (1807-1870)
Commander of the Confederate Army of Northern Virginia

Prayer is a strong wall and fortress of the church; it is a goodly Christian's weapon.

—MARTIN LUTHER (1483-1546)
German monk and leader of the Protestant Reformation
From "Of Prayer"

And Satan trembles when he sees
The weakest saint upon his knees.

—WILLIAM COWPER (1731-1800)
English poet
From "Exhortation to Prayer"

CHRISTIAN WITNESS

Christ was the word that spake it;
He took the bread and brake it;
And what that word did make it,
That I believe and take it.

—ELIZABETH I, QUEEN OF ENGLAND (1533-1603)*

---

*Before her coronation in 1558, Queen Elizabeth I gave this reply to a Catholic priest who inquired whether she believed in the real Presence in Holy Communion.

Here is my Creed. I believe in one God, Creator of the Universe. That he governs it by his Providence. That he ought to be worshipped. That the most acceptable service we render him is doing good to his other children. That the soul of Man is immortal and will be treated with justice in another life respecting its conduct in this.

—BENJAMIN FRANKLIN (1706-1790)
American writer and statesman

I Believe[†]

I believe that we all live on earth according to the teachings of Jesus, and that the greatest happiness will come to the world when man obeys His commandment, "Love ye one another."

I believe that every question between man and man is a religious question, and that every social wrong is a moral wrong.

I believe that we can live on earth according to the fulfillment of God's will, and that when the will of God is done on earth as it is done in heaven every man will love his fellow men and act towards them as he desires they should act towards him. I believe that the welfare of each is bound up in the welfare of all.

I believe that life is given us so we may grow in love, and I believe that God is in me as the sun is in the color and fragrance of a flower— the Light in my darkness, the Voice in my silence.

I believe that only in broken gleams has the Sun of Truth yet shone upon men.

I believe that love will finally establish the Kingdom of God on earth and that the Cornerstones of that Kingdom will be Liberty, Truth, Brotherhood, and Service.

I believe that no good shall be lost, and that all man has willed or hoped or dreamed of good shall exist forever.

I believe in the immortality of the soul because I have within me immortal longings.

I believe that the state we enter after death is wrought of our own motives, thoughts, and deeds.

I believe that in the life to come I shall have the senses I have not had here and that my home there will be beautiful with color, music, and speech, of flowers and faces I love.

Without this faith there would be little meaning in my life. I should be "a mere pillar of darkness in the dark." Observers in the full enjoyment of their bodily senses pity me, but it is because they do not see the golden chamber in my life where I dwell delighted; for, as dark as my path may seem to them, I carry a magic light in my heart. Faith, the spiritual strong searchlight, illumines the way, and although sinister doubts lurk in the shadow, I walk unafraid toward the Enchanted Wood where the foliage is always green, where joy abides, where nightingales nest and sing, and where life and death are one in the presence of the Lord.

> —HELEN KELLER (1880-1968)
> Blind and deaf writer and lecturer
> From *In Midstream: My Later Life*

We are subject to men who rule over us, but subject only in the Lord. If they command anything against Him, let us not pay the least heed to it.

> —JOHN CALVIN (1509-1564)
> French-born theologian and founder of Calvinism

❧CHRISTIANITY❧

The man without religion is as a ship without a rudder.

> —B. C. FORBES
> Founder, *Forbes*

Morality without religion is only a kind of dead reckoning,—an endeavor to find our place on a cloudy sea.

> —HENRY WADSWORTH LONGFELLOW (1807-1882)
> American poet and educator
> From *Kavanagh*

The Judeo-Christian tradition has formed us in the West; we are bound to it by ties which may often be invisible, but which are there nevertheless. It has formed the shape of our secularism; it has formed even the shape of modern atheism. For my part, I shall have to remain well within the Judeo-Christian tradition. I shall have to speak, without apology, of the Church, even when the Church is absent; of Christ, even when Christ is not recognized.

—FLANNERY O'CONNOR (1925-1964)
American novelist and short story writer
From "Novelist and Believer"

The strength of a country is the strength of its religious convictions.

—CALVIN COOLIDGE (1872-1933)
Thirtieth president of the United States

The religion of Jesus is better than all isms.

—DWIGHT L. MOODY (1837-1899)
American evangelist and founder, Moody Bible Institute

Religion is actually not a crutch; it is a cross. It is not an escape, it is a burden; not a flight, but a response. We speak here of a religion with teeth in it, the kind that demands self-sacrifice and surrender. One leans on a crutch, but a cross rests on us. A coward can use a crutch, but it takes a hero to embrace a cross.

—FULTON SHEEN (1895-1975)
American Roman Catholic bishop

The God of the Christians is a God who makes the soul feel that He is her only good, that her only rest is in Him, that her only delight is in loving Him; and who makes her at the same time abhor the obstacles which keep her back, and prevent her from loving God with all her strength.

—BLAISE PASCAL (1623-1662)
French scientist and philosopher
From *Pensées*

The world's plight is so precarious that we cannot survive without a return to order, and for us this can only be a Christian order.

—ANDREW LYTLE (1902—)
American educator, novelist, and essayist
From *Eden to Babylon*

Christianity's roots were small and humble—an itinerant rabbi preached and did miracles for three and a half years around the countryside of subjugated Israel. And today there are more than 1.8 billion professing believers in Him in most of the nations on earth! . . . Emperors and governors were the men with power in Christ's day. But now their bodies rot in their sepulchers, and their souls await the Final Judgment. They have no followers today. No one worships them. No one serves them or awaits their bidding.

—D. JAMES KENNEDY (1930—)
Presbyterian clergyman and founder, Coral Ridge Ministries
From *What If Jesus Had Never Been Born?*

There is another religion [true Christianity] that takes off fetters instead of putting them on—that breaks every yoke—that lifts up the bowed down. The Anti-slavery platform is based on this kind of religion. It spreads its table to the lame, the halt, and the blind. It goes down after a long neglected race. It passes, link by link till it finds the lowest link in humanity's chain—humanity's most degraded form in the most abject condition. It reaches down its arm and tells them to stand up.

—FREDERICK DOUGLASS (c.1817-1895)
African American abolitionist, orator, and escaped slave

The Christian way is different: harder and easier. Christ says, "Give me All. I don't want so much of your time and so much of your money and so much of your work: I want You. I have not come to torment your natural self, but to kill it. No half-measures are any good. I don't want to cut off a branch here and a branch there, I want to have the whole tree down. I don't want to drill the tooth, or crown it, or stop it, but to have it out. Hand over the whole natural self, all the desires which you think innocent as well as the ones you think wicked—the whole outfit. I will give you a new self instead. In fact, I will give you Myself: my own will shall become yours."

> —C. S. LEWIS (1898-1963)
> English novelist, essayist, and educator
> From *The Joyful Christian*

Of all the dispositions and habits which lead to political prosperity, Religion and Morality are indispensable supports. In vain would that man claim the tribute of Patriotism, who should labor to subvert these great Pillars of human happiness, these firmest props of the duties of men and citizens. The mere politician, equally with the pious man ought to respect and to cherish them. A volume could not trace all their connections with private and public felicity. Let it simply be asked where is the security for property, for reputation, for life, if the sense of religious obligation *desert* the oaths, which are the instruments of investigation in Courts of Justice? And let us with caution indulge the supposition, that morality can be maintained without religion. Whatever may be conceded to the influence of refined education on minds of peculiar structure, reason and experience both forbid us to expect that National morality can prevail in exclusion of religious principle.

'Tis substantially true, that virtue or morality is a necessary spring of popular government. The rule indeed extends with more or less force to every species of free Government. Who that is a sincere friend to it, can look with indifference upon attempts to shake the foundation of the fabric? . . .

Observe good faith and justice toward all Nations. Cultivate peace and harmony with all. Religion and morality enjoin this conduct; and can it be that good policy does not equally enjoin it? It will be worthy of a free, enlightened, and at no distant period, a great Nation to give to mankind the magnanimous and too novel example of a People always guided by an exalted justice and benevolence. Who can doubt that in the course of time and things the fruit of such a plan would richly repay any temporary advantages which might be lost by a steady adherence to it? Can it be, that Providence has not connected the permanent felicity of a Nation with its virtue? The experiment, at least, is recommended by every sentiment which ennobles human Nature. Alas! is it rendered impossible by its vices?

—GEORGE WASHINGTON (1732-1799)
First president of the United States
From his "Farewell Address" in 1796

Every Christian is to become a little Christ. The whole purpose of becoming a Christian is simply nothing else.

—C. S. LEWIS (1898-1963)
English novelist, essayist, and educator
From *Mere Christianity*

According to most philosophers, God in making the world enslaved it. According to Christianity, in making it, He set it free.

—G.K. CHESTERTON (1874-1936)
English journalist, novelist, and poet
Author, *Orthodoxy* and *The Father Brown Stories*

Christianity is in discord with the world, but in the Christian is the peace of Christ.

—MALCOLM MUGGERIDGE (1903-1990)
British journalist
From *Jesus Rediscovered*

I believe it is the religious people who are to be relied on in this Anti-slavery movement. Do not . . . class me with those who despise religion—do not identify me with the infidel. I love the religion of Christianity—which cometh from above—which is pure, peaceable, gentle, easy to be entreated, full of good fruits, and without hypocrisy.* I love that religion which sends its votaries to bind up the wounds of those who have fallen among thieves.

>—FREDERICK DOUGLASS (c.1817-1895)
>African American abolitionist, orator, and escaped slave

There was never law, or sect, or opinion did so much magnify goodness, as the Christian religion doth.

>—SIR FRANCIS BACON (1561-1626)
>English philosopher and statesman
>From "Of Goodness"

He who shall introduce into public affairs the principles of primitive Christianity will change the face of the world.

>—BENJAMIN FRANKLIN (1706-1790)
>American writer and statesman
>From a letter to the French ministry, written in March, 1778

Of all the systems of morality, ancient or modern, which have come under my observation, none appear to me so pure as that of Jesus.

>—THOMAS JEFFERSON (1743-1826)
>Third president of the United States

Christianity is the highest perfection of humanity.

>—SAMUEL JOHNSON (1709-1784)
>English lexicographer and poet

---

*paraphrase of James 3:17

Christians and camels receive their burdens kneeling.

>—AMBROSE BIERCE (1842-C.1914)
> American journalist and satirist
> From *The Devil's Dictionary*

❧ GOD'S WORLD ❧

If you get simple beauty and nought else, you get about the best God invents.

>—ROBERT BROWNING (1812-1889)
> English Victorian poet

. . . the fiery sun arriving in yet another promise kept by God.

>—LARRY WOIWODE (1941—)
> American novelist
> From *Acts*

I love to think of nature as an unlimited broadcasting station, through which God speaks to us every hour, if we will only tune in.

>—GEORGE WASHINGTON CARVER (1860-1943)
> African American chemist, botanist, and educator

[There is a] consistent scheme of the movement of the mechanism of the universe, set up for our benefit by the best and most law-abiding Architect of all things. . . .

>—NICOLAUS COPERNICUS (1473-1543)
> Polish astronomer
> From "Dedication of the Revolutions of the Heavenly Bodies"*

---

*an epistle to Pope Paul III which established the foundations of modern astronomy

Ever the powers of Nature stir,
For the laws of God are alive in her.
She makes, sets free, unites, leaves lone:
The Spirits above us, beneath us the stone.

   —JOHANN WOLFGANG VON GOETHE (1749-1832)
    German poet, novelist, and scientist
    From "For My Grandson"

Our Lord has written the promise of the resurrection not in books alone but in every leaf in the springtime.

   —MARTIN LUTHER (1483-1546)
    German monk and leader of the Protestant Reformation

"I am the Lord" rings everywhere like the refrain of the heavens.

   —CHARLES WILLIAMS (1886-1945)
    English poet, editor, playwright, and biographer
    From *He Came Down from Heaven*

There is no creature, regardless of its apparent significance, that fails to show us something of God's goodness.

   —THOMAS À KEMPIS (C.1379-1471)
    German monk
    From *The Imitation of Christ*

One of the hardest lessons we have to learn in this life, and one that many persons never learn, is to see the divine, the celestial, the pure, in the common, the near at hand—to see that heaven lies about us here in this world.

   —JOHN BURROUGHS (1837-1921)
    American naturalist and writer

Earth's crammed with heaven,
And every common bush afire with God.

> —ELIZABETH BARRETT BROWNING (1806-1861)
> English Victorian poet
> From "Aurora Lee"

SACRIFICE, OBEDIENCE, AND DUTY

Let us do all that we can in our day and generation in the cause of humanity. Every man has a mission from God to help his fellow-beings. Though we differ in faith, thank God there is one platform of charity and benevolence. We cannot, indeed, like our Divine Master, give sight to the blind, hearing to the deaf, speech to the dumb, and strength to the paralyzed limb, but we can work miracles of grace and mercy by relieving the distress of our suffering brethren. And never do we approach nearer to our Heavenly Father than when we alleviate the sorrows of others. Never do we perform an act more Godlike than when we bring sunshine to hearts that are dark and desolate. Never are we more like to God than when we cause the flowers of joy and of gladness to bloom in souls that were dry and barren before.

> —JAMES GIBBONS (1834-1921)
> Second American cardinal of the Roman Catholic Church

God never imposes a duty without giving time to do it.

> —JOHN RUSKIN (1819-1900)
> English art critic, writer, and social reformer
> From *Lectures on Architecture*

Life is a splendid gift. There is nothing small in it. For the greatest grow by God's law out of the smallest. But to live your life you must discipline it. You must not fritter it away in "fair purpose, erring act, inconstant will"; but must make your thoughts, your words, your acts, all work to the same end; that end not self; but God. That is what we call character.

> —FLORENCE NIGHTINGALE (1820-1910)
> English founder of modern nursing

God has never failed to make known to me the path of duty.

> —GROVER CLEVELAND (1837-1908)
> Twenty-second and twenty-fourth president of the United States
> From a letter written in 1906

The trivial round, the common task,
Would furnish all we ought to ask;
Room to deny ourselves; a road
To bring us, daily, nearer God.

> —JOHN KEBLE (1792-1866)
> English theologian and poet
> From *The Christian Year*

O Duty! if that name thou love
Who art a light to guide, a rod
To check the erring, and reprove;
Thou, who art victory and law
When empty terrors overawe;
From vain temptations dost set free;
And calm'st the weary strife of frail humanity!

> —WILLIAM WORDSWORTH (1770-1850)
> English Romantic poet
> From "Ode to Duty"

~ THANKFULNESS ~

It is the duty of all nations to acknowledge the providence of Almighty God, to obey His will, to be grateful for His benefits and humbly implore His protection and favor.

—GEORGE WASHINGTON (1732-1799)
First president of the United States

Because God's gifts put man's best dreams to shame.

—ELIZABETH BARRETT BROWNING (1806-1861)
English Victorian poet
From *Sonnets from the Portuguese*

The best things are nearest: breath in your nostrils, light in your eyes, flowers at your feet, duties at your hand, the path of God just before you.

—ROBERT LOUIS STEVENSON (1850-1894)
Scottish novelist and poet
Author, *Treasure Island*

The secret of my success? It is simple. It is found in the Bible: "In all thy ways acknowledge Him and He shall direct my paths."

—GEORGE WASHINGTON CARVER (1860-1943)
African American chemist, botanist, and educator

God's goodness hath been great to thee;
Let never a day nor night unhallowed pass,
But still remember what the Lord hath done.

—WILLIAM SHAKESPEARE (1564-1616)
English playwright and poet

⮬ FAITH AND REASON ⮬

Faith is to believe what we do not see; and the reward of this faith is to see what we believe.

> —ST. AUGUSTINE (354-430)
> Roman Catholic bishop of Hippo, North Africa
> Author, *Confessions* and *City of God*

If you fear
Cast all your cares on God;
*   that anchor holds.*

> —ALFRED, LORD TENNYSON (1809-1892)
> English Victorian poet laureate

'Twant me, 'twas the Lord. I always told him, "I trust to you. I don't know where to go or what to do, but I expect you to lead me," and he always did.

> —HARRIET TUBMAN (c.1820-1913)
> African American abolitionist and escaped slave

The greatest asset of a man, a business, or a nation is faith. The men who built this country and those who made it prosper during its darkest days were men whose faith in its future was unshakable.

Men of courage, they dared to go forward despite all hazards; men of vision, they always looked forward, never backward.

Christianity, the greatest institution humanity has ever known, was founded by twelve men, limited in education, limited in resources, but with an abundance of faith and divine leadership.

The vision essential to clear thinking; the common sense needed for wise decisions; the courage of convictions based on facts not fancies;

and the constructive spirit of faith as opposed to the destructive forces of doubt will preserve our Christian ways of life.

—THOMAS J. WATSON (1874-1956)
American businessman and philanthropist, founder of IBM

Faith is the root of all blessings. Believe, and you shall be saved; believe, and you must needs be satisfied; believe, and you cannot but be comforted and happy.

—JEREMY TAYLOR (1613-1667)
English Anglican bishop

He who keeps his faith only, cannot be discrowned.

—JAMES RUSSELL LOWELL (1819-1891)
American poet, essayist, and diplomat

Faith and love are apt to be spasmodic in the best minds. Men live on the brink of mysteries and harmonies into which they never enter, and with their hand on the door-latch they die outside.

—RALPH WALDO EMERSON (1803-1882)
American Transcendentalist poet and philosopher

Faith is not a suitcase you picked up on Sunday to carry to church, as now, but the source of vibrant application of scripture to every task.

—LARRY WOIWODE (1941—)
American novelist
From *Acts*

Without risk, faith is an impossibility.

—SØREN KIERKEGAARD (1813-1855)
Danish philosopher

I said to the man at the gate of the year, "Give me a light that I may go forth into the unknown." And the man replied, "Put your hand into the hand of God. That shall be to you better than a light, safer than a known way."

—GEORGE VI, KING OF ENGLAND (1895-1952)
From a New Year's message to the British people at the beginning of World War II

I believe in Christ like I believe in the sun, not just because I see it, but because by it I can see everything else.

—C. S. LEWIS (1898-1963)
English novelist, essayist, and educator
Author, *The Screwtape Letters* and *The Chronicles of Narnia*

All I have seen teaches me to trust the Creator for all I have not seen.

—RALPH WALDO EMERSON (1803-1882)
American Transcendentalist poet and philosopher

Man has not invented God:
He has developed faith
To meet a God already there.

—EDNA ST. VINCENT MILLAY (1892-1950)
American Pulitzer Prize-winning poet

This is what I found out about religion: It gives you courage to make the decisions you must make in a crisis and then the confidence to leave the result to a higher Power. Only by trust in God can a man carrying responsibility find repose.

—DWIGHT D. EISENHOWER (1890-1969)
Thirty-fourth president of the United States

Great souls are always loyally submissive, reverent to what is over them: only small mean souls are otherwise.

—THOMAS CARLYLE (1795-1881)
  Scottish essayist and historian

How does the fact that we turn to God in trust and faith relieve us of our fears? For one thing, when a man gets his mind on God, he gets it off himself. Fears, in reality, accompany excessive thinking about oneself. They are nurtured by the ego-centered attitude as a nest is warmed by a sitting hen. Our minds sit on the nest of our real and imaginary fears, mostly the latter, and soon we have hatched a flock of new little fears, and they grow up rapidly.

—NORMAN VINCENT PEALE (1898-1993)
  American clergyman and founder, *Guideposts*
  From *Faith Is the Answer*

Those great spiritual efforts, which the soul sometimes assays, are things on which it does not lay hold. It only leaps to them, not as upon a throne, for ever, but merely for an instant.

—BLAISE PASCAL (1623-1662)
  French scientist and philosopher
  From *Pensées*

Now, although the truth of the Christian faith . . . surpasses the capacity of reason, nevertheless that truth that human reason is naturally endowed to know cannot be opposed to the truth of the Christian faith.

—ST. THOMAS AQUINAS (1225-1274)
  Italian Dominican monk and principal theologian of the Roman Catholic Church
  From *On the Truth of the Catholic Faith*

Though men may with preaching be ministers unto God therein, and the man with his own free will obeying freely the inward inspiration of God be a weak worker with Almighty God therein, yet is the faith indeed the gracious gift of God Himself.

—ST. THOMAS MORE (1478-1535)
English statesman, writer, and martyr
From "The Need for a Foundation of Faith"

The steps of faith fall on the seeming void, but find the rock beneath.

—JOHN GREENLEAF WHITTIER (1807-1892)
American Quaker poet

Faith is the light of time, it alone recognizes truth without seeing it, touches what it cannot feel, looks upon this world as though it did not exist, sees what is not apparent. It is the key to celestial treasures, the key to the unfathomable mystery and knowledge of God.

—JEAN-PIERRE DE CAUSSADE (1675-1751)
French philosopher

He who made us would have been a pitiful bungler, if he had made the rules of our moral conduct a matter of science. For one man of science, there are thousands who are not. What would have become of them? Man was destined for society. His morality, therefore, was to be formed to this object. He was endowed with a sense of right and wrong, merely relative to this. . . . The moral sense, or conscience, is as much a part of man as his leg or arm. It is given to all human beings in a stronger or weaker degree, as force of members is given them in a greater or less degree. It may be strengthened by exercise, as may any particular limb of the body. This sense is submitted, indeed, in some degree, to the guidance of reason; but it is a small stock which is required for this; even a less one than what we call common sense.

State a moral case to a plowman and a professor. The former will decide it as well, and often better than the latter, because he has not been led astray by artificial rules. In this branch, therefore, read good books, because they will encourage, as well as direct your feelings. . . . [And] lose no occasion of exercising your dispositions to be grateful, to be generous, to be charitable, to be humane, to be true, just, firm, orderly, courageous, etc. Consider every act of this kind, as an exercise which will strengthen your moral faculties and increase your worth.

Religion. Your reason is now mature enough to examine this object. In the first place, divest yourself of all bias in favor of novelty and singularity of opinion. Indulge them in any other subject rather than that of religion. It is too important, and the consequences of error may be too serious. . . . Your own reason is the only oracle given you by heaven, and you are answerable, not for the rightness, but uprightness of the decision.

> —THOMAS JEFFERSON (1743-1826)
> Third president of the United States
> From a letter to his nephew Peter Carr, written in 1787

Two things are equally unaccountable to reason, and not the object of reasoning; the Wisdom of God and the Madness of Man.

> —ALEXANDER POPE (1688-1744)
> English poet and satirist

Faith is the force of life.

> —LEO TOLSTOY (1828-1910)
> Russian novelist and philosopher
> From *My Confession*

Through the dark and stormy night
Faith beholds a feeble light
Up the blackness streaking;
Knowing God's own time is best,
In a patient hope I rest
For the full day-breaking!

> —JOHN GREENLEAF WHITTIER (1807-1892)
>   American Quaker poet
>   From "Barclay of Ury"

God never wrought miracles to convince atheism, because his ordinary works convince it.

> —SIR FRANCIS BACON (1561-1626)
>   English philosopher and statesman
>   From "Of Atheism"

God is not dead, but modern man's loss of faith in him has led to despair.

> —WALKER PERCY (1916-1990)
>   American novelist

*Mock on, mock on, Voltaire, Rousseau;**
Mock on, mock on; 'tis all in vain!
You throw the sand against the wind,
And the wind blows it back again.

> —WILLIAM BLAKE (1757-1827)
>   English Romantic poet
>   From "Mock On"

---

*eighteenth-century French philosophers who argued against the existence of God

The most resolute efforts by Rational Atheists Societies and Militant Atheist Leagues succeed only in producing weird new faiths of their own. It appears literally impossible for us to believe in nothing.

—GEORGE ROCHE (1935—)
American educator
From *A World Without Heroes*

All we have gained then by our unbelief
Is a life of doubt diversified by faith,
For all one of faith diversified by doubt:
We called the chess-board white,—we call it black.

—ROBERT BROWNING (1812-1889)
English Victorian poet
From "Bishop Blougram's Apology"

Forth from his dark and lonely hiding-place,
(Portentous sight) the owlet Atheism,
Sailing on obscene wings athwart the noon,
Drops his blue-tinted lids, and holds them close,
And hooting at the glorious sun in Heaven,
Cries out, "Where is it?"

—SAMUEL TAYLOR COLERIDGE (1772-1834)
English Romantic poet
From "Fears in Solitude"

There is no strength in unbelief. Even the unbelief of what is false is no source of might. It is the truth shining from behind that gives the strength to disbelieve.

—GEORGE MACDONALD (1824-1905)
Scottish novelist and poet
From *The Marquis of Lossie*

Unbelief is blind.

> —JOHN MILTON (1608-1674)
> English poet
> From "Comus"

What is important in history is not only the events that occur but the events that obstinately do not occur. The outstanding non-event of modern times was the failure of religious belief to disappear. . . . What looked antiquated, even risible, in the 1980s was not religious belief but the confident predictions of its demise once provided by Feuerbach, Marx and Comte, Durkheim and Frazier, Wells, Shaw, Gide and Sartre, and countless others.

> —PAUL JOHNSON (1928—)
> English historian and philosopher
> From *Modern Times*

VIRTUE

The virtue of man ought to be measured, not by his extraordinary exertions, but by his everyday conduct.

> —BLAISE PASCAL (1623-1662)
> French scientist and philosopher

We often pray for purity, unselfishness, for the highest qualities of character, and forget that these things cannot be given, but must be earned.

> —LYMAN ABBOTT (1835-1922)
> American Congregationalist clergyman and writer

I cannot praise a fugitive and cloistered virtue, unexercised and unbreathed, that never sallies out and sees her adversary, but slinks out of the race where that immortal garland is to be run for, not without dust and heat.

  —JOHN MILTON (1608-1674)
   English poet
   From *Areopagitica*

Ye were not formed to live the life of brutes,
But virtue to pursue, and knowledge high.

  —DANTE ALIGHIERI (1265-1321)
   Italian poet
   Author, *The Divine Comedy*

His virtues walk'd their narrow round,
Nor made a pause, nor left a void;
And sure th' Eternal Master found
The single talent well employ'd.

  —SAMUEL JOHNSON (1709-1784)
   English lexicographer and poet
   "On the Death of Mr. Robert Levet"

If to do were as easy as to know what were good to do, chapels had been churches, and poor men's cottages princes' palaces. It is a good divine [theologian] that follows his own instructions; I can easier teach twenty what were good to be done, than be one of the twenty to follow mine own teaching.

  —WILLIAM SHAKESPEARE (1564-1616)
   English playwright and poet

Do all the good you can, in all the ways you can, to all the souls you can, in every place you can, at all the times you can, with all the zeal you can, as long as ever you can.

> —JOHN WESLEY (1703-1791)
> English evangelist and co-founder of Methodism

Think of no other greatness but that of the soul, no other riches but those of the heart.

> —JOHN QUINCY ADAMS (1767-1848)
> Sixth president of the United States

Good habits are not made on birthdays, nor Christian character at the new year. The workshop of character is everyday life. The uneventful and commonplace hour is where the battle is lost or won.

> —MALTBIE D. BABCOCK (1858-1901)
> American Presbyterian clergyman

Christianity is the good man's text; his life, the illustration.

> —JOSEPH P. THOMPSON (1819-1879)
> American Congregationalist clergyman

I have ever judged of the religion of others by their lives. For it is in our lives, and not from our works, that our religion must be read.

> —THOMAS JEFFERSON (1743-1826)
> Third president of the United States

'Tis not the dying for a faith that's so hard; 'tis the living up to it that is difficult.

> —WILLIAM MAKEPEACE THACKERAY (1811-1863)
> English novelist
> Author, *Vanity Fair*

The life of every man is a diary in which he means to write one story and writes another, and his humblest hour is when he compares the volume as it is with what he vowed to make it.

> —SIR JAMES M. BARRIE (1860-1937)
> Scottish-born journalist, novelist and playwright
> From *The Little Minister*

God is perfection, and whoever strives toward perfection is striving for something divine.

> —MICHELANGELO (1475-1564)
> Italian sculptor, painter, and architect

The Beatitudes cannot be taken alone: they are not ideals; they are hard facts and realities inseparable from the Cross of Calvary. What He taught was self-crucifixion: to love those who hate us; to pluck out eyes and cut off arms in order to prevent sinning; to be clean on the inside when the passions clamor for satisfaction on the outside; to forgive those who would put us to death; to overcome evil with good; to bless those who curse us; to stop mouthing freedom until we have justice, truth, and love of God in our hearts as the condition of freedom; to live in the world and still keep oneself unpolluted from it; to deny ourselves sometimes legitimate pleasures in order the better to crucify our egotism—all this is to sentence the old man in us to death.

> —FULTON SHEEN (1895-1975)
> American Roman Catholic bishop

What the Christian seeks is not greatness but goodness; not happiness but holiness; not power but purity; not feeling but fact; not information but wisdom.

> —MICHAEL BAUMAN (1950—)
> American teacher and theologian

Jesus begins the Beatitudes with a tremendous principle. . . . "Blessed are the poor in spirit, for theirs is the kingdom of Heaven" . . . You and I must discover our soft spot, our weak link, our ignorant area, our poverty pocket. And then we must become "poor in spirit" as well—face up to our poverty, humble our attitude, acknowledge our weakness, ask for help. Everybody is poor in his own way.

—ROBERT SCHULLER (1926—)
American Reformed evangelist and writer

I want a singleness of eye, a purity of intention, a central core to my life that will enable me to carry out these obligations and activities as well as I can. I want, in fact—to borrow from the language of the saints—to live "in grace" as much of the time as possible. . . . I would like to achieve a state of inner spiritual grace from which I could function and give as I was meant to in the eye of God.

—ANNE MORROW LINDBERGH (1907—)
American writer
From *Gift from the Sea*

This path for the followers of Christ, then, was a stonier road than ever men had been told to follow before. Its principles demanded a new sort of heroism, more severe than that of the Law of the Jews, more sacrificing of self than the old Roman virtue. Out of this teaching there would rise what were to be called the Christian "theological virtues" of faith, hope, and charity.

To have faith is to respond morally, through an act of will, to God's love and wisdom: to trust in "the Father of our Lord Jesus Christ." To have hope is to rejoice in the reality of the Lord, patient and confident. To have charity is to fulfill the Great Commandment, in act and in spirit, loving God and loving all men.

—RUSSELL KIRK (1918-1994)
American historian and lecturer
From *The Roots of American Order*

It is the content of our lives that determines their value. If we limit our-selves to supply the means of living, in what way have we placed our-selves above the cattle that graze the fields? Cattle can live in comfort. Their every need is amply supplied. Is it not when one exercises his rea-son, his love of beauty, his desire for friendship, his selection of the good from that which is not good, that he earns the right to call himself a man? I should be inclined to claim that the person who limits his inter-ests to the means of living without consideration of the content or meaning of his life is defeating God's great purpose when He brought into existence a creature with the intelligence and godlike powers that are found in man. It is in living wisely and fully that one's soul grows.

—ARTHUR COMPTON (1892-1962)
Physicist and Nobel laureate
From "The Aspiring Soul"

I am by no means convinced that we ought not all become Evangelicals. . . . Wisdom is better than wit and in the long run will cer-tainly have the laugh on her side; and don't be frightened by the idea of . . . acting more strictly up to the precepts of the New Testament than others.

—JANE AUSTEN (1775-1817)
English novelist
Author, *Pride and Prejudice*
From a letter to Fanny Knight, written in 1814

Even those who have renounced Christianity and attacked it in their innermost being still follow the Christian ideal, for hitherto neither their subtlety nor the ardor of their hearts has been able to create a higher ideal of man and of virtue than the ideal given by Christ of old.

—FYODOR DOSTOEVSKY (1821-1881)
Russian novelist
From *The Brothers Karamazov*

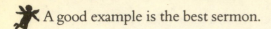 A good example is the best sermon.

—BENJAMIN FRANKLIN (1706-1790)
American writer and statesman

As one has to learn to read or to practice a trade, so one must learn to feel in all things, first and almost solely, the obedience of the universe to God. It is really an apprenticeship. Like every apprenticeship, it requires time and effort. . . . This does not mean that he will not suffer. Pain is the color of certain events. . . . When an apprentice gets hurt, or complains of being tired, the workmen and peasants have this fine expression: "It is the trade entering his body." Each time that we have some pain to go through, we can say to ourselves quite truly that it is the universe, the order, and beauty of the world and the obedience of creation to God that are entering our body. After that how can we fail to bless with tenderest gratitude the Love that sends us this gift?

—SIMONE WEIL (1909-1943)
French philosopher and mystic
From *Waiting for God*

LOVE

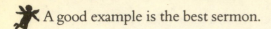 We can do no great things, only small things with great love.

—MOTHER TERESA (1910—)
Yugoslavian-born nun and Nobel laureate

If you love, you will suffer, and if you do not love, you do not know the meaning of a Christian life.

—DAME AGATHA CHRISTIE (1891-1976)
English mystery novelist
From *An Autobiography*

The Sermon on the Mount does not provide humanity with a complete guide to personal, social and economic problems. It sets forth spiritual attitudes, moral principles of universal validity, such as "Love your enemies," "Whatsoever ye would that men should do to you, do ye even so to them," and it leaves to Christians the task—the admittedly difficult task—of applying them in any given situation.

> —ROBERT JAMES MCCRACKEN (b.1904—)
> Scottish-born Canadian clergyman and writer

Just as there comes a warm sunbeam into every cottage window, so comes love—born of God's care for every separate need.

> —NATHANIEL HAWTHORNE (1804-1864)
> American novelist and short story writer

The Law of Love is this way. Jesus enjoined compassion: "I tell you to forgive seventy times seven." Yet the Christ was no preacher of an indiscriminate toleration of all human frailties: let man forgive his neighbor, but let all men tremble at the prospect of divine judgment.

> —RUSSELL KIRK (1918-1994)
> American historian and lecturer
> From *The Roots of American Order*

Of all earthly music, that which reaches farthest into heaven is the beating of a truly loving heart.

> —HENRY WARD BEECHER (1813-1887)
> American Congregationalist clergyman

Fear of God builds churches but love of God builds men.

> —LOUIS O. WILLIAMS (b.1908—)

Love all God's creation, the whole and every grain of sand in it. Love every leaf, every ray of God's light. Love the animals, love the plants, love everything. If you love everything you will perceive the divine mystery in things. Once you perceive it, you will begin to comprehend it better every day. And you will come at last to love the whole world with an all-embracing love.

> —FYODOR DOSTOEVSKY (1821-1881)
> Russian novelist
> From *The Brothers Karamazov*

At the heart of Jesus' ethical teaching stands the Great Commandment: "Thou shalt love the Lord with thy whole heart, with thy whole soul, with thy whole strength, with thy whole mind, and thy neighbor as thyself." So it had been written in the Law of the Jews, and every devout Jew repeated twice daily this precept. But by "neighbor," the Jews understood their immediate associates—at most, the community of Jews; while by that word "neighbor," Jesus meant all mankind.

"Do unto others as you would have others do unto you": this "Golden Rule" enunciated by Jesus is the spirit in which Christians are to fulfill that commandment to love neighbors. . . . In this, as in much else, the teaching of Christ urges men to be active in the service of God.

> —RUSSELL KIRK (1918-1994)
> American historian and lecturer
> From *The Roots of American Order*

It is true that virtually all peoples have traditions of compassion for the suffering, care for those in need, and concern for others. However, in most religious traditions, these movements of the heart are limited to one's own family, kin, nation, or culture. In some cultures, young males in particular have to be hard and insensitive to pain, so that they will be sufficiently cruel to enemies. Terror is the instrument intended to drive outsiders away from the territory of the tribe. In principle (though not always in practice), Christianity opposed this limitation on compassion. It taught people the impulse to reach out, especially to the most vulnerable, to the poor, the hungry, the wretched, those in prison, the hopeless, the sick, and others. It told humans to love their enemies.

—MICHAEL NOVAK (1933—)
American writer and philosopher
From "How Did Christ Revolutionize Political Economy?"

🌟 New Clothes for Old

When you see a flock of sheep feeding peacefully in a field, you probably say, "Oh . . . look at the pretty sheep!" Not for a moment do you think of all the trouble the shepherds have taken to tend those sheep through the cold winter.

If the lambs are born early in the year, before the snow has melted, many of them die of the cold. Sometimes the mother sheep dies as well. The shepherd is sad about this, as you can imagine.

Sometimes it happens that a mother sheep will die and leave a baby lamb. The shepherd does not want to lose the lamb as well, but what can he do? No other sheep will take the lamb and look after it. They are not like human beings, for they will only look after their own little ones.

So what do you suppose the shepherd does? Well, he looks over his flock, and finds a mother sheep who has just lost her lamb. He takes the poor dead lamb, removes its skin, and places it carefully over the body of the live lamb that has lost its mother. . . . It is just like putting on an overcoat, isn't it? Anyhow, the shepherd takes the poor little orphan lamb over to the mother sheep that has just lost her own baby. She smells the lamb all over, decides that it must surely be her own, and takes it to herself.

This gives us a beautiful illustration of what the love of Jesus does for us. Many times you must have heard the minister say in church that Jesus "covers us with the robe of His righteousness." Perhaps you have wondered just what he meant.

Now you can understand it easily, can't you? We are like the poor little orphan lamb. If we love Jesus, the slain Lamb, His goodness is wrapped, like a cloak, around us, and His Father accepts us, not because we are worthy of His love, but because He sees around us the glorious goodness of His own Son, and God welcomes us as His own dear children.

That doesn't mean, of course, that God is fooled, or that we can do what we like afterward. God truly accepts us because of what Jesus has done for us, but we must ever try by His grace to live to please Him. God wants us to be like Jesus through and through.

And that is where we differ from the poor little orphan lamb. He wears his covering only a few days until his mother gets used to him. We, however, must wear the righteousness of Jesus always, daily growing in grace and beauty of character.

> —ARTHUR S. MAXWELL (1896-1970)
> English-born American writer
> From *Uncle Arthur's Bedtime Stories*

TRUTH AND UNDERSTANDING

For it is but a feigned faith for a man to say to God secretly that he believeth Him, trusteth Him, and loveth Him, and then openly, where he should to God's honor tell the same tale, flatter God's enemies and do them pleasure and worldly worship, with the forsaking of God's faith before the world.

> —ST. THOMAS MORE (1478-1535)
> English statesman, writer, and martyr
> From "A Dialogue of Comfort Against Tribulation"

The pursuit of truth especially joins man to God. . . .

> —ST. THOMAS AQUINAS (1225-1274)
> Italian Dominican monk and principal theologian of the Roman
> Catholic Church
> From *On the Truth of the Catholic Faith*

Truth is the highest thing that man may keep.

> —GEOFFREY CHAUCER (c.1340-1400)
> English poet
> "The Franklin's Tale"

Truth is man's proper good, and the only immortal thing was given to our mortality to use.

> —BEN JONSON (1572-1637)
> English playwright

Servant of God, well done! well hast thou fought
The better fight, who single hast maintain'd
Against revolted multitudes the cause of truth.

> —JOHN MILTON (1608-1674)
> English poet
> From *Paradise Lost*

There are joys which long to be ours. God sends ten thousand truths, which come about us like birds seeking inlet; but we are shut up to them, and so they bring us nothing, but sit and sing awhile upon the roof, and then fly away.

> —HENRY WARD BEECHER (1813-1887)
> American Congregationalist clergyman

When I was young I was sure of everything; in a few years, having been mistaken a thousand times, I was not half so sure of most things as I was before; at present, I am hardly sure of anything but what God has revealed to me.

> —JOHN WESLEY (1703-1791)
> English evangelist and co-founder of Methodism

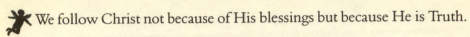 We follow Christ not because of His blessings but because He is Truth.

> —CHARLES COLSON (1930—)
> American writer and founder, Prison Fellowship
> From "A Message for all Seasons"

I have read in Plato and Cicero sayings that are very wise and beautiful; but I never read in either of them, "Come unto me all ye that labor and are heavy laden and I will give you rest."

> —ST. AUGUSTINE (354-430)
> Roman Catholic bishop of Hippo, North Africa
> Author, *Confessions* and *City of God*

God offers to every mind its choice between truth and repose. Take which you please—you can never have both.

> —RALPH WALDO EMERSON (1803-1882)
> American Transcendentalist poet and philosopher

To lie is so vile that even if it were speaking well of goodly things it would take something from God's grace; and truth is so excellent that if it praises but small things they become noble.

> —LEONARDO DA VINCI (1452-1519)
> Italian sculptor, painter, and architect

. . . Because he is intelligent the Christian, of all men, has to learn to discover with agonizing clarity what is conceivable by him about God.

> —KARL BARTH (1886-1968)
> Swiss Reformed theologian

Though the change from day to night is by a motion so gradual as scarcely to be perceived, yet when night is come we behold it very different from the day; and thus as people become wise in their own eyes, and prudent in their own sight, customs rise up from the spirit of this world, and spread by little, and little, until a departure from the simplicity that there is in Christ becomes as distinguishable as light from darkness, to such who are crucified to the world.

> —JOHN WOOLMAN (1720-1772)
> American Quaker clergyman and abolitionist
> From *Considerations on the True Harmony of Mankind*

MAN

Not every man is so great a coward as he thinks he is—nor yet so good a Christian.

> —ROBERT LOUIS STEVENSON (1850-1894)
> Scottish novelist and poet
> From *The Master of Ballantrae*

There are only three kinds of persons; those who serve God, having found Him; others who are occupied in seeking Him, not having found Him; while the remainder live without seeking Him, and without having found Him. The first are reasonable and happy, the last are foolish and unhappy; those between are unhappy and unreasonable.

> —BLAISE PASCAL
> French scientist and philosopher
> From *Pensées*

Every moment and every event of every man's life on earth plants something in his soul.

—THOMAS MERTON (1915-1968)
French-born Trappist monk and poet
From *New Seeds of Contemplation*

I decline to accept the end of man. . . . He is immortal not because he alone among creatures has an inexhaustible voice, but because he has a soul, a spirit capable of compassion and sacrifice and endurance. The poet's, the writer's duty is to write about these things. It is his privilege to help man endure by lifting his heart, by reminding him of the courage and honor and hope and pride and compassion and pity and sacrifice which have been the glory of his past. The poet's voice need not merely be the record of man, it can be one of the props, the pillars to help him endure and prevail.

—WILLIAM FAULKNER (1897-1962)
American novelist and short story writer
From his 1949 speech accepting the Nobel Prize for literature

I like insects for their stupidity. A paper wasp—*Polistes*—is fumbling at the stained-glass window on my right. I saw the same sight in the same spot last Sunday: Pssst! Idiot! Sweetheart! Go around by the door! I hope we seem as endearingly stupid to God—bumbling down into lamps, running half-wit across the floor, banging for days at the hinge of an opened door.

—ANNIE DILLARD (1945—)
Pulitzer Prize-winning American novelist and short story writer
From *Teaching a Stone to Talk*

A soul,—a spark of the never-dying flame that separates man from all the other beings of earth.

—JAMES FENIMORE COOPER (1789-1851)
American novelist
From *Afloat and Ashore*

In morals, as in physics, the stream cannot rise higher than its source. Christianity raises men from earth, for it comes from heaven; but human morality creeps, struts, or frets upon the earth's level, without wings to rise.

> —JOHN HENRY NEWMAN (1801-1890)
> English Roman Catholic cardinal

Lack of wealth is easily repaired; but poverty of soul is irreparable.

> —MICHEL DE MONTAIGNE (1533-1592)
> French essayist

≻FREEDOM≺

The God who gave us life, gave us liberty at the same time.

> —THOMAS JEFFERSON (1743-1826)
> Third president of the United States
> From "Summary View of the Rights of British America"

He is the best friend of American liberty who is most sincere and active in promoting pure and undefiled religion.

—JOHN WITHERSPOON (1723-1794)
Scottish-born American educator and Presbyterian clergyman
Signer of the Declaration of Independence

If we are not governed by God, then we will be ruled by tyrants.

—WILLIAM PENN (1644-1718)
English Quaker, founder of Pennsylvania

There never has been a period in which Common Law did not recognize Christianity as laying at its foundation.

—JOSEPH STORY (1779-1845)
United States Supreme Court justice
From an 1829 address at Harvard University

Kings then have not an absolute power in their regiment to do what pleases them; but their power is limited by God's word.

—JOHN KNOX (c.1505-1572)
Scottish preacher and reformer, founder of Presbyterianism

. . . [A] power ethical, politic, or moral to oppress is not from God and is not a power but a licentious derivation of a power and is no more from God, but from sinful nature and the old serpent, than a license to sin.

—SAMUEL RUTHERFORD (1600-1661)
Scottish Calvinist preacher and reformer
From *The Law and the Prince*

God grants liberty only to those who love it and are always ready to guard and defend it. Let our object be our country. And, by the blessing of God, may the country itself become a vast and splendid monument, not of oppression and terror, but of wisdom, of peace, and of liberty, upon which the world may gaze with admiration forever!

—DANIEL WEBSTER (1782-1852)
Statesman, attorney, and orator

God grant not only the love of liberty but a thorough knowledge of the rights of man may pervade all the nations of the earth—so that a philosopher may set his foot anywhere on its surface and say, "This is my Country."

—BENJAMIN FRANKLIN (1706-1790)
American writer and statesman

The basic need of the world is spirituality. The issue between free people and communism is not economic; . . . the issue is the preservation of the freedom of man as a living soul.

—DOUGLAS MACARTHUR (1880-1964)
American general, commander of Allied
forces in the Pacific (1941-1945)

Those who deny freedom to others deserve it not for themselves, and, under a just God, cannot long retain it.

—ABRAHAM LINCOLN (1809-1865)
Sixteenth president of the United States

Despotism may govern without faith, but Liberty cannot.

—ALEXIS DE TOCQUEVILLE (1805-1859)
French historian and statesman

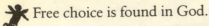 Free choice is found in God.

—St. Thomas Aquinas (1225-1274)
Italian Dominican monk and principal theologian of the
Roman Catholic Church
From *On the Truth of the Catholic Faith*

The Religion then of every man must be left to the conviction and conscience of every man; and it is the right of every man to exercise it as these may dictate. This right is in its nature an unalienable right. It is unalienable, because the opinions of men, depending only on the evidence contemplated by their own minds cannot follow the dictates of other men: It is unalienable also, because what is here a right towards men, is a duty towards the Creator.

—James Madison (1751-1836)*
Fourth president of the United States

It is those moral and spiritual qualities which rise alone in free men, which will fulfill the meaning of the word American. And with them will come centuries of further greatness to our country.

—Herbert Hoover (1874-1964)
Thirty-first president of the United States

Most important of all, the faith of America's founders affirmed the sanctity of each individual. Every human life—man or woman, child or adult, commoner or aristocrat, rich or poor—was equal in the eyes of the Lord. It also affirmed the responsibility of each individual.

—Lady Margaret Thatcher (1925—)
Prime Minister of Great Britain, 1979-1990
From "The Moral Foundations of Society"

---

*remarks in defense of religious freedom for Baptists and Quakers

There is no country in the world where the Christian religion retains a greater influence over the souls of men than in America. . . . Religion in America takes no direct part in the government of society, but it must be regarded as the first of their political institutions; for if it does not impart a taste for freedom, it facilitates the use of it. . . . I do not know whether all Americans have a sincere faith in their religion—for who can search the human heart?—but I am certain that they hold it indispensable to the maintenance of republican institutions.

—ALEXIS DE TOCQUEVILLE (1805-1859)
French historian and statesman
From *Democracy in America*

For freedom to exist, there have to be certain assumptions about the intrinsic worth of the individual. . . . Western freedom is the product of our faith, and the precepts of that faith are essential to its survival.

—M. STANTON EVANS (1934—)
Founder, National Journalism Center
From *The Theme Is Freedom*

Liberty is one of the choicest gifts that heaven hath bestowed upon man, and exceeds in volume all the treasures which the earth contains within its bosom or the sea covers. Liberty, as well as honor, man ought to preserve at the hazard of his life, for without it, life is insupportable.

—MIGUEL DE CERVANTES (1547-1616)
Spanish novelist, poet, and playwright
From *Don Quixote*

Man never fastened one end of a chain around the neck of his brother, that God did not fasten the other end around the neck of the oppressor.

—ALPHONSE DE LAMARTINE (1790-1869)
French poet and politician

. . . [T]he framers believed that the Constitution could not survive a people who did not believe in God or His laws. Whether Anglican or Pilgrim, Puritan or Baptist, Presbyterian, Catholic, or Quaker, our forefathers knew well those biblical passages that describe the sinful, fallen nature of man. In fact, the balance of power between people and government, between state and federal governments, and between the legislative, executive, and judicial branches of the federal government bears eloquent testimony to the founding fathers' belief in sinful man who should not be entrusted with too much power. "In God We Trust" was their motto, not "In Humanity We Trust."

They had just survived a bloody war with a king who talked of justice while forcing tyranny upon them. In that war they saw what men were made of, good and bad, and they concluded that without a people governed individually by God's laws, the nation would self-destruct.

George Washington said in his presidential farewell address that religion and morality are the two "great pillars of human happiness" and indispensable to "private and public felicity."

John Adams, our second president, said it this way: "We have no government armed with power capable of contending with human passions unbridled by morality and religion. Avarice, ambition, revenge, or gallantry would break the strongest cords of our Constitution as a whale goes through a net. Our Constitution was made only for a moral and religious people. It is wholly inadequate to the government of any other."

Thomas Jefferson, the third president, repeated the theme: "Can the liberties of a nation be sure when we remove their only firm basis, a conviction in the minds of the people, that these liberties are the gift of God? that they are not to be violated but with His wrath?"

> —PAT ROBERTSON (1930—)
> American evangelist and founder, Christian Broadcasting Network
> From *America's Dates with Destiny*

Every human soul is of infinite value, eternal, free; no human being, therefore, is so placed as not to have within his reach, in himself and others, objects adequate to infinite endeavor.

> —ARTHUR JAMES BALFOUR (1848-1930)
> English statesman and philosopher

The sacred rights of mankind are not to be rummaged for among old parchments or musty records. They are written, as with a sunbeam, in the whole volume of human nature, by the hand of the Divinity itself, and can never be erased or obscured by mortal power.

—ALEXANDER HAMILTON (1755-1804)
American attorney, banker, and statesman
First United States Secretary of the Treasury

All Christianity concentrates on the man at the crossroads. The vast and shallow philosophies, the huge syntheses of humbug, all talk about ages and evolution and ultimate developments. The true philosophy is concerned with the instant. Will a man take this road or that?—that is the only thing to think about, if you enjoy thinking. The eons are easy enough to think about, anyone can think about them. The instant is really awful: and it is because our religion has intensely felt the instant, that it has in literature dealt much with battle and in theology dealt much with hell. It is full of danger, like a boy's book: it is at an immortal crisis. . . . But the point is that a story is exciting because it has in it so strong an element of will, of what theology calls free will. You cannot finish a sum how you like. But you can finish a story how you like. When somebody discovered the Differential Calculus there was only one Differential Calculus he could discover. But when Shakespeare killed Romeo he might have married him to Juliet's old nurse if he had felt inclined. And Christendom has excelled in the narrative romance exactly because it has insisted on the theological free will.

—G.K. CHESTERTON (1874-1936)
English journalist, novelist, and poet
From *Orthodoxy*

OVERCOMING ADVERSITY

Let my heart be broken with the things that break the heart of God.

> —ROBERT PIERCE (1914-1978)
> American clergyman and founder, World Vision

No pain, no palm; no thorns, no throne; no gall, no glory; no cross, no crown.

> —WILLIAM PENN (1644-1718)
> English Quaker, founder of Pennsylvania
> From "No Cross, No Crown"

. . . Only God is able. It is faith in him that we must rediscover. With this faith we can transform bleak and desolate valleys into sunlit paths of joy and bring new light into the dark caverns of pessimism.

> —MARTIN LUTHER KING, JR. (1929-1968)
> African American Baptist clergyman, civil rights leader,
> and Nobel laureate
> From a sermon, "Our God Is Able"

The birthplace of Christianity was the tomb. The birthplace of splendor is desolation. Spring is conceived in the dark womb of Winter. And light is inevitably the offspring of darkness. . . . All this heaviness of night is surely but the prelude to a better dawn. The voice of God and the voice of Nature proclaim that the best is yet to be—always, the best is yet to be.

> —ROBERT CROMIE

It is the easiest thing in the world to obey God when he commands us to do what we like, and to trust Him when the path is all sunshine. The real victory of faith is to trust God in the dark, and through the dark.

—THEODORE L. CUYLER (1822-1909)
American Presbyterian clergyman and writer

We are always in the forge, or on the anvil; by trials God is shaping us for higher things.

—LYMAN BEECHER (1775-1863)
American Presbyterian clergyman and
co-founder, American Bible Society

Man sees himself lodged here in the mud and filth of the world, nailed and fastened to the most lifeless and stagnant part of the universe, in the lowest story of the house, at the furthest distance from the vault of Heaven, with the vilest animals; and yet, in his imagination, he places himself above the circle of the moon, and brings Heaven under his feet.

—MICHEL DE MONTAIGNE (1533-1592)
French essayist

Evil may have its hour, but God will have His day.

—FULTON SHEEN (1895-1975)
American Roman Catholic bishop

There is nothing that God has judged good for us that He has not given us the means to accomplish, both in the natural and moral world. If we cry, like children, for the moon, like children we must cry on.

—EDMUND BURKE (1729-1797)
Irish-born writer and statesman

The test of our religion is whether it fits us to meet emergencies. A man has no more character than he can command in a time of crisis.

—RALPH W. STOCKMAN

Christianity is not a Pollyanna religion. It doesn't claim that bad things won't happen to us. We are never told in the Old or New Testament that if we live a good life we'll never have any sickness or tragedy. However, we are promised in Isaiah 43: "Fear not, for I have redeemed you, I have called you by name; you are mine. When you pass through the waters . . . they shall not overwhelm you; when you walk through the fire you shall not be burned, and the flame shall not consume you. For I am the Lord your God."

—ROBERT SCHULLER (1926—)
American Reformed evangelist and writer

The crown of thorns is the condition of the crown of glory.

—FULTON SHEEN (1895-1975)
American Roman Catholic bishop

Do not lie in a ditch and say, *God help me*; use the lawful tools He hath lent thee.

—GEORGE CHAPMAN (c.1559-1634)
English dramatist, translator, and poet

We find thus by experience that there is no good applying to Heaven for earthly comfort. Heaven can give heavenly comfort; no other kind. And earth cannot give earthly comfort either. There is no earthly comfort in the long run.

—C. S. LEWIS (1898-1963)
English novelist, essayist, and educator
From *The Four Loves*

It is in A.D. 410, in Carthage in North Africa, that Augustine hears the desolating news that Rome has been sacked. If the days of the great Roman Empire are indeed over, he tells his flock, it is only what has happened sooner or later to every earthly kingdom. They must not lose heart; the world has grown old and is full of pressing tribulation, the world as they know it is passing away. Here truly, he says, we have no continuing city, but still we look for one; the cities that men build they sooner or later destroy, but there is also the City of God, which men did not build, and which they cannot destroy.

—MALCOLM MUGGERIDGE (1903-1990)
British journalist
From *Confessions of a Twentieth-Century Pilgrim*

Christendom bows humbly before the Cross. The crown of thorns has become the crown of light.

—JOHN SKELTON (C.1460-1529)
English poet
From *The Marquis of Montrose*

Now God be prais'd, that to believing souls gives light in darkness, comfort in despair!

—WILLIAM SHAKESPEARE (1564-1616)
English playwright and poet
From *Henry VI*

The moral principles and precepts contained in the Scriptures ought to form the basis of all our civil constitutions and laws. All the miseries and evils which men suffer from—vice, crime, ambition, injustice, oppression, slavery, and war—proceed from their despising or neglecting the precepts contained in the Bible.

—NOAH WEBSTER (1758-1843)
American lexicographer and philologist
Author, *The American Dictionary of the English Language*

It was granted me to carry away from my prison years on my bent back, which nearly broke beneath its load, the essential experience: how a human being becomes *evil* and how *good*. In the intoxication of my youthful successes I had felt myself to be infallible, and I was therefore cruel. In the surfeit of power I was a murderer and an oppressor. In my most evil moments I was convinced that I was doing good, and I was well supplied with systematic arguments. And it was only when, in the Gulag Archipelago,* on rotting prison straw that I sensed within myself the first stirrings of good. Gradually it was disclosed to me that the line separating good and evil passes, not through states, nor between classes, not between political parties either—but right through every human heart and through all human hearts. . . . And that is why I turn back to the years of my imprisonment and say, sometimes to the astonishment of those about me: "Bless you, prison!"

—ALEKSANDR SOLZHENITSYN (1918—)
Russian novelist and Nobel laureate

---

*Russian term for labor camps

SIN AND REDEMPTION

Calamity, war, famine, plague, death, adversity, disease, injury do not necessarily produce repentance. We may become better in a calamity but it does not necessarily make us repent. The essence of repentance is that we cannot be repentant until we confront our own self-righteousness with God's righteousness.

—FULTON SHEEN (1895-1975)
American Roman Catholic bishop

'Twas a thief that said the last kind word to Christ:
Christ took the kindness and forgave the theft."

—ROBERT BROWNING (1812-1889)
English Victorian poet
From "Giuseppe Capponsacchi"

Repentance must be something more than mere remorse for sins: it comprehends a change of nature befitting heaven.

—LEW WALLACE (1827-1905)
American general and novelist
From *Ben Hur*

Every man carries the bundle of his sins
Upon his own back.

—JOHN FLETCHER (1579-1625)
English dramatist
From *Rule a Wife and Have a Wife*

Sin is not hurtful because it is forbidden, but it is forbidden because it is hurtful.

—BENJAMIN FRANKLIN (1706-1790)
American writer and statesman
From *Poor Richard*

To abstain from sin when a man cannot sin is to be forsaken by sin, not to forsake it.

—ST. AUGUSTINE (354-430)
Roman Catholic bishop of Hippo, North Africa
From *Sermons*

Therefore I read you this counsel take,
Forsaketh sin, ere sin you forsake.

—GEOFFREY CHAUCER (C.1340-1400)
English poet
From "The Physician's Tale"

Who sins and mends commends himself to God.

—MIGUEL DE CERVANTES (1547-1616)
Spanish novelist, poet, and playwright
From *Don Quixote*

One leak will sink a ship; and one sin will destroy a sinner.

—JOHN BUNYAN (1628-1688)
English Baptist preacher
From *The Pilgrim's Progress*

Men are punished by their sins, not for them.

—ELBERT HUBBARD (1859-1915)
American editor, lecturer, and essayist
From "The Philistine"

Anger and just rebuke, and judgement giv'n,
That brought into this world a world of woe,
Sin and her shadow Death, and Misery
Death's harbinger.

> —JOHN MILTON (1608-1674)
> English poet
> From *Paradise Lost*

You need not choose evil; but have only to fail to choose good, and you drift fast enough toward evil. You do not need to say, "I will be bad," you have only to say, "I will not choose God's choice," and the choice of evil is already settled.

> —ATTRIBUTED TO SIR JOHN DAWSON (1820-1899)
> Canadian geologist and educator

I shall tell you a great secret, my friend. Do not wait for the last judgment; it takes place every day.

> —ALBERT CAMUS (1913-1960)
> French playwright, novelist, and Nobel laureate

There is only one way to put an end to evil, and that is to do good for evil.

> —LEO TOLSTOY (1828-1910)
> Russian novelist and philosopher
> Author, *War and Peace*

True wisdom comes from the overcoming of suffering and sin. All true wisdom is therefore touched with sadness.

> —WHITTAKER CHAMBERS (1901-1961)
> American journalist and Communist Party defector
> Author, *Witness*

We must acknowledge that there is such a thing as "the pleasures of sin"—temptation would not be so strong if this were not true. The answer is to make our love of God stronger than all temptation, and in that way to lead the good Christian life.

—PETER MARSHALL, SR. (1902-1949)
Scottish-born American Presbyterian clergyman

I have sinned, yes, I confess with no joy, but a broken and contrite heart, I'm assured, God will not despise.

—LARRY WOIWODE (1941—)
American novelist
From *Acts*

 Sin has many tools, but a lie is the handle which fits them all.

—OLIVER WENDELL HOLMES (1841-1935)
United States Supreme Court justice

Young twigs are easily bent and made to grow another way, old trees most difficultly. So persons in youth are more easily turned than others. Again, a young plant is much more easily plucked up by the roots than after it hath long stood and is rooted deep in the ground. So it is more easy to forsake sin in the beginning than after a long continuance in it.

—JONATHAN EDWARDS (1703-1758)
American Congregational clergyman and theologian*
From *Images or Shadows of Divine Things*

I myself see Christianity today as the only living spiritual force capable of undertaking the spiritual healing of Russia.

—ALEKSANDR SOLZHENITSYN (1918—)
Russian novelist and Nobel laureate

---

*In 1734, Edwards's forceful preaching helped bring an unprecedented religious revival that began in England to the colonies. It was known as the "Great Awakening."

We implore the mercy of God, not that He may leave us at peace in our vices, but that He may deliver us from them.

> —BLAISE PASCAL (1623-1662)
> French scientist and philosopher
> From *Pensées*

Sorrow wounds a person, but it is a clean wound and heals over in normal fashion. Sin, however, is like a splinter of infectious shrapnel received in battle. Whereas a soldier's body may be pierced by a piece of clean shrapnel and come to be solidly surrounded by healthy flesh, an unclean fragment will be a source of infection, causing various troublesome symptoms until removed. So, if a man commits a sin, his mind attempts to rationalize and justify it, in effect to throw tissue around it, but in vain. As the sin sinks deeper into the mind the infection spreads.

> —NORMAN VINCENT PEALE (1898-1993)
> American clergyman and founder, *Guideposts*
> From *Faith Is the Answer*

In moments of weakness and distress it is good to tread closely in God's footsteps.

> —ALEKSANDR SOLZHENITSYN (1918—)
> Russian novelist and Nobel laureate

If we lived in a state where virtue was profitable, common sense would make us good, and greed would make us saintly. And we'd live like animals or angels in the happy land that needs no heroes. But since in fact we see that avarice, anger, envy, pride, sloth, lust and stupidity commonly profit far beyond humility, chastity, fortitude, justice, and thought, and have to choose, to be human at all, . . . why then perhaps we must stand fast a little—even at the risk of being heroes.

> —ROBERT BOLT (1926-1995)
> American playwright
> From a speech by the character St. Thomas More in
> *A Man for All Seasons*

The Fall is a view of life. It is not the only enlightening, but the only encouraging view of life. It holds, as against the only real alternative philosophies, those of the Buddhist, or the Pessimist, or the Promethean, that we have misused a good world, and not merely been entrapped into a bad one. It refers evil back to the wrong use of the will, and thus declares that it can eventually be righted by the right use of the will. Every other creed except that one is some form of surrender to fate.

—G.K. CHESTERTON (1874-1936)
English journalist, novelist, and poet
Author, *Orthodoxy* and *The Father Brown Stories*

Roses grow upon briars, which is to signify that all temporal sweets are mixt with bitter. But what seems more especially to be meant by it is that pure happiness, the crown of glory, is to be come at in no other way than by bearing Christ's cross, by a life of mortification, self-denial, and labor, and bearing all things for Christ. The rose, that is chief of all flowers, is the last thing that comes out. The briary, prickly bush grows before that; the end and crown of all is the beautiful and fragrant rose.

—JONATHAN EDWARDS (1703-1758)
American Congregational clergyman and theologian
From *Images or Shadows of Divine Things*

For what is more consistent with faith than to acknowledge ourselves naked of all virtue, that we may be clothed by God; empty of all good, that we may be filled by Him, slaves to sin, that we may be liberated by Him; blind that we may be enlightened by Him; lame that we may be guided; weak, that we may be supported by Him; to divest ourselves of all ground of glorying, that He alone may be eminently glorious, and that we may glory in Him?

—JOHN CALVIN (1509-1564)
French-born Swiss theologian and founder of Calvinism
From "Dedication of the Institutes of Religion: An Address to His Majesty, Francis, King of France"

I no longer wished for a better world because I was thinking of the whole of creation, and in the light of this clearer discernment I have come to see that, though the higher things are better than the lower, the sum of all creation is better than the higher things alone.

—ST. AUGUSTINE (354-430)
Roman Catholic bishop of Hippo, North Africa
Author, *Confessions* and *City of God*

The history of the world is nothing but the history of the war waged by the powers of the world and of hell since the beginning against the souls humbly devoted to the divine action. In this war the advantages seem all on the side of pride, and yet humility always wins the day. The order of God has always remained victorious; those who have been on His side have triumphed with Him and are happy for eternity; injustice has never been able to protect the deserters. . . . The man who has wickedness in his mind always believes himself invincible. But, O God! how can we resist Thee? A single soul with hell and the world against it can fear nothing if it be on the side of surrender to God's order. . . . All who freely serve iniquity become the slaves of justice, and the divine action builds the Heavenly Jerusalem with the ruins of Babylon.

—JEAN-PIERRE DE CAUSSADE (1675-1751)
French philosopher

The one really strong case for Christianity is that even those who condemn sins have to confess them.

—G.K. CHESTERTON (1874-1936)
English journalist, novelist, and poet
Author, *Orthodoxy* and *The Father Brown Stories*

Only heaven means crowned, not conquered, when it says "Forgiven."

—ADELAIDE ANNE PROCTER (1825-1864)
"A Legend of Provence"

The quality of mercy is not strain'd. It droppeth as the gentle rain from heaven upon the place beneath: it is twice bless'd; it blesses him that gives and him that takes: 'tis mightiest in the mightiest; it becomes the throned monarch better than his crown; his scepter shows the force of temporal power, the attribute to awe and majesty, wherein doth sit the fear and dread of kings; but mercy is above this sceptered sway; it is an attribute of God himself. . . .

> —WILLIAM SHAKESPEARE (1564-1616)
> English playwright and poet
> From *The Merchant of Venice*

I beg them to remember that Our Lord caught me as so many others like me into His sheep fold straight out of the wilderness.

> —SIGRID UNDSET (1882-1949)
> Norwegian novelist and Nobel laureate
> From *Stages on the Road*

DEATH AND ETERNAL LIFE

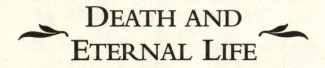

Fear not that thy life shall come to an end, but rather fear that it shall never have a beginning.

> —JOHN HENRY NEWMAN (1801-1890)
> English Roman Catholic cardinal

O what their joy and their glory must be,
Those endless sabbaths the blessed ones see!

> —PETER ABELARD (1079-1142)
> French monk, philosopher, and teacher

My sword I shall give to him that shall succeed me in my pilgrimage, and my courage and skill to him that can get it. My marks and scars I carry with me, to be a witness for me that I have fought His battles who now will be my regarder. When the day that He must go hence was come, many accompanied Him to the riverside, into which as He went He said: "Death where is thy sting?" And as He went down deeper He said: "Grave where is thy victory?" So He passed over, and all the trumpets sounded for Him on the other side.

—JOHN BUNYAN (1628-1688)
English Baptist preacher
From *Pilgrim's Progress*

What is this rest of death, sweet friend:
What is the rising up, and where?
I say, death is a lengthened prayer,
A longer night, a larger end.

—JOAQUIN MILLER [CINCINNATUS HINER MILLER] (1839-1913)
American jurist and "frontier poet"
From "A Song of the South"

Death's but a path that must be trod,
If man would ever pass to God.

—THOMAS PARNELL (1679-1718)
Irish poet
From "A Night-Piece on Death"

Death is but crossing the world, as friends do the seas; they live in one another still.

—WILLIAM PENN (1644-1718)
English Quaker, founder of Pennsylvania
From "Fruits of Solitude"

Her suffering ended with the day;
Yet lived she at its close,
And breathed the long, long night away
In statue-like repose.
But when the sun, in all his state,
Illumed the eastern skies,
She passed through Glory's morning gate,
And walked in Paradise.

—JAMES ALDRICH (1810-1856)
American verse writer
From "A Death-Bed"

So, like a prisoner awaiting his release, like a schoolboy when the end of term is near, like a migrant bird ready to fly south, like a patient in hospital anxiously scanning the doctor's face to see whether a discharge may be expected, I long to be gone. Extricating myself from the flesh I have too long inhabited, hearing the key turn in the lock of Time

—MALCOLM MUGGERIDGE (1903-1990)
British journalist
From *Confessions of a Twentieth-Century Pilgrim*

Think of yourself just as a seed patiently wintering in the earth; waiting to come up as a flower in the Gardener's good time, up into the real world, the real waking. I suppose that our whole present life, looked back on from there, will seem only a drowsy half-waking. We are here in the land of dreams. But cock-crow is coming. It is nearer now than when I began this letter.

—C. S. LEWIS (1898-1963)
English novelist, essayist, and educator
Author, *The Screwtape Letters* and *The Chronicles of Narnia*

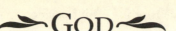 GOD

. . . the infinite mercy and goodness of God. . . .

> —SIR FRANCIS BACON (1561-1626)
> English philosopher and statesman

God is an infinite sea of substance.

> —ST. JOHN OF DAMASCUS (C.675-C.749)
> Syrian Eastern Orthodox monk and theologian

God is that, the greater than which cannot be conceived.

> —ST. ANSELM (C.1033-1109)
> Italian-born archbishop of Canterbury

. . . need, now as then,
Thee, God, who moldest men. . . .

> —ROBERT BROWNING (1812-1889)
> English Victorian poet
> From "Rabbi Ben Ezra"

God is our only hope. He alone will not fail us, for He came to abide in our midst as one of us, if we will but only open our hearts to receive Him. He came to glory in our glory, to suffer in our sufferings, and, in this hour of fears and tears God is no stranger to our lot. He is yoked to the same plough as we are!

> —FRANCIS JOSEPH SPELLMAN (1889-1967)
> American Roman Catholic cardinal

If we pretend to have reached either perfection or satisfaction, we have degraded ourselves and our work. God's work only may express that, but ours may never have that sentence written upon it, "Behold it was very good."

> —JOHN RUSKIN (1819-1900)
> English art critic, writer, and social reformer

.... suddenly I knew what millions of people around the world are discovering, that God is not remote. He is an ever-present source of comfort, power, and strength.

> —PAT ROBERTSON (1930—)
> American evangelist and founder, Christian Broadcasting Network
> From *America's Dates with Destiny*

Even though the historical world is a fallen world, it is . . . not devoid of reality. There is a moral order, and order of reason, which is real since God has taught us our duties. The reality of the moral order thus hinges on the reality of God.

> —GERHART NIEMEYER (1907—)
> German-born American political scientist and educator
> From *Between Nothingness and Paradise*

To be in act is for each being its good. But God is not only a being in act; He is His very act of being. . . . God is, therefore, *goodness itself*, and not only good.

> —ST. THOMAS AQUINAS (1225-1274)
> Italian Dominican monk and principal theologian of the Roman Catholic Church
> From *On the Truth of the Catholic Faith*

When there is no God, everything is permitted.

—FYODOR DOSTOEVSKY (1821-1881)
Russian novelist
From *The Brothers Karamazov*

In God there is no hunger that needs to be filled, only plenteousness that desires to give.

—C. S. LEWIS (1898-1963)
English novelist, essayist, and educator
From *The Four Loves*

When God began to make the world and put it into order and cause light to shine, it was a chaos, in a state of utter confusion, without form, and void, and darkness was upon the face thereof. So commonly things are in a state of great confusion before God works some great and glorious work in the church and in the world, or in some particular part of the church or world, and so oftentimes towards particular persons.

—JONATHAN EDWARDS (1703-1758)
American Congregational clergyman and theologian
From *Images or Shadows of Divine Things*

The tumults of the flesh were hushed, hushed the images of earth, and waters, and air; hushed also the poles of Heaven, yes the very soul hushed to herself, and by not thinking of self surmounting self, hushed all dreams and imaginary revelations, every tongue and every sign, and whatsoever only exists in transition. . . . And God alone speaks, not through any tongue of flesh, nor Angel's voice, nor sound of thunder, nor in the dark riddle of a similitude, that we might hear His Very Voice.

—ST. AUGUSTINE (354-430)
Roman Catholic bishop of Hippo, North Africa
Author, *Confessions* and *City of God*

. . . that Almighty and Eternal Being, whose gaze necessarily includes the whole of created things, and who surveys distinctly, though at once, mankind and man.

> —ALEXIS DE TOCQUEVILLE (1805-1859)
> French historian and statesman
> From *Democracy in America*

How are we to seek for Him? How are we to go toward Him? Even if we were to walk for hundreds of years, we should do no more than go 'round and 'round the world. Even in an airplane we could not do anything else. We are incapable of progressing vertically. We cannot take a step toward the heavens. God crosses the universe and comes to us.

> —SIMONE WEIL (1909-1943)
> French philosopher and mystic
> From *Waiting for God*

. . . God knows lowly things, and . . . this is not opposed to the nobility of His knowledge.

> —ST. THOMAS AQUINAS (1225-1274)
> Italian Dominican monk and principal theologian of the Roman
> Catholic Church
> From *On the Truth of the Catholic Faith*

God is the poet, men are but the actors.

> —HONORÉ DE BALZAC (1799-1850)
> French novelist

God Himself is the best Poet,
And the Real is his song.

> —ELIZABETH BARRETT BROWNING (1806-1861)
> English Victorian poet
> From "The Dead Pan"

God shall be my hope,
My stay, my guide and lantern to my feet.

—WILLIAM SHAKESPEARE (1564-1616)
English playwright and poet
From *Henry VI*

Who believes that equal grace
God extends in every place,
Little difference he scans
'Twixt a rabbit's God and man's.

—BRET HARTE (1839-1902)
American short story writer and diplomat
Author, *The Luck of Roaring Camp and Other Stories*
From "Battle Bunny: Envoy"

God is light
And never but in unapproached light
Dwelt from eternity.

—JOHN MILTON (1608-1674)
English poet
From *Paradise Lost*

When God dawns he dawns for all.

—MIGUEL DE CERVANTES (1547-1616)
Spanish novelist, poet, and playwright
From *Don Quixote*

Fear God, and where you go men will think they walk in hallowed cathedrals.

—RALPH WALDO EMERSON (1803-1882)
American Transcendentalist poet and philosopher
From "Conduct of Life: Worship"

Where there is peace, God is.

> —GEORGE HERBERT (1593-1633)
> English clergyman

All growth that is not towards God is growing to decay.

> —GEORGE MACDONALD (1824-1905)
> Scottish novelist and poet
> From *Within and Without*

In the faces of men and women I see God.

> —WALT WHITMAN (1819-1882)
> American poet
> From "Song of Myself"

Man proposes, but God disposes.

> —THOMAS À KEMPIS (C.1379-1471)
> German monk
> From *The Imitation of Christ*

God! Thou art love! I build my faith on that.

> —ROBERT BROWNING (1812-1889)
> English Victorian poet
> From "Paracelsus"

Yes, if you're a tramp in tatters,
While the blue sky bends above
You've got nearly all that matters—
You've got God and God is Love.

> —ROBERT W. SERVICE (c.1874-1958)
> Canadian novelist and poet
> From "Comfort"

Praise God from whom all Blessings flow;
Praise Him all creatures here below;
Praise Him above, ye Heavenly Host:
Praise Father, Son, and Holy Ghost.

—THOMAS KEN (1637-1711)
English theologian
From "Morning and Evening Hymn"

Let nothing disturb thee,
Let nothing affright thee,
All things are passing,
God changeth never.

—HENRY WADSWORTH LONGFELLOW (1807-1882)
American poet and educator
From "Santa Teresa's Bookmark"

God moves in a mysterious way
His wonders to perform;
He plants his footsteps in the sea,
And rides upon the storm.

—WILLIAM COWPER (1731-1800)
English poet
From "Light Shining Out of Darkness"

➤ JESUS ➤

Jesus Christ is a God whom we approach without pride and before whom we humble ourselves without despair.

> —BLAISE PASCAL (1623-1662)
> French scientist and philosopher
> From *Pensées*

One of the most amazing things ever said on this earth is Jesus' statement: "He that is greatest among you shall be your servant." Nobody has one chance in a billion of being thought really great after a century has passed except those who have been the servants of all. That strange realist from Bethlehem knew that.

> —HARRY EMERSON FOSDICK (1878-1969)
> American Baptist clergyman

"Was Christ a man like us?—Ah, let us try
If we then, too, can be such men as he!"

> —MATTHEW ARNOLD (1822-1888)
> English poet and literary critic
> From "Anti-Desperation"

One can sell Christ as Judas did, but one cannot buy Him.

> —FULTON SHEEN (1895-1975)
> American Roman Catholic bishop

He has turned aside the river of ages out of its course and lifted the centuries off their hinges.

> —UNKNOWN

The vine-wreathed god Rising, a stifled question from the silence,
Fronts the pierced Image with the crown of thorns.

> —GEORGE ELIOT [MARY ANN EVANS CROSS] (1819-1880)
> English novelist and poet
> From *Spanish Gypsy*

Jesus, whose name is not so much written as ploughed into the history of this world.

> —RALPH WALDO EMERSON (1803-1882)
> American Transcendentalist poet and philosopher
> From *Nature, Addresses, and Lectures*

In darkness there is no choice. It is light that enables us to see the differences between things; and it is Christ that gives us light.

> —J. C. (1795-1855) AND A. W. HARE (1792-1834)
> English clergymen
> From *Guesses at Truth*

The hands of Christ seem very frail,
For they were broken by a nail.
But only they reach Heaven at last
Whom these frail, broken hands hold fast.

> —RICHARD MORELAND (1880-1947)
> American poet
> From "His Hands"

All His glory and beauty come from within, and there He delights to dwell, His visits there are frequent, His conversation sweet, His comforts refreshing; and His peace passing all understanding.

> —THOMAS À KEMPIS (c.1379-1471)
> German monk
> From *The Imitation of Christ*

One Solitary Life

He was born in an obscure village, the child of a peasant woman. He grew up in another village, where He worked in a carpenter shop until He was thirty. Then for three years He was an itinerant preacher. He never wrote a book. He never held an office. He never had a family or owned a home. He didn't go to college. He never visited a big city. He never traveled two hundred miles from the place where He was born. He did none of the things that usually accompany greatness. He had no credentials except Himself.

He was only thirty-three when the tide of public opinion turned against Him. His friends ran away. One of them denied Him. He was turned over to His enemies and went through the mockery of a trial. He was nailed to the cross between two thieves.

While He was dying, His executioners gambled for His garments, the only property He had on earth. When He was dead, He was laid in a borrowed grave through the pity of a friend. Nineteen centuries have come and gone, and today He is the central figure of the human race.

All the armies that have ever marched, all the navies that have ever sailed, all the parliaments that have ever sat, all the kings that have ever reigned, put together, have not affected the life of man on this earth as much as that one solitary life.

—UNKNOWN

The central miracle asserted by Christians is the Incarnation. They say God became Man. Every other miracle prepares for this, or exhibits this, or results from this. Just as every natural event is the manifestation at a particular place and moment of Nature's total character, so every particular Christian miracle manifests at a particular place and moment the character and significance of the Incarnation.

—C. S. LEWIS (1898-1963)
English novelist, essayist, and educator
From *The Joyful Christian*

The Mystery of Jesus

Jesus suffers in His passions the torments which men inflict upon Him; but in His agony He suffers the torments which He inflicts on Himself; *turbare semetipsum* (to disturb oneself). This is a suffering from no human, but an almighty hand, for He must be almighty to bear it.

Jesus seeks some comfort at least in His three dearest friends, and they are asleep. He prays them to bear with Him for a little, and they leave Him with entire indifference, having so little compassion that it could not prevent their sleeping even for a moment. And thus Jesus was left alone to the wrath of God.

Jesus is alone on the earth, without anyone not only to feel and share His suffering, but even to know of it; He and Heaven were alone in that knowledge.

Jesus is in a garden, not of delight as the first Adam, where he lost himself and the whole human race, but in one of agony, where He saved Himself and the whole human race.

—BLAISE PASCAL (1623-1662)
French scientist and philosopher
From *Pensées*

Therefore, friends,
As far as to the sepulcher of Christ,
Whose soldier now, under whose blessed cross
We are impressed and engaged to fight . . .
To chase these pagans in those holy fields
Over whose acres walk'd those blessed feet,
Which fourteen hundred years ago were nail'd
For our advantage on the bitter cross.

—WILLIAM SHAKESPEARE (1564-1616)
English playwright and poet
From *Henry IV*

[The New Testament] talks about Christians being "born again"; it talks about them "putting on Christ"; about Christ "being formed in us"; about our coming to "have the mind of Christ."

Put right out of your head the idea that these are only fancy ways of saying that Christians are to read what Christ said and try to carry it out. . . . They mean that a real Person, Christ, here and now, in that very room where you are saying your prayers, is doing things to you. It is not a question of a good man who died two thousand years ago. It is a living Man, still as much a man as you, and still as much God as He was when He created the world, really coming and interfering with your very self; killing the old natural self in you and replacing it with the kind of self He has."

—C. S. LEWIS (1898-1963)
English novelist, essayist, and educator
From *Mere Christianity*

By a carpenter mankind was made, and only by that Carpenter can man be remade.*

—ERASMUS (c.1466-1536)
Dutch Roman Catholic priest, philosopher, and satirist

Official Christianity, of late years, has been having what is known as "a bad press." We are constantly assured that the churches are empty because preachers insist too much upon doctrine—"dull dogma," as people call it. The fact is the precise opposite. It is the neglect of dogma that makes for dullness. The Christian faith is the most exciting drama that ever staggered the imagination of man—and the dogma is the drama.

That drama is summarized quite clearly in the creeds of the Church, and if we think it dull it is because we either have never really read those amazing documents, or have recited them so often and so mechanically as to have lost all sense of their meaning. The plot pivots

---

*paraphrase of the Gospel of St. Mark

upon a single character, and the whole action is the answer to a single central problem: *What think ye of Christ?* Before we adopt any of the unofficial solutions (some of which are indeed excessively dull)— before we dismiss Christ as a myth, an idealist, a demagogue, a liar, or a lunatic—it will do no harm to find out what the creeds really say about Him. What does the Church think of Christ?

The Church's answer is categorical and uncompromising, and it is this: That Jesus Bar-Joseph, the carpenter of Nazareth, was in fact and in truth, and in the most exact and literal sense of the words, the God "by whom all things were made." His body and brain were those of a common man; His personality was the personality of God, so far as that personality could be expressed in human terms. He was not a kind of demon pretending to be human; He was in every respect a genuine living man. He was not merely a man so good as to be "like God"—He was God.

Now, this is not just a pious commonplace; it is not commonplace at all. For what it means is this, among other things: that for whatever reason God chose to make man as he is—limited and suffering and subject to sorrows and death—He had the honesty and the courage to take His own medicine. Whatever game He is playing with His creation, He has kept His own rules and played fair. He can exact nothing from man that He has not exacted from Himself.

He has himself gone through the whole of human experience, from the trivial irritations of family life and the cramping restrictions of hard work and lack of money to the worst horrors of pain and humiliation, defeat, despair, and death. When He was a man, He played the man. He was born in poverty and died in disgrace and thought it well worthwhile.

—DOROTHY SAYERS (1893-1957)
English novelist and essayist
From *Christian Letters to a Post-Christian World*

There is no historical task which so reveals a man's true self as the writing of a Life of Jesus.

—ALBERT SCHWEITZER (1875-1965)
German physician, missionary, and Nobel laureate in French Equatorial Africa

The Baptism of Christ

To be a Christian is to believe in the impossible. Jesus was God. Jesus was human.

This is what Scripture affirms. Yet theologians and philosophers and ordinary people have argued about it for nearly two thousand years. How could Jesus be both human and divine? That he was both is the basic affirmation of the Christian faith.

We human beings seem quite capable of accepting that light is a particle, and light is a wave. So why should it be more difficult for us to comprehend that Jesus was completely God and Jesus was completely human? Of course it takes imagination, but so does it take imagination for us to understand, as we watch a glorious sunset, that it is the planet earth that is turning, not the sun that is setting.

Those are the wonderful things that are beyond ordinariness—like love—that make life worth living.

Even for Jesus, the human being, his understanding of his Godness did not come all at once. There was a glimmer when he was a boy of twelve and talked with the elders in the Temple. But full understanding did not come until he was a young man and was baptized by his cousin John: John, who, years before, had recognized Jesus in the womb when pregnant Mary had visited Elizabeth.

John was reluctant to baptize Jesus, saying that he was not worthy even to lace up his sandals; but Jesus insisted, and as John baptized him in the River Jordan, the Holy Spirit came upon Jesus from above, and a thunder came from Heaven, and out of the thunder Jesus heard a voice saying: "This is my beloved son in whom I am well pleased."

And then Jesus knew who he was: a human being who was God. God who was human. A most Glorious Impossible.

—MADELEINE L'ENGLE (1919—)
Newbery Award-winning children's writer
From *The Glorious Impossible*

He came to die when He need not have died; He died to satisfy for what might have been pardoned without satisfaction; He paid a price which need not have been asked. . . . He died, not in order to exert a peremptory claim on the Divine justice, if I may so speak,—as if He were bargaining in the marketplace, or pursuing a plea in a court of law,—but in a more loving, generous, munificent way, did He shed that blood.

—JOHN HENRY NEWMAN (1801-1890)
    English Roman Catholic cardinal

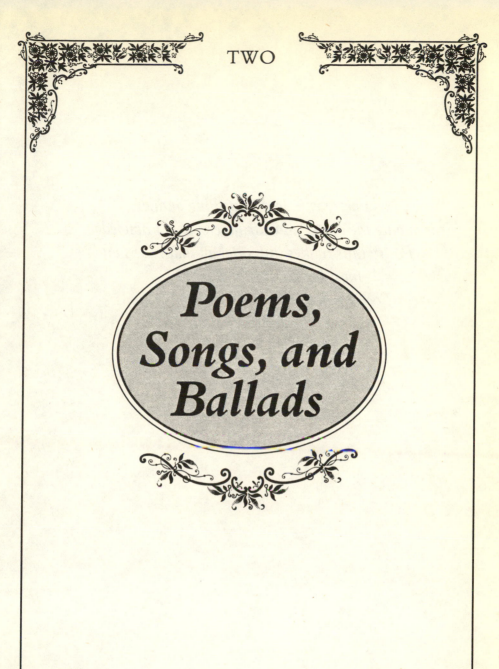

TWO

Poems, Songs, and Ballads

Poetry is indeed something divine.
It is at once the center and circumference of knowledge. . . .
Poetry thus makes immortal all that is best and
most beautiful in the world. . . .
Poetry redeems from decay the visitations
of the divinity in man.

PERCY BYSSHE SHELLEY (1792-1822)
English Romantic poet
From "A Defense of Poetry"

❧ PRAYERS ☙

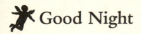 A Child's Evening Prayer

Ere on my bed my limbs I lay,
God grant me grace my prayers to say:
Oh God! preserve my mother dear
In strength and health for many a year;
And, O! preserve my father too,
And may I pay him reverence due;
And may I best thoughts employ
To be my parents' hope and joy;
And O! preserve my brothers both
From evil doings and from sloth,
And may we always love each other
Our friends, our father, and our mother:
And still, O Lord, to me impart
An innocent and grateful heart,
That after my great sleep I may
Awake to thy eternal day!

—SAMUEL TAYLOR COLERIDGE (1772-1834)
English Romantic poet

Good Night

Good night! Good night!
Far flies the light;
But still God's love
Shall shine above,
Making all bright,
Good night! Good night!

—VICTOR HUGO (1802-1885)
French novelist and poet
Author, *Les Misérables*

🕊 The Knight's Prayer

God be in my head
　And in my understanding;
God be in mine eyes
　And in my looking;
God be in my mouth
　And in my speaking;
God be in my heart
　And in my thinking;
God be at my end,
　And at my departing.

—UNKNOWN

The Prayers I Make†

The prayers I make will then be sweet indeed,
If Thou the spirit give by which I pray:
My unassisted heart is barren clay,
That of its native self can nothing feed.
Of good and pious works Thou art the seed,
That quickens only where Thou sayest it may;
Unless Thou show to us Thine own true way,
No man can find it: Father! Thou must lead.
Do Thou, then, breathe those thoughts into my mind
By which such virtue may in me be bred,
That in Thy holy footsteps I may tread;
The fetters of my tongue do Thou unbind,
That I may have the power to sing of Thee
And sound Thy praises everlastingly.*

—MICHELANGELO (1475-1564)
　Italian sculptor, painter, and architect

---

*The last six lines in this sonnet are attributed to Michelangelo's nephew.

Lord, Make Me an Instrument of Your Peace[†]

Lord, make me an instrument of Your peace.
Where there is hatred, let me sow love;
Where there is injury, pardon;
Where there is doubt, faith;
Where there is despair, hope;
Where there is darkness, light;
And where there is sadness, joy.
O, Divine Master, grant that I may not so much seek to be consoled as
*   to console;*
To be understood as to understand;
To be loved as to love;
For it is in giving that we receive;
It is in pardoning that we are pardoned;
It is in dying that we are born to eternal life.

—SAINT FRANCIS OF ASSISI (c.1182-1226)
    Italian friar and founder of the Franciscan Order

A Prayer of Thanksgiving

Lord, behold our family here assembled.
We thank Thee
For this place in which we dwell;
For the peace accorded us this day,
For the hope with which we expect tomorrow;
For the health, the work, the food
And the bright skies that make our lives delightful,
For our friends in all parts of the earth, and our friendly helpers. . . .
Let peace abound in our small company.

—ROBERT LOUIS STEVENSON (1850-1894)
    Scottish novelist and poet
    Author, *Treasure Island*

We Thank Thee

For flowers that bloom about our feet;
For tender grass, so fresh and sweet;
For song of bird and hum of bee;
For all things fair we hear or see
Father in Heaven, we thank Thee!

For blue of stream, for blue of sky;
For pleasant shade of branches high;
For fragrant air and cooling breeze;
For beauty of the blowing trees—
Father in Heaven, we thank Thee!

For mother-love, for father-care;
For brothers strong and sisters fair;
For love at home and school each day;
For guidance lest we go astray—
Father in Heaven, we thank Thee!

For Thy dear, everlasting arms,
That bear us o'er all ills and harms;
For blessed words of long ago,
That help us now Thy will to know—
Father in Heaven, we thank Thee!

—RALPH WALDO EMERSON (1803-1882)
American Transcendentalist poet and philosopher

Prayer for Gentleness to All God's Creatures

To all the humble beasts there be,
To all the birds on land and sea,
Great Spirit, sweet protection give
That Free and Happy they may live!
And to our hearts the rapture bring
Of love for every living thing;
Make us all one kin, and bless
Our ways with Christ's own gentleness.

—JOHN GALSWORTHY (1867-1933)
English novelist and Nobel laureate

Prayer for Generosity

Teach us good Lord, to serve Thee as Thou deservest:
To give and not count the cost;
To fight and not heed the wounds;
To toil and not to seek for rest;
To labor and not ask for reward
Save that of knowing that we do Thy will.

—ST. IGNATIUS OF LOYOLA (1491-1556)
Spanish founder of the Jesuit order

Prayer for Serenity

God, give us grace to accept with serenity the
things that cannot be changed, courage to change the
things that should be changed, and the wisdom to
distinguish the one from the other.

—REINHOLD NIEBUHR (1892-1971)
American philosopher

Grace and Thanksgiving

We thank, Thee, Lord for quiet upland lawns,
For misty loveliness of autumn dawns,
For gold and russet of the ripened fruit,
For yet another year's fulfillment, Lord.
We thank Thee now.

For joy of glowing color, flash of wings,
We thank Thee, Lord, for all the little things
That make the love and laughter of our days,
For home and happiness and friends, we praise
And thank Thee now.

—ELIZABETH GOULD (1848-1906)
American poet

The Blessing of Light

May the blessing of Light be on you,
Light without and light within.
May the blessed sunlight shine on you
And warm your heart till it glows
Like a great peatfire
And warm himself at it,
And also a friend.

—UNKNOWN

Lead Back Thy Old Soul†

Lord, what I once had done with youthful might,
Had I been from the first true to the truth,
Grant me, now old, to do—with better sight,
And humbler heart, if not the brain of youth;
So wilt Thou, in Thy gentleness and ruth,
Lead back thy old soul, by the path of pain,
Round to his best—young eyes and heart and brain.

—GEORGE MACDONALD (1824-1905)
Scottish novelist and poet
Author, *At the Back of the North Wind*

A Last Prayer

Father, I scarcely dare to pray,
So clear I see, now it is done,
How I have wasted half my day,
And left my work but just begun.

—HELEN HUNT JACKSON (1831-1885)
American novelist and poet

Others

Lord help me live from day to day
In such a self-forgetful way,
That even when I kneel to pray,
My prayer shall be for—others.

—CHARLES D. MEIGS (fl.1792)
American physician

The Day Is Done†

The day is done;
O God the Son,
Look down upon
Thy little one!

O God of Light,
Keep me this night,
And send to me
Thy angels bright.

I need not fear
If Thou art near;
Thou art my Savior,
Kind and dear.

—UNKNOWN

A Better Resurrection

I have no wit, no words, no tears;
    My heart within me like a stone
Is numbed too much for hopes or fears.
    Look right, look left, I dwell alone;
I lift mine eyes, but dimmed with grief
    No everlasting hills I see;
My life is in the falling leaf:
    O Jesus quicken me.

My life is like a faded leaf,
    My harvest dwindled to a husk:
Truly my life is void and brief
    And tedious in the barren dusk;
My life is like a frozen thing,
    No bud or greenness can I see;
Yet rise it shall—the sap of Spring;
    O Jesus rise in me.

My life is like a broken bowl,
    A broken bowl that cannot hold
One drop of water for my soul
    Or cordial in the searching cold;
Cast in the fire the perished thing;
    Melt and remold it, till it be
A royal cup for Him, my King:
    O Jesus drink of me.

—CHRISTINA ROSSETTI (1830-1894)
Italian-born poet

The Universal Prayer

Father of all! in every age,
  In every clime adored,
By saint, by savage, and by sage,
  Jehovah, Jove, or Lord!

Thou great First Cause, least understood,
  Who all my sense confined
To know but this, that Thou art good,
  And that myself am blind;

Yet gave me, in this dark estate,
  To see the good from ill;
And, binding nature fast in fate,
  Left free the human will:

What conscience dictates to be done,
  Or warns me not to do,
This, teach me more than hell to shun,
  That, more than heaven pursue.

What blessings Thy free bounty gives
  Let me not cast away;
For God is paid when man receives,
  To enjoy is to obey.

Yet not to earth's contracted span
  Thy goodness let me bound,
Or think Thee Lord alone of man,
  When thousand worlds are round:

Let not this weak, unknowing hand
  Presume Thy bolts to throw,
And deal damnation round the land
  On each I judge Thy foe.

If I am right, Thy grace impart
  Still in the right to stay;
If I am wrong, O teach my heart
  To find that better way!

Save me alike from foolish pride
　　And impious discontent
At aught Thy wisdom has denied,
　　Or aught Thy goodness lent.

Teach me to feel another's woe,
　　To hide the fault I see;
That mercy I to others show,
　　That mercy show to me.

Mean though I am, not wholly so,
　　Since quickened by Thy breath;
O lead me wheresoever I go,
　　Through this day's life or death!

This day be bread and peace my lot;
　　All else beneath the sun,
Thou know'st if best bestowed or not,
　　And let Thy will be done.

To Thee, whose temple is all space,
　　Whose altar, earth, sea, skies,
One chorus let all Being raise,
　　All Nature's incense rise!

—ALEXANDER POPE (1688-1744)
English poet and satirist

FAMILY, FRIENDS, CHURCH, AND COMMUNITY

To My Mother

Because the angels in the Heavens above,
Devoutly singing unto one another,
Can find, amid their burning terms of love,
None so devotional as that as "mother."

Therefore by that sweet name I have long called you,
Filling my heart of hearts where God installed you,
In setting my Virginia's spirit free,
My mother—my own mother, who died early,
Was but the mother of myself, but you
Are mother to the dead I loved so dearly,
Are thus more precious than the one I knew,
By that infinity with which my wife
Was dearer to my soul than its soul-life.

—EDGAR ALLAN POE (1809-1849)
American short story writer, poet, and critic

A Mother's Birthday

Lord Jesus, Thou hast known
    A mother's love and tender care:
And Thou wilt hear,
    While for my own
Mother most dear
I make this birthday prayer.

Protect her life, I pray,
    Who gave the gift of life to me;
And may she know,
    From day to day,
The deepening glow
Of joy that comes from Thee.

As once upon her breast
    Fearless and well content I lay,
So let her heart
    On Thee at rest,
Fell fear depart
And trouble fade away.

Ah, hold her by the hand,
    As once her hand held mine;
And though she may
    Not understand
Life's winding way,
Lead her in peace divine.

I cannot pay my debt
    For all the love that she has given;
But Thou, love's Lord,
    Wilt not forget
Her due reward,—
Bless her in earth and heaven.

—HENRY VAN DYKE (1852-1933)
American Presbyterian clergyman, educator, and novelist

The Hand That Rocks the Cradle

Blessing on the hand of women!
  Angels guard its strength and grace,
In the palace, cottage, hovel,
  Oh, no matter where the place;
Would that never storms assailed it,
  Rainbows ever gently curled;
For the hand that rocks the cradle
  Is the hand that rules the world.

Infancy's the tender fountain,
  Power may with beauty flow,
Mother's first to guide the streamlets,
  From them souls unresting grow—
Grow on for the good or evil,
  Sunshine streamed or evil hurled;
For the hand that rocks the cradle
  Is the hand that rules the world.

Woman, how divine your mission
  Here upon our natal sod!
Keep, oh, keep the young heart open
  Always to the breath of God!
All true trophies of the ages
  Are from mother-love impearled;
For the hand that rocks the cradle
  Is the hand that rules the world.

Blessings on the hand of women!
  Fathers, sons, and daughters cry,
And the sacred song is mingled
  With the worship in the sky—
Mingles where no tempest darkens,
  Rainbows evermore are hurled;
For the hand that rocks the cradle
  Is the hand that rules the world.

—WILLIAM ROSS WALLACE (1819–1881)
American poet

The Watcher

She always leaned to watch for us,
    Anxious if we were late,
In winter by the window,
    In summer by the gate;

And though we mocked her tenderly,
    Who had such foolish care,
The long way home would seem more safe
    Because she waited there.

Her thoughts were all so full of us,
    She never could forget!
And so I think that where she is
    She must be watching yet,

Waiting till we come home to her,
    Anxious if we are late—
Watching from Heaven's window,
    Leaning from Heaven's gate.

—MARGARET WIDDEMER (1880-1979)
American novelist and poet

My Mother

God made my mother on an April day,
From sorrow and the mist along the sea,
Lost birds' and wanderers' songs and ocean spray,
And the moon loved her wandering jealously.

Beside the ocean's din she combed her hair,
Singing the nocturne of the passing ships,
Before her earthly lover found her there
And kissed away the music from her lips.

She came unto the hills and saw the change
That brings the swallow and the geese in turns.
But there was not a grief she deemed strange,
For there is that in her which always mourns.

Kind heart she has for all on hill or wave
Whose hopes grew wings like ants to fly away.
I bless the God who such a mother gave
This poor bird-hearted singer of a day.

—FRANCIS LEDWIDGE (1891-1917)
Irish poet

A Prayer for Fathers

God bless fathers, all fathers old and young.
Bless the new father holding his son or daughter in his arms for the first time.
(Steady his trembling, Lord, make his arms strong.)
Give him the ambition and strength to provide for its physical needs.
But even more, give him the love and common sense to provide for its
hungering heart.
Give him the time and the will to be its friend.
Give him wisdom, give him patience, give him justice in discipline.
Make him a hero in his youngster's eyes.
So that the word "Father" will always mean a person to be respected, a fair and
mighty man.

And God bless older fathers too.
Fathers who are weary from working for their young.
Fathers who are sometimes disappointed, discouraged.
Fathers whose children don't always turn out the way they'd hoped;
fathers of children who seem thoughtless, ungrateful, critical, children who rebel.
Bless those fathers, Lord; comfort them.
And stay close to all these fathers when they must tell sons and daughters
good-bye,
When kids leave home, going off to college, or to marry, or to war—fathers need
to be steadied in their trembling then too, Lord.
(Mothers aren't the only ones who cry.)

Thou, our Heavenly Father, must surely understand these earthly fathers well.
We so often disappoint You, rebel against you, fail to thank You, turn away
   from You.
So, in Your infinite love (and infinite experience!) bless fathers, all fathers old
   and young.

    —MARJORIE HOLMES (1910—)
      American novelist and educator

A Thank You for Friends

There are all kinds of men
   Who have done me good turns,
That I still never think about,
   Not for a minute;
Yet if I were making up
   That sort of grace,
They would all of them have
   To be in it.

One man made up stories,
   Another wrote verses
I found, and liked,
   And I read them until I knew them,
Another one saw
   All the things they had written,
Then, being an artist,
   He drew them.

Another took wood
   And a saw and some glue,
And put each of them just
   In the place that would need it—
So that is the chair
   Where I sit with my book
And am so much at ease
   As I read it.

I'm forgetting the one
   Who read tale after tale
When I was too young
   To know letter from letter,
And the other who taught me them,
   Till in the end
I could read for myself—
   Which was better.

—RODNEY BENNETT

What Life Have You?[†]

What life have you if you have not life together?
There is no life that is not in community,
And no community not lived in praise of GOD.
Even the anchorite who meditates alone,
For whom the days and nights repeat the praise of GOD,
Prays for the Church, the Body of Christ incarnate.
And now you live dispersed on ribbon roads,
And no man knows or cares who is his neighbor
Unless his neighbor makes too much disturbance,
But all dash to and fro in motor cars,
Familiar with the roads and settled nowhere
Nor does the family even move about together,
But every son would have his motorcycle,
And daughters ride away on casual pillions.

Much to cast down, much to build, much to restore;
Let the work not delay, time and the arm not waste;
Let the clay be dug from the pit, let the saw cut the stone,
Let the fire not be quenched in the forge.

—T.S. ELIOT (1888-1965)
   American-born poet and Nobel laureate
   From "The Rock"

The Church Walking with the World

The Church and the World walked far apart
   On the changing shores of time,
The World was singing a giddy song
   And the Church a hymn sublime.
"Come, give me your hand," said the merry World,
   "And walk with me this way!"
But the good Church hid her snowy hands
   And solemnly answered "Nay,
I will not give you my hand at all,
   And I will not walk with you;
Your way is the way that leads to death;
   Your words are all untrue."

"Nay, walk with me but a little space,"
   Said the World with a kindly air;

"The road I walk is a pleasant road
   And the sun shines always there;
Your path is thorny and rough and rude,
   But mine is broad and plain;
My way is paved with flowers and dews,
   And yours with tears and pain;
The sky to me is always blue,
   No want, no toil I know;
The sky above you is always dark,
   Your lot is a lot of woe;
There's room enough for you and me
   To travel side by side."

Half shyly the Church approached the World
   And gave him her hand of snow;
And the old World grasped it and walked along,
   Saying, in accents low,
"Your dress is too simple to please my taste;
   I will give you pearls to wear
Rich velvets and silks for your graceful form,
   And diamonds to deck your hair."

The Church looked down at her plain white robes,
  And then at the dazzling World,
And blushed as she saw his handsome lip
  With a smile contemptuous curled.
"I will change my dress for a costlier one,"
  Said the Church, with a smile of grace;
Then her pure white garments drifted away,
  And the World gave, in their place,
Beautiful satins and shining silks,
  Roses and gems and costly pearls;
While over her forehead her bright hair fell
  Crisped in a thousand curls.

"Your house is too plain," said the proud old World,
  "I'll build you one like mine;
With walls of marble and towers of gold,
  And furniture ever so fine."
So he built her a costly and beautiful house;
  Most splendid it was to behold;
Her sons and her beautiful daughters dwelt there
  Gleaming in purple and gold;
Rich fairs and shows in the halls were held,
  And the World and his children were there.
Laughter and music and feasts were heard
  In the place that was meant for prayer.
There were cushioned seats for the rich and the gay,
  To sit in their pomp and pride;
But the poor who were clad in shabby array,
  Sat meekly down outside.

"You give too much to the poor," said the World.
  "Far more than you ought to do;
If they are in need of shelter and food,
  Why need it trouble you?
Go, take your money and buy rich robes,
  Buy horses and carriages fine;
Buy pearls and jewels and dainty food,
  Buy the rarest and costliest wine;

My children, they dote on all these things,
  And if you their love would win
You must do as they do, and walk in the ways
  That they are walking in."

So the poor were turned from her door in scorn,
  And she heard not the orphan's cry;
But she drew her beautiful robes aside,
  As the widows went weeping by.

Then the sons of the World and the Sons of the Church
  Walked closely hand and heart,
And only the Master, who knoweth all,
  Could tell the two apart.
Then the Church sat down at her ease, and said,
  "I am rich and my goods increase;
I have need of nothing, or aught to do,
  But to laugh, and dance, and feast."
The sly World heard, and he laughed in his sleeve,
  And mockingly said, aside—
"The Church is fallen, the beautiful Church;
And her shame is her boast and her pride."

The angel drew near to the mercy seat,
  And whispered in sighs her name—
Then the loud anthems of rapture were hushed,
  And heads were covered with shame
And a voice was heard at last by the Church
  From Him who sat on the throne,
"I know thy works, and how thou hast said
  'I am rich, and hast not known
That thou art naked, poor and blind
  And wretched before my face;'
Therefore from my presence cast I thee out,
  And blot thy name from its place."

—MATILDA C. EDWARDS

❧ GOD'S WORLD ❧

❧ Pippa's Song

> The year's at the spring
> And day's at the morn;
> Morning's at seven;
> The hillside's dew-pearled;
> The lark's on the wing;
> The snail's on the thorn;
> God's in His heaven—
> All's right with the world!

> —ROBERT BROWNING (1812-1889)
> English Victorian poet
> From "Pippa Passes"

❧ Nature's Creed

> I believe in the brook as it wanders
>   From hillside into glade;
> I believe in the breeze as it whispers
>   When evening's shadows fade.
> I believe in the roar of the river
>   As it dashes from high cascade;
> I believe in the cry of the tempest
>   'Mid the thunder's cannonade.
> I believe in the light of shining stars,
>   I believe in the sun and the moon;
> I believe in the flash of lightning,
>   I believe in the night-bird's croon.
> I believe in the faith of the flowers,
>   I believe in the rock and sod,
> For in all of these appeareth clear
>   The handiwork of God.

> —UNKNOWN

The Summer Sea

Soft soft wind, from out the sweet south sliding,
Waft thy silver cloud webs athwart the summer sea;
Thin thin threads of mist on dewy fingers twining
Weave a veil of dappled gauze to shade my babe and me.

Deep deep love, within thine own abyss abiding,
Pour Thyself abroad, O Lord, on earth and air and sea;
Worn weary hearts within Thy holy temple hiding,
Shield from sorrow, sin, and shame my helpless babe and me.

—CHARLES KINGSLEY (1819-1875)
English clergyman, social reformer, and novelist
Song from *The Water Babies*

 # The Robin's Song

God bless the field and bless the furrow,
Stream and branch and rabbit burrow,
Hill and stone and flower and tree,
From Bristol town to Wetherby—
Bless the sun and bless the sleet,
Bless the lane and bless the street,
Bless the night and bless the day,
From Somerset and all the way
To the meadows of Cathay;
Bless the minnow, bless the whale,
Bless the rainbow and the hail,
Bless the nest and bless the leaf,
Bless the righteous and the thief,
Bless the wing and bless the fin,
Bless the air I travel in,
Bless the mill and bless the mouse,
Bless the miller's bricken house,
Bless the earth and bless the sea,
God bless you and God bless me!

—UNKNOWN

Arbor Day Song

Of nature broad and free,
Of grass and flower and tree,
   Sing we today.
God hath pronounced it good,
So we, his creatures would
Offer to field and wood
   Our heartfelt lay.

To all that meets the eye,
In earth, or in sky,
   Tribute we bring.
Barren this world would be,
Bereft of shrub and tree;
Now Gracious Lord to Thee,
   Praises we sing.

May we Thy hand behold,
As bud and leaf unfold,
See but Thy thought;
   Nor heedlessly destroy,
Nor pass unnoticed by;
But be our constant joy
   All Thou hast wrought.

As each small bud and flower!
Speaks of the Maker's power,
   Tells of His love;
So we, Thy children dear,
Would live from year to year,
Show forth Thy goodness here,
   And then above.

—MARY A. HEERMANS

A Passing Glimpse

I often see flowers from a passing car
That are gone before I can tell what they are.

I want to get out of the train and go back
To see what they were beside the track.

I name all the flowers I am sure they weren't:
Not fireweed loving where woods have burnt—

Not bluebells gracing a tunnel mouth—
Not lupine living on sand and drouth.

Was something brushed across my mind
That no one on earth will ever find?

Heaven gives its glimpses only to those
Not in position to look too close.

—ROBERT FROST (1874-1963)
American Pulitzer Prize-winning poet

I Love All Beauteous Things[†]

I love all beauteous things,
I seek and adore them;
God hath no better praise,
And man in his hasty days
Is honored for them.

I too will something make
And joy in the making;
Altho' tomorrow it seem
Like the empty words of a dream
Remembered on waking.

—ROBERT BRIDGES (1844-1930)
English poet laureate

High Flight*

Oh, I have slipped the surly bonds of earth,
And danced the skies on laughter-silvered wings;
Sunward I've climbed and joined the tumbling mirth
Of sun-split clouds—and done a hundred things
You have not dreamed of—wheeled and soared and swung
High in the sunlit silence. Hov'ring there,
I've chased the shouting wind along and flung
My eager craft through footless halls of air.
Up, up the long delirious, burning blue
I've topped the wind-swept heights with easy grace,
Where never lark, or even eagle, flew;
And, while with silent, lifting mind I've trod
The high untrespassed sanctity of space,
Put out my hand, and touched the face of God.

—JOHN GILLEPSIE MAGEE, JR. (1922-1941)
Royal Canadian air force pilot

Is There Care in Heaven?†

And is there care in heaven? and is there love
In heavenly spirits to these creatures base
That may compassion of their evils move?
There is:—else much more wretched were the case
Of men than beasts: But oh! the exceeding grace
Of highest God that loves His creatures so,
And all His works with mercy doth embrace. . . .

—EDMUND SPENSER (c. 1552-1599)
English poet
Author, *The Faerie Queene*

---

*This sonnet was written on the back of a letter to the author's mother. After his death in combat at age 19, it was made the official poem of the British flying forces and was posted at all air bases.

Like an Angel[†]

How like an angel came I down!
How bright are all things here!
When first among His works I did appear,
Oh, how their Glory me did crown!
The world resembled His Eternity,
In which my soul did walk;
And everything that I did see
Did with me talk.

The skies in their magnificence,
The lively, lovely air;
Oh, how divine, how soft, how sweet, how fair!
The stars did entertain my sense,
And all the work of God so bright and pure,
So rich and great did seem
As if they ever must endure
In my esteem.

—THOMAS TRAHERNE (c. 1636-1674)
English poet

The Evening Clouds[†]

Those evening clouds, that setting ray,
And beauteous tints, serve to display
Their great Creator's praise;
Then let the short-lived thing call'd man,
Whose life's comprised within a span,
To Him his homage raise.

We often praise the evening clouds,
And tints so gay and bold,
But seldom think upon our God,
Who tinged these clouds with gold.

—SIR WALTER SCOTT (1771-1832)
Scottish novelist and poet
Author, *Ivanhoe*

God's World

O world, I cannot hold thee close enough!
  Thy winds, thy wide grey skies!
  Thy mists, that roll and rise!
Thy woods, this autumn day, that ache and sag
  And all but cry with colour! That gaunt crag
  To crush! To lift the lean of that black bluff!
World, World, I cannot get thee close enough!

Long have I known a glory in it all,
  But never knew I this:
  Here such a passion is
As stretcheth me apart,—Lord, I do fear
Thou'st made the world too beautiful this year.
My soul is all but out of me,—let fall
No burning leaf; prithee,* let no bird call.

—EDNA ST. VINCENT MILLAY (1892-1950)
American Pulitzer Prize-winning poet

April and May

April cold with dropping rain
Willows and lilacs brings again,
The whistle of returning birds,
And the trumpet-lowing of the herds.
The scarlet maple-keys betray
What potent blood hath modest May,
What fiery force the earth renews,
The wealth of forms, the flush of hues;
What joy in rosy waves outpoured
Flows from the heart of Love, the Lord.

—RALPH WALDO EMERSON (1803-1882)
American Transcendentalist poet and philosopher

---

*pray thee, or please

Miracles

Why, who makes much of a miracle?
As to me, I know of nothing else but miracles,
Whether I walk the streets of Manhattan,
Or dart my sight over the roofs of houses toward the sky,
Or wade with naked feet along the beach just
        in the edge of the water,
Or stand under trees in the woods,
Or talk by day with anyone I love, or sleep in the bed
        at night with anyone I love,
Or sit at table at dinner with the rest,
Or look at strangers opposite me riding in the car,
Or watch honeybees busy around the hive
        of a summer forenoon,
Or animals feeding in the fields,
Or birds, or the wonderfulness of insects in the air,
Or the wonderfulness of the sundown, or of stars
        shining so quiet and bright,
Or the exquisite delicate curve of the new moon in spring;
These with the rest, one and all, are to me miracles,
The whole referring, yet each distinct and in its place,
To me every hour of the light and dark is a miracle,
Every cubic inch of space is a miracle,
Every foot of the interior swarms with the same
To me the sea is a continual miracle,
The fishes that swim—the rocks—the motion of the waves—
        the ships with men in them,
What stranger miracles are there?

      —WALT WHITMAN (1819-1882)
       American poet

All Things Bright and Beautiful

All things bright and beautiful,
  All creatures great and small,
All things wise and wonderful,
  The Lord God made them all.

Each little flower that opens,
  Each little bird that sings,
He made their glowing colors,
  He made their tiny wings.

The rich man in his castle,
  The poor man at his gate,
God made them, high or lowly,
  And order'd their estate.

The purple-headed mountain,
  The river running by,
The sunset and the morning,
  That brightens up the sky;—

The cold wind in the winter,
  The pleasant summer sun,
The ripe fruits in the garden,—
  He made them every one.

The tall trees in the greenwood,
  The meadows where we play,
The rushes by the water
  We gather every day;—

He gave us eyes to see them,
  And lips that we might tell,
How great is God Almighty,
  Who has made all things well.

—CECIL FRANCES ALEXANDER (1818-1895)
English poet and hymn writer

i thank You God for most this amazing

i thank You God for most this amazing
day: for the leaping greenly spirits of trees
and a blue true dream of sky; and for everything
which is natural which is infinite which is yes

(i who have died am alive again today,
and this is the sun's birthday; this is the birth
day of life and of love and wings: and of the gay
great happening illimitably earth)

how should tasting touching hearing seeing
breathing any—lifted from the no
of all nothing—human merely being
doubt unimaginable You?

(now the ears of my ears awake and
now the eyes of my eyes are opened)

—e.e. cummings (1894–1962)
American poet

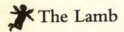 ## The Lamb

Little lamb, who made thee?
    Dost thou know who made thee,

Gave thee life, and bade thee feed
By the stream and o'er the mead.
Gave thee clothing of delight,
Softest clothing, woolly, bright;
Gave thee such a tender voice,
Making all the vales rejoice?

Little lamb, who made thee?
    Dost thou know who made thee?

Little lamb, I'll tell thee;
    Little lamb, I'll tell thee;

He is called by thy name,
For He calls Himself a Lamb;
He is meek, and He is mild,
He became a little child.
I a child, and thou a lamb,
We are called by His name.
Little lamb, God bless thee!
   Little lamb, God bless thee!

—WILLIAM BLAKE (1757-1827)
English Romantic poet

God's Grandeur

The world is charged with the grandeur of God.
   It will flame out, like shining from shook foil;
   It gathers to a greatness, like the ooze of oil
Crushed. Why do men then now not reck* His rod?
Generations have trod, have trod, have trod;
   And all is seared with trade; bleared, smeared with toil;
   And wears man's smudge and shares man's smell: the soil
Is bare now, nor can foot feel, being shod.

And for all this, nature is never spent;
   There lives the dearest freshness deep down things;
And though the last lights off the black West went
   Oh, morning, at the brown brink eastward, springs—
Because the Holy Ghost over the bent
   World broods with warm breast and ah! bright wings.

—GERARD MANLEY HOPKINS (1844-1889)
English Jesuit priest and teacher

---

*take heed of

Robin's Song

Robins sang in England
    Frost or rain or snow,
All the long December days
    Endless years ago.

Robins sang in England
    Before the Legions came,
Before our English fields were tilled
    Or England was a name.

Robins sang in England
    When forests dark and wild
Stretched across from sea to sea
    And Jesus was a child.

Listen! In the frosty dawn
    From his leafless bough
The same brave song he ever sang
    A robin's singing now.

—RODNEY BENNETT

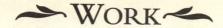 WORK

Envoy* to the Toiling of Felix

The legend of Felix is ended, the toiling of Felix is done;
The Master has paid him his wages, the goal of his journey is won;
He rests, but he never is idle; a thousand years pass like a day,
In the glad surprise of Paradise where work is sweeter than play.

Yet often the King of that country comes out from his tireless host,
And walks in this world of the weary as if He loved it the most;
For here in the dusty confusion, with eyes that are heavy and dim,
He meets again the laboring men who are looking and longing
*   for Him.*

He cancels the curse of Eden, and brings them a blessing instead:
Blessed are they that labor, for Jesus partakes of their bread.
He puts His hand to their burdens, He enters their homes at night:
Who does his best shall have as a guest the Master of life and light.

And courage will come with His presence, and patience return at
*   His touch,*
And manifold sins be forgiven to those who love Him much;
The cries of envy and anger will change to the songs of cheer,
The toiling age will forget its rage when the Prince of Peace
*   draws near.*

This is the gospel of labor, ring it, ye bells of the kirk
The Lord of Love came down from above, to live with the men
*   who work.*
This is the rose that He planted, here in the thorn-curst soil:
Heaven is blest with perfect rest, but the blessing of Earth is toil.

—HENRY VAN DYKE (1852-1933)
   American Presbyterian clergyman, educator, and novelist

---

*Dedication

Work

Work!
Thank God for the might of it,
The ardor, the urge, the delight of it,
Work that springs from the heart's desire,
Setting the brain and the soul on fire—
Oh, what is so good as the heat of it,
And what is so glad as the beat of it,
And what is so kind as the stern command,
Challenging brain and heart and hand?

Work!
Thank God for the pride of it,
For the beautiful, conquering tide of it;
Sweeping the life in its furious flood,
Thrilling the arteries, cleansing the blood,
Mastering stupor and dull despair,
Moving the dreamer to do and dare.
Oh, what is so good as the urge of it,
And what is so glad as the surge of it,
And what is so strong as the summons deep,
Rousing the torpid soul from sleep?

Work!
Thank God for the pace of it,
For the terrible, keen, swift race of it;
Fiery steeds in full control,
Nostrils a-quiver to greet the goal.
Work, the Power that drives behind,
Guiding the purposes, taming the mind,
Holding the runaway wishes back,
Reining the will to one steady track,
Speeding the energies faster, faster,
Triumphing over disaster.
Oh, what is so good as the pain of it,
And what is so kind as the cruel goad,
Forcing us on through the rugged road?

Work!
Thank God for the swing of it,
For the clamoring, hammering ring of it,
Passion and labor daily hurled
On the mighty anvils of the world,
Oh, what is so fierce as the flame of it?
And what is so huge as the aim of it?
Thundering on through dearth and doubt,
Calling the plan of the Maker out.
Work, the Titan: Work, the friend,
Shaping the earth to a glorious end,
Draining the swamps and blasting the hills,
Doing whatever the Spirit wills—
Rending a continent apart,
To answer the dream of the Master heart,
Thank God for a world where none may shirk—
Thank God for the splendor of work!

—ANGELA MORGAN [LAURAN PAINE] (B.1916)
American novelist, historian, and poet

 Work

Let me but do my work from day to day,
In field or forest, at the desk or loom,
In roaring market-place or tranquil room;
Let me but find it in my heart to say,
When vagrant wishes beckon me astray,
"This is my work; my blessing, not my doom;
Of all who live, I am the one by whom
This work can best be done in the right way."

Then shall I see it not too great, nor small,
To suit my spirit and to prove my powers;
Then shall I cheerfully greet the laboring hours,
And cheerfully turn, when the long shadows fall
At eventide, to play and love and rest,
Because I know for me my work is best.

—HENRY VAN DYKE (1852-1933)
American Presbyterian clergyman, educator, and novelist

Song of Work

Work while the sun climbeth high in the heaven,
Work in the noon-day's dust and heat,
Work till the evening its blessing hath given,
Work while the moon keeps vigil sweet.
Work while the verdant grasses are springing,
Work in the summer's radiant glow,
Work in the autumn with gladness and singing,
Work in the time of frost and snow.

*Labor is noble and rich is its guerdon,**
Sweet after toil comes peaceful rest.
Take on thy shoulders, rejoicing, the burden,
Pleasure is good, but work is best.
Great is our Lord, of labor the master,
Follow the path His feet have trod.
Strive, with the joy of all honest endeavor;
Then at the last, find rest with God.

> —MARY BLAKE (1840-1907)
> Irish poet

The Glory of the Garden

Then seek your job with thankfulness and work till further orders,
If it's only netting strawberries or killing slugs on borders;
And when your back stops aching and your hands begin to harden,
You will find yourself a partner in the Glory of the Garden.

Oh, Adam was a gardener, and God who made him sees
That half a proper gardener's work is done upon his knees,
So when your work is finished, you can wash your hands and pray
For the Glory of the Garden, that it may not pass away!
And the Glory of the Garden shall never pass away!

> —RUDYARD KIPLING (1865-1936)
> English journalist, novelist, poet, and Nobel laureate
> Author, *The Jungle Book*

---

*reward

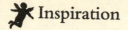 **Inspiration**

Whate'er we leave to God, God does,
And blesses us;
The work we choose should be our own,
God lets alone.

—HENRY DAVID THOREAU (1817-1862)
American Transcendentalist philosopher and essayist
Author, *Walden*

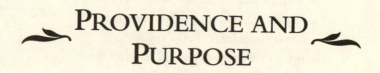

PROVIDENCE AND PURPOSE

Under the Leaves

Oft have I walked these woodland paths,
Without the blessed foreknowing
That underneath the withered leaves
The fairest buds were growing.

Today the south-wind sweeps away
The types of autumn's splendor,
And shows the sweet arbutus flowers,—
Spring's children, pure and tender.

O prophet-flowers!—with lips of bloom,
Outvying in your beauty
The pearly tints of ocean shells,—
Ye teach me faith and duty!

Walk life's dark ways, ye seem to say,
With love's divine foreknowing
That where man sees but withered leaves,
God sees sweet flowers growing.

—ALBERT LAIGHTON (1829-1887)
American attorney and verse writer

Sometime

Sometime, when all life's lessons have been learned,
    And sun and stars forevermore have set,
The things which our weak judgments here have spurned,
    The things o'er which we grieved with lashes wet,
Will flash before us out of life's dark night,
    As stars shine most in deeper tints of blue;
And we shall see how all God's plans are right,
    And how what seemed reproof was love most true.

And we shall see how, while we frown and sigh,
    God's plans go on as best for you and me;
How, when we called, He heeded not our cry,
    Because His wisdom to the end could see.
And even as prudent parents disallow
    Too much of sweet to craving babyhood,
So God, perhaps, is keeping from us now
    Life's sweetest things, because it seemeth good.

And if, sometimes, commingled with life's wine,
    We find the wormwood, and rebel and shrink,
Be sure a wiser hand than yours or mine
    Pours out the potion for our lips to drink;
And if some friend you love is lying low,
    Where human kisses cannot reach his face,
Oh, do not blame the loving Father so,
    But wear your sorrow with obedient grace!

And you shall shortly know that lengthened breath
    Is not the sweetest gift God sends His friend,
And that, sometimes, the sable pall of death
    Conceals the fairest boon His love can send;
If we could push ajar the gates of life,
    And stand within, and all God's workings see,
We could interpret all this doubt and strife,
    And for each mystery could find a key.

But not today. Then be content, poor heart;
    God's plans, like lilies pure and white, unfold;
We must not tear the close-shut leaves apart,—
    Time will reveal the chalices of gold.
And if, through patient toil, we reach the land
    Where tired feet, with sandals loosed, may rest,
When we shall clearly see and understand,
    I think that we will say, "God knew the best!"

—MAY RILEY SMITH (1842-1927)
American poet

This World Is Not Conclusion[†]

This world is not conclusion;
    A sequel stands beyond,
Invisible, as music,
    But positive, as sound.
It beckons and it baffles;
    Philosophies don't know,
And through a riddle, at the last,
    Sagacity must go.
To guess it puzzles scholars;
    To gain it, men have shown
Contempt of generations,
    And crucifixion known.

—EMILY DICKINSON (1830-1886)
American poet

Providence

Lo, the lilies of the field,
How their leaves instruction yield!
Hark to Nature's lesson given,
By the blessed birds of heaven!
Every bush and tufted tree
Warbles sweet philosophy:
Mortal, fly from doubt and sorrow;
God provideth for the morrow.

Say, with richer crimson glows
The kingly mantle than the rose?
Say, have kings more wholesome fare
Than we citizens of air?
Barns nor hoarded grain have we,
Yet we carol merrily.
Mortal, fly from doubt and sorrow;
God provideth for the morrow.

One there lives, whose guardian eye
Guides our humble destiny;
One there lives, who, Lord of all,
Keeps our feathers lest they fall.
Pass we blithely then the time,
Fearless of the snare and lime,
Free from doubt and faithless sorrow:
God provideth for the morrow.

—REGINALD HEBER (1783-1826)
English Anglican bishop of Calcutta

The Hidden Line, or The Destiny of Men

There is a time, we know not when,
    A point we know not where,
That marks the destiny of men
    To glory or despair.

There is a line by us unseen,
    That crosses every path;
The hidden boundary between
    God's patience and his wrath.

To pass that limit is to die,
    To die as if by stealth;
It does not quench the beaming eye,
    Or pale the glow of health.

The conscience may be still at ease,
 The spirits light and gay;
That which is pleasing still may please,
 And care be thrust away.

But on that forehead God has set
 Indelibly a mark,
Unseen by man, for man as yet
 Is blind and in the dark.

And yet the doomed man's path below
 May bloom as Eden bloomed;
He did not, does not, will not know,
 Or feel that he is doomed.

He knows, he feels that all is well,
 And every fear is calmed;
He lives, he dies, he wakes in hell,
 Not only doomed, but damned.

Oh! where is that mysterious borne
 By which our path is crossed;
Beyond which, God himself hath sworn,
 That he who goes is lost.

How far may we go on in sin?
 How long will God forbear?
Where does hope end, and where begin
 The confines of despair?

An answer from the skies is sent;
 "Ye that from God depart,
While it called today, repent,
 And harden not your heart."

  —J. ADDISON ALEXANDER (1809-1860)
  American educator

❧ THANKFULNESS ❧

On Jordan's Bank†

On Jordan's bank the Baptist's cry
Announces that the Lord is nigh;
Awake and hearken for he brings
Glad tidings of the King of kings.

Then cleansed be every breast from sin;
Make straight the way of God within,
And let each heart prepare a home
Where such a mighty guest may come.

For Thou art our salvation, Lord,
Our refuge, and our great reward;
Without Thy grace we waste away
Like flowers that wither and decay.

To heal the sick stretch out Thine hand,
And bid the fallen sinner stand;
Shine forth, and let Thy light restore
Earth's own true loveliness once more.

All praise, eternal Son, to Thee,
Whose advent doth Thy people free;
Whom with the Father we adore
And Holy Ghost for evermore.

—CHARLES COFFIN (1676-1749)
French Latinist and hymnist

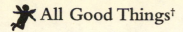 # All Good Things[†]

> *Thou, O God,*
> *dost sell us all good things*
> *at the price of labor.*

> —LEONARDO DA VINCI (1452-1519)
> Italian sculptor, painter, and architect

Thanksgiving for the Earth

> *Praised be our Lord for our brother the sun,*
> *Most comely is he, and bright,*
> *Praised be our Lord for our sister the moon,*
> *With her pure and lovely light.*
> *Praised be our Lord for the sparkling bright stars*
> *Encircling the dome of night.*
>
> *Praised be our Lord for the wind and the rain,*
> *For clouds, for dew and the air;*
> *For the rainbow set in the sky above*
> *Most precious and kind and fair.*
> *For all these things tell the love of our Lord,*
> *The love that is everywhere.*
>
> *Praised be our Lord for our Mother the earth,*
> *Most gracious is she, and good.*
> *With her gifts of flowers and nuts and fruit,*
> *Of grass and corn and wood.*
> *For she it is who upholds us in life*
> *And gives us our daily food.*
>
> *Praised be our Lord for the turn of the year,*
> *For new-born life upspringing;*
> *For buds and for blossoms, for lambs and babes,*
> *For thrush and blackbird singing.*
> *May praise, like the lark, leap up from our hearts,*
> *To heaven's gate upwinging.*

> —ELIZABETH GOUDGE (1900-1984)
> English novelist and poet

This Day

> This day might be
> The day I somehow always thought to see,
> And that should come to bless me past the scope
> And measure of my farthest reaching hope.
>
> Today, maybe the things that were concealed,
> Before the first day was, shall be revealed;
> Before the sun shall sink into the west
> The tired earth may have fallen on his breast,
> And into heaven the world have passed away.
>
> At any rate, it is another day!

—WILLIAM DEAN HOWELLS (1837-1920)
Novelist and editor, *Atlantic Monthly*

A Hundred Prayers of Praise†

> The presence of God:
> he picked me up
> and swung me like a bell
> I saw the trees
> on fire, rang
> a hundred prayers of praise

—ANNIE DILLARD (1945—)
American Pulitzer Prize-winning novelist
From *Tickets for a Prayer Wheel*

TIME

A Name in the Sand

Alone I walked the ocean strand;
A pearly shell was in my hand:
I stooped and wrote upon the sand
My name—the year—the day.
As onward from the spot I passed,
One lingering look behind I cast;
A wave came rolling high and fast,
And washed my lines away.

And so, methought, 'twill shortly be
With every mark on earth from me:
A wave of dark oblivion's sea
Will sweep across the place
Where I have trod the sandy shore
Of time, and been, to be no more,
Of me—my day—the name I bore,
To leave nor track nor trace.

And yet, with Him who counts the sands
And holds the waters in His hands,
I know a lasting record stands
Inscribed against my name,
Of all this mortal part has wrought,
Of all this thinking soul has thought,
And from these fleeting moments caught
For glory or for shame.

—HANNAH FLAGG GOULD (1789-1865)
American poet

Timeless Halls†

He came unto the timeless halls
where shining fall the countless years,
and endless reigns the Elder King
. . . beyond the world were visions showed
forbid to those who dwell within.

—J.R.R. TOLKIEN
From a song in *The Fellowship of the Ring*

The Water Mill

Listen to the water mill,
  —Through the livelong day;
How the clicking of the wheel
  Wears the hours away.
Languidly the autumn wind
  Stirs the withered leaves;
On the field the reapers sing,
  Binding up the sheaves;
And a proverb haunts my mind,
  And as a spell is cast,
The mill will never grind
  With the water that has passed."

Autumn winds revive no more
  Leaves strewn o'er earth and main.
The sickle never more shall reap
  The yellow, garnered grain;
And the rippling stream flows on
  Tranquil, deep and still,
Never gliding back again
  To the water mill.
Truly speaks the proverb old,
  With a meaning vast:
"The mill will never grind
  With the water that has passed."

Take the lesson to thyself,
    Loving heart and true;
Golden years are fleeting by,
    Youth is passing, too.
Learn to make the most of life,
    Lose no happy day!
Time will never return again—
    Sweet chances thrown away.
Leave no tender word unsaid,
    But love while love shall last:
"The mill will never grind
    With the water that has passed."

Work, while yet the sun does shine,
    Men of strength and will
Never does the streamlet glide
    Useless by the mill.
Wait not till tomorrow's sun
    Beams brightly on thy way;
All that thou canst call thine own
    Lies in this word: "Today!"
Power, intellect and health
    Will not always last:
"The mill will never grind
    With the water that has passed."

O the wasted hours of life
    That have swiftly drifted by!
O the good we might have done!
    Gone, lost without a sight
Love that we might once have saved
    By a single kindly word;
Thoughts conceived, but ne'er expressed,
    Perishing unpenned, unheard
Take the proverb to thy soul!
    Take, and clasp it fast:
"The mill will never grind
    With the water that has passed."

O love thy God and fellow man
Thyself consider last;
For come it will when thou must scan
Dark errors of the past.
And when the fight of life is o'er
And earth recedes from view.
And heaven in all its glory shines.
'Midst the good, the pure, the true
Then you will see more clearly
The proverb, deep and vast:
"The mill will never grind
With the water that has passed."

—SARAH DOUDNEY (1843-1926)
English writer

Divine Delight

Dark, dark this mind, if ever in vain it rove
The face of man in search of hope and love;
Or, turning inward from earth's sun and moon,
Spin in cold solitude thought's mazed cocoon
Fresh hang Time's branches.
Hollow in space outcry.
The grave-toned trumpets of Eternity.
"World of divine delight," heart whispereth,
Though all its all lie but 'twixt birth and death.

—WALTER DE LA MARE (1873-1956)
English novelist and poet

🏃 God's Time†

With God a day endures alway,
A thousand years are but a day.

—ROBERT BROWNING (1812-1889)
English Victorian poet
From "The Boy and the Angel"

FAITH AND REASON

Faith of Our Fathers

Faith of our fathers! living still
In spite of dungeon, fire, and sword:
O how our hearts beat high with joy
Whenever we hear that glorious word!
Faith of our fathers! holy faith!
We will be true to thee till death!

Our fathers, chained in prisons dark,
Were still in heart and conscience free:
How sweet would be their children's fate,
If they, like them, could die for thee!
Faith of our fathers! holy faith!
We will be true to thee till death!

Faith of our fathers! we will love
Both friend and foe in all our strife:
And preach thee, too, as love knows how,
By kindly words and virtuous life.
Faith of our fathers! holy faith!
We will be true to thee till death!

—FREDERICK W. FABER (1814-1863)
English clergyman and poet

Faith Came Singing[†]

Faith came singing into my room
And other guests took flight.
Grief, anxiety, fear and gloom,
Sped out into the night.

—ELIZABETH CHENEY (1918—)
American poet

Rock of Ages

Rock of Ages, cleft for me,
Let me hide myself in Thee;
Let the water and the blood,
From thy wounded side which flowed,
Be of sin the double cure,
Save from wrath and make me pure.

Could my tears forever flow,
Could my zeal no languor know,
These for sins could not atone;
Thou must save, and Thou alone:
In my hands no price I bring;
Simply to Thy cross I cling.

While I draw this fleeting breath,
When my eyes shall close in death,
When I rise to worlds unknown,
And behold Thee on Thy throne:
Rock of Ages, cleft for me,
Let me hide myself in Thee.

—AUGUSTUS M. TOPLADY (1740-1778)
English theologian and hymn writer

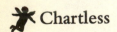 ## Chartless

I never saw a moor,
I never saw the sea;
Yet know I how the heather looks,
And what a wave must be.

I never spoke with God,
Nor visited in heaven;
Yet certain am I of the spot
As if the chart were given.

—EMILY DICKINSON (1830-1886)
American poet

Whoever Plants a Seed†

There is no unbelief;
Whoever plants a seed beneath the sod
And waits to see it push away the clod,
He trusts in God.

Whoever says when clouds are in the sky,
"Be patient, heart; light breaketh by and by,"
Trusts the Most High.

Whoever sees 'neath winter's field of snow,
The silver harvest of the future grow,
God's power must know.

—ELIZABETH YORK CASE (1840-1911)
American verse writer

Faith and Reason†

Dim as the borrow'd beams of moon and stars
To lonely, weary, wandering travelers,
Is reason to the soul; and as on high,
Those rolling fires discover but the sky,
Not light us here; so Reason's glimmering ray
Was lent, not to assure us of our doubtful way,
But guide us upward to a better day.
And as those nightly tapers disappear,
When day's bright lord ascends our hemisphere;
So pale grows Reason at Religion's sight;
So dies, and so dissolves in supernatural light.

—JOHN DRYDEN (1631-1700)
English dramatist, critic, and poet laureate
From "The Layman's Faith"

Shall We Gather at the River?

Shall we gather at the river
Where bright angel feet have trod,
With its crystal tide forever
Flowing from the throne of God?

CHORUS: Yes, we'll gather at the river,
The beautiful, the beautiful river,
Gather with the saints at the river
That flows from the throne of God.

On the margin of the river,
Where bright angel feet have trod,
We shall walk and worship ever,
All the happy, golden day.

On the bosom of the river,
Where the Savior King we own,
We shall meet and sorrow never,
'Neath the glory of the throne.

Soon we'll reach the shining river,
Soon our pilgrimage will cease;
Soon our happy hearts will quiver
With the melody of peace.

—ROBERT LOWRY (1826-1899)
American Baptist clergyman

The Agnostic

The tired agnostic longs for prayer
More than the blest can ever do:
Between the chinks in his despair,
From out his forest he peeps through
Upon a clearing sunned so bright
He cups his eyeballs from its light.

He for himself who would decide
What thing is black, what thing is white,
Whirls with the whirling spectrum wide,
Runs with the running spectrum through
Red, orange, yellow, green and blue

And purple,—turns and stays his stride
Abruptly, reaching left and right
To catch all colours into light—
But light evades him: still he stands
With rainbows streaming through his hands.

He knows how half his hours are spent
In blue or purple discontent,
In red or yellow hate or fright,
And fresh young green whereon a blight
Sits down in orange overnight.

Yet worships still the ardent sod
For every ripped and ribboned hue,
For warmth of sun and breath of air,
And beauty met with everywhere;
Not knowing why, not knowing who
Pumps in his breath and sucks it out,
Nor unto whom his praise is due.

Yet naught nor nobody obeys
But his own heart, which bids him, "Praise!"
This, knowing that doubled were his days
Could he but rid his mind of doubt—
Yet will not rid him, in such ways
Of awful dalliance with despair—
And, though denying, not betrays.

—EDNA ST. VINCENT MILLAY (1892-1950)
American Pulitzer Prize-winning poet

The Convert

After one moment I bowed my head
And the whole world turned over and came upright,
And I came out where the old road shone white,
I walked the ways and heard what all men said,
Forests of tongues, like autumn leaves unshed,
Being not unlovable but strange and light;
Old riddles and new creeds, not in despite
But softly, as men smile about the dead.

The sages have a hundred maps to give
That their crawling cosmos like a tree,
They rattle reason out through many a sieve
That stores the sand and lets the gold go free:
And all these things are less than dust to me
Because my name is Lazarus and I live.

—G.K. CHESTERTON (1874-1936)
English journalist, novelist, and poet
Author, *Orthodoxy* and *The Father Brown Stories*

The Pilgrim

Who would true valor see,
Let him come hither!
One here will constant be,
Come wind, come weather;
There's no discouragement
Shall make him once relent
His first avow'd intent
To be a Pilgrim.

Whoso beset him round
With dismal stories,
Do but themselves confound
His strength the more is.
No lion can him fright;
He'll with a giant fight;
But he will have a right
To be a Pilgrim.

Nor enemy, nor friend,
  Can daunt his spirit;
He knows he at the end
  Shall life inherit:
Then, fancies, fly away;
He'll fear not what men say;
He'll labor, night and day,
  To be a Pilgrim.

—JOHN BUNYAN (1628-1688)
English Baptist preacher
Author, *Pilgrim's Progress*

By Faith Alone†

No earthly object is more base and vile
Than I, without Thee, miserable am.
My spirit now, midst errors multiform,
Weak, wearied, and infirm, pardon implores.
O Lord most high! extend to me that chain
Which with itself links every gift divine:
Chiefest to my faith I bid my soul aspire,
Flying from sense, whose path conducts to death.
The rarer be this gift of gifts, the more
May it to be abound; and still the more,
Since the world yields not true content and peace
By faith alone the font of bitter tears
Can spring within my heart, made penitent:
No other key unlocks the gates of heaven.

—MICHELANGELO (1475-1564)
Italian sculptor, painter, and architect

O World

O world, thou choosest not the better part!
It is not wisdom to be only wise,
And on the inward vision close the eyes,
But it is wisdom to believe the heart.

Columbus found a world, and had no chart,
Save one that faith deciphered in the skies;
To trust the soul's invincible surmise
Was all his science and his only art.
Our knowledge is a torch of smoky pine
That lights the pathway but one step ahead
Across a void of mystery and dread.
Bid, then, the tender light of faith to shine
By which alone the mortal heart is led
Unto the thinking of the thought divine.

—GEORGE SANTAYANA (1863-1952)
Spanish-born philosopher and poet

 VIRTUE

On Virtue

O thou bright jewel in my aim I strive
To comprehend thee. Thine own words declare
Wisdom is higher than a fool can reach
I cease to wonder and no more attempt
Thine height t' explore or fathom thy profound.
But O my soul sink not into despair.
Virtue is near thee and with a gentle hand
Would now embrace thee, hovers o'er thine head.
Fain would the heaven born soul with her converse,
Then seek, then court her for her promis'd bliss.
. . . Attend me Virtue, through my youthful years!
O leave me not to the false joys of time!
But guide my steps to endless life and bliss.

—PHILLIS WHEATLEY (c. 1753-1784)
African American poet
From "On Virtue"

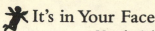 ## It's in Your Face

You don't have to tell how you live each day,
You don't have to say if you work or play,
A tried, true barometer serves in the place
However you live, it will show in your face.
. . . What you wear in your heart you wear in your face.
. . . If you live close to God, in His infinite grace,
You don't have to tell it, it shows in your face.

—UNKNOWN

The Divine Image

To Mercy, Pity, Peace and Love,
All pray in their distress:
And to these virtues of delight
Return their thankfulness.

For Mercy, Pity, Peace and Love
Is God our Father dear,
And Mercy, Pity, Peace and Love
Is man, His child and care.

For Mercy has a human heart,
Pity a human face,
And love, the human form divine,
And Peace, the human dress.

Then every man of every clime,
That prays in his distress,
Prays to the human form divine,
Love, Mercy, Pity, Peace.

And all must love the human form,
In heathen, Turk, or Jew,
Where Mercy, Love, and Pity dwell
There God is dwelling too.

—WILLIAM BLAKE (1757-1827)
English Romantic poet

Life Sculpture

Chisel in hand stood a sculptor boy
With his marble block before him,
And his eyes lit up with a smile of joy,
As an angel dream passed o'er him.

He carved the dream on that shapeless stone,
With many a sharp incision;
With Heaven's own light the sculptor shone—
He'd caught that angel vision.

Children of life are we, as we stand
With our lives uncarved before us,
Waiting the hour when, at God's command,
Our life dream shall pass o'er us.

If we carve it then on the yielding stone,
With many a sharp incision,
Its heavenly beauty shall be our own,
Our lives that angel vision.

—WILLIAM CROSWELL DEANE

❧ LOVE ❧

The Day with a White Mark

All day I have been tossed and whirled in a preposterous happiness:
Was it an elf in the blood? or a bird in the brain? or even part
Of the cloudily crested, fifty-league-long, loud uplifted wave
Of a journeying angel's transit roaring over and through my heart?

My garden's spoiled, my holidays are canceled, the omens harden;
The plann'd and unplann'd miseries deepen; the knots draw tight.
Reason kept telling me all day my mood was out of season.
It was, too. In the dark ahead the breakers only are white.

Yet I—I could have kissed the very scullery taps. The color of
My day was like a peacock's chest. In at each sense there stole
Ripplings and dewy sprinkles of delight that with them drew
Fine threads of memory through the vibrant thickness of the soul.

As though there were transparent earths and luminous trees should grow there,
*   And shining roots worked visibly far down below one's feet,*
So everything, the tick of the clock, the cock crowing in the yard
Probing my soil, woke diverse buried hearts of mine to beat,

Recalling either adolescent heights and the inaccessible
Longings and ice-sharp joys that shook my body and turned me pale,
Or humbler pleasures, chuckling as it were in the ear, mumbling
Of glee, as kindly animals talk in a children's tale.

Who knows if ever it will come again, now the day closes?
No one can give me, or take away, that key. All depends
On the elf, the bird, or the angel. I doubt if the angel himself
Is free to choose when sudden heaven in man begins or ends.

—C. S. LEWIS (1898-1963)
    English novelist, essayist, and educator
    Author, *The Screwtape Letters* and *The Chronicles of Narnia*

From All That Dwell Below the Skies

From all that dwell below the skies
Let the Creator's praise arise;
Let the Redeemer's name be sung
Through every land by every tongue.

Eternal are Thy mercies, Lord;
Eternal truth attends Thy word:
Thy praise shall sound from shore to shore,
Till suns shall rise and set no more.

In every land begin the song;
To every land the strains belong:
In cheerful sounds all voices raise
And fill the world with loudest praise.

—ISAAC WATTS (1674-1748)
Dissenter and pastor of Mark Lane Chapel, London

How Do I Love Thee?†

How do I love thee? Let me count the ways.
I love thee to the depth and breadth and height
My soul can reach, when feeling out of sight
For the ends of Being and ideal Grace.
I love thee to the level of every day's
Most quiet need, by sun and candle-light.
I love thee freely, as men strive for Right;
I love thee purely, as they turn from Praise.
I love thee with the passion put to use
In my old griefs, and with my childhood's faith.
I love thee with a love I seemed to lose
With my lost saints,—I love thee with the breath,
Smiles, tears, of all my life!—and, if God choose,
I shall but love thee better after death.

—ELIZABETH BARRETT BROWNING (1806-1861)
English Victorian poet

Who Adores the Maker[†]

If it be true that any beauteous thing
Raises the pure and just desire of man
From earth to God, the eternal fount of all,
Such I believe my love; for as in her
So fair, in whom I all besides forget
I view the gentle work of her Creator,
I have no care for any other thing
Whilst thus I love. Nor is it marvelous,
Since the effect is not of my own power,
If the soul doth by nature, tempted forth,
Enamored through the eyes,
Repose upon the eyes, which it resembleth,
And through them riseth to the primal love,
As to its end, and honors in admiring;
For who adores the Maker must love his work.

—MICHELANGELO (1475-1564)
Italian sculptor, painter, and architect

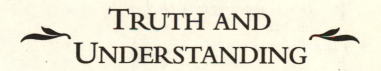

TRUTH AND UNDERSTANDING

In His Name[†]

In the name of Him who caused Himself to be,
Creating ever from eternity,
In His name who made faith and trust and love,
The strength of things and man's activity,
Oft-named and yet unfathomed mystery.

—JOHANN WOLFGANG VON GOETHE (1749-1832)
German poet, novelist, and scientist
From "Prelude"

God Our Refuge

If there had anywhere appeared in space
   Another place of refuge where to flee,
Our hearts had taken refuge in that place,
   And not with Thee.

For we against creation's bars had beat
   Like prisoned eagles, through great worlds had sought
Though but a foot of ground to plant our feet,
   Where Thou wert not.

And only when we found in earth and air,
   In heaven or hell, that such might nowhere be—
That we could not flee from Thee anywhere,
   We fled to Thee.

—RICHARD CHEVENIX TRENCH (1807–1886)
Anglican archbishop of Dublin and instigator of
the *Oxford English Dictionary*

"I Am the Way"

Thou art the Way.
Hadst Thou been nothing but the goal,
   I cannot say
If Thou hadst ever met my soul.

I cannot see—
I, child of process—if there lies
   An end for me,
Full of repose, full of replies.

I'll not reproach
The road that winds, my feet that err.
   Access, approach
Art Thou, Time, Way, and Wayfarer.

—ALICE MEYNELL (1847–1922)
English poet and literary magazine editor

I Believe in Him[†]

Who dare name His name
And say, "I believe in Him?"
Who dare silence the heart
And say, "I believe Him not?"
The All-enfolder,
The All-upholder,
Does He not hold, uphold
You and me and Himself?
Is not the sky arched overhead
And the earth set firm at our feet?
Do not the great stars rise,
Look down with immortal love?
And I look into your eyes?
Does not the whole world press
Into your heart and brain,
And the eternal secret float
All round you, hidden and plain?
Fill to the brim your soul
From that full blessedness,
Then name it as you will
Love, Rapture, God!
I have no name for it, none!
The heart is all, and the name
Nothing but clamor and smoke
Clouding the glow of the sky.

—JOHANN WOLFGANG VON GOETHE (1749-1832)
German poet, novelist, and scientist
From *Faust*

Truth[†]

Truth forever on the scaffold, Wrong forever on the throne,—
Yet that scaffold sways the future, and, behind the dim unknown,
Standeth God within the shadow, keeping watch above his own.

—JAMES RUSSELL LOWELL (1819-1891)
American poet, essayist, and diplomat
From *The Present Crisis*

As Spring the Winter

As spring the winter doth succeed
And leaves the naked trees do dress,
The earth all black is clothed in green.
At sunshine each their joy express.

My sun's return with healing wings,
My soul and body doth rejoice,
My heart exults and praises sings
To Him that heard my wailing voice.

My winter's past, my storms are gone,
And former clouds seem now all fled,
But if they must eclipse again,
I'll run where I was succored.

I have a shelter from the storm,
A shadow from the fainting heat,
I have access to His throne,
Who is a God so wondrous great.

O hath thou made my pilgrimage
Thus pleasant, fair, and good,
Blessed me in youth and elder age,
My Baca* made a springing flood.

O studious am what I shall do
To show my duty with delight;
All I can give is but thine own
And at most a simple mite.**

—ANNE BRADSTREET (1612-1672)
Puritan writer and America's first poet

---

*Hebrew for "weeping"
**small sum

See in Me†

Thy fishes breathe but where Thy waters roll;
Thy birds fly but within Thy airy sea;
My soul breathes only in Thy infinite soul
I breathe, I think, I love, I live but Thee.
Oh, breathe, oh, sink—O Love, live into me;
Unworthy is my life till all divine,
Till Thou see in me only what is thine.

—GEORGE MACDONALD (1824-1905)
Scottish novelist and poet
Author, *At the Back of the North Wind*

MAN

Mortals†

To bind me faithful to my calling high,
By birth was given me beauty's light
Lantern and mirror of two noble arts;
And other faith is falsity.
This bears the soul alone to its proud height;
To paint, to sculpture, this all strength imparts
And other judgments foolish are and blind,
Which draw from sense the beauty that can move,
And bear to Heaven each heart with wisdom sane.
No road divine our eyes infirm may find;
The mortal may not from that world remove
Whence without grace to hope to rise is vain.

—MICHELANGELO (1475-1564)
Italian sculptor, painter, and architect

To Cry to Thee[†]

> *O that Thou*
> *shouldst give dust*
> *a tongue*
> *to cry to Thee.*

> —GEORGE HERBERT (1593-1633)
> English clergyman

On Being Human

> *Angelic minds, they say, by simple intelligence*
> *Behold the Forms of nature. They discern*
> *Unerringly the Archetypes, all the verities*
> *Which mortals lack or indirectly learn.*
> *Transparent in primordial truth, unvarying,*
> *Pure Earthness and right Stonehood from their clear,*
> *High eminence are seen; unveiled, the seminal*
>   *Huge Principles appear.*

> *The Tree-ness of the tree they know—the meaning of*
> *Arboreal life, how from earth's salty lap*
> *The solar beam uplifts it, all the holiness*
> *Enacted by leaves' fall and rising sap;*
> *But never an angel knows the knife-edged severance*
> *Of sun from shadow where the trees begin,*
> *The blessed cool at every pore caressing us*
>   *An angel has no skin.*

> *They see the Form of Air; but mortals breathing it*
> *Drink the whole summer down into the breast.*
> *The lavish pinks, the field new-mown, the ravishing*
> *Sea-smells, the wood-fire smoke that whispers* Rest.
> *The tremor on the rippled pool of memory*
> *That from each smell in widening circles goes,*
> *The pleasure and the pang—can angels measure it?*
>   *An angel has no nose.*

The nourishing of life, and how it flourishes
On death, and why, they utterly know; but not
The hill-born, earthy spring, the dark cold bilberries
The ripe peach from the southern wall still hot,
Full-bellied tankards foamy-topped, the delicate
Half-lyric lamb, a new loaf's billowy curves,
Nor porridge, nor the tingling taste of oranges—
    An angel has no nerves.

Far richer they! I know the senses' witchery
Guards us, like air, from heavens too big to see;
Imminent death to man that barb'd sublimity
And dazzling edge of beauty unsheathed would be.
Yet here, within this tiny, charm'd interior,
This parlor of the brain, their Maker shares
With living men some secrets in a privacy
Forever ours, not theirs.

    —C. S. LEWIS (1898-1963)
      English novelist, essayist, and educator
      Author, *The Screwtape Letters* and *The Chronicles of Narnia*

The Wants of Man*

"Man wants but little here below,
Nor wants that little long."
'Tis not with me exactly so;
But 'tis so in the song.
My wants are many and, if told,
Would muster many a score;
And were each wish a mint of gold,
I still should long for more.

---

*In this poem, the author intends to mock the "wants of man" and thus make the point that they are unimportant compared to the mercy of God, which should be his only true desire.

What first I want is daily bread—
And canvas-backs—and wine
And all the realms of nature spread
Before me, when I dine.
Four courses scarcely can provide
My appetite to quell;
With four choice cooks from France beside,
To dress my dinner well.

What next I want, at princely cost,
Is elegant attire:
Black sable furs for winter's frost,
And silks for summer's fire,
And Cashmere shawls, and Brussels lace
My bosom's front to deck—
And diamond rings my hands to grace,
And rubies for my neck.

I want (who does not want?) a wife—
Affectionate and fair;
To solace all the woes of life,
And all its joys to share.
Of temper sweet, of yielding will,
Of firm, yet placid mind—
With all my faults to love me still
With sentiment refined.

And as Time's car incessant runs,
And Fortune fills my store,
I want of daughters and of sons
From eight to half a score.
I want (alas! can mortal dare
Such bliss on earth to crave?)
That all the girls be chaste and fair,
The boys all wise and brave.

I want a warm and faithful friend,
To cheer the adverse hour;
Who ne'er to flatter will descend,
Nor bend the knee to power—
A friend to chide me when I'm wrong,
My inmost soul to see;
And that my friendship prove as strong
For him as his for me.

I want the seals of power and place,
The ensigns of command;
Charged by the People's unbought grace
To rule my native land
Nor crown nor scepter would I ask
But from my country's will,
By day, by night, to ply the task
Her cup of bliss to fill.

I want the voice of honest praise
To follow me behind,
And to be thought in future days
The friend of human kind,
That after ages, as they rise,
Exulting may proclaim
In choral union to the skies
Their blessings on my name.

These are the Wants of mortal Man—
I cannot want them long,
For life itself is but a span,
And earthly bliss—a song.
My last great Want—absorbing all—
Is, when beneath the sod,
And summoned to my final call,
The Mercy of My God.

—JOHN QUINCY ADAMS (1767-1848)
Sixth president of the United States

🏃 Young and Old

When all the world is young, lad,
And all the trees are green;
And every goose a swan, lad,
And every lass a queen;
Then hey for boot and horse, lad,
And round the world away;
Young blood must have its course, lad,
And every dog his day.

When all the world is old, lad,
And all the trees are brown;
And all the sport is stale, lad,
And all the wheels run down:
Creep home, and take your place there,
The spent and maimed among:
God grant you find one face there
You loved when all was young.

—CHARLES KINGSLEY (1819-1875)
English clergyman, social reformer, and novelist
From *The Water Babies*

❧ LEGENDS AND HEROES ❧

🏃 The Late Passenger

The sky was low, the sounding rain was falling dense and dark,
And Noah's sons were standing at the window of the Ark.

The beasts were in, but Japhet said, "I see one creature more
Belated and unmated there come knocking at the door."

"Well let him knock," said Ham, "Or let him drown or learn to swim.
We're overcrowded as it is; we've got no room for him."

"And yet it knocks, how terribly it knocks," said Shem, "Its feet
Are hard as horn—but oh the air that comes from it is sweet."

"Now hush," said Ham, "You'll waken Dad, and once he comes to see
What's at the door, it's sure to mean more work for you and me."

Noah's voice came roaring from the darkness down below,
"Some animal is knocking. Take it in before we go."

Ham shouted back, and savagely he nudged the other two,
"That's only Japhet knocking down a brad-nail in his shoe."

Said Noah, "Boys, I hear a noise that's like a horse's hoof."
Said Ham, "Why, that's the dreadful rain that drums upon the roof."

Noah tumbled up on deck and out he put his head;
His face went gray, his knees were loosed, he tore his beard and said,

"Look, look! It would not wait. It turns away. It takes its flight.
Fine work you've made of it, my sons, between you all tonight!

"Even if I could outrun it now, it would not turn again—Not now.
Our great discourtesy has earned its high disdain.

"Oh noble and unmated beast, my sons were all unkind;
In such a night what stable and what manger will you find?

"Oh golden hoofs, oh cataracts of mane, oh nostrils wide
With indignation! Oh the neck wave-arched, the lovely pride!

"Oh long shall be the furrows ploughed across the hearts of men
Before it comes to stable and to manger once again,

"And dark and crooked all the ways in which our race shall walk,
And shriveled all their manhood like a flower with broken stalk,

"And all the world, oh Ham, may curse the hour when you were born;
Because of you the Ark must sail without the Unicorn."

—C. S. Lewis (1898-1963)
English novelist, essayist, and educator
Author, *The Screwtape Letters* and *The Chronicles of Narnia*

Provençal Legend

On his little grave and wild,
Faustinus, the martyr child,
    Candytufts and mustards grow.
Ah, how many a June has smiled
    On the turf he lies below.

Ages gone they laid him there,
Quit of sun and wholesome air,
    Broken flesh and tortured limb,
Leaving all his faith the heir
    Of his gentle hope and him.

Yonder, under pagan skies,
Bleached by rains, the circus lies,
    Where they brought him from his play
Comliest his of sacrifice,
    Youth and tender April day.

"Art thou not the shepherd's son?—
There the hills thy lambkins run?—
    These the fields thy brethren keep?"
On a higher hill than yon
    Doth my Father lead His sheep."

"Bring thy ransom then," they say,
"Gold enough to pave the way
    From the Temple to the Rhone."
When he came, upon his day,
    Slender, tremulous, alone,

Mustard flowers like these he pressed,
Golden, flame-like, to his breast,
    Blooms the early weanlings eat
When his Triumph brought him rest,
    Yellow bloom lay at his feet.

Golden play days came: the air
Called him, weanlings bleated there,
    Roman boys ran fleet with spring;
Shorn of youth and usage fair,
    Hope nor hilltop days they bring.

But the shepherd children still
Come at Easter, warm or chill,
    Come with violets gathered wild
From his sloping pasture hill,
Playfellows who would fulfill
    Playtime to that martyr child.

—WILLA CATHER (1876-1947)
American novelist and short story writer

George Washington

This was the man God gave us when the hour
Proclaimed the dawn of Liberty begun;
Who dared a deed, and died when it was done,
Patient in triumph, temperate in power,—
Not striving like the Corsican to tower
To heaven, nor like great Philip's greater son
To win the world and weep for worlds unwon,
Or lose the star to revel in the flower.
The lives that serve the eternal verities
Alone do mold mankind, Pleasure and pride
Sparkle awhile and perish, as the spray
Smoking across the crests of the cavernous seas
Is impotent to hasten or delay
The everlasting surges of the tide.

—JOHN HALL INGHAM

🦋 Good King Wenceslas

Good King Wenceslas looked out
    On the Feast of Stephen,
When the snow lay round about,
    Deep, and crisp, and even.

Brightly shone the moon that night
    Though the frost was cruel,
When a poor man came in sight,
    Gath'ring winter fuel.

"Hither, page, and stand by me,
    If thou know'st it, telling,
Yonder peasant, who is he?
    Where and what his dwelling?"

"Sire, he lives a good league hence,
    Underneath the mountain;
Right against the forest fence,
    By Saint Agnes' fountain."

"Bring me flesh, and bring me wine,
    Bring me pine-logs hither;
Thou and I shall see him dine,
    When we bear them thither."

Page and monarch, forth they went,
Forth they went together;
Through the rude wind's wild lament
And the bitter weather.

"Sire, the night is darker now,
    And the wind blows stronger;
Fails my heart, I know not how,
    I can go no longer."

"Mark my footsteps, good my page;
    Tread thou in them boldly:
Thou shalt find the winter rage
    Freeze thy blood less coldly."

In his master's steps he trod,
    Where the snow lay dinted;
Heat was in the very sod
    Where the saint had printed.

Therefore, Christian men, be sure,
    Wealth or rank possessing,
Ye who now will bless the poor,
    Shall yourselves find blessing.

—UNKNOWN

Columbus

Give me white paper!
This which you use is black and rough with smears
Of sweat and grime, and fraud, and blood and tears,
Crossed with the story of men's sins and fears,
Of battle and of famine all these years,
When all God's children had forgot their birth
And drudged and fought and died like beasts of earth.

"Give me white paper!"
One storm-trained seaman listened to the word;
What no man saw he saw, he heard what no man heard.
In answer he compelled the sea
To eager man to tell
The secret she had kept so well!
Left blood and guilt and tyranny behind—
Sailing still west the hidden shore to find;
For all mankind that unstained scroll unfurled,
Where God might write anew the story of the World.

—EDWARD EVERETT HALE (1822-1909)
American Unitarian clergyman
Author, *The Man Without a Country*

The Pilgrim Fathers

The breaking waves dashed high
    On a stern and rock-bound coast,
And the woods against a stormy sky
    Their giant branches tossed;

And the heavy night hung dark
    The hills and waters o'er,
When a band of exiles moored their bark
    On the wild New England shore.

Not as the conqueror comes,
    They, the true-hearted came;
Not with the roll of stirring drums,
    And the trumpet that sings of fame;

Not as the flying come,
    In silence and in fear;
They shook the depths of the desert gloom
    With their hymns of lofty cheer.

Amidst the storm they sang,
    And the stars heard and the sea;
And the sounding aisles of the dim woods rang
    To the anthem of the free!

The ocean eagle soared
    From his nest by the white wave's foam;
And the rocking pines of the forest roared—
    This was their welcome home!

There were men with hoary hair
    Amidst that pilgrim band;
Why had they come to wither there
    Away from their childhood's land?

There was woman's fearless eye,
    Lit by her deep love's truth;
There was manhood's brow serenely high,
    And the fiery heart of youth.

What sought they thus afar?
    Bright jewels of the mine?
The wealth of seas, the spoils of war?
    They sought a faith's pure shrine!

Aye, call it holy ground,
    The soil where they first trod,
They have left unstained what there they found—
    Freedom to worship God.

—FELICIA HEMANS (1793-1835)
English poet

🧚 Washington, the Brave, the Wise, the Good[†]

Washington, the brave, the wise, the good.
Supreme in war, in council, and in peace.
Valiant without ambition, discreet without fear, confident without presumption.
In disaster calm; in success, moderate; in all, himself.
The hero, the patriot, the Christian.
The father of nations, the friend of mankind,
Who, when he had won all, renounced all, and sought in the bosom of his
    family and of nature, retirement, and in the hope of religion, immortality.

—UNKNOWN
Inscription at Mount Vernon

Abraham Lincoln

Whence came this man? As if on the wings
    Of the winds of God that blew!
He moved, undaunted, mid captains and kings,
    And, not having learned, he knew I
Was he son of the soil, or child of the sky?
    Or, pray, was he both? Ah me!
How little they dreamed, as the storm rolled nigh,
    What he was, and was to be!

When trembled the lamps of hopes, or quite
    Blew out in that furious gale,
He drew his light from the Larger Light
    Above him that did not fail:
Heaven-led all trials and perils among,
    As unto some splendid goal
He fared right onward, unflinching—this strong
    God-gifted, heroic soul!

We know him now how noble his part,
    And how clear was his vision then!
With the firmest hand and the kindliest heart
    Of them all—this master of men!
Of the pride of power or the lust of self,
    Oh never a taint we find:
He lost himself in the larger self
    Of his country and all mankind.

There are those called great, or good, by right
    But as long as the long roll is,
Not many the names, with the double light
    Of greatness and goodness like his.
Thrice happy the nation that holds him dear
    Who never can wholly die,
Never cease to bestow of his counsel and cheer,
    As the perilous years go by!

For after the trumpets have ceased to blow,
    And the banners are folded away,
And the stress and the splendor forgotten, we know,
    Of a truth, in that judgment day,
That whatso'er else, in the Stream that rolls,
    May sink and be utterly gone,
The souls of the men who were true to their souls
    Forever go marching on!

There are those whose like, it was somehow planned,
*   We never again shall see;*
But I would to God there were more in the land
*   As true and as simple as he,—*
As he who walked in our common ways,
*   With the seal of a king on his brow;*
Who lived as a man among men his days,
*   And belongs to the ages now!*

—SAMUEL VALENTINE COLE (1851-1925)
American poet

The Ballad of John Henry

John Henry was a little baby boy
You could hold him in the palm of your hand.
He gave a long and lonesome cry,
"Going to be a steel-driving man, Lord, Lord,
Going to be a steel-driving man."

They took John Henry to the tunnel,
Put him in the lead to drive,
The rock was so tall, John Henry so small,
That he laid down his hammer and he cried, "Lord, Lord,"
Laid down his hammer and he cried.

John Henry started on the right hand,
The steam drill started on the left,
"Before I'd let that steam drill beat me down,
I'd hammer my fool self to death, Lord, Lord,
Hammer my fool self to death."

John Henry told his captain,
"A man ain't nothing but a man,
Before I let your steam drill beat me down
I'll die with this hammer in my hand, Lord, Lord,
Die with this hammer in my hand."

Now the captain told John Henry,
"I believe my tunnel's sinking in."
"Stand back, Captain, and don't you be afraid,
That's nothing but my hammer catching wind, Lord, Lord,
That's nothing but my hammer catching wind."

John Henry told his captain,
"Look yonder, boy, what do I see?
Your drill's done broke and your hole's done choke,
And you can't drive steel like me, Lord, Lord,
You can't drive steel like me."

John Henry hammering in the mountain,
'Til the handle of his hammer caught on fire,
He drove so hard till he broke his poor heart,
Then he laid down his hammer and he died, Lord, Lord,
He laid down his hammer and he died.

They took John Henry to the tunnel,
And they buried him in the sand,
And every locomotive come rolling by
Say, "There lies a steel-driving man, Lord, Lord,
There lies a steel-driving man."

—Unknown

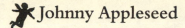

Johnny Appleseed

These apple trees were planted here
A century ago—
A hundred years of springtime bloom,
A hundred years of snow.

A hundred apple autumns
With the wild geese flying by,
A hundred years of applesauce
And steaming apple pie.

The man who planted apple trees
Once stood here on this land,
A sack of seeds upon his back,
A Bible in his hand.

Young Hannah Goodwin saw him first,
A stranger lean and lorn;
His face was thin, his feet were bare,
His clothing old and worn.

The Goodwin family asked him in
To dine and talk awhile.
America was lonely then;
He'd traveled many a mile.

He said he'd gladly stay to sup
But could not linger here;
He had to go plant apple trees
Across the great frontier.

He said it was a wide, wild land,
A lonesome land, and long.
He said his apples, sharp and sweet,
Would make the country strong.

The family listened while he spoke
Of forests green and grand,
Of prairies vast with waving grass,
Of rivers ribbed in sand.

He spoke of families like their own,
All moving bravely west
With guns and tots and cooking pots
To claim the wilderness.

He said he'd bring them apple trees,
Our Lord's gift to the earth;
He said the sun would warm his seeds,
The rain would give them birth.

He said that each good orchard grown
Would bear fruit as God planned,
And give the yearning pioneers
A taste of the Promised Land.

The Goodwin family wished him well,
And watched him leave alone.
He carried neither gun nor knife;
No weapon did he own.

For though he walked alone and lorn
Through the dangerous land and wild,
He said he'd harm no creature born;
Each one was God's own child.

Young Hannah heard the tales of him
All through her growing years,
As he brought apples, sharp and sweet,
To other pioneers.

She heard he walked through day and night
And through the winds that moan.
She heard he walked in snow and rain
That chilled him to the bone.

And where he walked she heard he gave
His blessing, softly thrown:
The scattered seeds among the weeds,
The sweet fruit wisely grown.

She heard he loved the forest land
And all its creatures, too:
Wild deer and hare, wild wolf and bear,
And every bird that flew.

She heard the Indians trusted him;
He knew the things they knew:
Which plants would heal or make a meal,
Which streams ran clear and true.

He walked all the trails and heard all the tales;
His orchards spread and grew,
And where he went the deep, rich scent
Of apple blossoms grew.

Old Hannah Goodwin saw him last
When many years had gone.
He came in by the orchard gate
A quiet hour past dawn.

Old Hannah knew that gentle smile,
That face so long and thin.
There was a Bible in his hand;
He spoke of where he'd been.

He'd walked all through America
And all his seeds he'd sown.
He'd planted apples, sharp and sweet,
And swiftly they had grown.

There was spicy apple cider now
Out on the western plain.
There was applesauce in Iowa
And apple pie in Maine.

Apples 'cross the wide Missouri
And down the Ohio.
Sharp and sweet across the land,
They made our country grow.

Old Hannah Goodwin offered thanks
For her own trees grown so tall.
He said no thanks were owed to him:
The Lord had made them all.

"To grow a country or a tree
Takes just a planter who
Will seed and tend till in the end
The earth's best dreams come true."

He said farewell and traveled on
And did not come again,
But in this orchard, sharp and sweet,
His apples still remain.

Old Hannah Goodwin talked of him
In apple time each year
When the orchard came to harvest
And the air was crisp and clear.

She'd ask children to remember
And to thank the Lord indeed
For apples sharp and sweet
And Johnny Appleseed.

—REEVE LINDBERGH (1946—)
American poet and daughter of Charles and Anne Lindbergh

King Robert of Sicily

Robert of Sicily, brother of Pope Urbane
And Valmond, Emperor of Allemaine,
Appareled in magnificent attire
With retinue of many a knight and squire,
On St. John's eve, at vespers, proudly sat
And heard the priests chant the Magnificat. *
And as he listened, o'er and o'er again

---

*The hymn from the Book of Luke which begins, "My soul doth magnify the Lord."

Repeated, like a burden or refrain,
He caught the words, "Deposuit potentes
De sede, et exaltavit humiles";
And slowly lifting up his kingly head,
He to a learned clerk beside him said,
"What mean these words?"
The clerk made answer meet,
"He has put down the mighty from their seat,
And has exalted them of low degree."
Thereat King Robert muttered scornfully,
"'Tis well that such seditious words are sung
Only by priests, and in the Latin tongue;
For unto priests, and people be it known,
There is no power can push me from my throne,"
And leaning back he yawned and fell asleep,
Lulled by the chant monotonous and deep.

When he awoke, it was already night;
The church was empty, and there was no light,
Save where the lamps, that glimmered few and faint,
Lighted a little space before some saint.
He started from his seat and gazed around,
But saw no living thing and heard no sound.
He groped towards the door, but it was locked;
He cried aloud, and listened, and then knocked,
And uttered awful threatenings and complaints,
And imprecations upon men and saints.
The sounds re-echoed from the roof and walls
As if dead priests were laughing in their stalls.

At length the sexton, hearing from without
The tumult of the knocking and the shout,
And thinking thieves were in the house of prayer,
Came with his lantern, asking, "Who is there?"
Half choked with rage, King Robert fiercely said,
"Open; 'tis I, the King! Art thou afraid?"
The frightened sexton, muttering, with a curse,
"This is some drunken vagabond, or worse!"

Turned the great key and flung the portal wide;
A man rushed by him at a single stride,
Haggard, half-naked, without hat or cloak,
Who neither turned, nor looked at him, nor spoke,
But leaped into the blackness of the night,
And vanished like a specter from his sight.

Robert of Sicily, brother of Pope Urbane
And Valmond, Emperor of Allemaine,
Despoiled of his magnificent attire,
Bare-headed, breathless, and besprent with mire,
With sense of wrong and outrage desperate,
Strode on and thundered at the palace gate;
Rushed through the court-yard, thrusting in his rage
To right and left each seneschal and page,
And hurried up the broad and sounding stair,
His white face ghastly in the torches' glare.
From hall to hall he passed with breathless speed;
Voices and cries he heard, but did not heed,
Until at last he reached the banquet-room,
Blazing with light, and breathing with perfume.
There on the dais sat another king,
Wearing his robes, his crown, his signet ring—
King Robert's self in features, form, and height,
But all transfigured with angelic light!
It was an Angel; and his presence there
With a divine effulgence filled the air,
An exaltation, piercing the disguise,
Though none the hidden Angel recognize.

A moment speechless, motionless, amazed,
The throneless monarch on the Angel gazed,
Who met his look of anger and surprise
With the divine compassion of his eyes!
Then said, "Who art thou, and why com'st thou here?"
To which King Robert answered with a sneer,
"I am the King, and come to claim my own
From an impostor, who usurps my throne!"

And suddenly, at these audacious words,
Up sprang the angry guests, and drew their swords;
The Angel answered, with unruffled brow,
"Nay, not the King, but the King's Jester; thou
Henceforth shalt wear the bells and scalloped cape,
And for thy counselor shalt lead an ape;
Thou shalt obey my servants when they call,
And wait upon my henchmen in the hall!"

Deaf to King Robert's threats and cries and prayers,
They thrust him from the hall and down the stairs;
A group of tittering pages ran before,
And they opened wide the folding door,
His heart failed, for he heard, with strange alarms,
The boisterous laughter of the men-at-arms,
And all the vaulted chamber roar and ring
With the mock plaudits of "Long live the King!"
Next morning, waking with the day's first beam,
He said within himself, "It was a dream!"
But the straw rustled as he turned his head;
There were the cap and bells beside his bed;
Around him rose the bare, discolored walls,
Close by, the steeds were champing in their stalls,
And in the corner, a revolting shape,
Shivering and chattering, sat the wretched ape.
It was no dream; the world he loved so much
Had turned to dust and ashes at his touch!

Days came and went; and now returned again
To Sicily the old Saturnian reign;
Under the Angel's governance benign
The happy island danced with corn and wine,
And deep within the mountain's burning breast
Enceladus, the giant, was at rest.

Meanwhile King Robert yielded to his fate,
Sullen and silent and disconsolate.
Dressed in the motley garb that Jesters wear,
With look bewildered, and a vacant stare,

Close shaven above the ears, as monks are shorn,
By courtiers mocked, by pages laughed to scorn,
His only friend the ape, his only food
What others left—he still was unsubdued,
And when the Angel met him on his way,
And half in earnest, half in jest, would say,
Sternly, though tenderly, that he might feel
The velvet scabbard held a sword of steel,
"Art thou the King?" the passion of his woe
Burst from him in resistless overflow,
And lifting high his forehead, he would fling
The haughty answer back, "I am, I am the King!"

Almost three years were ended, when there came
Ambassadors of great repute and name
From Valmond, Emperor of Allemaine,
Unto King Robert, saying that Pope Urbane
By letter summoned them forthwith to come
On Holy Thursday to his city of Rome.
The Angel with great joy received his guests,
And gave them presents of embroidered vests,
And velvet mantles with rich ermine lined,
And rings and jewels of the rarest kind.
Then he departed with them o'er the sea
Into the lovely land of Italy,
Whose loveliness was more resplendent made
By the mere passing of that cavalcade
With plumes, and cloaks, and housings, and the stir
Of jeweled bridle and of golden spur.

And lo! among the menials, in mock state,
Upon a piebald steed, with shambling gait,
His cloak of foxtails flapping in the wind,
The solemn ape demurely perched behind,
King Robert rode, making huge merriment
In all the country towns through which they went.

The Pope received them with great pomp, and blare
Of bannered trumpets, on St. Peter's square,
Giving his benediction and embrace,
Fervent, and full of apostolic grace.
While with congratulations and with prayers
He entertained the Angel unawares,
Robert, the Jester, bursting through the crowd,
Into their presence rushed, and cried aloud:
"I am the King! Look and behold in me
Robert, your brother, King of Sicily!
This man, who wears my semblance to your eyes,
Is an impostor in a king's disguise.
Do you not know me? Does no voice within
Answer my cry, and say we are akin?"
The Pope in silence, but with troubled mien,
Gazed at the Angel's countenance serene;
The Emperor, laughing, said, "It is strange sport
To keep a madman for thy Fool at court!"
And the poor, baffled Jester, in disgrace
Was hustled back among the populace.

In solemn state the Holy Week went by,
And Easter Sunday gleamed upon the sky;
The presence of the Angel, with its light,
Before the sun rose, made the city bright,
And with new fervor filled the hearts of men,
Who felt that Christ indeed had risen again.
Even the Jester, on his bed of straw,
With haggard eyes the unwonted splendor saw;
He felt within a power unfelt before,
And kneeling humbly on his chamber floor,
He heard the rushing garments of the Lord
Sweep through the silent air, ascending heavenward.

And now the visit ending, and once more
Valmond returning to the Danube's shore,
Homeward the Angel journeyed, and again
The land was made resplendent with his train,

Flashing along the towns of Italy
Unto Salerno, and from thence by sea.
And when once more within Palermo's wall,
And, seated on the throne in his great hall,
He heard the Angelus* from convent towers,
As if the better world conversed with ours,
He beckoned to King Robert to draw nigher,
And with a gesture bade the rest retire,
And when they were alone, the Angel said
"Art thou the King?" Then, bowing down his head,
King Robert crossed both hands upon his breast,
And meekly answered him, "Thou knowest best!
My sins as scarlet are; let me go hence,
And in some cloister's school of penitence,
Across those stones that pave the way to heaven,
Walk barefoot, till my guilty soul be shriven!"

The Angel smiled, and from his radiant face
A holy light illumined all the place,
And through the open window, loud and clear,
They heard the monks chant in the chapel near,
Above the stir and tumult of the street,
"He has put down the mighty from their seat,
And has exalted them of low degree!"
And through the chant a second melody
Rose like the throbbing of a single string:
"I am an Angel, and thou art the King!"
King Robert, who was standing near the throne,
Lifted his eyes, and lo! he was alone!
But all appareled as in days of old,
With ermined mantle and with cloth of gold;
And when his courtiers came they found him there,
Kneeling upon the floor, absorbed in silent prayer.

—HENRY WADSWORTH LONGFELLOW (1807-1882)**
American poet and educator

---

*prayer bell
**Longfellow was perhaps the most prolific Christian author of the nineteenth century. He was also the first American poet whose bust was placed in the Poet's Corner of Westminster Abbey.

❧ FREEDOM ❧

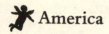 America

My country, 'tis of thee,
Sweet land of liberty,
　　Of thee I sing;
Land where my fathers died,
Land of the pilgrims' pride,
From every mountain-side
　　Let freedom ring.

My native country, thee,
Land of the noble free,—
　　Thy name I love;
I love thy rocks and rills,
Thy woods and tempted hills;
My heart with rapture thrills
　　Like that above.

Let music swell the breeze,
And ring from all the trees;
　　Sweet freedom's song;
Let mortal tongues awake,
Let all that breathe partake,
Let rocks their silence break,—
　　The sound prolong.

Our fathers' God, to thee,
Author of liberty,
　　To Thee I sing;
Long may our land be bright
With freedom's holy light;
Protect us by Thy might,
　　Great God our King.

—SAMUEL FRANCIS SMITH (1808-1895)
American Baptist clergyman and poet

🏃 The Star-Spangled Banner

O say, can you see, by the dawn's early light,
What so proudly we hailed at the twilight's last gleaming?
Whose broad stripes and bright stars, through the perilous fight,
O'er the ramparts we watched were so gallantly streaming!
And the rocket's red glare, the bombs bursting in air,
Gave proof through the night that our flag was still there;
O! say, does that star-spangled banner yet wave
O'er the land of the free, and the home of the brave?

On that shore dimly seen through the mists of the deep,
Where the foe's haughty host in dread silence reposes,
What is that which the breeze, o'er the towering steep,
As it fitfully blows, now conceals, now discloses?
Now it catches the gleam of the morning's first beam,
In full glory reflected now shines on the stream;
'Tis the star-spangled banner; O long may it wave
O'er the land of the free, and the home of the brave!

And where is that band who so vauntingly swore
That the havoc of war and the battle's confusion
A home and a country should leave us no more?
Their blood has washed out their foul footsteps' pollution.
No refuge could save the hireling and slave
From the terror of flight, or the gloom of the grave;
And the star-spangled banner in triumph doth wave
O'er the land of the free, and the home of the brave.

O! thus be it ever, when freemen shall stand
Between their loved homes and the war's desolation!
Blest with victory and peace, may the heav'n-rescued land
Praise the power that hath made and preserved us a nation.
Then conquer we must, when our cause it is just,
And this be our motto—"In God is our trust":
And the star-spangled banner in triumph shall wave
O'er the land of the free, and the home of the brave.

—FRANCIS SCOTT KEY (1779-1843)
American poet and attorney

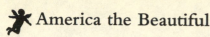 America the Beautiful

O beautiful for spacious skies,
For amber waves of grain,
For purple mountain majesties
Above the fruited plain!
America! America!
God shed His grace on thee,
And crown thy good with brotherhood
From sea to shining sea.

O beautiful for pilgrim feet,
Whose stern, impassioned stress
A thoroughfare for freedom beat
Across the wilderness!
America! America!
God mend thine every flaw,
Confirm thy soul in self-control,
Thy liberty in law!

O beautiful for heroes proved
In liberating strife,
Who more than self their country loved,
And mercy more than life!
America! America!
May God thy gold refine
Till all success be nobleness
And every gain divine!

O beautiful for patriot's dream
That sees beyond the years
Thine alabaster cities gleam
Undimmed by human tears!
America! America!
God shed His grace on thee
And crown thy good with brotherhood
From sea to shining sea!

—KATHERINE LEE BATES (1859-1929)
American educator

Battle Hymn of the Republic

Mine eyes have seen the glory of the coming of the Lord:
He is trampling out the vintage where the grapes of wrath are stored;
He hath loosed the fateful lightning of his terrible swift sword:
His truth is marching on.

I have seen him in the watch-fires of a hundred circling camps;
They have builded him an altar in the evening dews and damps;
I can read his righteous sentence by the dim and flaring lamps:
His day is marching on.

I have read a fiery gospel, writ in burnished rows of steel:
"As ye deal with my contemners, so with you my grace shall deal;
Let the Hero, born of woman, crush the serpent with his heel,
Since God is marching on."

He has sounded forth the trumpet that shall never call retreat;
He is sifting out the hearts of men before his judgment-seat:
O, be swift, my soul, to answer him! be jubilant, my feet!
Our God is marching on.

In the beauty of the lilies Christ was born across the sea,
With a glory in his bosom that transfigures you and me;
As he died to make men holy, let us die to make men free,
While God is marching on.

He is coming like the glory of the morning on the wave,
He is wisdom to the mighty, he is honor to the brave,
So the world shall be his footstool, and the soul of wrong his slave,
Our God is marching on!

—JULIA WARD HOWE (1819-1910)
American author, abolitionist, and social reformer

🦖 Go Down, Moses

When Israel was in Egypt's land:
    Let my people go;
Oppress'd so hard they could not stand,
    Let my people go.

Chorus: Go down, Moses,
Way down in Egypt's land,
Tell old Pharaoh,
Let my people go.

"Thus saith the Lord," bold Moses said,
    Let my people go;
"If not I'll smite your first-born dead,"
    Let my people go.

No more shall they in bondage toil,
    Let my people go;
Let them come out with Egypt's spoil,
    Let my people go.

When Israel out of Egypt came,
    Let my people go;
And left the proud oppressive land,
    Let my people go.

O, 'twas a dark and dismal night,
    Let my people go;
When Moses led the Israelites,
    Let my people go.
'Twas they that led the armies through,
    Let my people go.

                                —UNKNOWN

Free at Last

> Free at last, free at last,
> I thank God that I am free at last;
> Free at last, free at last,
> I thank God that I am free at last;
> Some of these mornings bright and fair,
> I thank God I'm free at last,
> Going to meet King Jesus in the air,
> I thank God I'm free at last.

> —UNKNOWN

Onward, Christian Soldiers

> Onward, Christian soldiers,
> Marching as to war,
> With the cross of Jesus
> Going on before!
> Christ the royal Master
> Leads against the foe;
> Forward into battle,
> See His banners go.
> Onward, Christian soldiers,
> Marching as to war,
> With the cross of Jesus
> Going on before!
>
> Like a mighty army
> Moves the Church of God;
> Brothers we are treading
> Where the saints have trod;
> We are not divided,
> All one body we,
> One in hope and doctrine,
> One in charity.
> Onward, Christian soldiers,
> Marching as to war,
> With the cross of Jesus
> Going on before!

Onward, then, ye people!
Join our happy throng!
Blend with ours your voices
In the triumph song!
Glory, laud, and honor,
Unto Christ, the King;
This through countless ages
Men and angels sing.
Onward, Christian soldiers,
Marching as to war,
With the cross of Jesus
Going on before!

—SABINE BARING-GOULD (1834-1924)
English clergyman and writer

 Creed

Lord, let me not in service lag,
Let me be worthy of our flag;
Let me remember, when I'm tried,
The sons heroic who have died
In freedom's name, and in my way
Teach me to be as brave as they.

In all I am, in all I do,
Unto our flag I would be true;
For God and country let me stand.
Unstained of soul and clean of hand,
Teach me to serve and guard and love
The Starry Flag which flies above.

—EDGAR A. GUEST (1881-1959)
English journalist and poet

Our Nation Forever

Ring out to the stars the glad chorus!
Let bells in sweet melody chime;
Ring out to the sky bending o'er us
The chant of a nation sublime:
One land with a history glorious!
One God and one faith all victorious!

The songs of the camp-fires are blended,
The North and the South are no more;
The conflict forever is ended,
From the lakes to the palm-girded shore.

One people united forever
In hope greets the promising years;
No discord again can dissever
A Union cemented by tears.

The past shall retain but one story—
A record of courage and love;
The future shall cherish one glory,
While the stars shine responsive above.

With emotions of pride and of sorrow,
Bring roses and lilies today;
In the dawn of the nation's tomorrow
We garland the blue and the gray.
One land with a history glorious!
One God and one faith all victorious!

—WALLACE BRUCE (fl. 1865)*

---

*Sung at a Union concert of Northern and Southern songs in the Chautauqua Amphitheatre, 1883

Land of Our Birth

Land of our Birth, we pledge to thee
Our love and toil in the years to be:
When we are grown and take our place,
As men and women with our race.

Father in Heaven who lovest all,
O help Thy children when they call;
That they may build from age to age
An undefiled heritage.

Teach us to rule ourselves alway,
Controlled and cleanly night and day;
That we may bring, if need arise,
No maimed or worthless sacrifice.

Teach us the strength that cannot seek,
By deed or thought, to hurt the weak:
That, under Thee, we may possess
Man's strength to comfort man's distress.

Teach us delight in simple things,
And mirth that has no bitter springs;
Forgiveness free of evil done,
And Love to all men 'neath the sun!

Land of our birth, our faith, our pride,
For whose dear sake our fathers died;
O Motherland, we pledge to thee
Head, heart and hand through the years to be.

—RUDYARD KIPLING (1865-1936)
English journalist, novelist, poet, and Nobel laureate
Author, *The Jungle Book*

OVERCOMING ADVERSITY

The Shepherd Boy's Song

He that is down, needs fear no fall;
    He is that is low, no pride;
He that is humble ever shall
    Have God to be his guide.

I am content with what I have,
Little be it or much;
And, Lord, contentment still I crave,
    Because thou savest such.

Fulness to such a burden is,
    That go on pilgrimage;
Here little, and hereafter bliss,
Is best from age to age.

—JOHN BUNYAN (1628-1688)
English Baptist preacher
Author, *Pilgrim's Progress*

He Knows He Has Wings!†

What matter it though life uncertain be
    To all? What though its goal
Be never reached? What though it fall and flee—
    Have we not each a soul?
Be like the bird that on a bough too frail
    To bear him gaily swings;
He carols though the slender branches fail—
    He knows he has wings!

—VICTOR HUGO (1802-1885)
French novelist and poet
Author, *Les Misérables*

On My Blindness[†]

What I consider how my light is spent, *
Ere half my days, in this dark world and wide,
And that one talent which is death to hide
Lodged with me useless, though my soul more bent
To serve therewith my Maker, and present
My true account, lest He returning chide,
"Doth God exact day-labor, light denied?"
I fondly ask. But Patience, to prevent
That murmur, soon replies, "God doth not need
Either man's work or his own gifts; who best
Bear His mild yoke, they serve Him best. His state
Is kingly: thousands at His bidding speed,
And post o'er land and ocean without rest;
They also serve who only stand and wait."

—JOHN MILTON (1608-1674)
English poet
Author, *Paradise Lost*

Jesus to His Disciples

I have instructed you to follow me
What way I go;
The road is hard, and stony,—as I know;
Uphill it climbs, and from the crushing heat
No shelter will be found
Save in my shadow: wherefore follow me; the footprints of my feet
Will be distinct and clear;
However trodden on, they will not disappear.

And see ye not at last
How tall I am?—
Even at noon I cast
A shadow like a forest far behind me on the ground.

—EDNA ST. VINCENT MILLAY (1892-1950)
American Pulitzer Prize-winning poet

---

*Milton's blindness became complete at age forty-four.

The Old Rugged Cross

On a hill far away stood an old rugged cross,
The emblem of suffering and shame;
And I love that old cross,
Where the dearest and best
For a world of sinners was slain.

Chorus: So I'll cherish the old rugged cross
Till my trophies at last I lay down;
I will cling to the old rugged cross
And exchange it someday for a crown.

Oh, that old rugged cross, so despised by the world,
Has a wondrous attraction for me;
For the dear Lamb of God left His glory above
To bear it to dark Calvary.

In the old rugged cross, stained with blood so divine,
A wondrous beauty I see;
For 'twas on that old cross that Jesus suffered and died
To pardon and sanctify me.

To the old rugged cross I will ever be true,
Its shame and reproach gladly bear;
Then He'll call me some day to my home far away,
Where His glory forever I'll share.

—GEORGE BENNARD (1873-1958)
American Methodist evangelist

Nearer to Thee

Nearer, my God, to Thee,
Nearer to Thee!
E'en though it be a cross
That raiseth me;
Still all my song shall be,
Nearer, my God, to Thee,
Nearer to Thee!

Though like the wanderer,
*   The sun gone down,*
Darkness be over me,
*   My rest a stone;*
Yet in my dreams I'd be
Nearer, my God, to Thee,
*   Nearer to Thee!*

There let the way appear
*   Steps unto heaven;*
All that Thou send'st to me
*   In mercy given;*
Angels to beckon me
Nearer, my God, to Thee,
*   Nearer to Thee!*

Then, with my waking thoughts
*   Bright with Thy praise,*
Out of my stony griefs
*   Bethel I'll raise;*
So by my woes to be
Nearer, my God, to Thee,
*   Nearer to Thee!*

Or if on joyful wing
*   Cleaving the sky,*
Sun, moon, and stars forgot,
*   Upward I fly,*
Still all my song shall be,
Nearer, my God, to Thee,
*   Nearer to Thee!*

—SARAH FLOWER ADAMS (1805-1848)
English verse and hymn writer

"My Peace I Give Unto You"

Blessed are the eyes that see
The things that You have seen,
Blessed are the feet that walk
The ways where You have been.

Blessed are the eyes that see
The Agony of God,
Blessed are the feet that tread
The paths His feet have trod.

Blessed are the souls that solve
The paradox of Pain,
And find the path that, piercing it,
Leads through to peace again.

—G. A. STUDDERT KENNEDY (1883-1929)
English World War I chaplain

A Mighty Fortress Is Our God

A mighty fortress is our God,
A bulwark never failing;
Our helper he, amid the flood
Of mortal ills prevailing.
For still our ancient foe
Doth seek to work us woe;
His craft and pow'r are great,
And arm'd with cruel hate,
On earth is not his equal.

Did we in our own strength confide,
Our striving would be losing;
Were not the right man on our side,
The man of God's own choosing.
Dost ask who that may be?
Christ Jesus, it is he;
Lord Sabaoth his name,
From age to age the same,
And he must win the battle.

And though this world, with demons fill'd,
Should threaten to undo us,
We will not fear, for God hath willed
His truth to triumph through us.
The Prince of darkness grim,
We tremble not for him;
His rage we can endure,
For lo, his doom is sure—
One little word shall fell him.

God's word above all earthly pow'rs,
No thanks to them, abideth;
The Spirit and the gifts are ours
Through him who with us sideth.
Let goods and kindred go,
This mortal life also
The body they may kill,
God's truth abideth still,
His kingdom is forever.

—MARTIN LUTHER (1483-1546)
German monk and leader of the Protestant Reformation

Griefs

I measure every grief I meet
  With analytic eyes;
I wonder if it weighs like mine,
  Or has an easier size.

I wonder if they bore it long,
  Or did it just begin?
I could not tell the date of mine,
  It feels so old a pain.

I wonder if it hurts to live,
  And if they have to try,
And whether, could they choose between,
  They would not rather die.

I wonder if when years have piled—
    Some thousands—on the cause
Of early hurt, if such a lapse
    Could give there any pause;

Or would they go on aching still
    Through centuries above,
Enlightened to a larger pain
    By contrast with the love.

The grieved are many, I am told;
    The reason deeper lies,—
Death is but one and comes but once,
    And only nails the eyes.

There's grief of want, and grief of cold,—
    A sort they call "despair";
There's banishment from native eyes,
    In sight of native air.

And though I may not guess the kind
    Correctly, yet to me
A piercing comfort it affords
    In passing Calvary,

To note the fashions of the cross,
    Of those that stand alone,
Still fascinated to presume
    That some are like my own.

        —EMILY DICKINSON (1830-1886)
        American poet

What the Chimney Sang

Over the chimney the night wind sang,
And chanted a melody no one knew;
And the woman stopped as her babe she tossed,
And thought of the one she had long since lost,
And said, as the teardrops back she forced:
"I hate the wind in the chimney!"

Over the chimney the night wind sang,
And chanted a melody no one knew;
And the children said, as they closer drew:
"'Tis some witch is cleaving the black night through,
'Tis a fairy trumpet that just then blew,
And we fear the wind in the chimney!"

Over the chimney the night wind sang,
. And chanted a melody no one knew;
And the man, as he sat on his hearth below,
Said to himself: "It will surely snow,
And fuel is dear and wages are low,
And I'll stop the leak in the chimney."

Over the chimney the night wind sang,
And chanted a melody no one knew;
And the prophet listened and smiled,
For he was man, and woman, and child,
And said: "It is God's own harmony,
This wind we hear in the chimney."

—BRET HARTE (1836-1902)
American short story writer and diplomat
Author, *The Luck of Roaring Camp and Other Stories*

Victory in Defeat

Defeat may serve as well as victory
To shake the soul and let the glory out.
When the great oak is straining in the wind,
The boughs drink in new beauty, and the trunk
Sends down a deeper root on the windward side.
Only the soul that knows the mighty grief
Can know the mighty rapture. Sorrows come
To stretch out spaces in the heart for joy.

—EDWIN MARKHAM (1852-1940)
American poet and lecturer

The Cross Hath Lifted[†]

> The Cross hath lifted
> Love, Heaven-gifted,
> Never let it go:
> And the Cross shall take me,
> Lift me, break me,
> For all the world to know.
>
> —JACOPONE DA TODI

A Psalm of Life

> Tell me not, in mournful numbers,
>   "Life is but an empty dream!"
> For the soul is dead that slumbers,
>   And things are not what they seem.
>
> Life is real! Life is earnest;
>   And the grave is not its goal;
> "Dust thou art, to dust returnest,"
>   Was not spoken of the soul.
>
> Not enjoyment, and not sorrow,
>   Is our destined end or way;
> But to act, that each tomorrow
>   Find us farther than today.
>
> Art is long, and Time is fleeting,
>   And our hearts, though stout and brave,
> Still like muffled drums, are beating,
>   Funeral marches to the grave.
>
> In the world's broad field of battle,
>   In the bivouac of life,
> Be not like dumb, driven cattle!
>   Be a hero in the strife!
>
> Trust no Future, however pleasant!
>   Let the dead Past bury its dead!
> Act—act in the living Present!
>   Heart within, and God o'erhead!

Lives of great men all remind us
  We can make our lives sublime,
And, departing, leave behind us
  Footprints on the sands of time;

Footprints, that perhaps another,
  Sailing o'er life's solemn main,
A forlorn and shipwrecked brother,
  Seeing, shall take heart again.

Let us, then, be up and doing,
  With a heart for any fate;
Still achieving, still pursuing,
  Learn to labor and to wait.

—HENRY WADSWORTH LONGFELLOW (1807-1882)
American poet and educator

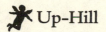 Up-Hill

Does the road wind up-hill all the way?
  Yes, to the very end.
Will the day's journey take the whole long day?
  From morn to night, my friend.

But is there for the night a resting-place?
  A roof for when the slow dark hours begin.
May not the darkness hide it from my face?
  You cannot miss that inn.

Shall I meet other wayfarers at night?
  Those who have gone before.
Then must I knock, or call when just in sight?
  They will not keep you standing at that door.

Shall I find comfort, travel-sore and weak?
  Of labor you shall find the sum.
Will there be beds for me and all who seek?
  Yea, beds for all who come.

—CHRISTINA ROSSETTI (1830-1894)
Italian-born poet

⤚ SIN AND REDEMPTION ⤙

Amazing Grace

Amazing grace, how sweet the sound,
That saved a wretch like me!
I once was lost, but now am found,
Was blind, but now I see.

'Twas grace that taught my heart to fear,
And grace my fears relieved;
How precious did that grace appear
The hour I first believed!

Through many dangers, toils, and snares,
I have already come;
'Tis grace has brought me safe thus far,
And grace will lead me home.

The Lord has promised good to me,
His word my hope secures;
He will my shield and portion be
As long as life endures.

When we've been there ten thousand years,
Bright shining as the sun,
We've no less days to sing God's praise
Than when we'd first begun.

—JOHN NEWTON (1725-1807)
English slavetrader turned abolitionist clergyman

A Hymn to God the Father

Wilt Thou forgive that sin where I begun,
*   Which is my sin, though it were done before?*
Wilt Thou forgive those sins through which I run,
*   And do them still, though still I do deplore?*

Wilt Thou forgive that sin by which I won
*   Others to sin, and made my sin their door?*
Wilt Thou forgive that sin which I did shun
*   A year or two, but wallowed in a score?*
*   When Thou hast done, Thou has not done,*
*   For I have more.*

I have a sin of fear, that when I've spun
*   My last thread, I shall perish on the shore;*
Swear by Thyself that at my death Thy sun
*   Shall shine as it shines now, and heretofore;*
*   And having done that, Thou hast done,*
*   I have no more.*

—JOHN DONNE (c. 1571-1631)
   English poet and dean of St. Paul's Cathedral

Hear Me, O God!†

Hear me, O God!
 A broken heart
 Is my best part:
Use still Thy rod
 That I may prove
 Therein my love.

If Thou hadst not
 Been stern to me,
 But left me free,
I had forgot
 Myself and Thee.

For sin's so sweet,
 As minds ill bent
 Rarely repent,
Until they meet
 Their punishment.

Who more can crave
 Than Thou
 That gav'st a son
To free a slave
 First made of nought,
 With all since bought?

Sin, Death, and Hell,
 His glorious name
 Quite overcame,
Yet I rebel,
 And slight the same.

But I'll come in,
 Before my loss
 Me farther toss,
As sure to win
 Under His cross.

—BEN JONSON (1572-1637)
English playwright

The First Psalm

The man in life wherever placed,
    Hath happiness in store,
Who walks not in the wicked's way,
    Nor learns their guilty lore.

Nor from the seat of scornful pride
    Casts forth his eyes abroad,
But with humility and awe
    Still walks before his God.

That man shall flourish like the trees,
    Which by the streamlets grow;
The fruitful top is spread on high,
    And firm the root below.

Be he who blossom buds in guilt,
    Shall to the ground be cast,
And, like the rootless stubble, tost
    Before the sweeping blast.

For why? that God the good adore
    Hath given them peace and rest,
But hath decreed that wicked men
    Shall never be truly blest.

—ROBERT BURNS (1759-1796)
Scottish poet

The Character of a Happy Life

How happy is he born and taught,
    That serveth not another's will;
Whose armor is his honest thought,
    And simple truth his utmost skill!

Whose passions not his masters are,
    Whose soul is still prepared for death,
Untied unto the worldly care
    Of public fame, or private breath;

Who envies none that chance doth raise,
Or vice; who never understood
How deepest wounds are given by praise;
Nor rules of state, but rules of good:

Who hath his life from rumors freed,
Whose conscience is his strong retreat;
Whose state can neither flatterers feed,
Nor ruin make oppressors great;

Who God doth late and early pray,
More of his grace than gifts to lend;
And entertains the harmless day
With a religious book or friend;

This man is freed from servile bands,
Of hope to rise, or fear to fall;
Lord of himself, though not of lands;
And having nothing, yet hath all.

—HENRY WOTTON (1568-1639)
English diplomat and poet

Recessional

God of our fathers, known of old,
Lord of our far-flung battle-line,
Beneath whose awful Hand we hold
Dominion over palm and pine—
Lord God of Hosts, be with us yet,
Lest we forget—lest we forget!

The tumult and the shouting dies,
The Captains and the Kings depart:
Still stands Thine ancient sacrifice,
A humble and a contrite heart.
Lord God of Hosts, be with us yet,
Lest we forget—lest we forget!

Far-called, our navies melt away;
    On dune and headland sinks the fire:
Lo, all our pomp of yesterday
    Is one with Nineveh and Tyre!*
Judge of nations, spare us yet,
Lest we forget—lest we forget!

If, drunk with sight of power, we loose
    Wild tongues that have not Thee in awe—
Such boasting as the Gentiles use
    Or lesser breeds without the Law—
Lord God of Hosts, be with us yet,
Lest we forget—lest we forget!

For heathen heart that puts her trust
    In reeking tube and iron shard—
All valiant dust that builds on dust,
And guarding, calls not Thee to guard—
For frantic boast and foolish word.
    Thy mercy on Thy people, Lord!

—RUDYARD KIPLING (1865-1936)
English journalist, novelist, poet, and Nobel laureate
Author, *The Jungle Book*

The Fool's Prayer

The royal feast was done; the King
    Sought some new sport to banish care,
And to his jester cried: "Sir Fool,
    Kneel now, and make for us a prayer!"

The jester doffed his cap and bells,
    And stood the mocking court before;
They could not see the bitter smile
    Behind the painted grin he wore.

---

*the ancient capitals of Assyria and Phoenicia which were destroyed

He bowed his head, and bent his knee
    Upon the Monarch's silken stool;
His pleading voice arose: "O Lord,
    Be merciful to me, a fool!

"No pity, Lord, could change the heart
    From red with wrong to white as wool;
The rod must heal the sin: but Lord,
    Be merciful to me, a fool!

"'Tis not by guilt the onward sweep
    Of truth and right, O Lord, we stay;
'Tis by our follies that so long
    We hold the earth from heaven away.

"These clumsy feet, still in the mire,
    Go crushing blossoms without end;
These hard, well-meaning hands we thrust
    Among the heart-strings of a friend.

"The ill-timed truth we might have kept—
    Who knows how sharp it pierced and stung?
The word we had not sense to say—
    Who knows how grandly it had rung!

"Our faults, no tenderness should ask,
    The chastening stripes must cleanse them all;
But for our blunders—oh, in shame
    Before the eyes of heaven we fall.

"Earth bears no balsam for mistakes;
    Men crown the knave, and scourge the tool
That did his will; but Thou, O Lord,
    Be merciful to me, a fool!"

The room was hushed; in silence rose
    The King, and sought his gardens cool,
And walked apart, and murmured low,
"Be merciful to me, a fool!"

      —EDWARD ROWLAND SILL (1841-1887)
      American educator and poet

DEATH AND ETERNAL LIFE

On Death[†]

And I press on with a lighter heart
Through all the ways of the endless rings.
The pure word of the living God
Moves in the depths of them and sings.

Unhampered now by fierce desire
We follow and find no ending here
Till in the light of eternal Love
We melt, we disappear.

> —JOHANN WOLFGANG VON GOETHE (1749-1832)
> German poet, novelist, and scientist
> From *The Divan of East and West*

Afraid?

Afraid? Of whom am I afraid?
Not death; for who is he?
The porter of my father's lodge
As much abasheth me.

Of life? 'Twere odd I fear a thing
That comprehendeth me
In one or more existences
At Deity's decree.

Of resurrection? Is the east
Afraid to trust the morn
With her fastidious forehead?
As soon impeach my crown!

> —EMILY DICKINSON (1830-1886)
> American poet

Wayfaring Stranger

I'm just a poor, wayfaring stranger,
A-traveling through this world of woe;
But there's no sickness, toil, nor danger
In that bright world to which I go.
I'm going there to meet my father,
I'm going there no more to roam,

Chorus: I'm just a-going over Jordan,
I'm just a-going over home.

I know dark clouds will gather round me
I know my way is steep and rough,
But beauteous fields lies just beyond me
Where souls redeemed their vigil keep.
I'm going there to meet my mother,
She said she'd meet me when I come.

I want to wear a crown of glory
When I get home to that bright land;
I want to shout Salvation's story,
In concert with that bloodwashed band.
I'm going there to meet my savior,
To sing his praise forever more.

—UNKNOWN

Swing Low, Sweet Chariot

I looked out over Jordan, and what did I see,
Coming for to carry me home?
A band of angels coming after me,
Coming for to carry me home.

Chorus: Swing low, sweet chariot,
Coming for to carry me home;
Swing low, sweet chariot,
Coming for to carry me home.

If you get there before I do,
Coming for to carry me home,
Tell all my friends I'm coming too,
Coming for to carry me home.

The brightest day that ever I saw,
Coming for to carry me home,
'Twas good old Moses and Aaron, too,
When Jesus wash'd my sins away,
Coming for to carry me home.

I'm sometimes up and sometimes down,
Coming for to carry me home,
But still my soul feels heavenly bound,
Coming for to carry me home.

—UNKNOWN

As from the Darkening Gloom*

As from the darkening gloom a silver dove
Upsoars, and darts into the Eastern light,
On pinions that naught moves but pure delight,
So fled thy soul into the realms above,
Regions of peace and everlasting love;
Where happy spirits, crown'd with circlets bright
Of starry beam, and gloriously bedight,**
Taste the high joy none but the blest can prove.
There thou or joinest the immortal quire
In melodies that even Heaven fair
Fill with superior bliss, or, at desire
Of the omnipotent Father, cleavest the air
On holy message sent—What pleasure's higher
Wherefore does any grief our joy impair?

—JOHN KEATS (1795-1821)
English Romantic poet

---

*a sonnet written upon the death of Keats's grandmother in 1814
**arrayed

Bound for the Promised Land

On Jordan's stormy banks I stand
And cast a wishful eye,
To Canaan's fair and happy land
Where my possessions lie.

Chorus: I am bound for the Promised Land
O who will come and go with me?

O the transporting rapturous scene
That rises to my sight,
Sweet fields arrayed in living green
And rivers of delight.

There generous fruits that never fail
On trees immortal grow;
There rocks and hills and brooks and vales
With milk and honey flow.

Soon will the Lord my soul prepare
For joys beyond the skies,
Where never-ceasing pleasures roll,
And praises never die.

—UNKNOWN

Broad Is the Road†

Broad is the road that leads to death
And thousands walk together there;
But wisdom shows a narrow path
With here and there a travel'r.

"Deny thyself, and take thy cross"
Is the Redeemer's great command;
Nature must call her gold but dross,
If she would gain this heav'nly hand.

—ISAAC WATTS (1674-1748)
Dissenter and pastor of Mark Lane Chapel, London

Triumph O'er Death[†]

By fire the artist molds the ductile steel
Into the beauteous forms his thought defines;
And fire expels the alloys, which else conceal
The gold's pure luster and its mass refines.
Nor can the Phoenix, matchless bird, resume
Its plumes except it burn. Be it my doom
Thus into death to burn, since Heaven assigns
Triumph o'er death to such in realms of light,
O death how sweet! O conflagration bright!
If thus resolved to ashes, upward springs
The soul, no more a mortal home to claim;
Or rather, if transmuted into flame,
Which has by Nature's law a heavenward aim,
I'm wafted thither on immortal wings.

—MICHELANGELO (1475-1564)
Italian sculptor, painter, and architect

A Sonnet

Poor soul, the center of my sinful earth,
Fool'd by these rebel powers that thee array,
Why dost thou pine within, and suffer dearth,
Painting thy outward walls so costly gay?
Why so large cost, having so short a lease,
Dost thou upon thy fading mansion spend?
Shall worms, inheritors of this excess,
Eat up thy charge? is this thy body's end?
Then, Soul, live thou upon thy servant's loss,
And let that pine to aggravate thy store;
Buy terms divine in selling hours of dross;
Within be fed, without be rich no more:
So shalt thou feed on death, that feeds on men,
And, death once dead, there's no more dying then.

—WILLIAM SHAKESPEARE (1564-1616)
English playwright and poet

The Dying Christian to His Soul

Vital spark of heavenly flame!
Quit, O quit this mortal frame!
Trembling, hoping, lingering, flying,
O! the pain, the bliss of dying!
Cease, fond nature, cease thy strife,
And let me languish into life!

Hark! they whisper: angels say,
Sister spirit, come away!
What is this absorbs me quite?
Steals my senses, shuts my sight,
Drowns my spirit, draws my breath?
Tell me, my soul, can this be death?

The world recedes; it disappears!
Heaven opens on my eyes! my ears
With sounds seraphic ring!
Lend, lend your wings! I mount! I fly!
O Grave! where is thy victory?
O Death! where is thy sting?*

—ALEXANDER POPE (1688-1744)
English poet and satirist

The End of the Play

The play is done; the curtain drops,
    Slow falling to the prompter's bell:
A moment yet the actor stops,
    And looks around, to say farewell.
It is an irksome word and task;
    And, when he's laughed and said his say,
He shows, as he removes the mask,
    A face that's anything but gay.

---

*The last two lines are from 1 Corinthians, 15:55.

One word, ere yet the evening ends,
    Let's close it with a parting rhyme,
And pledge a hand to all young friends,
    As fits the merry Christmas-time.
On life's wide scene you, too, have parts,
    That Fate ere long shall bid you play;
Good night! with honest gentle hearts
    A kindly greeting go alway!

Good night!—I'd say, the griefs, the joys,
    Just hinted in this mimic page,
The triumphs and defeats of boys,
    Are but repeated in our age.
I'd say, your woes were not less keen,
    Your hopes more vain than those of men;
Your pangs or pleasures of fifteen
    At forty-five played o'er again.

I'd say, we suffer and we strive,
    Not less or more as men than boys;
With grizzled beards at forty-five,
    As erst at twelve in corduroys.
And if, in time of sacred youth,
    We learned at home to love and pray,
Pray Heaven that early Love and Truth
    May never wholly pass away.

And in the world, as in the school,
    I'd say, how fate may change and shift;
The prize be sometimes with the fool,
    The race not always to the swift.
The strong may yield, the good may fall,
    The great man be a vulgar clown,
The knave be lifted over all,
    The kind cast pitilessly down.

Who knows the inscrutable design?
    Blessed be He who took and gave!
Why should your mother, Charles, not mine,
    Be weeping at her darling's grave?
We bow to Heaven that will'd it so,
    That darkly rules the fate of all.
That sends the respite or the blow,
    That's free to give, or to recall.

This crowns his feast with wine and wit:
    Who brought him to that mirth and state?
His betters, see, below him sit,
    Or hunger hopeless at the gate.
Who bade the mud from Dives' wheel
    To spurn the rags of Lazarus?
Come, brother, in that dust we'll kneel,
    Confessing Heaven that ruled it thus.

So each shall mourn, in life's advance,
    Dear hopes, dear friends, untimely killed;
Shall grieve for many a forfeit chance,
    And longing passion unfulfilled.
Drives our English hearts of oak
    Seaward round the world.
Come, as came our fathers,
    Heralded by thee,
Conquering from the eastward,
    Lords by land and sea.
Come; and strong within us
    Stir the Vikings' blood;
Bracing brain and sinew;
    Blow, thou wind of God!

—WILLIAM MAKEPEACE THACKERAY (1811-1863)
    English novelist
    Author, *Vanity Fair*

Crossing the Bar

Sunset and evening star
  And one clear call for me!
And may there be no moaning of the bar
  When I put out to sea,

But such a tide as moving seems asleep,
  Too full for sound and foam,
When that which drew from out the boundless deep
  Turns again home.

Twilight and evening bell,
  And after that the dark!
And may there be no sadness of farewell,
  When I embark;

For tho' from our borne of Time and Place
  The flood may bear me far,
I hope to see my Pilot face to face
  When I have crossed the bar.

—ALFRED, LORD TENNYSON (1809-1892)
English Victorian poet laureate

The Last Invocation

At the last, tenderly,
From the walls of the powerful fortress'd house,
From the clasp of the knitted locks, from the keep of the well-closed doors,
Let me be wafted.

Let me glide noiselessly forth;
With the key of softness unlock the locks—with a whisper,
Set open the doors O soul.

Tenderly—be not impatient,
(Strong is your hold O mortal flesh,
Strong is your hold O love).

—WALT WHITMAN (1819-1892)
American poet

The Passionate Man's Pilgrimage

Give me my scallop shell* of quiet,
My staff of faith to walk upon,
My scrip** of joy, immortal diet,
My bottle of salvation:
My gown of glory, hope's true gauge,
And thus I'll make my pilgrimage.

Blood must be my body's balmer.
No other balm will there be given
Whilst my soul like a white palmer
Travels to the land of heaven,
Over the silver mountains,
Where spring the nectar fountains;
And there I'll kiss
The bowl of bliss,
And drink my eternal fill
On every milken hill.
My soul will be a-dry before,
But after it, will ne'er thirst more.

And by the happy, blissful way
More peaceful pilgrims I shall see,
That have shook off their gowns of clay,
And go appareled fresh like me.
I'll bring them first
To slake their thirst,
And then to taste those nectar suckets
As the clear wells
Where sweetness dwells,
Drawn up by saints in crystal buckets.

---

*the badge worn by pilgrims
**pilgrim's wallet

And when our bottles and all we
Are filled with immortality;
Then the holy paths we'll travel
Strewed with rubies thick as gravel,
Ceilings of diamonds, sapphire floors,
High walls of coral and pearl bowers.

From thence to heaven's bribeless hall
Where no corrupted voices brawl,
No conscience molten into gold,
Nor forg'd accusers bought and sold,
No cause deferred, nor vain-spent journey,
For there Christ is the King's attorney:
Who pleads for all without degrees,
And he hath angels,* but no fees.

When the grand twelve million jury
Of our sins with sinful fury,
Gainst our souls black verdicts give,
Christ pleads his death, and then we live.
Be thou my speaker, taintless pleader,
Unblotted lawyer, true proceeder,
Thou movest salvation even for alms,
Not with a bribed lawyer's palms.

And this is my eternal plea,
To him that made heaven, earth, and sea,
Seeing my flesh must die so soon,
And want a head to dine next noon,
Just at the stroke when my veins start and spread
Set on my soul an everlasting head.
Then I am ready like a palmer fit,
To tread those blest paths which before I writ.

       —SIR WALTER RALEIGH (c.1552-1618)
        Explorer, adventurer, and advisor to Queen Elizabeth I

---

*a pun on the "angel-noble," an Elizabethan coin

Prospice*

Fear death?—to feel the fog in my throat,
　　The mist in my face,
When the snows begin, and the blasts denote
　　I am nearing the place,
The power of the night, the press of the storm,
　　The post of the foe;
Where he stands, the Arch Fear in a visible form,
　　Yet the strong man must go:
For the journey is done and the summit attained,
　　And the barriers fall,
Though a battle's to fight ere the guerdon** be gained,
　　The reward of it all.
I was ever a fighter, so—one fight more,
　　The best and the last!
I would hate that death bandaged my eyes, and forbore,
　　And bade me creep past.
No! let me taste the whole of it, fare like my peers
　　The heroes of old,
Bear the brunt, in a minute pay glad life's arrears
　　Of pain, darkness, and cold.
For sudden the worst turns the best to the brave,
　　The black minute's at end,
And the elements' rage, the fiend-voices that rave,
　　Shall dwindle, shall blend,
Shall change, shall become first a peace out of pain,
　　Then a light, then thy breast,
O thou soul of my soul! I shall clasp thee again,
　　And with God be the rest!

—ROBERT BROWNING (1812-1889)
English Victorian poet

---

*Look Forward
**reward

L'Envoi*

When Earth's last picture is painted, and the
    tubes are twisted and dried,
When the oldest colors have faded, and the
    youngest critic has died,
We shall rest, and, faith, we shall need it—lie
    down for an eon or two,
Till the Master of All Good Workmen shall set us
    to work anew!

And those who were good shall be happy: they
    shall sit in a golden chair;
They shall splash at a ten-league canvas with
    brushes of comet's hair;
They shall find real saints to draw from—
    Magdalene, Peter, and Paul;
They shall work for an age at a sitting and never
    be tired at all!

And only the Master shall praise us, and only
    the Master shall blame;
And no one shall work for money, and no one
    shall work for fame;
But each for the joy of the working, and each,
    in his separate star,
Shall draw the Thing as he sees It for the God of
    Things as They Are!

—RUDYARD KIPLING (1865-1936)
    English journalist, novelist, poet, and Nobel laureate
    Author, *The Jungle Book*

---

*The End

Then Sings My Soul

Who can tell a man's real pain
when he learns the news at last
that he must die? Sure we all know
none of us is going anywhere

except in some pineslab box or its fine
expensive equal. But don't we put it off
another day, and then another and another,
as I suppose we must to cope? And so

with Lenny, Leonardo Rodriguez, a man
in the old world mold, a Spaniard
of great dignity and a fine humility,
telling us on this last retreat for men

that he had finally given up praying
because he didn't want to hear
what God might want to tell him now:
that he wanted Lenny soon in spite

of the hard facts that he had his kids
his still beautiful wife, and an agèd
mother to support. I can tell you now
it hit us hard him telling us because

for me as for the others he'd been
the model, had been a leader, raised
in the old Faith of San Juan de la Cruz
and Santa Teresa de Avila, this toreador

waving the red flag at death itself,
horns lowered and hurling down on him.
This story has no ending because there is
still life and life means hope. But

on the third day, at the last Mass, we were
all sitting in one big circle like something
out of Dante*—fifty laymen, a priest, a nun—
with Guido DiPietro playing his guitar

and singing an old hymn in that tenor voice
of his, and all of us joining in at the refrain,
Then sings my soul, my Savior God to thee,
How great thou art, how great thou art.

and there I was on Lenny's left, listening
to him sing, his voice cracked with resignation,
how great thou art, until angry glad tears
began rolling down my face, surprising me. . . .

Lord, listen to the sound of my voice.
Grant Lenny health and long life. Or,
if not that, whatever strength and peace
he needs His family likewise, and

his friends. Grant me too the courage
to face death when it shall notice me,
when I shall still not understand why
there is so much sorrow in the world.

Teach me to stare down those lowered horns
on the deadend street that shall have no alleys
and no open doors. And grant me the courage
then to still sing to thee, how great thou art.

> —PAUL MARIANI (1940—)
> American educator, biographer, and poet

---

*medieval Italian religious poet, author of *The Divine Comedy*

Joy, Shipmate, Joy!

Joy, shipmate, joy!
(Pleased to my soul at death I cry)
Our life is closed, our life begins,
The long, long anchorage we leave,
The ship is clear at last, she leaps!
She swiftly courses from the shore,
Joy, shipmate, joy!

—WALT WHITMAN (1819-1882)
American poet

Peace

Now, God be thanked Who has matched us with His hour,
And caught our youth, and wakened us from sleeping,
With hand made sure, clear eye, and sharpened power,
To turn, as swimmers in cleanness leaping,

Glad from a world grown old and cold and weary,
Leave the sick hearts that honor could not move,
And half-men, and their dirty songs and dreary,
And all the little emptiness of love.

Oh! we who have known shame, we have found release there,
Where there's no ill, no grief, but sleep has mending
Naught broken save this body, lost but breath;
Nothing to shake the laughing heart's long peace there
But only agony, and that has ending;
And the worst friend and enemy is Death.

—RUPERT BROOKE (1887-1915)
English poet

🦋 The Christian's "Good-Night"

Sleep on, beloved, sleep, and take thy rest;
Lay down thy head upon thy Savior's breast;
We love thee well, but Jesus loves thee best—
Good-night! Good-night! Good-night!

Calm is thy slumber as an infant's sleep,
But thou shalt wake no more to toil and weep;
Thine is a perfect rest, secure and deep—
Good-night! Good-night! Good-night!

Until the shadows from this earth are cast;
Until He gathers in His sheaves at last;
Until the twilight gloom be overpast—
Good-night! Good-night! Good-night!

Until the Easter glory lights the skies;
Until the dead in Jesus shall arise,
And He shall come, but not in lowly guise—
Good-night! Good-night! Good-night!

Until made beautiful by Love Divine,
Thou, in the likeness of thy Lord shalt shine,
And He shall bring that golden crown of thine—
Good-night! Good-night! Good-night!

Only Good-night, beloved—not Farewell
A little while, and all His saints shall dwell
In hallowed union, indivisible—
Good-night! Good-night! Good-night!

Until we meet again before His throne,
Clothed in the spotless robe He gives His own;
Until we know even as we are known—
Good-night! Good-night! Good-night!

—SARAH DOUDNEY (1843-1926)
English writer

Last Lines

No coward soul is mine,
No trembler in the world's storm-troubled sphere:
    I see Heaven's glories shine,
And faith shines equal, arming me from fear.

 O God, within my breast,
Almighty, ever-present Deity!
    Life—that in me has rest,
As I—undying Life—have power in Thee!

 Vain are the thousand creeds
That move men's hearts: unutterably vain;
    Worthless as withered weeds,
Or idlest froth amid the boundless main,

 To waken doubt in one
Holding so fast by thine infinity;
    So surely anchored on
The steadfast rock of immortality.

 With wide-embracing love
Thy Spirit animates eternal years,
    Pervades and broods above,
Changes, sustains, dissolves, creates, and rears.

 Though earth and man were gone,
And suns and universes ceased to be,
    And Thou were left alone,
Every existence would exist in Thee.

 There is not room for Death,
Nor atom that his might could render void:
    Thou—Thou are Being and Breath,
And what Thou art may never be destroyed.

        —EMILY BRONTË (1818-1848)
          English Victorian poet and novelist
          Author, *Wuthering Heights*

Death, Be Not Proud

Death, be not proud, though some have called thee
  Mighty and dreadful, for thou are not so;
  For those whom thou think'st thou dost overthrow
Die not, poor Death, nor yet canst thou kill me.
From rest and sleep, which but thy pictures be,
  Much pleasure—then, from thee much more must flow;
  And soonest our best men with thee do go,
Rest of their bones and soul's delivery.
Thou'rt slave to fate, chance, kings, and desperate men,
  And dost with poison, war, and sickness dwell;
  And poppy or charms can make us sleep as well,
And better than thy stroke. Why swell'st thou then?
  One short sleep past, we wake eternally,
  And death shall be no more. Death, thou shalt die.

—JOHN DONNE (c. 1571-1631)
English poet and dean of St. Paul's Cathedral

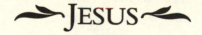

JESUS

O Simplicitas*

An angel came to me
And I was unprepared
To be what God was using.
Mother I was to be.
A moment I despaired,
Thought briefly of refusing.
The angel knew I heard.
According to God's word
I bowed to this strange choosing.

A palace should have been
The birthplace of a king
(I had no way of knowing).
We went to Bethlehem;
It was so strange a thing.
The wind was cold, and blowing,
My cloak was old, and thin.
They turned us from the inn;
The town was overflowing.

God's Word, a child so small,
Who still must learn to speak,
Lay in humiliation.
Joseph stood, strong and tall.
The beasts were warm and meek
And moved with hesitation.
The Child born in a stall?
I understood it: all.
Kings came in adoration.

Perhaps it was absurd:
The stable set apart,
The sleepy cattle lowing;
And the incarnate Word
Resting against my heart.
My joy was overflowing.
The shepherds came, adored
The folly of the Lord,
Wiser than all men's knowing.

—MADELEINE L'ENGLE (1919—)
Newbery Award-winning children's writer
Author, *A Wrinkle in Time*

---

*O Simplicity

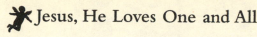

Jesus, He Loves One and All

Jesus, He loves one and all,
Jesus, He loves children small,
Their souls are waiting round His feet
On high before His mercy seat.

While He wandered here below
Children small to Him did go,
At His feet they knelt and prayed,
On their heads His hands He laid.

Came a Spirit on them then,
Better than of mighty men,
A Spirit faithful, pure, and mild,
A Spirit fit for king and child.

Oh! that Spirit give to me,
Jesu Lord, where'er I be!

—CHARLES KINGSLEY (1819-1875)
English clergyman, social reformer, and novelist

That Holy Thing

They all were looking for a king
To slay their foes and lift them high:
Thou cam'st, a little baby thing
That made a woman cry.

O Son of Man, to right my lot
Naught but Thy presence can avail;
Yet on the road Thy wheels are not,
Nor on the sea Thy sail!

My how or when Thou wilt not heed,
But come down Thine own secret stair,
That Thou mayst answer all my need—
Yea, every bygone prayer.

—GEORGE MACDONALD (1824-1905)
Scottish novelist and poet
Author, *At the Back of the North Wind*

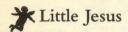 # Little Jesus

Little Jesus was Thou shy
Once, and just as small as I?
And what did it feel like to be
Out of Heaven and just like me?
Didst Thou sometimes think of there,
And ask where all the angels were?
I should think that I would cry
For my house all made of sky;
I would look about the air,
And wonder where the angels were;
And at waking 'twould distress me—
Not an angel there to dress me
Hadst Thou ever any toys,
Like us little girls and boys?
And didst Thou play in Heaven with all
The angels that were not too tall,
With stars for marbles? Did the things
Play "Can you see me?" through their wings?
And did Thy mother let Thee spoil
Thy robes with playing on our soil?
How nice to have them always new
In Heaven, because 'twas quite clean blue!

Didst thou kneel at night to pray,
And didst Thou join Thy hands this way?
And did they tire sometimes, being young,
And make the prayers seem very long?
And dost Thou like it best that we
Should join our hands to pray to Thee?
I used to think before I knew,
The prayer not said unless we do.
And did Thy mother at the night
Kiss Thee and fold the clothes in right?
And didst Thou feel quite good in bed,
Kissed, and sweet, and Thy prayers said?

Thou canst not have forgotten all
That it feels like to be small:
And Thou knowest I cannot pray
To Thee in my father's way—
When Thou wast so little, say,
Couldst Thou talk in Thy Father's way?
So, a little child, come down
And hear a little child's tongue like Thy own;
Take me by the hand and walk,
And listen to my baby talk;
To Thy Father show my prayer
(He will look, Thou art so fair)
And say: O Father, I, Thy Son,
Bring the prayer of a little one;
And He will smile, the children's tongue,
Has not changed since Thou wast young.

> —FRANCIS THOMPSON (1859-1907)
> English poet

Guiltless Blood[†]

Perhaps the Christian volume is the theme,—
 How guiltless blood for guilty man was shed;
How He, who bore in heaven the second name,
 Had not on earth whereon to lay his head:
 How his first followers and servants sped
The precepts sage they wrote to many a land;
 How he, who lone in Patmos banished,*
Saw in the sun a mighty angel stand,
And heard great Babylon's doom pronounced by Heaven's command.

> —ROBERT BURNS (1759-1796)
> Scottish poet
> From *The Cotter's Saturday Night*

---

*Aegean Sea island off the coast of Asia Minor where St. John the Divine reputedly wrote the Book of Revelation

Unto Us a Son Is Given

> *Given, not lent,*
> *And not withdrawn—once sent,*
> *This infant of mankind, this One,*
> *Is still the little welcome Son.*
>
> *New every year,*
> *New born and newly dear,*
> *He comes with tidings and a song,*
> *The ages long, the ages long:*
>
> *Even as the cold*
> *Keen winter grows not old,*
> *As childhood is so fresh, foreseen,*
> *And spring in the familiar green.*
>
> *Sudden as sweet*
> *Come the expected feet.*
> *All joy is young, and new all art,*
> *And He, too, whom we have by heart.*

—ALICE MEYNELL (1847-1922)
English poet and literary magazine editor

A Legend

> *Christ, when a child, a garden made,*
> *And many roses flourished there,*
> *He watered them three times a day,*
> *To make a garland for his hair.*
>
> *And when in time the roses bloomed*
> *He called the children in to share;*
> *They tore the flowers from every stem*
> *And left the garden stript and bare.*

"How wilt thou weave thyself a crown
  Now that thy roses all are dead?"
"Ye have forgotten that the thorns
  Are left for me," the Christ-child said.

They plaited then a crown of thorns
  And laid it rudely on his head.
A garland for his forehead made
  For roses drops of blood instead.

—TSCHAIKOVSKY (1840-1893)
Russian composer

At the Manger Mary Sings

O shut your bright eyes that mine must endanger
With their watchfulness; protected by its shade
Escape from my care; what can you discover
From my tender look but how to be afraid?
Love but can confirm the more it would deny.
  Close your bright eye.

Sleep. What have you learned from the womb that bore you
But an anxiety your Father cannot feel?
Sleep. What will the flesh that I gave do for you,
Or my mother love, but tempt you from His will?
Why was I chosen to teach His Son to weep?
  Little one, sleep.

Dream. In human dreams earth ascends to heaven
Where no one need pray nor ever feel alone.
In your first few hours of life here, O have you
Chosen already what death must be your own?
How soon will you start on the Sorrowful Way?
  Dream while you may.

—W. H. AUDEN (1907-1973)
English poet

THANKSGIVING DAY

The First Thanksgiving

When the Pilgrims
first gathered together to share
with their Indian friends
in the mid-autumn air,
they lifted their voices
in jubilant praise
for the bread on the table,
the berries and maize,
for fields and for forests,
for the turkey and the deer,
for bountiful crops
they were blessed with that year.
They were thankful for these
and they feasted away,
and as they were thankful,
we're thankful today.

—JACK PRETLUSKY

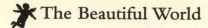# The Beautiful World

Here's a song of praise for a beautiful world,
For the banner of blue that's above it unfurled,
For the streams that sparkle and sing to the sea,
For the bloom in the glade and the leaf on the tree;
Here's a song of praise for a beautiful world.

Here's a song of praise for the mountain peak,
Where the wind and the lightning meet and speak,
For the golden star on the soft night's breast,
And the silvery moonlight's path to rest;
Here's a song of praise for a beautiful world.

Here's a song of praise for the rippling notes
That come from a thousand sweet bird throats,
For the ocean wave and the sunset glow,
And the waving fields where the reapers go;
Here's a song of praise for a beautiful world.

Here's a song of praise for the ones so true,
And the kindly deeds they have done for you;
For the great earth's heart, when it's understood,
Is struggling still toward the pure and good;
Here's a song of praise for a beautiful world.

Here's a song of praise for the One who guides,
For He holds the ships and He holds the tides.
And underneath and around and above
The world is lapped in the light of His love;
Here's a song of praise for a beautiful world.

—W. L. CHILDRESS

The First Thanksgiving Day

In Puritan New England a year had passed away
Since first beside the Plymouth coast the English Mayflower lay,
When Bradford, the good Governor, sent fowlers forth to snare
The turkey and the wild-fowl, to increase the scanty fare:—
"Our husbandry hath prospered, there is corn enough for food,
Though the peas be parched in blossom, and the grain indifferent good.
Who blessed the loaves and fishes for the feast miraculous
And filled the widow's cruse, He hath remembered us!

"Give thanks unto the Lord of Hosts, by whom we all are fed,
Who granted us our daily prayer, 'Give us our daily bread!'
By us and by our children let this day be kept for aye,
In memory of His bounty, as the land's Thanksgiving Day."

Each brought his share of Indian meal the pious feast to make,
With the fat deer from the forest and the wild fowl from the brake.
And chanted hymn and prayer were raised—though eyes with tears were dim—
"Be Lord He hath remembered us, let us remember Him!"

Then Bradford stood up at their head and lifted up his voice:
"The corn is gathered from the field, I call you to rejoice;
Thank God for all His mercies, from the greatest to the least,
Together we have fasted, friends, together let us feast.
And let these altars, wreathed with flowers
And piled with fruits, awake again
Thanksgivings for the golden hours,
The early and the latter rain!"

      —JOHN GREENLEAF WHITTIER (1807-1892)
       American Quaker poet

Thanksgiving Day

With steadfast and unwavering faith, with hard and patient toil,
The Pilgrims wrung their harvest from a strange and sterile soil.
And when the leaves turned red and gold beneath the autumn sun,
They knelt beside the scanty sheaves their laboring hands had won,
And each grave elder, in his turn, with bowed and reverent head,
Gave thanks to bounteous Heaven for the miracle of bread.

And so was born Thanksgiving Day. That little dauntless band,
Beset by deadly perils in a wild and alien land,
With hearts that held no fear of death, with stern, unbending wills,
And faith as firmly founded as the grim New England hills,
Though pitiful the yield that sprang from that unfruitful sod,
Remembered in their harvest time the goodly grace of God.

God grant us grace to look on this, our glorious native land,
As but another princely gift from His almighty hand.
May we prove worthy of His trust and keep its every shore
Protected from the murderous hordes that bear the torch of war,
And be the future bright or dark God grant we never may
Forget the reverent spirit of that first Thanksgiving Day.

—J. J. MONTAGUE (1873-1941)
American journalist and verse writer

CHRISTMAS

 ## The Shepherd Who Stayed

There are in Paradise
Souls neither great nor wise,
Yet souls who wear no less
The crown of faithfulness.

My master bade me watch the flock by night;
My duty was to stay. I do not know
What thing my comrades saw in that great light,
I did not heed the words that bade them go,
I know not were they maddened or afraid;
    I only know I stayed.

The hillside seemed on fire; I felt the sweep
Of wings above my head; I ran to see
If any danger threatened these my sheep.
What though I found them folded quietly,
What though my brother wept and plucked my sleeve,
    They were not mine to leave.

Thieves in the wood and wolves upon the hill,
My duty was to stay. Strange though it be,
I had no thought to hold my mates, no will
To bid them wait and keep the watch with me.
I had not heard that summons they obeyed;
    I only know I stayed.

Perchance they will return upon the dawn
With word of Bethlehem and why they went.
I only know that watching here alone,
I know a strange content.
I have not failed that trust upon me laid;
    I ask no more—I stayed.

—THEODOSIA GARRISON (b.1874)
American poet

Everywhere, Everywhere Christmas Tonight

Christmas in lands of the fir tree and pine,
Christmas in lands of the palm tree and vine;
Christmas where snow peaks stand solemn and white,
Christmas where cornfields lie sunny and bright;
  Everywhere, everywhere Christmas tonight!

Christmas where children are hopeful and gay,
Christmas where old men are patient and gray;
Christmas where peace, like a dove in its flight;
Broods o'er brave men in the thick of the fight;
  Everywhere, everywhere Christmas tonight!

For the Christ child who comes is the Master of all;
No palace too great—no cottage too small.
The angels who welcome Him sing from the height,
"In the city of David, a King in His might."
  Everywhere, everywhere Christmas tonight!

Then let every heart keep its Christmas within
Christ's pity for sorrow, Christ's hatred of sin,
Christ's care for the weakest, Christ's courage for right,
Christ's dread of the darkness, Christ's love of the light,
  Everywhere, everywhere Christmas tonight!

So the stars of the midnight which compass us round,
Shall see a strange glory and hear a sweet sound,
And cry, "Look the earth is aflame with delight,
O sons of the morning rejoice at the sight."
  Everywhere, everywhere Christmas tonight!

—PHILLIPS BROOKS (1835-1893)
American Episcopal bishop of Massachusetts

A Child of the Snows

There is heard a hymn when the panes are dim;
    And never heard before or again,
When the nights are strong with a darkness long,
    And the dark is alive with rain.

Never we know but in sleet and snow,
    The place where the great fires are,
That the midst of the earth is a raging mirth
    And the heart of the earth a star.

And at night we win to the ancient inn
    Where the child in the frost is furled,
We follow the feet where all souls meet
    At the inn at the end of the world.

The gods lie dead where the leaves lie red,
    For the flame of the sun is flown,
The gods lie cold where the leaves lie gold,
    And a Child comes forth alone.

—G.K. CHESTERTON (1874–1936)
English journalist, novelist, and poet
Author, *Orthodoxy* and *The Father Brown Stories*

The House of Christmas

There fared a mother driven forth
Out of an inn to roam;
In the place where she was homeless
All men are at home.
The crazy stable close at hand,
With shaking timber and shifting sand,
Grew a stronger thing to abide and stand
Than the square stones of Rome.

For men homesick in their homes,
And strangers under the sun,
And they lay their heads in a foreign land
Whenever the day is done.
Here we have battle and blazing eyes,
And chance and honor and high surprise,
But our homes are under miraculous skies
Where the yule tale was begun.

A Child in a foul stable,
Where the beasts feed and foam;
Only where He was homeless
Are you and I at home;
We have hands that fashion and heads that know,
But our hearts we lost—how long ago!
In a place no chart nor ship can show
Under the sky's dome.

This world is wild as an old wive's tale,
And strange the plain things are,
The earth is enough and the air is enough
For our wonder and our war;
But our rest is as far as the fire-drake swings
And our peace is put in impossible things
Where classed and thundered unthinkable wings
Round an incredible star.

To an open house in the evening
Home shall men come,
To an older place than Eden
And a taller town than Rome.
To the end of the way of the wandering star,
To the things that cannot be and that are,
To the place where God was homeless
And all men are at home.

—G.K. CHESTERTON (1874-1936)
English journalist, novelist, and poet
Author, *Orthodoxy* and *The Father Brown Stories*

The Oxen

Christmas Eve and twelve of the clock.
    "Now they are all on their knees,"
An elder said as we sat in a flock
    By the embers in fireside ease.

We pictured the meek and mild creatures where
    They dwelt in their strawy pen,
Nor did it occur to one of us there
    To doubt they were kneeling then.

So fair a fancy few would weave
    In those years! Yet, I feel,
If someone said on Christmas Eve,
    "Come; see the oxen kneel

"In the lonely barton* by yonder coomb**
    Our childhood used to know,"
I should go with him in the gloom,
Hoping it might be so.

        —THOMAS HARDY (1840-1928)
        English novelist and poet

An Offertory

Oh, the beauty of the Christ Child,
    The gentleness, the grace,
The smiling, loving tenderness,
    The infantile embrace!
All babyhood he holdeth,
    All motherhood enfoldeth—
Yet who hath seen his face?

---

*shelter for cattle
**narrow valley

Oh, the nearness of the Christ Child,
    When, for a sacred space,
He nestles in our very homes—
    Light of the human race!
We know Him and we love Him,
    No man to us need prove Him—
Yet who hath seen his face?

    —MARY MAPES DODGE (1831-1905)
      American children's short story writer
      Author, *Hans Brinker, or The Silver Skates*

EASTER

Most Glorious Lord of Life

(A Sonnet for Easter)

Most glorious Lord of life, that on this day
    Didst make they triumph over death and sin;
    And having harrowed hell didst bring away
    Captivity thence captive, us to win:
This joyous day, dear Lord, with joy begin,
    And grant that we for whom Thou diddest die
    Being with Thy dear blood clean washed from sin,
    May love for ever in felicity.
And that Thy love we weighing worthily
    May likewise love Thee for the same again;
    And for Thy sake that all like dear didst buy,
    With love may one another entertain.
So let us love, dear love, like as we ought.
Love is the lesson which the Lord us taught.

    —EDMUND SPENSER (c. 1552-1599)
      English poet
      Author, *The Faerie Queene*

Nature's Easter Music

The flowers from the earth have arisen
    They are singing their Easter-song;
Up the valleys and over the hillsides
    They come, an unnumbered throng.

Oh, listen! The wild flowers are singing
    Their beautiful song without words!
They are pouring the soul of their music
    Through the voices of happy birds.

Every flower to a bird has confided
    The joy of its blossoming birth—
The wonders of its resurrection
    From its grave, the frozen earth.

For you, chirp the wren and the sparrow,
    Little Eyebright, Anemone pale!
Gay Columbine, orioles are chanting
    Your trumpet-note, loud on the gale.

The Buttercup's thanks for the sunshine
    The gold finch's twitter reveals;
And the Violet trills, through the bluebird,
    Of the heaven that within her she feels.

The song-sparrow's exquisite warble
    Is born in the heart of the Rose—
Of the wild-rose, shut in its calyx,
    Afraid of belated snows.

And the melody of the wood-thrush
    Floats up from the nameless and shy
White blossoms that stay in the cloister
    Of pine-forests, dim and high.

The dust of the roadside is vocal:
    There is music from every clod;
Bird and breeze are the wild-flowers' angels,
    Their messages bearing to God.

"We arise and we praise Him together!"
With a flutter of petals and wings,
The anthem of spirits immortal
Rings back from created things.

And nothing is left wholly speechless:
For the dumbest life that we know
May utter itself through another,
And double its gladness so.

—LUCY LARCOM (1824-1893)
American poet

Easter Week

See the land, her Easter keeping,
Rises as her Maker rose.
Seeds, so long in darkness sleeping,
Burst at last from winter snows.
Earth with heaven above rejoices,
Fields and gardens hail the spring;
Shaughs* and woodlands ring with voices,
While the wild birds build and sing.
You to whom your Maker granted
Powers to those sweet birds unknown,
Use the craft by God implanted;
Use the reason not your own.
Here, while heaven and earth rejoices,
Each his Easter tribute bring—
Work of fingers, chant of voices,
Like the birds who build and sing.

—CHARLES KINGSLEY (1819-1875)
English clergyman, social reformer, and novelist

---

*thickets

At Easter Time

> The little flowers came through the ground,
>   At Easter time, at Easter time;
> They raised their heads and looked around,
>   At happy Easter time.
> And every pretty bud did say,
>   "Good people, bless this holy day,
> For Christ is risen," the angels say
>   At happy Easter time!"
> The pure white lily raised its cup
>   At Easter time, at Easter time;
> The crocus to the sky looked up
>   At happy Easter time.
> "We'll hear the song of Heaven!" they say,
>   "Its glory shines on us today.
> Oh! may it shine on us always
>   At holy Easter time!"
>
> 'Twas long and long and long ago,
>   That Easter time, that Easter time;
> But still the pure white lilies blow
>   At happy Easter time.
> And still each little flower doth say,
>   "Good Christians, bless this holy day,
> For Christ is risen, the angels say
>   At blessed Easter time!"

—LAURA E. RICHARDS (1850-1943)
Pulitzer Prize-winning biographer and novelist

Seven Stanzas at Easter

> Make no mistake if he rose at all
> it was as his body;
> if the cell's dissolution did not reverse, the molecules reknit,
>   the amino acids rekindle,
> the church will fall.

It was not as the flowers,
each soft Spring recurrent;
it was not as his Spirit in the mouths and fuddled eyes of the
    eleven apostles;
it was as his flesh: ours.

The same hinged thumbs and toes,
the same valved heart
that—pierced—died, withered, decayed, and then regathered
    out of his Father's might
new strength to enclose.

Let us not mock God with metaphor,
analogy, sidestepping transcendence;
making of the event a parable, a sign painted in the faded
    credulity of earlier ages:
let us walk through the door.

The stone is rolled back, not papier-maché,
not a stone in a story,
but the vast rock of materiality that in the slow grinding
    of time will eclipse for each of us
the wide light of day.

And if we will have an angel at the tomb,
make it a real angel,
weighty with Max Planck's* quanta, vivid with hair, opaque
    in the dawn light, robed in real linen
spun on a definite loom.

Let us not seek to make it less monstrous,
for our own convenience, our own sense of beauty,
lest, awakened in one unthinkable hour, we are embarrassed
    by the miracle,
and crushed by remonstrance.

—JOHN UPDIKE (1932—)
    American Pulitzer Prize-winning novelist, short story writer and poet

---

*Max Planck (1858-1947) was a German physicist who proposed that energy exists only in quanta, or discrete amounts. This theory helped usher in the era of modern physics

Easter Night

All night had shout of men and cry
    Of woeful women filled His way;
Until that noon of somber sky
    On Friday, clamor and display
Smote Him; no solitude had He,
    No Silence, since Gethsemane.

Public was Death; but Power, but Might,
    But Life again, but Victory,
Were hushed within the dead of night,
    The shutter'd dark, the secrecy.
And all alone, alone, alone
He rose again behind the stone.

—ALICE MEYNELL (1847-1922)
English poet and literary magazine editor

When Mary Thro' the Garden Went

When Mary thro' the garden went,
    There was no sound of any bird,
And yet, because the night was spent,
    The little grasses lightly stirred,
The flowers awoke, the lilies heard.

When Mary thro' the garden went,
    The dew lay still on flower and grass,
The waving palms above her sent
    Their fragrance out as she did pass,
No light upon the branches was.

When Mary thro' the garden went,
    Her eyes, for weeping long, were dim,
The grass beneath her footsteps bent,
    The solemn lilies, white and slim,
These also stood and wept for Him.

When Mary thro' the garden went,
She sought, within the garden ground,
One for Whom her heart was rent,
One Who for her sake was bound,
One Who sought and she was found.

—MARY E. COLERIDGE (1816-1907)
English essayist, historical novelist, and great-niece
of Samuel Taylor Coleridge

Stories
for Younger
Readers

PROVIDENCE AND PURPOSE

A Handful of Clay

Henry Van Dyke

Often, we are convinced that we are special beings destined for greatness. While it is natural to have high aims and ambitions, we mustn't forget that God may have a different purpose—at once humbler and grander—in mind for us, the "common clay" of the world. The author of this story, Henry van Dyke (1852-1933), was a New England Presbyterian clergyman and educator who wrote a number of popular novels and collections of short stories.

There was a handful of clay in the bank of a river. It was only common clay, coarse and heavy; but it had high thoughts of its own value, and wonderful dreams of the great place which it was to fill in the world when the time came for its virtues to be discovered.

Overhead, in the spring sunshine, the trees whispered together of the glory which descended upon them when the delicate blossoms and leaves began to expand, and the forest glowed with fair, clear colors, as if the dust of thousands of rubies and emeralds were hanging, in soft clouds, above the earth.

The flowers, surprised with the joy of beauty, bent their heads to one another, as the wind caressed them, and said: "Sisters, how lovely you have become. You make the day bright."

The river, glad of new strength and rejoicing in the unison of all its waters, murmured to the shores in music, telling of its release from icy fetters, its swift flight from the snow-clad mountains, and the mighty work to which it was hurrying—the wheels of many mills to be turned, and great ships to be floated to the sea.

Waiting blindly in its bed, the clay comforted itself with lofty hopes.

"My time will come," it said. "I was not made to be hidden forever. Glory and beauty and honor are coming to me in due season."

One day the clay felt itself taken from the place where it had waited so long. A flat blade of iron passed beneath it, and lifted it, and tossed it into a cart with other lumps of clay, and it was carried far away, as it seemed, over a rough and stony road. But it was not afraid, nor discouraged, for it said to itself: "This is necessary. The path to glory is always rugged. Now I am on my way to play a great part in the world."

But the hard journey was nothing compared with the tribulation and distress that came after it. The clay was put into a trough and mixed and beaten and stirred and trampled. It seemed almost unbearable. But there was consolation in the thought that something very fine and noble was certainly coming out of all this trouble. The clay felt sure that, if it could only wait long enough, a wonderful reward was in store for it.

Then it was put upon a swiftly turning wheel, and whirled around until it seemed as if it must fly into a thousand pieces. A strange power pressed it and molded it as it revolved, and through all the dizziness and pain it felt that it was taking a new form.

Then an unknown hand put it into an oven, and fires were kindled about it—fierce and penetrating—hotter than all the heats of summer that had ever brooded upon the bank of the river. But through all, the clay held itself together and endured its trials, in the confidence of a great future.

"Surely," it thought, "I am intended for something very splendid, since such pains are taken with me. Perhaps I am fashioned for the ornament of a temple, or a precious vase for the table of a king."

At last the baking was finished. The clay was taken from the furnace and set down upon a board, in the cool air, under the blue sky. The tribulation was passed. The reward was at hand.

Close beside the board there was a pool of water, not very deep, nor very clear, but calm enough to reflect, with impartial truth, every image that fell upon it. There, for the first time, as it was lifted from the board, the clay saw its new shape, the reward of all its patience and pain, the consummation of its hopes—a common flower-pot, straight and stilt, red and ugly. And then it felt that it was not destined for a king's house, nor for a palace of art, because it was made without glory or beauty or honor; and it murmured against the unknown maker, saying, "Why hast thou made me thus?"

Many days it passed in sullen discontent. Then it was filled with earth, and something—it knew not what—but something rough and brown and dead-looking, was thrust into the middle of the earth and covered over.

The clay rebelled at this new disgrace. "This is the worst of all that has happened to me, to be filled with dirt and rubbish. Surely I am a failure."

But presently it was set in a greenhouse, where the sunlight fell warm upon it, and water was sprinkled over it, and day by day as it waited, a change began to come to it. Something was stirring within it— a new hope. Still it was ignorant, and knew not what the new hope meant.

One day the clay was lifted again from its place, and carried into a great church. Its dream was coming true after all. It had a fine part to play in the world. Glorious music flowed over it. It was surrounded with flowers. Still it could not understand. So it whispered to another vessel of clay, like itself, close beside it, "Why have they set me here? Why do all the people look toward us?"

And the other vessel answered, "Do you not know? You are carrying a royal scepter of lilies. Their petals are white as snow, and the heart of them is like pure gold. The people look this way because the flower is the most wonderful in the world. And the root of it is in your heart."

Then the clay was content, and silently thanked its maker, because, though an earthen vessel, it held so great a treasure.

➤ THANKFULNESS ➤

The Ears of Wheat
The Brothers Grimm

Jakob Grimm (1785-1863) was a folklorist and specialist in languages. His brother Wilhelm (1786-1859) was a novelist. Together, they collected and wrote down virtually all the popular fairy tales and legends of their native Germany. In this particular fable retold by the Brothers Grimm, we are instructed in what happens when we forget the blessings of God and waste his bounty.

Ages upon ages ago, says the German grandmother, when angels used to wander on earth, the ground was more fruitful than it is now. Then the stalks of wheat bore not fifty- or sixty-fold, but four times five hundred-fold. Then the wheat ears grew from the bottom to the top of the stalk. But the men of the earth forgot that this blessing came from God, and they became idle and selfish.

One day a woman went through a wheat-field, and her little child, who accompanied her, fell into a puddle and soiled her frock. The mother tore off a handful of the wheat-ears and cleaned the child's dress with them.

Just then an angel passed by and saw her. Wrathfully he spoke: "Wasteful woman, no longer shall the wheatstalks produce ears. You mortals are not worthy of the gifts of Heaven!"

Some peasants who were gathering wheat in the fields heard this, and falling on their knees, prayed and entreated the angel to leave the wheat alone, not only on their account, but for the sake of the little birds who otherwise must perish of hunger.

The angel pitied their distress, and granted a part of the prayer. And from that day to this the ears of wheat have grown as they do now.

The Master of the Harvest

Mrs. Alfred Gatty

(Adapted)

In times of hardship and in times of plenty, we should always turn, as the woman in this story does, to Scripture in order to find our way. And we should never forget that all good things come from God. The author, the wife of an English clergyman, wrote many short stories in the late 19th century.

The Master of the Harvest walked by the side of his cornfields in the springtime. A frown was on his face, for there had been no rain for several weeks, and the earth was hard from the parching of the east winds. The young wheat had not been able to spring up.

So as he looked over the long ridges that stretched in rows before him, he was vexed and began to grumble and say:

"The harvest will be backward, and all things will go wrong."

Then he frowned more and more, and uttered complaints against Heaven because there was no rain; against the earth because it was so dry; against the corn because it had not sprung up.

And the Master's discontent was whispered all over the field, and along the ridges where the corn-seed lay. And the poor little seeds murmured:

"How cruel to complain! Are we not doing our best? Have we let one drop of moisture pass by unused? Are we not striving every day to be ready for the hour of breaking forth? Are we idle? How cruel to complain!"

But of all this the Master of the Harvest heard nothing, so the gloom did not pass from his face. Going to his comfortable home he repeated to his wife the dark words, that the drought would ruin the harvest, for the corn was not yet sprung up.

Then his wife spoke cheering words, and taking her Bible she wrote some texts upon the flyleaf, and after them the date of the day.

And the words she wrote were these:

The eyes of all wait upon Thee; and Thou givest them their meat in due season. Thou openest Thine hand and satisfiest the desire of every living thing. How excellent is Thy loving-kindness, O God! therefore the children of men put their trust under the shadow of Thy wings. Thou hast put gladness in my heart, more than in the time that their corn and their wine increased.

And so a few days passed as before, and the house was gloomy with the discontent of the Master. But at last one evening there was rain all over the land, and when the Master of the Harvest went out the next morning for his early walk by the cornfields, the corn had sprung up at last.

The young shoots burst out at once, and very soon all along the ridges were to be seen rows of tender blades, tinting the whole field with a delicate green. And day by day the Master of the Harvest saw them, and was satisfied, but he spoke of other things and forgot to rejoice.

Then a murmur rose among the corn-blades.

"The Master was angry because we did not come up; now that we have come forth why is he not glad? Are we not doing our best? From morning and evening dews, from the glow of the sun, from the juices of the earth, from the freshening breezes, even from clouds and rain, are we not taking food and strength, warmth and life? Why does he not rejoice?"

And when the Master's wife asked him if the wheat was doing well he answered, "Fairly well," and nothing more.

But the wife opened her Book, and wrote again on the flyleaf:

Who hath divided a watercourse for the overflowing of waters, or a way for the lightning of thunder, to cause it to rain on the earth where no man is, on the wilderness wherein there is no man, to satisfy the desolate and waste ground, and to cause the bud of the tender herb to spring forth? For He maketh small the drops of water; they pour down rain according to the vapor thereof, which the clouds do drop and distill upon man abundantly. Also can any understand the spreadings of the clouds, or the noise of his tabernacle?

Very peaceful were the next few weeks. All nature seemed to rejoice in the fine weather. The corn-blades shot up strong and tall. They burst into flowers and gradually ripened into ears of grain. But alas! the Master of the Harvest had still some fault to find. He looked at the ears and saw that they were small. He grumbled and said: "The yield will be less than it ought to be. The harvest will be bad."

And the voice of his discontent was breathed over the cornfield where the plants were growing and growing. They shuddered and murmured: "How thankless to complain! Are we not growing as fast as we can? If we were idle would we bear corn-ears at all? How thankless to complain!"

Meanwhile a few weeks went by, and a drought settled on the land. Rain was needed, so that the corn-ears might fill. And behold, while the wish for rain was yet on the Master's lips, the sky became full of heavy clouds, darkness spread over the land, a wild wind arose, and the roaring of thunder announced a storm. And such a storm! Along the ridges of corn-plants drove the rainladen wind, and the plants bent down before it and rose again like the waves of the sea. They bowed down and they rose up. Only where the whirlwind was the strongest they fell to the ground and could not rise again.

And when the storm was over, the Master of the Harvest saw here and there patches of overweighted corn, yet dripping from the thundershower, and he grew angry with them, and forgot to think of the long ridges where the corn-plants were still standing tall and strong, and where the corn-ears were swelling and rejoicing.

His face grew darker than ever. He railed against the rain. He railed against the sun because it did not shine. He blamed the wheat because it might perish before the harvest.

"But why does he always complain?" moaned the corn-plants.

"Have we not done our best from the first? Has not God's blessing been with us? Are we not growing daily more beautiful in strength and hope? Why does not the Master trust, as we do, in the future richness of the harvest?"

Of all this the Master of the Harvest heard nothing. But his wife wrote on the flyleaf of her Book:

He watereth the hills from his chambers, the earth is satisfied with the fruit of thy works. He causeth the grass to grow for the cattle and herb for the service of man, that he may bring forth food out of the earth, and wine that maketh glad the heart of man, and oil to make his face to shine, and bread which strengtheneth man's heart.

And day by day the hours of sunshine were more in number. And by degrees the green corn-ears ripened into yellow, and the yellow turned into gold, and the abundant harvest was ready, and the laborers were not wanting.

Then the bursting corn broke out into songs of rejoicing. "At least we have not labored and watched in vain! Surely the earth hath yielded her increase! Blessed be the Lord who daily loadeth us with benefits! Where now is the Master of the Harvest? Come, let him rejoice with us!"

And the Master's wife brought out her Book and her husband read the texts she had written even from the day when the corn-seeds were held back by the first drought, and as he read a new heart seemed to grow within him, a heart that was thankful to the Lord of the Great Harvest. And he read aloud from the Book:

> Thou visitest the earth and waterest it; thou greatly enrichest it with the river of God which is full of water; thou preparest them corn, when thou hast so provided for it. Thou waterest the ridges thereof abundantly; thou settlest the furrows thereof; thou makest it soft with showers; thou blessest the springing thereof. Thou crownest the year with thy goodness, and thy paths drop fatness. They drop upon the pastures of the wilderness, and the little hills rejoice on every side. The pastures are clothed with flocks. The valleys also are covered over with corn; they shout for joy, they also sing. O that men would praise the Lord for His goodness, and for his wonderful works to the children of men!

Homesick at Home

G.K. Chesterton

Written in 1896 by English journalist, novelist, and poet G.K. Chesterton (1874-1936), this poignant story reminds us that sometimes we have to lose something to really appreciate it. "Homesick at Home" opens with a mysterious riddle and proceeds to answer it with the tale of a man who left his family and his home in order to find them again.

One, seeming to be a traveler, came to me and said, "What is the shortest journey from one place to the same place?"

The sun was behind his head, so that his face was illegible.

"Surely," I said, "to stand still."

"That is no journey at all," he replied. "The shortest journey from one place to the same place is round the world."

And he was gone.

■

White Wynd had been born, brought up, married, and made the father of a family in the White Farmhouse by the river. The river enclosed it on three sides like a castle: On the fourth side there were stables and beyond that a kitchen-garden and beyond that an orchard and beyond that a low wall and beyond that a road and beyond that a pine wood and beyond that a cornfield and beyond that slopes meeting the sky, and beyond that—but we must not catalogue the whole earth, though it is a great temptation. White Wynd had known no other home but this. Its walls were the world to him and its roof the sky.

This is what makes his action so strange.

In his later years he hardly ever went outside the door. And as he grew lazy he grew restless: angry with himself and everyone. He found himself in some strange way weary of every moment and hungry for the next.

His heart had grown stale and bitter towards the wife and children whom he saw every day, though they were five of the good faces of the earth. He remembered, in glimpses, the days of his toil and strife for bread, when, as he came home in the evening, the thatch of his home burned with gold as though angels were standing there. But he remembered it as one remembers a dream.

Now he seemed to be able to see other homes, but not his own. That was merely a house. Prose had got hold of him: the sealing of the eyes and the closing of the ears.

At last something occurred in his heart: a volcano; an earthquake; an eclipse; a daybreak; a deluge; an apocalypse. We might pile up colossal words, but we should never reach it.

Eight hundred times the white daylight had broken across the bare kitchen as the little family sat at breakfast. And the eight hundred and first time the father paused with the cup he was passing in his hand.

"That green cornfield through the window," he said dreamily, "shining in the sun. Somehow, somehow it reminds me of a field outside my own home."

"Your own home?" cried his wife. "This is your home."

White Wynd rose to his feet, seeming to fill the room. He stretched forth his hand and took a staff. He stretched it forth again and took a hat. The dust came in clouds from both of them.

"Father," cried one child. "Where are you going?"

"Home," he replied.

"What can you mean? This is your home. What home are you going to?"

"To the White Farmhouse by the river."

"This is it!"

He was looking at them very tranquilly when his eldest daughter caught sight of his face.

"Oh, he is mad!" she screamed, and buried her face in her hands.

He spoke calmly. "You are a little like my eldest daughter," he said. "But you haven't got the look, no, not the look which is a welcome after work."

"Madam," he said, turning to his thunderstruck wife with a stately courtesy. "I thank you for your hospitality, but indeed I fear I have trespassed on it too long. And my home—"

"Father, Father, answer me! Is not this your home?"

The old man waved his stick.

"The rafters are cobwebbed, the walls are rain-stained. The doors bind me, the rafters crush me. There are littlenesses and bickerings and heartburnings here behind the dusty lattices where I have dozed too long. But the fire roars, and the door stands open. There is bread and raiment, fire and water and all the crafts and mysteries of love. There is rest for heavy feet on the matted floor, and for starved heart in the pure faces, far away at the end of the world, in the house where I was born."

"Where, where?"

"In the White Farmhouse by the river."

And he passed out of the front door, the sun shining on his face.

And the other inhabitants of the White Farmhouse stood staring at each other.

White Wynd was standing on the timber bridge across the river, with the world at his feet.

And a great wind came flying from the opposite edge of the sky (a land of marvelous pale golds) and met him. Some may know what that first wind outside the door is to a man. To this man it seemed that God had bent back his head by the hair and kissed him on the forehead.

He had been weary with resting, without knowing that the whole remedy lay in sun and wind and his own body. Now he half believed that he wore the seven-leagued boots.

He was going home. The White Farmhouse was behind every wood and beyond every mountain wall. He looked for it as we all look for fairyland, at every turn of the road. Only in one direction he never looked for it, and that was where, only a thousand yards behind him, the White Farmhouse stood up, gleaming with thatch and whitewash against the gusty blue of morning.

He looked at the dandelions and crickets and realized that he was gigantic. We are too fond of reckoning always by mountains. Every object is infinitely vast as well as infinitely small.

He stretched himself like one crucified in an uncontainable greatness.

"Oh God, who hast made me and all things, hear four songs of praise. One for my feet that Thou hast made strong and light upon Thy daisies. One for my head, which Thou hast lifted and crowned above the four corners of Thy heaven. One for my heart, which Thou hast made a heaven of angels singing Thy glory. And one for that pearl-tinted cloudlet far away above the stone pines on the hill."

He felt like Adam newly created. He had suddenly inherited all things, even the suns and stars.

Have you ever been out for a walk?

The story of the journey of White Wynd would be an epic. He was swallowed up in huge cities and forgotten: Yet he came out on the other side. He worked in quarries, and in docks in country after country. Like a transmigrating soul, he lived a series of existences: a knot of vagabonds, a colony of workmen, a crew of sailors, a group of fisher-men, each counted him a final fact in their lives, the great spare man with eyes like two stars, the stars of an ancient purpose.

But he never diverged from the line that girdles the globe.

On a mellow summer evening, however, he came upon the strangest thing in all his travels. He was plodding up a great dim down, that hid everything, like the dome of the earth itself.

Suddenly a strange feeling came over him. He glanced back at the waste of turf to see if there were any trace of boundary, for he felt like one who has just crossed the border of elfland. With his head a belfry of new passions, assailed with confounding memories, he toiled on the brow of the slope.

The setting sun was raying out a universal glory. Between him and it, lying low on the fields, there was what seemed to his swimming eyes a white cloud. No, it was a marble palace. No, it was the White Farmhouse by the river.

He had come to the end of the world. Every spot on earth is either the beginning or the end, according to the heart of man. That is the advantage of living on an oblate spheroid.

It was evening. The whole swell of turf on which he stood was turned to gold. He seemed standing in fire instead of grass. He stood so still that the birds settled on his staff.

All the earth and the glory of it seemed to rejoice round the madman's homecoming. The birds on their way to their nests knew him, Nature herself was in his secret, the man who had gone from one place to the same place.

But he leaned wearily on his staff. Then he raised his voice once more.

"O God, who hast made me and all things, hear four songs of praise. One for my feet, because they are sore and slow, now that they draw near the door. One for my head, because it is bowed and hoary, now that Thou crownest it with the sun. One for my heart, because Thou hast taught it in sorrow and hope deferred that it is the road that makes the home. And one for that daisy at my feet."

He came down over the hillside and into the pine wood. Through the trees he could see the red and gold sunset settling down among the white farm-buildings and the green apple-branches. It was his home now. But it could not be his home till he had gone out from it and returned to it. Now he was the Prodigal Son.

He came out of the pine wood and across the road. He surmounted the low wall and tramped through the orchard, through the kitchen garden, past the cattle-sheds. And in the stony courtyard he saw his wife drawing water.

⤝ Faith and Reason ⤞

A Lesson of Faith
Mrs. Alfred Gatty
(Adapted)

This second story by Mrs. Gatty, the wife of an English clergyman, is about a caterpillar who teaches us the vital importance of faith in an unforgettable way.

L et me hire you as a nurse for my poor children," said a butterfly to a quiet caterpillar, who was strolling along a cabbage-leaf in her odd, lumbering fashion.

"See these little eggs," continued the butterfly; "I do not know how long it will be before they come to life, and I feel very sick. If I should die, who will take care of my baby butterflies when I am gone? Will you, kind, mild, green caterpillar? They cannot, of course, live on your rough food. You must give them early dew, and honey from the flowers, and you must let them fly about only a little way at first. Dear me! it is a sad pity that you cannot fly yourself. Dear, dear! I cannot think what made me come and lay my eggs on a cabbage-leaf! What a place for young butterflies to be born upon! Here, take this gold-dust from my wings as a reward. Oh, how dizzy I am! Caterpillar! you will remember about the food—"

And with these words the butterfly drooped her wings and died. The green caterpillar, who had not had the opportunity of even saying "yes" or "no" to the request, was left standing alone by the side of the butterfly's eggs.

"A pretty nurse she has chosen, indeed, poor lady!" exclaimed she, "and a pretty business I have in hand. Why did she ever ask a poor crawling creature like me to bring up her dainty little ones! Much they'll mind me, truly, when they feel the gay wings on their backs and can fly away."

However, the poor butterfly was gone, and there lay the eggs on the cabbage-leaf, and the green caterpillar had a kind heart, so she resolved to do her best.

"But two heads are better than one," said she; "I will consult some wise animal on the matter."

Then she thought and thought till at last she thought of the lark, and she fancied that because he went up so high, and nobody knew where he went to, he must be very clever and know a great deal.

Now in the neighboring cornfield there lived a lark, and the caterpillar sent a message to him, begging him to come and talk to her. When he came, she told him all her difficulties and asked him how she was to feed and rear the little butterfly creatures.

"Perhaps you will be able to inquire and learn something about it the next time you go up high," said the caterpillar timidly.

"Perhaps I can," answered the lark; and then he went singing upwards into the bright, blue sky, till the green caterpillar could not hear a sound, nor could she see him. So she began to walk round the butterfly's eggs, nibbling a bit of the cabbage-leaf now and then as she moved along.

"What a time the lark has been gone!" she cried at last. "I wonder where he is just now. He must have flown higher than usual this time. How I should like to know where he goes, and what he hears in that curious blue sky! He always sings going up and coming down, but he never lets any secret out."

And the green caterpillar took another turn round the butterfly's eggs.

At last the lark's voice began to be heard again. The caterpillar almost jumped for joy, and it was not long before she saw her friend descend with hushed note to the cabbage bed.

"News, news, glorious news, friend caterpillar!" sang the lark, "but the worst of it is, you won't believe me!"

"I believe anything I am told," said the caterpillar hastily.

"Well, then, first of all, I will tell you what those little creatures are to eat—"and the lark nodded his head toward the eggs. "What do you think it is to be? Guess!"

"Dew and honey out of the flowers, I am afraid!" sighed the caterpillar.

"No such thing, my good friend," cried the lark exultantly; "you are to feed them with cabbage-leaves!"

"Never!" said the caterpillar indignantly. "It was their mother's last request that I should feed them on dew and honey."

"Their mother knew nothing about the matter," answered the lark; "but why do you ask me, and then disbelieve what I say? You have neither faith nor trust."

"Oh, I believe everything I am told," said the caterpillar.

"Nay, but you do not," replied the lark. "Why, caterpillar, what do you think those little eggs will turn out to be?"

"Butterflies, to be sure," said the caterpillar.

"*Caterpillars!*" sang the lark; "and you'll find it out in time." And the lark flew away.

"I thought the lark was wise and kind," said the mild, green caterpillar to herself, once more beginning to walk round the eggs, "but I find that he is foolish and saucy instead. Perhaps he went up *too* high this time. How I wonder what he sees, and what he does up yonder!"

"I would tell you if you would believe me," sang the lark, descending once more.

"I believe everything I am told," answered the caterpillar.

"Then I'll tell you something else," cried the lark. "You *will one day be a butterfly yourself!*"

"Wretched bird," exclaimed the caterpillar, "you are making fun of me. You are now cruel as well as foolish! Go away! I will ask your advice no more."

"I told you you would not believe me," cried the lark.

"I believe everything I am told," persisted the caterpillar, "everything that it is *reasonable* to believe. But to tell me that butterflies' eggs are caterpillars, and that caterpillars leave off crawling and get wings and become butterflies! Lark! you do not believe such nonsense yourself! You know it is impossible!"

"I know no such thing," said the lark. "When I hover over the cornfields, or go up into the depths of the sky, I see so many wonderful things that I know there must be more. O caterpillar! it is because you *crawl*, and never get beyond your cabbage-leaf, that you call anything *impossible*."

"Nonsense," shouted the caterpillar, "I know what's possible and what's impossible. Look at my long, green body and many legs, and then talk to me about having wings! Fool!"

"More foolish you!" cried the indignant lark, "to attempt to reason about what you cannot understand. Do you not hear how my song swells with rejoicing as I soar upwards to the mysterious wonder-world above? Oh, caterpillar, what comes from thence, receive as I do—on trust."

"What do you mean by that?" asked the caterpillar.

"*On faith*," answered the lark.

"How am I to learn faith?" asked the caterpillar.

At that moment she felt something at her side. She looked round—eight or ten little green caterpillars were moving about, and had already made a hole in the cabbage-leaf. They had broken from the butterfly's eggs!

Shame and amazement filled the green caterpillar's heart, but joy soon followed. For as the first wonder was possible, the second might be so too.

"Teach me your lesson, lark," she cried.

And the lark sang to her of the wonders of the earth below and of the heaven above. And the caterpillar talked all the rest of her life of the time when she should become a butterfly.

But no one believed her. She nevertheless had learned the lark's lesson of faith, and when she was going into her chrysalis, she said:

"I shall be a butterfly some day!"

LOVE

The Loveliest Rose in the World
Hans Christian Andersen

(Adapted by Frances Jenkins Olcott)

There are many kinds of love: the love between husbands and wives; the love between parents and children; the love between friends; and so on. Each is a wonderful kind of love, but what is the greatest love in the world? The Danish poet, novelist, and writer of fairy tales Hans Christian Andersen (1805-1875) has an answer.

Once there reigned a queen, in whose garden were found the most glorious flowers at all seasons and from all the lands of the world. But more than all others she loved the roses, and she had many kinds of this flower, from the wild dog-rose with its applescented green leaves to the most splendid, large, crimson roses. They grew against the garden walls, wound themselves around the pillars and windframes, and crept through the windows into the rooms, and all along the ceilings in the halls. And the roses were of many colors, and of every fragrance and form.

But care and sorrow dwelt in those halls. The queen lay upon a sickbed, and the doctors said she must die.

"There is still one thing that can save her," said the wise man who was also in attendance upon the Queen. "Bring her the loveliest rose in the world, the rose that is the symbol of the purest, the brightest love. If that is held before her eyes ere they close, she will not die."

Then old and young came from every side with roses, the loveliest that bloomed in each garden, but they were not of the right sort. The flower was to be plucked from the Garden of Love. But what rose in all that garden expressed the highest and purest love?

And the poets sang of the loveliest rose in the world—of the love of maid and youth, and of the love of dying heroes.

"But they have not named the right flower," said the wise man. "They have not pointed out the place where it blooms in its splendor. It is not the rose that springs from the hearts of youthful lovers, though this rose will ever be fragrant in song. It is not the bloom that sprouts from the blood flowing from the breast of the hero who dies for his country, though few deaths are sweeter than his, and no rose is redder than the blood that flows then. Nor is it the wondrous flower to which man devotes many a sleepless night and much of his fresh life—the magic flower of science."

"But I know where it blooms," said a happy mother, who came with her pretty child to the bedside of the dying queen. "I know where the loveliest rose of love may be found. It springs in the blooming cheeks of my sweet child, when, waking from sleep, it opens its eyes and smiles tenderly at me."

"Lovely is this rose, but there is a lovelier still," said the wise man.

"I have seen the loveliest, purest rose that blooms," said a woman. "I saw it on the cheeks of the queen. She had taken off her golden crown. And in the long, dreary night she carried her sick child in her arms. She wept, kissed it, and prayed for her child."

"Holy and wonderful is the white rose of a mother's griefs," answered the wise man, "but it is not the one we seek."

"The loveliest rose in the world I saw at the altar of the Lord" said the good Bishop, as the young maidens went to the Lord's Table. Roses were blushing and pale roses shining on their fresh cheeks. A young girl stood there. She looked with all the love and purity of her spirit up to heaven. That was the expression of the highest and purest love."

"May she be blessed," said the wise man, "but not one of you has yet named the loveliest rose in the world."

Then there came into the room a child, the queen's little son.

"Mother," cried the boy, "only hear what I have read."

And the child sat by the bedside and read from the Book of Him who suffered death upon the cross to save men, and even those who were not yet born. "Greater love there is not."

And a rosy glow spread over the cheeks of the queen, and her eyes gleamed, for she saw that from the leaves of the Book there bloomed the loveliest rose, that sprang from the blood of Christ shed on the cross.

"I see it!" she said, "he who beholds this, the loveliest rose on earth, shall never die."

In the Beginning

Max Lucado

From Tell Me the Story

In this story, Max Lucado (1955—), one of today's most popular contemporary Christian writers, weaves a beautiful tale about the beginning of the world. He depicts a loving God who fashioned many wonders in order to delight His best creation of all— us. And each of us, says Lucado, has a bit of His love inside, like "a light within."

The Father was dreaming. I could see it in His eyes—the sparkle. It was there again.

"What is it You see, my King?"

He didn't turn, but kept His gaze fixed on the great emptiness—the massive, boundless, unending space. The more He looked, the more His eyes would dance. I knew He saw something.

I looked in the same direction. I leaned forward and stared intently. All I saw was emptiness. All I ever saw was emptiness.

I hadn't seen the sphere that He had pulled out of the sky. "Where was that?" I asked as He began molding it in His hands.

"It was there," He replied, looking outward. I looked and saw nothing. When I turned, He was smiling. He knew a seraph's vision was too limited.

The same thing happened with the water. "Where did this come from?" I asked, touching the strange substance.

"I saw it, Michael." He chuckled as He filled an ocean from His palm. "And when I saw it, I made it. I saw it near the stars."

"The what?"

"The stars." Out into the void He reached. When He pulled back His hand, He kept it closed as if to entice me to lean forward. I did. And just as my face was near, He opened His hand. A burst of light escaped, and I looked up just in time to see it illuminate His face, too. Once again, He was smiling.

"Watch how they sparkle," He reveled. And with the flip of His wrist, the palmful of diamonds soared into the blackness until they found their destiny, and there they hung.

"Won't the children love them?" the Maker said as together we watched the twinkling begin.

I still wasn't sure what or who these "children" were, but I knew they occupied a place in the Dream like nothing else. Ever since the Dream started, the Father spoke often of these children—what they would be like, how they would respond.

I remember once, the Father held the sphere in one hand and motioned to me with the other. "Come. See what the children will see." He then put His fingers to His lips and blew gently. Off His fingertips floated tiny whiffs of white cotton balls of fluff.

"What do they do?" I asked as the train of puffs sailed toward the globe.

"Oh Michael," He boomed with excitement, "they do everything. They give shade. They give rain. But most of all, My children can watch them pass and, if they look closely, they will see Me."

That was the way He thought about everything. All the Dream was for the children. And in all the Dream was the Father. With a waterfall, He said, "I made it small so they could run in and out." With the dandelion, "This is just the right size for the children to blow," and the rivers in the canyon: "They can sit right here and watch the water race into the valley."

"But where are the children?" I once asked, looking into the same space from whence had come the rest of the Dream.

"Oh, not out there," responded the Artist. There was urgency in His voice as He repeated, "Not out there."

But that is all the Father said. And that's all I asked.

With the coming of the creatures, I almost forgot. We laughed so much as He made them. Each one was special. The tiny wing for the mosquito. The honk so unlike any other sound for the goose. The shell for the turtle. The darting eyes of the owl.

He even let me decorate a few. I put violet in the butterfly wings, and He loved my idea to stretch the elephant's nose.

What fun it was as the heavens gave birth to fowl and fish, reptile and rodent! No more had the little ones scurried off His palm than the giant ones appeared. He grabbed the giraffe and stretched its neck, and He put a hole in the whale's head ("so it will come to the surface and breathe and the children will see it").

"What will we call them all?" I asked.

"I'll leave that up to the children."

The children—I'd almost forgotten. But He hadn't. As the last winged creature left His fingers, He turned and looked at me and I knew.

"It's time?"

"Yes, it's time."

I expected to see His eyes dance again. But they didn't. I anticipated eagerness. But He didn't begin. For a long period, He sat looking out into the void—longer than normal.

"Do You see the children?"

"No. They are not to be found out there."

"Then what do You see?"

"I see their deeds."

He spoke softly. The joy was gone from His voice.

"What? What is it? What is it You see?"

Perhaps it was because He thought I needed to know. Or maybe because He needed someone else to know. I'm not sure why, but He did what He had never done. He let me see. As if the sky were a curtain, He took it and pulled it back.

Before I could see it, I could smell it. The stench stung my eyes. "It's greed you smell," He explained. "A love for foolish, empty things."

I started to turn away. But my King didn't, so I didn't. I looked again.

It was so dark—a darkness unlike the starless sky—a blackness unlike the void. This darkness moved. It crept. It shadowed and swayed. It was a living soot. He knew my thoughts and spoke.

His words were slow and spaced. "They will put it out."

"What?"

"They will destroy that which makes them Mine."

It was then I saw it for the first time. He reached into Himself—deep into His own self and pulled it out. A flame. A shining circle.

It glowed brilliantly in His palm. Much brighter than the constellations He had spread about or the sun He'd ignited.

"This is . . . " I began.

"This is part of Me," He finished and added what I couldn't have imagined. "And out of Me, I will make My children."

For the first time I saw. I saw why the children were so treasured. I saw the uniqueness in them. They bore His light—the universe He created, the children He fathered.

"But the darkness?" I had to ask. "Why?"

"Just as I chose, so must they choose. Else they won't be Mine."

Just then His face lifted. His eyes brightened. "But they won't all forget Me. Look."

Into tomorrow I gazed. At first I saw nothing. Just swarthy darkness billowing. But then, as I searched, I saw. First, only one, then a cluster, then more—lights they were. Flickers of candles, weakened but not lost in the blackness. Like the stars He had cast against the black heavens, these flames flickered in a sable sea.

"It's My children." There was pride in His voice. "My children remember."

The look on His face, I cannot forget. His eyes had sparkled when He suspended the planets in space; His cheeks had danced as He heard the cat purr. I had seen His face alive before—but not like now. For at this moment—when He saw His children alight in the darkness—when He saw those who were seeking Him—He celebrated. His countenance exploded with joy. His head flew back, and laughter shook the stars.

"My children, My children, My children," were His only words. And then, He paused, wiped the tears from His face, and pledged a promise for all Heaven to hear.

"You haven't forgotten Me; I won't forget you."

Then He turned to me. "To the work, Michael; we've much to do. We must make the Dream come true."

And I thought making animals was a delight. "No two will be alike," He vowed as He began reaching into Himself for balls of light. "Some big, some small. Some timid, some bold. Some with big ears, some with little." And off His palm they came. Generation chosen. Destination determined. Each with a different thread of character or shape of body.

But each with a bit of Him—a light within.

And He even let me help. "Look what I made, Father," I told him. "I call them freckles. Let me show You how they work."

And He smiled.

Legends and Heroes

The Legend of the Stranger Child
Count Franz Pocci

While you are reading this story, you hear a loud knock. You open the door and discover a stranger asking for help. What should you do? In the Old Testament there are many instances in which the stranger is an angel sent by God. And in the New Testament—as in the legend below—we learn that the stranger may be Christ Himself. Count Franz Pocci (1807-1876) was a German author and illustrator.

There once lived a laborer who earned his daily bread by cutting wood. His wife and two children, a boy and girl, helped him with his work.

The boy's name was Valentine, and the girl's, Marie. They were obedient and pious and the joy and comfort of their poor parents.

One winter evening, this good family gathered about the table to eat their small loaf of bread, while the father read aloud from the Bible. Just as they sat down there came a knock on the window, and a sweet voice called: "O let me in! I am a little child, and I have nothing to eat, and no place to sleep. I am so cold and hungry! Please, good people, let me in!"

Valentine and Marie sprang from the table and ran to open the door, saying: "Come in, poor child, we have but very little ourselves, not much more than thou hast, but what we have we will share with thee."

The stranger child entered and going to the fire began to warm his cold hands.

The children gave him a portion of their bread, and said: "Thou must be very tired; come, lie down in our bed, and we will sleep on the bench here before the fire."

Then answered the Stranger Child: "May God in Heaven reward you for your kindness."

They led the little guest to their small room, laid him in their bed, and covered him closely, thinking to themselves: "Oh! how much we have to be thankful for! We have our nice warm room and comfortable bed, while this child has nothing but the sky for a roof, and the earth for a couch."

When the parents went to their bed, Valentine and Marie lay down on the bench before the fire, and said one to the other: "The stranger child is happy now, because he is so warm! Good-night!"

Then they fell asleep.

They had not slept many hours when little Marie awoke, and touching her brother lightly, whispered: "Valentine, Valentine, wake up! wake up! Listen to the beautiful music at the window."

Valentine rubbed his eyes and listened. He heard the most wonderful singing and the sweet notes of many harps:

> *Blessed Child,*
> *Thee we greet,*
> *With sound of harp*
> *And singing sweet.*

> *Sleep in peace,*
> *Child so bright,*
> *We have watched thee*
> *All the night.*

> *Blest the home*
> *That holdeth Thee,*
> *Peace, and love,*
> *Its guardians be.*

The children listened to the beautiful singing, and it seemed to fill them with unspeakable happiness. Then creeping to the window they looked out.

They saw a rosy light in the east, and, before the house in the snow, stood a number of little children holding golden harps and lutes in their hands, and dressed in sparkling, silver robes.

Full of wonder at this sight, Valentine and Marie continued to gaze out at the window, when they heard a sound behind them, and turning saw the Stranger Child standing near. He was clad in a golden garment, and wore a glistening, golden crown upon his soft hair. Sweetly he spoke to the children: "I am the Christ Child, who wanders about the world seeking to bring joy and good things to loving children. Because you have lodged me this night I will leave with you my blessing."

As the Christ Child spoke, He stepped from the door, and breaking off a bough from a fir tree that grew near, planted it in the ground, saying: "This bough shall grow into a tree, and every year it shall bear Christmas fruit for you."

Having said this, He vanished from their sight, together with the silver-clad, singing children—the angels.

And, as Valentine and Marie looked on in wonder, the fir bough grew, and grew, and grew, into a stately Christmas tree laden with golden apples, silver nuts, and lovely toys. And after that, every year at Christmas time, the tree bore the same wonderful fruit.

And you, dear boys and girls, when you gather around your richly decorated trees—think of the two poor children who shared their bread with a Stranger Child, and be thankful.

The Wonder Tree
Friedrich Adolph Krummacher

(Adapted)

What are miracles? Are they grand, mysterious events that happen in the blink of an eye? Or are they as familiar and undramatic as the slow springing from the earth of the fig, the date, and the pomegranate? Perhaps miracles are commonplace, suggests this legend by German theologian and writer Friedrich Adolph Krummacher (1768-1845). If so, our appreciation for them, and for He who is the maker of all miracles, should grow rather than diminish.

One day in the springtime, Prince Solomon was sitting under the palm trees in the royal gardens, when he saw the Prophet Nathan walking near.

"Nathan," said the Prince, "I would see a wonder."

The prophet smiled. "I had the same desire in the days of my youth," he replied.

"And was it fulfilled?" asked Solomon.

"A man of God came to me," said Nathan, "having a pomegranate seed in his hand. 'Behold,' he said, 'what will become of this.' Then he made a hole in the ground, planted the seed, and covered it over. When he withdrew his hand the clods of earth opened, and I saw two small leaves coming forth. But scarcely had I beheld them when they joined together and became a small stem wrapped in bark; and the stem grew before my eyes, and it grew thicker and higher and became covered with branches.

"I marveled, but the man of God motioned me to be silent. 'Behold' said he, 'new creations begin.'

"Then he took water in the palm of his hand and sprinkled the branches three times, and, lo! the branches were covered with green leaves, so that a cool shade spread above us, and the air was fined with perfume.

"'From whence come this perfume and this shade?' cried I.

"'Dost thou not see' he answered, 'these crimson flowers bursting from among the leaves, and hanging in clusters?'

"I was about to speak, but a gentle breeze moved the leaves, scattering the petals of the flowers around us. Scarcely had the falling flowers reached the ground when I saw ruddy pomegranates hanging beneath the leaves of the tree, like almonds on Aaron's rod. Then the man of God left me, and I was lost in amazement."

"Where is he, this man of God?" asked Prince Solomon eagerly. "What is his name? Is he still alive?"

"Son of David," answered Nathan, "I have spoken to thee of a vision."

When the prince heard this he was grieved to the heart. "How couldst thou deceive me thus?" he asked.

But the prophet replied: "Behold in thy father's gardens thou mayest daily see the unfolding of wonder trees. Doth not this same miracle happen to the fig, the date, and the pomegranate? They spring from the earth, they put out branches and leaves, they flower, they fruit, not in a moment, perhaps, but in months and years, but canst thou tell the difference betwixt a minute, a month, or a year in the eyes of Him with whom one day is as a thousand years, and a thousand years as one day?"

They Heard the Angels Sing

Arthur S. Maxwell

The Seventh Day Adventists were organized in 1863 in Europe and the United States. They are a devout sect, believing that Christ will return in person, strictly observing the Sabbath on Saturdays, and pursuing charitable work around the world. Here is a 20th-century legend told by English-born American author Arthur Maxwell (1896-1970) about what happened to a group of Seventh Day Adventist missionaries in Indonesia. This legend teaches us about the literal saving power of faith.

B ang! Boom! Bang! Boom! Boom! The bombs were dropping all around. Buildings were burning and falling. People were screaming and crying.

Already most of the city of Surabaya had been destroyed in the terrible bombardment. Thousands of men, women, and children had been killed.

Almost all the churches had been bombed, all except the little Adventist church, where Christian and Ketty, with their father and mother and some friends, were talking together, wondering how long their lives would be spared, and whether it would be their turn next to die.

As the bursting bombs came ever nearer and nearer, they could see, through the windows, great fires blazing all about them. Father, who was the minister of the church, then urged them all to take refuge in the baptismal tank. It was not much of an air-raid shelter, but the best they had.

This tank, which was behind the pulpit, was not very large or deep, but they all crowded into it. Then they began to pray.

What a prayer meeting was that!

Father prayed, and Mother, and then the children.

Christian, just twelve years old, remembered the Thirty-fourth Psalm, especially where it says, "The angel of the Lord encampeth round about them that fear him, and delivereth them."

Over and over again he pleaded, "Send the angels, Lord, to encamp round about us and deliver us. Send the angels, Lord! Send the angels!"

Then little Ketty, who was only four, began to plead: "Dear Jesus, Thou hast promised to send Thine angels. Keep Thy promise. Oh, Jesus, send the angels!"

So they prayed.

And God in heaven heard.

What happened next may seem to some unbelievable, but it really happened. I know this minister well. He is one of God's noblest servants, and he told me the story himself.

As they prayed, the planes passed over, and the bombs fell farther and farther away. When the sky seemed clear again, Father went out into the church to see if all was well. It was. Not a spark of fire had fallen on the building.

As he stood there, thanking God for His goodness, there came a loud knocking on the door. Going to see who it could be at such a time, he found two policemen there, with many angry civilians behind them.

"Who was singing in this church just now?" they demanded.

"Singing?" he said. "Singing? Nobody. The church has been empty."

"You're not telling the truth," they said. "We heard the singing, and we want to know what you mean by singing in here when the city is burning and people are dying all around you."

"Come in and see for yourself," said Father.

They came, and found the place empty, and went away wondering.

So did Father. What could the police mean by saying that there had been singing in the church? He had not heard any.

Then the bombers returned. Again the dreadful hum of their engines became louder and louder. Once more the bombs began to fall. So Father hurried back to the baptismal tank and told the others the strange story the police had told him.

Then they prayed again. Once more, as the noise and terror of it all mounted about them, Christian and Ketty lifted up their voices to God, saying, "Send the angels! Send the angels, Jesus! Keep Your promise! Send the angels!"

And then *they* heard it too, that strange, sweet sound. Above the din of destruction, above the bombing and the burning, they heard the sound of singing. Beautiful singing, such as they had never heard before. And it was coming from the church, just as the police had said.

And the song? It sounded, so he told me, just like the old, familiar hymn:

All the way my Savior leads me;
What have I to ask beside?
Can I doubt His tender mercy,
Who through life has been my guide?
Heavenly peace, divinest comfort,
Here by faith in Him to dwell!
For I know whate'er befall me,
Jesus doeth all things well.

When the bombers had passed, all hurried out of the baptismal tank into the church. They found the building empty, without a sign that anyone had been there. Then again there came the loud knocking at the door, as police and people came to find out what it all meant. When, once more, they found nobody there save this handful of grownups and children, they were amazed and could not believe their eyes.

But father understood now. So did Christian and Ketty. They knew their prayers had been answered. They knew that God had sent His angels to protect them, and they—O joy, O wonder of wonders—they had heard them singing!

Today that Adventist church still stands in Surabaya, a monument to God's protecting power over His people in time of trouble, a testimony that the angels of the Lord still encamp round about them that fear Him, to deliver them.

Columbus at La Rabida

Washington Irving

(Adapted)

As schoolchildren, we memorize the line, "In 1492, Columbus sailed the ocean blue." We are taught that Christopher Columbus (1451-1506) was a sailor from Genoa, Italy, that he convinced the Queen of Spain to finance his expedition to find a shorter route to the Far East, and that instead he discovered the New World. But seldom do we learn that it was faith in God that inspired his explorations and sustained him when all seemed lost. Washington Irving (1783-1859), better known as the author of "The Legend of Sleepy Hollow" and "Rip Van Winkle," became fascinated with this aspect of Columbus's life when he served as United States Minister to Spain in 1842-1846.

About half a league from the little seaport of Palos de Moguer, in Andalusia, there stood, and continues to stand at the present day, an ancient convent of Franciscan friars, dedicated to Santa Maria de Rabida.

One day a stranger on foot, in humble guise, but of a distinguished air, accompanied by a small boy, stopped at the gate of the convent and asked of the porter a little bread and water for his child. While receiving this humble refreshment, the prior of the convent, Juan Perez de Marchena, happened to pass by, and was struck with the appearance of the stranger. Observing from his air and accent that he was a foreigner, he entered into conversation with him and soon learned the particulars of his story.

That stranger was Columbus.

Accompanied by his little son Diego, he was on his way to the neighboring town of Huelva, to seek a brother-in-law, who had married a sister of his deceased wife.

The prior was a man of extensive information. His attention had been turned in some measure to geographical and nautical science. He was greatly interested by the conversation of Columbus, and struck with the grandeur of his views. When he found, however, that the voyager was on the point of abandoning Spain to seek the patronage of the court of France, the good friar took the alarm.

He detained Columbus as his guest, and sent for a scientific friend to converse with him. That friend was Garcia Fernandez, a physician of Palos. He was equally struck with the appearance and conversation of the stranger. Several conferences took place at the convent, at which veteran mariners and pilots of Palos were present.

Facts were related by some of these navigators in support of the theory of Columbus. In a word, his project was treated with a deference in the quiet cloisters of La Rabida and among the seafaring men of Palos which had been sought in vain among sages and philosophers.

Among the navigators of Palos was one Martin Alonzo Pinzon, the head of a family of wealth, members of which were celebrated for their adventurous expeditions. He was so convinced of the feasibility of Columbus's plan that he offered to engage in it with purse and person, and to bear the expenses of Columbus in an application to court. Fray Juan Perez, being now fully persuaded of the importance of the proposed enterprise, advised Columbus to repair to the court, and make his propositions to the Spanish sovereigns, offering to give him a letter of recommendation to his friend, the prior of the Convent of Prado and confessor to the queen, and a man of great political influence; through whose means he would, without doubt, immediately obtain royal audience and favor. Martin Alonzo Pinzon, also, generously furnished him with money for the journey, and the friar took charge of his youthful son, Diego, to maintain and educate him in the convent.

Thus aided and encouraged and elated with fresh hopes, Columbus took leave of the little *junto* at La Rabida, and set out, in the spring of 1486, for the Castilian court, which had just assembled at Cordova, where the sovereigns were fully occupied with their chivalrous enterprise for the conquest of Granada. But alas! success was not yet! for Columbus met with continued disappointments and discouragements, while his projects were opposed by many eminent prelates and Spanish scientists as being against religion and unscientific. Yet in spite of this opposition, by degrees the theory of Columbus began to obtain proselytes. He appeared in the presence of the king with modesty, yet self-possession, inspired by a consciousness of the dignity and importance of his errand; for he felt himself, as he afterwards declared in his letters, animated as if by a sacred fire from above, and considered himself an instrument in the hand of Heaven to accomplish its great designs. For nearly seven years of apparently fruitless solicitation, Columbus followed the royal court from place to place, at times encouraged by the sovereigns, and at others neglected.

At last he looked round in search of some other source of patronage, and feeling averse to subjecting himself to further tantalizing delays and disappointments of the court, determined to repair to Paris. He departed, therefore, and went to the Convent of La Rabida to seek his son Diego. When the worthy Friar Juan Perez de Marchena beheld Columbus arriving once more at the gate of his convent after nearly seven years of fruitless effort at court, and saw by the humility of his garb the poverty he had experienced, he was greatly moved; but when he found that he was about to carry his proposition to another country, his patriotism took alarm.

The friar had once been confessor to the queen, and knew that she was always accessible to persons of his sacred calling. He therefore wrote a letter to her, and at the same time entreated Columbus to remain at the convent until an answer could be received. The latter was easily persuaded, for he felt as if on leaving Spain he was again abandoning his home.

The little council at La Rabida now cast round their eyes for an ambassador to send on this momentous mission. They chose one Sebastian Rodriguez, a pilot of Lepe, one of the most shrewd and important personages in this maritime neighborhood. He so faithfully and successfully conducted his embassy that he returned shortly with an answer.

Isabella had always been favorably disposed to the proposition of Columbus. She thanked Juan Perez for his timely services and requested him to repair immediately to the court, leaving Columbus in confident hope until he should hear further from her. This royal letter, brought back by the pilot at the end of fourteen days, spread great joy in the little *junto* at the convent.

No sooner did the warm-hearted friar receive it than he saddled his mule, and departed, privately, before midnight to the court. He journeyed through the countries of the Moors, and rode into the new city of Santa Fe where Ferdinand and Isabella were engaged in besieging the capital of Granada.

The sacred office of Juan Perez gained him a ready admission into the presence of the queen. He pleaded the cause of Columbus with enthusiasm. He told of his honorable motives, of his knowledge and experience, and his perfect capacity to fulfill the undertaking. He showed the solid principles upon which the enterprise was founded, and the advantage that must attend its success, and the glory it must shed upon the Spanish Crown.

Isabella, being warm and generous of nature and sanguine of disposition, was moved by the representations of Juan Perez, and requested that Columbus might be again sent to her. Bethinking herself of his poverty and his humble plight, she ordered that money should be forwarded to him, sufficient to bear his traveling expenses, and to furnish him with decent raiment.

The worthy friar lost no time in communicating the result of his mission. He transmitted the money, and a letter, by the hand of an inhabitant of Palos, to the physician, Garcia Fernandez, who delivered them to Columbus. The latter immediately changed his threadbare garb for one more suited to the sphere of a court, and purchasing a mule, set out again, reanimated by hopes, for the camp before Granada.

This time, after some delay, his mission was attended with success. The generous spirit of Isabella was enkindled, and it seemed as if the subject, for the first time, broke upon her mind in all its real grandeur. She declared her resolution to undertake the enterprise, but paused for a moment, remembering that King Ferdinand looked coldly on the affair, and that the royal treasury was absolutely drained by the war.

Her suspense was but momentary. With an enthusiasm worthy of herself and of the cause, she exclaimed: "I undertake the enterprise for my own crown of Castile, and will pledge my jewels to raise the necessary funds." This was the proudest moment in the life of Isabella. It stamped her renown forever as the patroness of the discovery of the New World.

Salvaging Scrap
Shirley Graham and George D. Lipscomb

One of America's greatest heroes is George Washington Carver (1860-1943). His shining example of service in the name of the Lord speaks to all men. An African American, Carver was born into slavery, but once freed he became an outstanding chemist and botanist and did much to help in the fight against racial prejudice. Every aspect of his life was tied to his Christianity, as this story, written in the early part of this century, reveals.

Nobody could have had a more discouraging beginning than George Washington Carver. Born of slave parents, orphaned as a baby, then bought by the poor farmer Carver for the price of a horse, little George grew up a sickly child with a serious speech defect. Yet against great odds of poverty and being a Negro, his perseverance saw him through college and graduate studies to become one of America's most ingenious scientists. His philosophy was "Throw away nothing, everything can be used." And he produced paints and stains out of common clay, 118 products from the sweet potato, over 300 from peanuts, and many other products from waste material. He won international fame for his work in soil improvement and is said to have invented the science of *ersatz* or substitutes, in which field he accomplished miracles. And the character of this gentle and truly religious man was such that he never thought of making money out of these things, only of giving service to mankind. Dr. Carver gave all his savings to Tuskegee Institute to be used for research. Here is his story:

■

The two men met on the steps of the administration building at Tuskegee and for a few minutes stood talking. They were often to stand thus together in the years to come and always they made a striking contrast. Tall, broad-shouldered, robust, deep-voiced Booker T. Washington, with his leonine head, strong features, and tawny complexion, and George Washington Carver, slender figure poised lightly on his feet, narrow, slightly sloping shoulders, delicate features, high-pitched voice, and eyes the burning center of his dusky face. This was the fall of 1896 and, as he looked out over the school grounds, Carver later confessed that he was appalled, almost bewildered.

"I had never seen anything like it. There was yellow soil and red and purple and brown and riveted and banded, and all sorts of things, except grass or plants. There were erosion gullies in which an ox could get lost!"

Yet a few miles away, beside the railroad tracks at Chehaw, he discovered Neviusia, a rare deciduous shrub which he had been taught grew only under the most careful cultivation.

At the time of Dr. Carver's arrival, Dr. Washington apologized that the carriage had not been at Chehaw when his train arrived.

"I'd forgotten that you might not know about the short line on to Tuskegee. Conductors don't always inform our visitors," he explained.

"The boys told me you sent your fine surrey and best horses to meet all 'big folks.'" Carver's eyes twinkled. "They wondered why you bothered today!"

Washington laughed and regarded this young scientist with keen appreciation. His lack of ostentation, and his quiet, simple dignity delighted him. But he was puzzled also. Who was this man? Where had he come from?

Carver did not consume the time talking about himself. He asked a dozen keen and searching questions which made Washington wonder even more. Then he said he'd like to see the laboratory.

Washington replied at once: "We'll go to the Agricultural Hall. It's our newest building, put up by the students. They," he added, "are mighty proud of it."

"But, the laboratory," began Carver. Washington held up his hand.

"Also—it has plenty of space."

Carver regarded him with a quizzical expression around his eyes.

"I see. You mean you're giving me the space and—"

"God has given you the brains!" finished Dr. Washington.

"Well," said Carver, dryly, "I guess, together, we ought to manage a laboratory." And then they both chuckled.

They looked at each other, the chuckle grew to laughter, and the two great souls knit as one. Never in the close companionship, ending only with Booker T. Washington's death, did their understanding, loyalty, or faith in one another waver. Not even death changed that. For when the offers came from round the world, with gold and fame and everything men seek, Carver said simply:

"I promised Dr. Washington I'd work at Tuskegee. He's gone, but Tuskegee and work and needs remain."

No laboratory, no greenhouses, no gardens! Carver did not voice his dismay, and if he thought with longing of all he'd left behind, no one knew. Quietly he rounded up the few students in Agriculture.

It did not take him long to discover that "farming" was the most unpopular subject in the curriculum. Most of the boys had come to Tuskegee to get away from farm work. They wanted to learn a "trade" or "skill." Anybody could farm! Their frankly expressed attitude is told by T. M. Campbell in his delightful little book, *The Movable School Goes to the Negro Farmer*:

> Custom and environment in my home community had schooled me in the idea that all work other than farming could be done only by white people. But when I reached Tuskegee and observed such activities as saw-milling, brick-making, the construction of houses, carriages, wagons, and buggies and the making of tin utensils, harness mattresses, brooms, clothes, shoes—all done by Negroes—it

was to me like entering a new Heaven. I could scarcely believe such things were possible.

To make the subject of agriculture even more undesirable, some teachers in other departments sought to punish students by assigning them to "the farm." But among the students whom Dr. Carver first met were Jacob Jones, now a lawyer in Oklahoma, and Walter Keys, who engaged himself to this new teacher as helper, J. H. Palmer, who served all the remainder of his life at Tuskegee, and some time later, Thomas Monroe Campbell, first Negro to be appointed field agent in the United States Department of Agriculture, and Sanford Lee, county agricultural agent in the State of Georgia.

How was he best to reach these boys who, with no elementary background, no knowledge of general science or even books as taught in Northern high schools, wanted to know how to make things grow? Sanford H. Lee has described something of Dr. Carver's method:

My very first recollection of him was my first morning in his class. As he always did, before going right into the subject at hand, he gave us about ten minutes' general talk. I remember his words so well— "To him, who in the love of Nature holds communion with her visible forms, she speaks a various language!" All of us stared at this strange man from "up North." What on earth was he talking about? Then, looking hard at us, he continued: "Young people, I want to beg of you always keep your eyes and ears open to what Mother Nature has to teach you. By so doing you will learn many valuable things every day of your life." How many times have I heard him quote Bryant's *Thanatopsis* both to his classes and on other occasions. In fact, it was rather difficult for him to begin the discussion of any lesson without quoting some favorite author, or from the Psalms. "O Lord, how manifold are Thy works, in wisdom hast Thou made them all." This was one of his favorites.

To this day, I seldom begin a day without thinking of that familiar Bryant quotation—"To him who in the love of nature—"

As a county agent, every year, I learn much more from my chickens and orchard and flowers than I do from books. They "tell" me something every time I walk among them—just as Dr. Carver told us they would.

The word went out among the students that the new teacher was "different." Students who had been sent to "farming" for punishment decided to remain. The first campaign to salvage waste was being organized!

One morning the new teacher closed his talk with a little poem. He said it was called "Things Not Done Before." Whether he wrote the lines himself or found them somewhere is not known. The final verses are:

> *The few who strike out without map or chart*
> *Where never a man has been,*
> *From the beaten path they draw apart*
> *To see what no man has seen.*
> *Their deeds they hunger alone to do,*
> *Though battered and bruised and sore,*
> *They blaze the trail for the many who*
> *Do nothing not done before.*
>
> *The things that haven't been done before*
> *Are the tasks worthwhile today;*
> *Are you one of the flock that follows, or*
> *Are you one who will lead the way?*
> *Are you one of the timid souls that quail*
> *At the jeers of a doubting crew,*
> *Or dare you, whether you win or fail,*
> *Strike out for the goal that's new.*

His voice lilted on the question, and raising his eyes he looked into the faces of his students. They smiled back at him, and he said:

"Today, we're going to do something which has never been done before. We're going out and find the things we need for our laboratory. We're going into town and look through every scrap heap. We'll go to the back doors and ask the lady of the house for old kitchen utensils she can't use. We need containers of all kinds, and lamps, and pans in which to cook."

He showed them pictures of crucibles, and beakers, distilling apparatus and extracting apparatus. From his box he took out tubes and small glass cases. "These are the kind of things we need. God knows our need. He will direct us! Shall we go?"

"Yes, sir!" they said, and followed him.

It was an exciting hunt. The students had caught his crusading spirit. They searched up and down alleys, raked through trash and dump heaps, politely but firmly accosted housewives, gathered hollow reeds from the swamp, which "teacher" said could be used for pipettes. When evening came, they met with all their findings. Carver praised each one. What he could not use at once, he set aside, saying, "There is no waste, save of time. All of these things can be used again." Thus spoke the first and pioneer chemurgist.* Only now is the country awakening to the truth of his words.

You may see that first laboratory equipment today preserved in the Carver Museum: a large lantern, its chimney still shining bright; jugs, large and small—one of them marked "Vinegar"; a bent skillet, saucepans, broken bottles, tops of cans, an oil lamp, pieces of rubber. With this discarded scrap Carver began to rebuild Alabama.

A twenty-acre patch of ground was assigned to him—"no-good" ground. Hogs rooted among the weeds and rubbish on it. He and his students first cleaned it off and then he asked for a two-horse plow. No one down that way had ever seen a two-horse plow, but Dr. Washington okayed his request and one was sent for. When it arrived and Carver hitched it up and began to turn the soil, observers slapped their thighs and rocked with laughter. The idea of a professor plowing! Even his students were a bit chagrined. But he was good-natured about it, even joking with the farmers who gathered round. Their mirth changed to pity, then.

At his bidding, the students brought back muck from the swamps and leaf-mold from the woods. He plowed these under, then told them to clean the barns and bring the "drippings." The farmers were appalled when after all this work, instead of planting cotton, he planted cowpeas!

When the students harvested the spindly cowpeas with a miserable pea in each stalk, they were disgusted. All this for something to throw

---

*Today, chemurgy is a widely recognized and highly valued science that involves the use of agricultural products in the manufacture of industrial goods.

to the hogs! But the teacher surprised them by saying, "Now I'll show you how to cook them!"

Well, Northerners were a bit crazy anyhow! But one evening they all sat down to a delicious meal prepared by their professor. Never had they tasted such food. Afterward, he explained each dish—prepared from cowpeas! The word got around and other students asked to join his classes. People began to talk.

When he planted sweet potatoes on his tract, they simply looked on, saying nothing. But when the tract yielded eighty bushels to an acre, their eyes opened. In the spring he said to his now greatly augmented class:

"Now, we shall see. I've been rotating crops on this land. It has been rested, *refreshed*, and enriched. Now, we'll try cotton."

This they could understand. Long before the cotton was picked, farmers came from near and far to gaze in wonder at the perfect stalks, and when he harvested a five hundred-pound bale of cotton from one acre, whites and blacks regarded him with deep respect. Never had such a thing been done in that vicinity!

Meanwhile, Carver was acquainting himself with the neighborhood. Each morning at four he arose and went to the woods or swamp. To the discouraged people of Alabama, he began to say and to write that all around them was untold wealth; that the state had more varieties of trees than could be found in all of Europe—twenty-two species of oak, pine trees, the longleaf, shortleaf, upland spruce, lowland spruce, slash, yellow—all valuable hard woods. The yellow poplar, with its yellowish-green blossoms, often reached a height of one hundred and twenty feet. There were twenty varieties of the white-blooming haw tree, magnificent evergreen trees, rare yellow-blooming magnolias. And that spring he found more wildflowers than he had ever known existed!

When the country people saw him gathering plants and scooping up different kinds of soil, they said, "This man's a rootdoctor!"

And they came to Carver with their aches and pains. He, recognizing that most of them were suffering from the hidden hunger of pellagra, began to prescribe wild grasses and weeds which, tested, proved rich in vitamins. He showed them how to brew teas from certain roots, and cooked and let them taste weeds which grew beside the road. They sang his praises, bowed, and called him "Doctor."

They came to him for more advice. He gave it freely and went among them demonstrating how to apply fertilizer. He put into children's language explanations of the interlocked relations of plants and animals and soil and rain and air and sun.

He tested many soils, and because he never threw anything away, the jars and jugs full of clay accumulated and even piled in heaps upon the trays. One bright Saturday morning, Walter Keys, in a burst of energy, decided to clean up for the professor.

He first tackled the dirt in the corner—dumping it all into a large basket. He was just about to carry it out when Carver entered the laboratory. With his hand still on the door, he asked, "What are you doing?"

"Gonna clean up this place, wash all the tubes, and get everything in order for you, sir."

Walter waited expectantly for his teacher's customary expression of appreciation. Instead, he asked sharply, "Where are you taking that clay?"

"You've finished with this." Walter was positive. "All of it's been tested, so I'm throwing it out."

"Oh, no," Carver protested, "I—"

What on earth did he want with the clay? He himself wasn't sure, except that— Leaning over the basket, he ran his fingers through the gritty stuff. Slowly, he asked, "Walter, what do you see there?"

Now Walter had been with him long enough to know that his teacher expected him really "to see." He didn't want to disappoint him, but— He frowned and studied the basket of dirt. All he could see was hard, lumpy, gritty clay of various hues.

"Well, sir—it's—it's got some grit in it, and some's lumpy and some's sort of sandy— Oh, yes,"—his voice brightened—"there's a few weeds and roots."

"But—the colors—the colors, boy, don't you see them—yellow and red and purple and brown? Why so many colors?"

Walter shrugged his shoulders. He had been looking at similar clay all his life.

"Oh, that! That's just the way clay *is*!"

"But—why?" Carver insisted.

Walter was stumped!

"No," said Carver, waving his hand, "don't throw it out. There is a reason. I'll have to talk to God about this."

Walter pushed the basket into the corner. Like Farmer Carver, so many years ago, he was a little shocked. He knew about praying. He knew you should fall on your knees, close your eyes, and choose the very best words while you asked God to "forgive your sins," "redeem your soul," and "save" you from "the devil and all his works." He'd heard lots of praying. But he certainly couldn't imagine God, "up on His great white throne, bending His ear" to listen to anybody "talking" about clay—not even the Professor.

The Professor had gone out quietly. He was in deep thought. He turned his footsteps toward the swamp, and soon the spreading branches of sweet gum trees linked with Spanish moss shut out the sun. The marshy ground tangled with muscadine vines, and mosses slushed beneath his feet. But he went on, his eyes catching a glimpse of wild hydrangea, with its spikes of thickly clustered white flowers. How lovely they were! Just then his foot caught and he fell flat into a mud hole. He was not hurt, but scrambled up quickly.

Poisonous snakes inhabited such places and, as he wiped away the sticky, oozy mud with his handkerchief, he kept sharp watch. He rubbed hard, but though the mud came off, the stains remained. This was a pretty pickle, he thought ruefully. He looked down at the handkerchief. It was a brilliant blue! He shook the mud off, even rinsed the cloth out in the muddy water. Grit and sand were removed, but the blue remained. For a while he studied it and then said aloud:

"Thanks, Mr. Creator! Thank you very much. At last, I see!"

He hurried back to the laboratory. Walter had gone. Trays and test tubes were clean and shining. Forgetting all about his grimly appearance, Carver pulled out the basket of clay and after arranging a tray dumped a handful of the red clay on it, smoothing it out with his palm. Then, tilting the tray a little, he held a dipper of water above it and allowed the water to slowly drip over the clay. Small rocks and grit began to wash away. He emptied the dipper, and tilting the tray in the opposite direction repeated the process. This he did until there remained on the tray only a thin, pasty coating of red. He touched this lightly with his finger and smeared the finger across a sheet of paper.

Holding the paper close to the window he studied it a long time. Then he nodded his head.

"Paint! The people down here are walking on paint—good paint—durable paint!"

For several days and nights he worked alone. He carefully separated his clays according to their colors and washed them clean. Then with intense heat he reduced the clay to finest powder, mixed the powder with oils, with water, hot and then cold, tested them on woods, on canvas, with brush and with fingers. Finally, he told his students.

Shortly after this, a group of white farmers asked Carver to come to their church and tell the people of their community something about soil improvement. The place was some distance away, near Montgomery, but Carver gladly agreed to go.

Walter drove him over, after carefully cleaning and shining the buggy. They found the church with little trouble, since it had been described as new and still unpainted. Carver's talk was well received. Many of the farmers came up to shake his hand. One of them said, "We're poor folks over here and sure needed your talk!"

"I hope I've been some help."

"Our cotton's been falling off steady. We got this church up, and haven't even been able to raise enough money to paint it."

"Now, that's too bad," said Carver sympathetically.

"Yes, 'tis," joined in another man, "weather's going to come down and our nice building's going to be ruined."

"Is paint so expensive?" Carver was thinking rapidly.

"Down this way it costs a heap. If crops are good this season, I reckon we'll have a rally and raise the money. That'll be after the spring rains, though," the man added regretfully.

Carver smiled at him.

"This is God's house, and it deserves the best. I'll give you paint, good paint."

Several people turned around and stared at the shabby, darkfaced professor. They had heard a great deal about Tuskegee. And they knew the school was always needing money. Yet here was one of its teachers offering to give them enough paint to paint their church. Well! But Carver was speaking gently:

"Lift up your eyes, good people, to the hills of God. See all the gorgeous colors with which he has decked them? We'll take just a little from his bounteous store of pure and lasting coloring, and with it paint your church!"

They really couldn't believe him. But a few days later a little wagon drew up in front of the church. Carver and several students climbed down. From the back they took pails of blue paint, Carver directing everything. And the next Sunday morning the people worshipped in a church which matched the sky in color, its steeple pointing upward proudly. The rains fell and the paint neither cracked nor peeled.

God's good earth gives freely of itself. Nothing is wasted and God's colors do not fade.

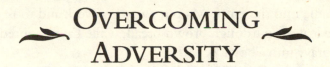

OVERCOMING ADVERSITY

The Four Days' Blizzard
Laura Ingalls Wilder

From The Long Winter

Laura Ingalls Wilder (1867-1957) was an American children's author who wrote nine popular autobiographical novels depicting the adventures of her Midwestern pioneer family. The books were also the basis for a long-running television series called Little House on the Prairie. *This chapter from the sixth of Mrs. Wilder's books tells of a terrible blizzard—the fourth the Ingalls family had to endure one brutal winter in the early 1870s. Forced to burn hay for fuel and down to their last stores of grain, they still refuse to give up, and they credit their faith with giving them the courage to go on.*

All day, while Laura turned the coffee mill or twisted hay, she remembered that Cap Garland and the younger Wilder brother were driving across the trackless snow-fields, going in search of wheat to bring to town.

That afternoon she and Mary went out in the back yard for a breath of air and Laura looked fearfully to the northwest, dreading to see the low-lying rim of darkness that was the sure sign of a coming blizzard. There was no cloud, but still she distrusted the bright sunshine. It was too bright and the snow-covered prairie, glittering as far as eye could see, seemed menacing. She shivered.

"Let's go in, Laura," Mary said. "The sunshine is too cold. Do you see the cloud?"

"There is no cloud," Laura assured her. "But I don't like the weather. The air feels savage, somehow."

"The air is only air," Mary replied. "You mean it is cold."

"I don't either mean it's cold. I mean it's savage!" Laura snapped.

They went back into the kitchen through the lean-to entryway.

Ma looked up from Pa's sock that she was darning. "You didn't stay out long, girls," she said. "You should get what fresh air you can, before the next storm."

Pa came into the entry. Ma put away her work and took from the oven the loaf of sourdough brown bread, while Laura poured the thin codfish gravy into a bowl.

"Gravy again. Good!" Pa said, sitting down to eat. The cold and the hard work of hauling hay had made him hungry. His eyes glittered at sight of the food. Nobody, he said, could beat Ma at making good bread, and nothing was better on bread than codfish gravy. He made the coarse bread and the gruel of groundwheat flour with a bit of salt fish in it seem almost a treat.

"The boys have a fine day for their trip," he said. "I saw where one of the horses went down in Big Slough, but they got him out with no trouble."

"Do you think they will get back all right, Pa?" Carrie asked timidly, and Pa said, "No reason why not, if this clear weather holds."

He went out to do the chores. The sun had set and the light was growing dim when he came back. He came through the front room so they knew that he had gone across the street to get the news. They knew when they saw him that it was not good news.

"We're in for it again," he said, as he hung his coat and cap on the nail behind the door. "There's a cloud coming fast."

"They didn't get back?" Ma asked him.

"No," Pa said.

Ma silently rocked and they all sat silent while the dusk deepened.

Grace was asleep in Mary's lap. The others drew their chairs closer to the stove, but they were still silent, just waiting, when the jar of the house came and the roar and howl of the wind.

Pa rose with a deep breath. "Well, here it is again."

Then suddenly he shook his clenched fist at the northwest. "Howl! blast you! howl!" he shouted.

"We're all here safe! You can't get at us! You've tried all winter but we'll beat you yet! We'll be right here when spring comes!"

"Charles, Charles," Ma said soothingly. "It is only a blizzard. We're used to them."

Pa dropped back in his chair. After a minute he said, "That was foolish, Caroline. Seemed for a minute like that wind was something alive, trying to get at us."

"It does seem so, sometimes," Ma went on soothing him.

"I wouldn't mind so much if I could only play the fiddle," Pa muttered, looking down at his cracked and stiffened hands that could be seen in the glow of fire from the cracks of the stove.

In all the hard times before, Pa had made music for them all. Now no one could make music for him. Laura tried to cheer herself by remembering what Pa had said; they were all there, safe. But she wanted to do something for Pa. Then suddenly she remembered. "We're all here!" It was the chorus of the "Song of the Freed Men."

"We can sing!" she exclaimed, and she began to hum the tune.

Pa looked up quickly. "You've got it, Laura, but you are a little high. Try it in B flat," he said.

Laura started the tune again. First Pa, then the others, joined in, and they sang:

> *When Paul and Silas were bound in jail,*
> *Do thy-self-a no harm,*
> *One did sing and the other did pray*
> *Do thy-self-a no harm.*
>
> *We're all here, we're all here,*
> *Do thy-self-a no harm,*
> *We're all here, we're all here,*
> *Do thy-self-a no harm.*

> *If religion was a thing that money could buy,*
> *Do thy-self-a no harm,*
> *The rich would live and the poor would die,*
> *Do thy-self-a no harm.*

Laura was standing up now and so was Carrie, and Grace was awake and singing with all her might:

> *We're all here, we're all here!*
> *Do thy-self-a no harm.*
> *We're all here, we're all here!*
> *Do thy-self-a no harm!*

"That was fine!" Pa said. Then he sounded a low note and began:

> *De old Jim riber, I float down,*
> *I ran my boat upon de groun'*
> *De drif' log come with a rushin' din,*
> *An' stove both ends of my or boat in.*

"Now, all together on the chorus!" And they all sang:

> *It will neber do to gib it up so,*
> *It will neber do to gib it up so,*
> *It will neber do to gib it up so, Mr. Brown!*
> *It will neber do to gib it up so!*

When they stopped singing, the storm seemed louder than ever. It was truly like a great beast worrying the house, shaking it, growling and snarling and whining and roaring at the trembling walls that stood against it.

After a moment Pa sang again, and the stately measures were suited to the thankfulness they were all feeling:

> *Great is the Lord*
> *And greatly to be praised*
> *In the city of our God,*
> *In the mountain of His holiness.*

Then Ma began:

> *When I can read my title clear*
> *To mansions in the skies,*
> *I'll bid farewell to every fear*
> *And wipe my weeping eyes.*

The storm raged outside, screaming and hammering at walls and windows, but they were safely sheltered, and huddled in the warmth of the hay fire they went on singing.

It was past bedtime when the warmth died from the stove, and because they could not waste hay they crept from the dark, cold kitchen through the colder darkness upstairs and to the beds.

Under the quilts, Laura and Mary silently said their prayers, and Mary whispered, "Laura."

"What?" Laura whispered.

"Did you pray for them?"

"Yes," Laura answered. "Do you think we ought to?"

"It isn't like asking for anything for ourselves," Mary replied. "I didn't say anything about the wheat. I only said please to save their lives if it's God's will."

"I think it ought to be," Laura said. "They were doing their best. And Pa lived three days in that Christmas blizzard when we lived on Plum Creek."

All the days of that blizzard nothing more was said about Cap Garland and the young Wilder brother. If they had found shelter they might live through the storm. If not, nothing could be done for them. It would do no good to talk.

The constant beating of the winds against the house, the roaring, shrieking, howling of the storm, made it hard even to think. It was possible only to wait for the storm to stop. All the time, while they ground wheat, twisted hay, kept the fire burning in the stove, and huddled over it to thaw their chapped, numb hands and their itching, burning, chilblained feet, and while they chewed and swallowed the coarse bread, they were all waiting until the storm stopped.

It did not stop during the third day or the third night. In the fourth morning it was still blowing fiercely.

"No sign of a letup." Pa said when he came in from the stable. "This is the worst yet."

After a while, when they were all eating their morning bread, Ma roused herself and answered, "I hope everyone is all right in town."

There was no way to find out. Laura thought of the other houses, only across the street, that they could not even see. For some reason she remembered Mrs. Boast. They had not seen her since last summer, nor Mr. Boast since the long-ago time when he brought the last butter.

"But we might as well be out on a claim too," she said. Ma looked at her, wondering what she meant, but did not ask. All of them were only waiting for the blizzard noises to stop.

That morning Ma carefully poured the last kernels of wheat into the coffee mill.

There was enough to make one last small loaf of bread. Ma scraped the bowl with the spoon and then with her finger to get every bit of dough into the baking pan.

"This is the last, Charles," she said.

"I can get more," Pa told her. "Almanzo Wilder was saving some seed wheat. I can get to it through the blizzard if I have to."

Late that day, when the bread was on the table, the walls stopped shaking. The howling shrillness went away and only a rushing wind whistled under the eaves. Pa got up quickly, saying, "I believe it's stopping!"

He put on his coat and cap and muffler and told Ma that he was going across the street to Fuller's Store. Looking through peepholes that they scratched in the frost, Laura and Carrie saw snow blowing by on the straight wind.

Ma relaxed in her chair and sighed, "What a merciful quiet."

The snow was settling. After a while Carrie saw the sky and called Laura to see it. They looked at the cold, thin blue overhead and at the warm light of sunset on the low-blowing snow. The blizzard really was ended. And the northwest sky was empty.

"I hope Cap Garland and young Mr. Wilder are somewhere safe," Carrie said. So did Laura, but she knew that saying so would not make any difference.

DEATH AND ETERNAL LIFE

The Angel
Hans Christian Andersen

Early fairy tales often dealt with the difficult subject of death. One reason was because infant mortality was high, and many unfortunate children were unable to lead healthy, long lives. They needed a way to confront their fears and understand what lay beyond their earthly existence. The Danish poet, novelist and writer of fairy tales Hans Christian Andersen (1805-1875) writes here about the angels who watch over young children and carry them to Heaven.

"Whenever a good child dies, an angel of God comes down from Heaven, takes the dead child in his arms, spreads out his great white wings, and flies with him over all the places which the child has loved during his life. Then he gathers a large handful of flowers which he carries up to the Almighty, that they may bloom more brightly in Heaven than they do on earth. And the Almighty presses the flowers to His heart, but He kisses the flower that pleases Him best, and it receives a voice and is able to join the song of the chorus of bliss."

These words were spoken by an angel of God as he carried a dead child up to Heaven, and the child listened as if in a dream. Then they passed over well-known spots where the little one had often played, and through beautiful gardens full of lovely flowers.

"Which of these shall we take with us to Heaven to be transplanted there?" asked the angel.

Close by grew a slender, beautiful rosebush, but some wicked hand had broken the stem, and the half-opened rosebuds hung all faded and withered on the trailing branches.

"Poor rosebush" said the child. "Let us take it with us to Heaven, that it may bloom above in God's garden."

The angel took up the rosebush. Then he kissed the child and the little one half-opened his eyes. The angel gathered also some beautiful flowers, as well as a few humble buttercups and heartsease.

"Now we have flowers enough," said the child, but the angel only nodded. He did not fly upward to Heaven.

It was night and quite still in the great town. Here they remained, and the angel hovered over a small narrow street in which lay a large heap of straw, ashes, and sweepings from houses of people who had moved away. There lay fragments of plates, pieces of plaster, rags, old hats, and other rubbish. Amidst all of this confusion, the angel pointed to the pieces of a broken flowerpot, and to a lump of earth which had fallen out of it. The earth had been kept from falling to pieces by the roots of a withered field flower which had been thrown amongst the rubbish.

"We will take this with us," said the angel. "I will tell you why as we fly along."

And as they flew the angel related the history.

"Down in that narrow lane, in a low cellar, lived a poor sick boy. He had been afflicted from his childhood, and even in his best days he could just manage to walk up and down the room on crutches once or twice, but no more. During some days in summer the sunbeams would lie on the floor of the cellar for about half an hour. In this spot the poor sick boy would sit warming himself in the sunshine and watching the red blood through his delicate fingers as he held them before his face. Then he would say he had been out, though he knew nothing of the green forest in its spring verdure till a neighbor's son brought him a green bough from a beech tree. This he would place over his head, and fancy that he was in the beech wood while the sun shone and the birds caroled gaily.

"One spring day the neighbor's boy brought him some field flowers, and among them was one to which the roots still adhered. This he carefully planted in a flowerpot, and placed in a window seat near his bed. And the flower had been planted by a fortunate hand, for it grew, put forth fresh shoots, and blossomed every year. It became a splendid flower garden to the sick boy, and his little treasure upon earth. He watered it and cherished it, and took care it should have the benefit of every sunbeam that found its way into the cellar, from the earliest morning ray to the evening sunset. The flower entwined itself even in his dreams. For him it bloomed; for him it spread its perfume. And it gladdened his eyes, and to the flower he turned, even in death, when the Lord called him. He has been one year with God. During that time the flower has stood in the window, withered and forgotten, till cast out among the sweepings into the street, on the day the lodgers moved. And this poor flower, withered and faded as it is, we have added to our nosegay, because it gave more real joy than the most beautiful flower in the garden of a queen."

"But how do you know all this?" asked the child whom the angel was carrying to Heaven.

"I know it, "said the angel, "because I was the poor sick boy who walked upon crutches, and I know my own flower well."

Then the child opened his eyes and looked into the glorious happy face of the angel, and at the same moment they found themselves in that heavenly home where all is happiness and joy. And God pressed the dead child to His heart, and wings were given him so that he could fly with the angel, hand in hand. Then the Almighty pressed all the flowers to His heart. But He kissed the withered field flower, and it received a voice. Then it joined in the song of the angels, who surrounded the throne, some near, and others in a distant circle, but all equally happy. They all joined in the chorus of praise, both great and small—the good, happy child and the poor field flower, that once lay withered and cast away on a heap of rubbish in a narrow dark street.

A Child's Dream of a Star

Charles Dickens

How should we teach children to cope with the loss of someone they love? One way is to read this gentle, compassionate story by England's foremost Victorian novelist, Charles Dickens (1812-1870). It conveys the tragedy of parting in this world and the joy of reuniting in Heaven.

There was once a child, and he strolled about a good deal, and thought of a number of things. He had a sister, who was a child too, and his constant companion. These two used to wonder all day long. They wondered at the beauty of the flowers; they wondered at the height and blueness of the sky; they wondered at the depth of the bright water; they wondered at the goodness and the power of God who made the lovely world.

They used to say to one another, sometimes, supposing all the children upon earth were to die, would the flowers, and the water, and the sky be sorry? They believed they would be sorry. For, said they, the buds are the children of the flowers, and the little playful streams that gambol down the hillsides are the children of the water; and the smallest bright specks playing at hide-and-seek in the sky all night must surely be the children of the stars; and they would all be grieved to see their playmates, the children of men, no more.

There was one clear, shining star that used to come out in the sky before the rest, near the church spire, above the graves. It was larger and more beautiful, they thought, than all the others, and every night they watched for it, standing hand in hand at a window. Whoever saw it first, cried out, "I see the star!" And often they cried out both together, knowing so well when it would rise, and where. So they grew to be such friends with it, that, before lying down in their beds, they always looked out once again, to bid it good night; and when they were turning round to sleep, they used to say, "God bless the star!"

But while she was still very young, oh, very, very young, the sister drooped, and came to be so weak that she could no longer stand in the window at night; and then the child looked sadly out by himself, and when he saw the star, turned round and said to the patient pale face on the bed, "I see the star!" and then a smile would come upon the face, and a little weak voice used to say, "God bless my brother and the star!"

And so the time came, all too soon! when the child looked out alone, and when there was no face on the bed; and when there was a little grave among the graves, not there before; and when the star made long rays down toward him, as he saw it through his tears.

Now, these rays were so bright, and they seemed to make such a shining way from earth to Heaven, that when the child went to his solitary bed, he dreamed about the star; and dreamed that, lying where he was, he saw a train of people taken up that sparkling road by angels. And the star, opening, showed him a great world of light, where many more such angels waited to receive them.

All these angels, who were waiting, turned their beaming eyes upon the people who were carried up into the star; and some came out from the long rows in which they stood, and fell upon the people's necks, and kissed them tenderly, and went away with them down avenues of light, and were so happy in their company, that lying in his bed he wept for joy.

But there were many angels who did not go with them, and among them one he knew. The patient face that once had lain upon the bed was glorified and radiant, but his heart found out his sister among all the host.

His sister's angel lingered near the entrance of the star, and said to the leader among those who had brought the people thither:

"Is my brother come?"

And he said, "No."

She was turning hopefully away when the child stretched out his arms, and cried, "Oh sister, I am here! Take me!" and then she turned her beaming eyes upon him, and it was night; and the star was shining into the room, making long rays down toward him as he saw it through his tears.

From that hour forth, the child looked out upon the star as on the home he was to go to, when his time should come; and he thought that he did not belong to the earth alone, but to the star too, because of his sister's angel gone before.

There was a baby born to be a brother of the child; and while he was so little that he never yet had spoken word, he stretched his tiny form out on his bed, and died.

Again the child dreamed of the opened star, and of the company of angels, and the train of people, and the rows of angels with their beaming eyes all turned upon those people's faces.

Said his sister's angel to the leader:

"Is my brother come?"

And he said, "Not that one, but another."

As the child beheld his brother's angel in her arms, he cried, "Oh, sister, I am here! Take me!" And she turned and smiled upon him, and the star was shining.

He grew to be a young man, and was busy at this books when an old servant came to him and said:

"Thy mother is no more. I bring her blessing on her darling son!"

Again at night he saw the star, and all that former company. Said his sister's angel to the leader:

"Is my brother come?"

And he said, "Thy mother!"

A mighty cry of joy went forth through all the star, because the mother was reunited to her two children. And he stretched out his arms and cried, "Oh, mother, sister, and brother, I am here! Take me!" And they answered him, "Not yet," and the star was shining.

He grew to be a man, whose hair was turning gray, and he was sitting in his chair by the fireside, heavy with grief, and with his face bedewed with tears, when the star opened once again.

Said his sister's angel to the leader, "Is my brother come?"

And he said, "Nay, but his maiden daughter."

And the man who had been the child saw his daughter, newly lost to him, a celestial creature among those three, and he said, "My daughter's head is on my sister's bosom, and her arm is around my mother's neck, and at her feet there is the baby of old time, and I can bear the parting from her, God be praised!"

And the star was shining.

Thus the child came to be an old man, and his once smooth face was wrinkled, and his steps were slow and feeble, and his back was bent. And one night as he lay upon his bed, his children standing round, he cried as he had cried so long ago:

"I see the star!"

They whispered to one another, "He is dying."

And he said, "I am. My age is falling from me like a garment, and I move toward the star as a child. And oh, my Father, now I thank Thee that it has so often opened, to receive those dear ones who await me!"

And the star was shining; and it shines upon his grave.

THANKSGIVING DAY

The First Thanksgiving
Lena Barksdale

The message of this Thanksgiving tale is summed up by the Pilgrim woman who says to her granddaughter: "Be true to God and honest and kind to your neighbor." Would that all men could follow such simple, heartfelt advice! It is easy to forget that we must make God's will, not our own, the guide of our actions and that we must always be ready to share what we have—freely and unstintingly—with others. The author of this story, Lena Barksdale (1887-1964), was an American writer of children's fiction.

I am ready to begin," said Grandma. "Where's Hannah? Come here, child, and sit on this stool at my feet. It's where your mother used to sit, my dear, when she was your age, and you must sit here today, and hear your old grandmother tell about Thanksgiving in Pilgrim days.

"It was a long time ago, my children, that First Thanksgiving, as we like to call it, though people have always given thanks for good harvests, I am sure, and they always will. But this first feast of ours in Plymouth more than forty years ago was different, I think, from any other harvest feast ever held before, or any that can ever be held again.

"Your grandfather and I were little more than children then, but we could work along with the older people. Every pair of hands counted, and if some were a little smaller none made note of it. There was much work to be done. We did what we could gladly. We'd had a long voyage, and many good people died of a strange sickness on the ship. We had thought to land in Virginia, where there were many English settlers before us. It might well be that they would be pleased to see us, and would gladly show us how to make our homes snug and comfortable against the cold, and teach us the ways of this new land. But God had other plans for us. In His wisdom He brought us here to a rocky, bleak, frozen land, as it seemed to us then, lying in stretches of desolate shore, empty of houses, where there was no one to welcome us.

"We lived on the ship for many weeks, but as soon as it seemed reasonably safe we women were set ashore to wash our linen, which sorely needed cleansing after our tedious voyage. It was good to feel solid earth under our feet again, but we dared not venture far, nor go out of sight of our protectors, for none knew where the Indians were, or how they might greet us. The men would go forth in parties armed with their muskets, taking the long boat or the shallop, and landing here and there to spy out the land and find a fair place to build our town. We women on the ship could only pray for their safe return when they ventured forth.

"Once when some of the men were returning to the ship they brought a boatload of juniper boughs that they had cut. We burned it in our stoves, taking comfort in the spicy smell of it. That was our first welcoming from the land.

"At last the men came to an agreement where to build the town, and they set to cutting down trees to build the houses, each man working diligently, and the day came when we were all set ashore, with our gear, and the ship sailed away and left us. We were often cold, and hungry and afraid that winter, but we got along.

"Later, you know, Squanto came and lived with us for a time, and he taught us to plant the corn when the oak leaf was the size of a mouse's ear, and as we planted the seed, he had us throw two fish in each hole to enrich the soil, so that the yield would be more abundant. He caught good eels for us, and taught us many other things, useful for us to know. We could not have known many of these things otherwise, our lives having been so different in Holland, and before that, in England. Do not forget, my children, it was an Indian who first befriended us and guided us in the new land. Massasoit, their sagamore,* also became our friend and made a treaty of peace with us.

"In the sweet spring weather I'll never forget how comforting it was to see the trees come into leaf, and the little wild flowers blooming along the streams and in the woods. We found onions and watercress, fresh

---

*chief

and tasty to the palate. It was such simple things as these that made us begin to love the land, and feel at home at last.

"So it was that by the time our first harvest was ripe and gathered into the storing sheds that we had provided, we knew beyond any doubt that we had found a good comfortable land where we were free and could live our lives without anyone meddling. That's the great thing, children, and don't any of you forget it. God has given us freedom here to think and to worship as seems right to us. Remember to be upright in all your dealings with one another and with the Indians. Be true to God and honest and kind to your neighbor. That is what being free means, and if we forget it we shall suffer, and rightly so. Your grandpa's been true and fine all his long life, and so must you children be."

Grandma's eyes were very bright and her voice shook a little as she looked into the faces of her strong sons and daughters and all the grandchildren. After a moment she went on:

"Then when the first harvest was in and we knew none would go hungry that winter, nor cold, because our houses were built of stout timbers and there was a great store of wood to burn, our governor and the other men decided we would have a feast and invite Massasoit to come and bring some of his braves to eat it with us. They set a day, and sent a messenger to invite Massasoit, who was pleased to accept, and who sent five deer as a gift toward the feast. For days all the women and girls were busy roasting and baking and shining the pewter. The boys cut many fresh trenchers from stout poplar wood, and spoons too, though we knew our guests would not bother overmuch with spoons, preferring to use their fingers. The men brought in wild turkey, geese, and duck in abundance, as well as deer. Your grandfather brought down his first deer, and that was a proud day for him. We had found cranberries growing wild that summer, and the women found ways of using them, and our harvest had yielded plenty of corn, some of which we had laboriously ground for bread, and some we had cracked for hominy. We were so happy preparing the food for that feast. You never know how wonderful it is to have plenty all 'round you until you've gone hungry as we went hungry that first winter. So we set about preparing a lavish abundance of food for our guests, but we didn't know how many guests were coming."

Grandma smiled, and the older people chuckled. They knew how many guests had come!

"It's just as well we didn't know," she went on, "we couldn't have worked any harder, and we would have worried for fear we didn't have enough. Such a good smell of roasting and baking filled the village as put us all in fine humor. Maybe Massasoit and his men smelt that good smell away off in their town. Anyway, ninety of them came, and I was the first to see them. It happened this way:

"We brought our food together at the common house that morning, all the victuals that had been cooked in the several houses where the most skillful housewives lived. We women had put on our best caps and fresh kerchiefs, and we were busily laying out the trenchers when someone remembered a basket of fresh loaves left by mistake in one of the more distant houses. I was sent to fetch it, and as I came out of the door with the basket on my arm, I looked across the fields and saw our guests coming down the trail from the woods. Of course we were used to the Indians and their outlandish ways of dressing by that time, and I thought not at all about how different they were from us, but only that they made a brave and proper sight. Tall, strong men they were, some with feathers stuck in the bands around their heads. Their long straight hair shone with bear's grease. They wore deerskins over their shoulders, and some wore long tight hose that met the leather girdles around their waists. A few had their faces painted in black or red or yellow, to suit each man's fancy. I could see the wildcat skin that one important brave had thrown over his arm. I could tell Massasoit a great way off because of the heavy chain of white bone beads that he was wont to wear around his neck. He was also wearing the copper chain with a jewel in it that our people gave him when he first visited us many months before. They came along the trail, single file as was their custom, and as I watched I saw more and more coming, until it seemed to me, in my foolish fancy, that all the Indians in America were coming to our feast. Then as I stood there idly watching, it came over me that no one else in the town had seen them, and I ran to the common house as fast as I could because I knew our elders must be warned in time to go out and greet them properly.

"All the people were dismayed to learn my news, and we were much put to it to welcome our guests and serve them graciously, for we could never let them suspect that we had looked for no more than a score. We bustled around and prepared more tables out of doors. Fortunately, it was not excessively cold. Anyway, we were used to the cold and of course they were. We had built fires outside to take off the chill, and the best carpet and cushions for their principal men were ready to be spread. So by the time the Indians had got through passing that smelly pipe of theirs around among themselves and our men, the food was ready, and our guests were more than ready to eat it. But of course if you didn't know them, you would never have guessed it. It was their habit to move slowly and deliberately, as if they were pretending the food was not there until the time came to fall to. Never in all my life have I seen so many people eat so much. Those Indians must have been hollow to the knees. One big brave grabbed a whole turkey and gnawed away at it until there was nothing left but bare bones. Then he was ready to begin on a steak of venison, which he ate along with two or three tankards of beer. He finished off with a whole pie.

"Later on they wrestled, ran races, sang, danced and played games, probably some of the same games that you children played this morning. The Indians could outrun and outwrestle our boys, but when our boys began teaching the Indians some of our English games the Indians didn't win so often. It wouldn't have been wise to let them think they could beat us in everything. It was a great day, and our guests liked it so well that they wrapped up in their deerskins and spent the night in the town, and the next day, and the next after that, we did it all over again. Of course, there wasn't quite so much to eat after the first day, but the Indians didn't care. They were used to having a big feast, and then not bothering much about food for several days. But even at that it kept us busy cooking. We didn't mind because we had plenty, and if it meant peace and goodwill between ourselves and the Indians, we women were only too glad to do our part to help. But when it was all over and the Indians finally left, we had to do a lot of cleaning up. Soon after that the cold shut down on us and our second winter in Plymouth began. So that," said Grandma, "is the story of our First Thanksgiving."

⮞CHRISTMAS⮜

The Wooden Shoes of Little Wolff

François Coppée

(Adapted)

François Coppée (1842-1908) was a French novelist and playwright who often focused on how religion can help alleviate the sorrows of the poor. His story here is based on a popular legend, and it prompts the question: How many of us would give away the last thing we owned—secretly and without any hope of recompense or recognition—to an anonymous beggar on the streets? When we have plenty to spare, we can afford to be generous, but what about when we are cold and starving? The sacrifice of the poor little boy in this story, made so cheerfully and willingly, reflects the true nature of Christian charity.

Once upon a time, so long ago that the world has forgotten the date, in a city of the North of Europe, the name of which is so hard to pronounce that no one remembers it, there was a boy, just seven years old, whose name was Wolff. He was an orphan and lived with his aunt, a hard-hearted, avaricious old woman who never kissed him but once a year, on New Year's Day; and who sighed with regret every time she gave him a bowl of soup.

The poor boy was so sweet-tempered that he loved the old woman in spite of her bad treatment, but he could not look without trembling at the wart, decorated with four gray hairs, which grew on the end of her nose.

As Little Wolff's aunt was known to have a house of her own and a woolen stocking full of gold, she did not dare to send her nephew to the school for the poor. But she wrangled so that the schoolmaster of the rich boys' school was forced to lower his price and admit Little Wolff among his pupils. The bad schoolmaster was vexed to have a boy so meanly clad and who paid so little, and he punished Little Wolff severely without cause, ridiculed him, and even incited against him his comrades, who were the sons of rich citizens. They made the orphan their drudge and mocked at him so much that he was as miserable as the stones in the street, and hid himself away in corners to cry.

Then the Christmas season came.

On the eve of the great day, the schoolmaster was to take all his pupils to the midnight church service, and then to conduct them home again to their parents' houses.

Now as the winter was very severe, and a quantity of snow had fallen within the past few days, the boys came to the place of meeting warmly wrapped up, with fur-lined caps drawn down over their ears, padded jackets, gloves and knitted mittens, and good strong shoes with thick soles. Only Little Wolff presented himself shivering in his thin everyday clothes, and wearing on his feet socks and wooden shoes.

His naughty comrades tried to annoy him in every possible way, but the orphan was so busy warming his hands by blowing on them and was suffering so much from chilblains, that he paid no heed to the taunts of the others. Then the band of boys, marching two by two, started for the parish church.

It was comfortable inside the church, which was brilliant with lighted tapers. And the pupils, made lively by the gentle warmth, the sound of the organ, and the singing of the choir, began to chatter in low tones. They boasted of the midnight treats awaiting them at home. The son of the mayor had seen, before leaving the house, a monstrous goose larded with truffles so that it looked like a black-spotted leopard. Another boy told of the fir tree waiting for him, on the branches of which hung oranges and sugar-plums. Then they talked about what the Christ Child would bring them, or what he would leave in their shoes which they would certainly be careful to place before the fire when they went to bed. And the eyes of the little rogues, lively as a crowd of mice, sparkled with delight as they thought of the many gifts they would find on waking—the pink bags of burnt almonds, the bonbons, lead soldiers standing in rows, menageries, and magnificent jumping-jacks, dressed in purple and gold.

Little Wolff, alas! knew well that his miserly old aunt would send him to bed without any supper; but as he had been good and industrious all the year, he trusted that the Christ Child would not forget him, so he meant that night to set his wooden shoes on the hearth.

The midnight service was ended. The worshipers hurried away, anxious to enjoy the treats awaiting them in their homes. The band of pupils, two by two, following the schoolmaster, passed out of the church.

Now, under the porch, seated on a stone bench, in the shadow of an arched niche, was a child asleep—a little child dressed in a white garment and with bare feet exposed to the cold. He was not a beggar, for his dress was clean and new, and beside him upon the ground, tied in a cloth, were the tools of a carpenter's apprentice.

Under the light of the stars, his face, with its closed eyes, shone with an expression of divine sweetness, and his soft, curling blond hair seemed to form an aureole of light about his forehead. But his tender feet, blue with the cold on this cruel night of December, were pitiful to see!

The pupils so warmly clad and shod, passed with indifference before the unknown child. Some, the sons of the greatest men in the city, cast looks of scorn on the barefooted one. But Little Wolff, coming last out of the church, stopped deeply moved before the beautiful, sleeping child.

"Alas!" said the orphan to himself, "how dreadful! This poor little one goes without stockings in weather so cold! And, what is worse, he has no shoe to leave beside him while he sleeps, so that the Christ Child may place something in it to comfort him in all his misery."

And carried away by his tender heart, Little Wolff drew off the wooden shoe from his right foot, placed it before the sleeping child; and as best as he was able, now hopping, now limping, and wetting his sock in the snow, he returned to his aunt.

"You good-for-nothing!" cried the old woman, full of rage as she saw that one of his shoes was gone. "What have you done with your shoe, little beggar?"

Little Wolff did not know how to lie, and, though shivering with terror as he saw the gray hairs on the end of her nose stand upright, he tried, stammering, to tell his adventure.

But the old miser burst into frightful laughter. "Ah! the sweet young master takes off his shoe for a beggar! Ay! master spoils a pair of shoes for a barefoot! This is something new, indeed! Ah! well, since things are so, I will place the shoe that is left in the fireplace, and tonight the Christ Child will put in a rod to whip you when you wake. And tomorrow you shall have nothing to eat but water and dry bread, and we shall see if the next time you will give away your shoe to the first vagabond that comes along."

And saying this the wicked woman gave him a box on each ear, and made him climb to his wretched room in the loft. There the heart-broken little one lay down in the darkness, and, drenching his pillow with tears, fell asleep.

But in the morning, when the old woman, awakened by the cold and shaken by her cough, descended to the kitchen, oh! wonder of wonders!

She saw the great fireplace filled with bright toys, magnificent boxes of sugar-plums, riches of all sorts, and in front of all this treasure, the wooden shoe which her nephew had given to the vagabond, standing beside the other shoe which she herself had placed there the night before, intending to put in it a handful of switches.

And as Little Wolff, who had come running at the cries of his aunt, stood in speechless delight before all the splendid Christmas gifts, there came great shouts of laughter from the street.

The old woman and the boy went out to learn what it was all about, and saw the gossips gathered around the public fountain. What could have happened? Oh, a most amusing and extraordinary thing! The children of all the rich men of the city, whose parents wished to surprise them with the most beautiful gifts, had found nothing but switches in their shoes!

Then the old woman and Little Wolff remembered with alarm all the riches that were in their own fireplace, but just then they saw the pastor of the parish church arriving with his face full of perplexity.

Above the bench near the church door, in the very spot where the night before a child, dressed in white, with bare feet exposed to the great cold, had rested his sleeping head, the pastor had seen a golden circle wrought into the old stones. Then all the people knew that the beautiful, sleeping child, beside whom had lain the carpenter's tools, was the Christ Child himself, and that he had rewarded the faith and charity of Little Wolff.

Baboushka and the Three Kings

(Told by Ruth Robbins)

This wonderfully sentimental Russian folk tale is an example of how nearly every culture has tried to personalize the story of the Nativity. Doubtless there are versions of "Baboushka and the Three Kings" told at Christmastime in France, Spain, Belgium, Poland, Brazil, Mexico, Ethiopia, Polynesia, Japan, China, and elsewhere around the globe.

Long ago and far away, on a winter's evening, the wind blew hard and cold around a small hut. Inside the hut Baboushka was sweeping and scrubbing, and feeding wood to the stove. The old woman took pride in the clean comfort of her meager home.

The swirling snow drifted and deepened outside. Baboushka's hut felt snug around her; her warm stove was the center of a cold world.

As the day turned into night, a trumpet call sounded on the wind. A train of travelers was approaching. Leading the procession was a magnificent sleigh drawn by three white horses. In the sleigh rode three men, splendid figures, wearing jeweled crowns and cloaks of crimson and ermine. Men on horseback followed the sleigh, and behind them men trudged on foot.

The procession stopped at the door of Baboushka's hut. Baboushka heard a knock. When she lifted the latch, the three strangers stood in the doorway. The poor woman looked in wonder at their elegant dress, their frosted beards, their kind eyes. What manner of men were these?

In answer to her thought, one of the three smiled and said, "We have been following a bright star to a place where a babe is born. Now we have lost our way in the snow. Come with us, Baboushka. Help us to find the child, to offer him gifts, and to rejoice in his birth."

Baboushka shivered in the cold. She hugged a shawl tightly around her thin shoulders. "Good sirs, come in and warm yourselves by the stove. I've not yet finished my day's work. And I shudder to go out on such a cruel night. Morning is wiser than evening. Rest here this night, and I will go with you in the dawn."

"There is no time to linger, Baboushka," answered the strangers. "If you cannot come with us now, we must continue our journey." They turned and disappeared into the storm.

Baboushka went back to her sweeping and scrubbing. Her work

finished, she sat down to a lonely supper by the stove. She felt a sudden tenderness and joy for the newborn child. What grand gentlemen, those three! "They did seem like kings," she said aloud. "It is no ordinary babe they seek. Yes! I must go and follow them!"

To find the new babe, to offer him her gift, was now her one yearning. This thought burned in her mind like a candle in the dark.

Baboushka awoke before dawn and made ready for her journey. Into her sack she carefully placed a few poor but precious gifts. As the new day began, she stepped out onto the quiet snow. The old woman hunted for the path made by the travelers, but the snow had covered their way.

Stopping one person and then another, and still another, she asked, "In what direction did the three kings go; they who were seeking the child?"

Neither old nor young could tell her.

Baboushka stood watching the children at play in the new snow, the dogs yelping and dancing around her. But she must not delay; she must push her way ahead.

From village to village and door to door, she went, asking, "Have you seen the child?" Always she received the same answer; no one had seen him.

Never stopping, Baboushka wandered on, searching for the child but never finding him.

And it is said that every year, at the season when the birth of the child was first heralded, Baboushka renews her search across that land with new hope.

And it is said that every year little children await the coming of Baboushka. They find joy in the poor but precious gifts she leaves behind her in the silent night.

The Legend of the First Christmas Tree
Elizabeth Goudge

Elizabeth Goudge (1900-1984) was an English poet and novelist who wrote dozens of books for children and adults. Here she tells of a fir tree standing above Bethlehem that watches over "his people" as a shepherd watches over his flock. His only wish is to be useful as the first fir tree in Eden, and it is a wish that comes true on the first Christmas.

There were trees in and about Bethlehem in those days. There were oleander, almond, and quince trees in the gardens, vines and olives on the terraced hillsides, oak trees, mulberries, figs, and citrons. They did not grow thickly; there were no forests or tangled copses; they never hid the rocky hillsides, the far glimpse of the mountains, or the great stretch of the sky; the strength of these things could always be seen through their leaves and branches; but they flung a veil of beauty over the harshness of the land, and their bounty made to the people who lived there all the difference between death and life.

The gaunt old fir tree up above them all on the hill where the sheep were folded watched them as spring passed to summer and summer to autumn. He rejoiced in the pink and white fruit blossoms flung like spray against the blue sky, in the tender green of the new young mulberry leaves and the shimmering silver of the olives. He waved his arms in satisfaction when he saw the citrons hanging among their leaves like small golden suns, the rich clusters of the grapes, the mulberries, and figs that would give food and drink to his people. For he always thought of the people of this country as *his* people, simply because he loved them. He had stood there high on the hillside, looking down on them all, for longer than anyone could remember. He knew all about them, for the people of Bethlehem loved to climb the hill and sit and talk to each other beneath his branches, and he would listen and remember all that they said. And when they were sad they would come and sit alone at his feet and he would hear their broken murmurs. And he would hear the shepherds talking, too, when they were taking care of the sheep. In this way he would learn not only about the personal joys and sorrows of his people but about all that happened to them as a nation. He would hear old men talking of the past history of Israel, and sometimes on Sabbath days he would hear the scholars among them repeating to each other the hallowed words of the Prophets and speaking in low soft voices of the Redeemer, He that should come, the Wonderful, the Councilor, the Prince of Peace. And sometimes he would hear one of the shepherd boys singing aloud the songs of the shepherd boy David, and that he liked the best of all, because in the loveliness of the words and the sweetness of the music he found great comfort for his grief.

For he suffered great grief because of his uselessness to the people he loved. Those other trees gave so much but he had neither fruit nor blossom, nothing but his fir cones, which he sometimes dropped hopefully on the heads of his people, knowing them good to burn; but they seldom bothered to pick them up. He had not even beauty to delight his people for he was an ugly old tree, fantastically twisted by all the winter storms he had endured through all the years. He was no good to anyone, as far as he could see, except perhaps to the sheep who liked to rub themselves against him when they itched. And perhaps very occasionally to those who sat by themselves among his twisted roots and to whom he murmured softly, opening to them the treasure of the wisdom of the trees.

But did they listen to it? They would sit very still, leaning back against his trunk with their eyes half shut against the sun or leaning forward with their elbows on their knees and their chins in their hands, staring at the far blue distance, and he would tell them many things. But if they heard they gave no sign. Yet he persevered, never quite despairing, cradling them among his roots as he talked as a mother cradles her babe in her arms. All trees are wise, possessing a wisdom of a much higher order than man can attain to in this world, but fir trees are wiser than all the others, and this fir tree especially possessed a knowledge of good and evil that had come to him not only from his own lifetime of looking, listening, and remembering, but from the wisdom of all his ancestors, stretching back and back to the first fir tree of all, a very wise tree that had grown in the first garden of all, the one that the Lord God planted eastward of Eden and made so very fair.

That first fir tree was not in the least like his descendants. He was the most beautiful tree in the garden. In spring his blossoms were lovelier than those of the almond, his leaves were pure silver like the olive, but larger, and shaped like hands placed palm to palm in prayer, and his fruit was of a brighter gold than that of the citron. It must have been of the wisdom and beauty of that first fir tree that King Solomon was thinking when he said that a word fitly spoken is like apples of gold in pictures of silver. But the Lord God had forbidden the man and woman who lived in the garden to eat those golden apples, for they were not yet ready for the wisdom of them. The fir tree knew that and whenever they came near him he did his best to hide his golden apples under his sil-

330 THE CHRISTIAN'S TREASURY

ver leaves, lest those frail mortal creatures should be tempted by them. And he talked to them too, whispering softly and silverly when they sat at his feet cradled in his comfortable roots, explaining to them that being human beings and not gods they could not know evil unless they practiced it, and so they must refrain from that knowledge and be content to know only good. Love God, he told them, be humble, obedient, and contented children, and all will be well with you. But they paid no attention to the fir tree. They wanted to be arrogant gods, ordering other people about, instead of loving children humbly doing what they were told. And so they ate of the fruit of the tree.

It was not in the least the fir tree's fault but he felt that it was. He was so grief-stricken that his heart broke within him and the sap dried up in his body. His golden fruit withered to hard brown cones and his silver leaves rolled up into tiny dry spears. He died of grief there in the garden, his cones tumbling to the ground. But there were seeds in the cones and the birds and the winds carried them away from the garden and his children took root and grew up all over the world.

But they never again were beautiful as their ancestor had been in the first days. They grew upon bare hillsides, torn by winds and lightnings, wailing and lamenting for the sin of the world, bearing no life, neither flowers nor leaves nor fruit. But they retained their deep and heavenly wisdom and whenever they could they would gather men and women and children about them and tell them the things that they knew. These descendants of Adam and Eve paid no more attention than Adam and Eve had done, but they did come to have a special love for fir trees, and in almost every country in the world there grew up an idea that if you had a fir tree near your dwelling you were lucky. They were such comforting trees. They never blew down in a storm or changed with the seasons. In them was no variableness or shadow of turning.

Everyone at Bethlehem felt like that about the fir tree upon the hill. He did not know it. He was quite unaware that when things went wrong with them they came and curled themselves up among his roots, even as they were unaware that it was because he had chosen to share their sorrow and pain that they found him so satisfying, a sort of shadow of what they longed for.

A God Who was eternal, unchangeable, and yet Who at the same time shared all things with them, that was the paradox that they wanted, whether they knew it or not. And this was what the fir tree wanted for them, longing for it with increasing passion and desperation as the years went by. He saw that it was the one thing that would save them. The love and obedience they had withheld in the garden they would perhaps give to a God like that. If this God could Himself be obedient and loving, then, when they strove to be like Him (for always it seemed that these ridiculous human creatures had to emulate God), they would not destroy themselves, as they had done in the garden, but save their souls alive. If this could only happen, thought the fir tree, he believed that he would be so happy that his stiff needles would unfurl into silver leaves again and his hard brown cones turn into golden fruit. "The desert shall rejoice and blossom as the rose," he had heard them say, when they sat at his feet and talked of the coming of the Redeemer of Israel. Something like that, he was sure, would happen to him.

And it did. It was midwinter, with the sky swept bare of clouds and ablaze with those angelic stars which men believe sing as they sweep upon their way. But as yet they were too far away to be heard. The world was in profoundest quietness and night in the midst of her swift course. The shepherds were heavy-eyed that night, and the fir tree was awake guarding the sheep for them. He did this very often, awaking them with a low warning murmur if any danger threatened. But nothing threatened tonight; indeed it seemed to the fir tree that just for tonight the earth was swept as clear of evil as the sky of clouds, so that a deep serenity possessed him, from his topmost spike of needles down to his deepest root. A mighty love possessed him too, both for the stars blazing like great angels in the sky above him and for the weary men and beasts sleeping beneath his branches. He had a feeling that he would have liked to link the two together in love, to stretch up his arms to the sky and pull down the stars upon the earth.

"Glory to God in the highest and on earth peace." Who was singing? The fir tree looked down at his feet, where little Reuben, the shepherd boy who so delighted him by singing the songs of David to the music of his pipe, was curled up like a dormouse among his roots. But Reuben was fast asleep. Besides, this was not one voice singing, it was many voices, and they were singing at a vast distance. Yet the music was drawing nearer, rising and dying away, then rising again more powerfully, like the ebb and flow of a great wind. But nothing stirred upon the earth and no wind that ever blew could sound those notes of breath-taking beauty, a beauty that shook the fir tree from top to bottom yet left him with his serenity even deeper than before. "Arise, shine, for thy light is come, and the glory of the Lord is risen upon thee." It was the stars themselves that were singing, and they were coming down to earth. The fir tree gave a great shout of triumph and held up his arms to them, and then the singing was sweeping over him in great waves of glorious sound and he was drenched and drowned in light, so blinded and deafened by glory that in his body all his senses died, and for a little while it seemed that he ceased to be.

When he came to himself it was still and quiet again, the stars were once more back in the sky and the shepherds had gone. But he knew where they had gone, for during the time when he had seemed to cease to be he had been told good tidings of great joy. Yes, they'd gone, and gone quickly, taking their gifts with them. Yes, they'd gone—all except one, all except young Reuben—what ailed the child? The fir tree looked down at Reuben and Reuben looked up at the fir tree, wide-eyed with delight, his cheeks scarlet and his mouth wide open, jigging on his toes and letting out a long shrill whistle of ecstasy as a small boy will when he is beside himself with pleasure at some astounding sight. The fir tree could see the excited small boy as clearly as though a thousand candles were burning, and for a moment or two he was at a loss to know where the light was coming from. Then he saw that it was coming from himself. The stars, when they went back to their appointed places, had not withdrawn their gift of light. Every withered needle on him had become a leaf of silver and every hard dry cone a golden fruit. He stood there robed in light, glorious and beautiful as a young god in the dawning of the world.

"Take me!" he cried to Reuben. "Take me!" Would the child understand? They never did understand when he spoke to them. But Reuben did; he was young enough. He reached up and broke off the glowing branch that the fir tree held out to him and raced off with it down the hill to Bethlehem. He ran so fast that he was not far behind the other shepherds, and when they had presented their gifts he knelt down and presented his. He stuck it upright in a pitcher beside the manger, all bright and glowing, and when the Baby saw it He laughed. It was the first Christmas tree.

The next morning the fir tree looked as usual, but he did not feel as usual, for all his grief had gone. It had happened. The Lord God had visited and redeemed His people. He cried aloud in delight and stretched up his branches to the clear blue sky. "A hallowed day hath dawned upon us," he cried. "Come, ye nations, and worship the Lord; for on this day a great light hath descended upon the earth."

And besides his overwhelming joy in this great light he had his own private reason for happiness. He saw the future of the fir trees, his children and descendants. They might stand hard and dry and gaunt upon their hillsides through the spring and summer and autumn, when other trees were giving their blossom and leaves and fruit, but when the December birthday of the Son of God came round once more, and other trees were stripped and bare, it was they who would keep watch beside the manger, robed in silver and gold, bringing joy to the hearts of little children and peace and goodwill to men.

Playing Pilgrims[†]
Louisa May Alcott

From Little Women

Louisa May Alcott (1832-1888) was not only a writer but a Union nurse during the Civil War. She wrote Little Women *in 1869, basing it on her own family and experiences. In this excerpt, the March sisters learn that it truly is "more blessed to give than to receive," and they fondly recall their old pastime of playing devout pilgrims like John Bunyan's character, Christian, on the way to the Celestial City.*

"Christmas won't be Christmas without any presents," grumbled Jo, lying on the rug.

"It's so dreadful to be poor!" sighed Meg, looking down at her old dress.

"I don't think it's fair for some girls to have plenty of pretty things, and other girls nothing at all," added little Amy, with an injured sniff.

"We've got father and mother and each other," said Beth contentedly, from her corner.

The four young faces on which the firelight shone brightened at the cheerful words, but darkened again as Jo said sadly: "We haven't got Father, and shall not have him for a long time." She didn't say "perhaps never," but each silently added it, thinking of Father far away, where the fighting was.

Nobody spoke for a minute; then Meg said in an altered tone: "You know the reason mother proposed not having any presents this Christmas was because it is going to be a hard winter for everyone; and she thinks we ought not to spend money for pleasure, when our men are suffering so in the army. We can't do much, but we can make our little sacrifices, and ought to do it gladly. But I am afraid I don't," and Meg shook her head as she thought regretfully of all the pretty things she wanted.

"But I don't think the little we should spend would do any good. We've each got a dollar, and the army wouldn't be much helped by our giving that. I agree not to expect anything from mother or you, but I do want to buy *Undine and Sintram* for myself; I've wanted it *so* long," said Jo, who was a bookworm.

"I have planned to spend mine on new music," said Beth, with a little sigh, which no one heard but the hearth brush and kettle holder.

"I shall get a nice box of Faber's drawing pencils; I really need them," said Amy decidedly.

"Mother didn't say anything about our money, and she won't wish us to give up everything. Let's each buy what we want, and have a little fun; I'm sure we work hard enough to earn it," cried Jo, examining the heels of her shoes in a gentlemanly manner.

"I know *I* do—teaching those tiresome children nearly all day, when I'm longing to enjoy myself at home," began Meg, in the complaining tone again.

"You don't have half such a hard time as I do," said Jo. "How would you like to be shut up for hours with a nervous, fussy old lady, who keeps you trotting, is never satisfied, and worries you till you're ready to fly out of the window or cry?"

"It's naughty to fret; but I do think washing dishes and keeping things tidy is the worst work in the world. It makes me cross; and my hands get so stiff, I can't practice well at all," and Beth looked at her rough hands with a sigh that anyone could hear that time.

"I don't believe any of you suffer as I do," cried Amy; "for you don't have to go to school with impertinent girls, who plague you if you don't know your lessons, and laugh at your dresses, and label your father if he isn't rich, and insult you when your nose isn't nice."

"If you mean *libel*, I'd say so, and not talk about *labels*, as if Papa was a pickle bottle," advised Jo, laughing.

"I know what I mean, and you needn't be *statirical* about it. It's proper to use good words, and improve your *vocabilary*," returned Amy, with dignity.

"Don't peck at one another, children. Don't you wish we had the money Papa lost when we were little, Jo? Dear me, how happy and good we'd be, if we had no worries!" said Meg, who could remember better times.

"You said, the other day, you thought we were a deal happier than the King children, for they were fighting and fretting all the time, in spite of their money."

"So I did, Beth. Well, I think we are; for, although we do have to work, we make fun for ourselves, and are a pretty jolly set, as Jo would say."

"Jo does use such slang words!" observed Amy, with a reproving look at the long figure stretched on the rug. Jo immediately sat up, put her hands in her pockets, and began to whistle.

"Don't, Jo; it's so boyish!"

"That's why I do it."

"I detest rude, unladylike girls!"

"I hate affected, niminy-piminy chits!"

"'Birds in their little nests agree,'" sang Beth, the peacemaker, with such a funny face that both sharp voices softened to a laugh, and the "pecking" ended for that time.

"Really, girls, you are both to be blamed," said Meg, beginning to lecture in her elder-sisterly fashion. "You are old enough to leave off boyish tricks and to behave better, Josephine. It didn't matter so much when you were a little girl; but now you are so tall, and turn up your hair, you should remember that you are a young lady."

"I'm not! And if turning up my hair makes me one, I'll wear it in two tails till I'm twenty," cried Jo, pulling off her net, and shaking down a chestnut mane. "I hate to think I've got to grow up, and be Miss March, and wear long gowns, and look as prim as a China aster! It's bad enough to be a girl, anyway, when I like boys' games and work and manners! I can't get over my disappointment in not being a boy; and it's worse than ever now, for I'm dying to go and fight with Papa, and I can only stay at home and knit, like a poky old woman!" And Jo shook the blue army sock till the needles rattled like castanets, and her ball bounded across the room.

"Poor Jo! It's too bad, but it can't be helped; so you must try to be contented with making your name boyish, and playing brother to us girls," said Beth, stroking the rough head at her knee with a hand that all the dishwashing and dusting in the world could not make ungentle in its touch.

"As for you, Amy," continued Meg, "you are altogether too particular and prim. Your airs are funny now; but you'll grow up an affected little goose, if you don't take care. I like your nice manners and refined ways of speaking, when you don't try to be elegant; but your absurd words are as bad as Jo's slang."

"If Jo is a tomboy and Amy a goose, what am I, please?" asked Beth, ready to share the lecture.

"You're a dear, and nothing else," answered Meg warmly; and no one contradicted her, for the "Mouse" was the pet of the family.

As young readers like to know "how people look," we will take this moment to give them a little sketch of the four sisters, who sat knitting away in the twilight, while the December snow fell quietly without, and the fire crackled cheerfully within. It was a comfortable old room, though the carpet was faded and the furniture very plain; for a good picture or two hung on the walls, books filled the recesses, chrysanthemums and Christmas roses bloomed in the windows, and a pleasant atmosphere of home peace pervaded it.

Margaret, the eldest of the four, was sixteen, and very pretty, being plump and fair, with large eyes, plenty of soft, brown hair, a sweet mouth, and white hands, of which she was rather vain. Fifteen-year-old Jo was very tall, thin, and brown, and reminded one of a colt; for she never seemed to know what to do with her long limbs, which were very much in her way. She had a decided mouth, a comical nose, and sharp, gray eyes, which appeared to see everything, and were by turns fierce, funny, or thoughtful. Her long, thick hair was her one beauty; but it was usually bundled into a net, to be out of her way. Round shoulders had Jo, big hands and feet, a flyaway look to her clothes, and the uncomfortable appearance of a girl who was rapidly shooting up into a woman, and didn't like it. Elizabeth—or Beth, as everyone called her—was a rosy, smoothhaired, bright-eyed girl of thirteen, with a shy manner, a timid voice, and a peaceful expression, which was seldom disturbed. Her father called her "Little Tranquillity," and the name suited her excellently; for she seemed to live in a happy world of her own, only venturing out to meet the few whom she trusted and loved. Amy, though the youngest, was a most important person—in her own opinion at least. A regular snow-maiden, with blue eyes, and yellow hair curling on her shoulders, pale and slender, and always carrying herself like a young lady mindful of her manners. What the characters of the four sisters were we will leave to be found out.

The clock struck six; and, having swept up the hearth, Beth put a pair of slippers down to warm. Somehow the sight of the old shoes had a good effect upon the girls; for Mother was coming, and everyone brightened to welcome her. Meg stopped lecturing, and lighted the lamp, Amy got out of the easy chair without being asked, and Jo forgot how tired she was as she sat up to hold the slippers nearer to the blaze.

"They are quite worn out; Marmee must have a new pair."

"I thought I'd get her some with my dollar," said Beth.

"No, I shall!" cried Amy.

"I'm the oldest," began Meg, but Jo cut in with a decided—"I'm the man of the family now Papa is away, and I shall provide the slippers, for he told me to take special care of Mother while he was gone."

"I'll tell you what we'll do," said Beth; let's each get her something for Christmas, and not get anything for ourselves."

"That's like you, dear! What will we get?" exclaimed Jo.

Everyone thought soberly for a minute; then Meg announced, as if the idea was suggested by the sight of her own pretty hands, "I shall give her a nice pair of gloves."

"Army shoes, best to be had," cried Jo.

"Some handkerchiefs, all hemmed," said Beth.

"I'll get a little bottle of cologne; she likes it, and it won't cost much, so I'll have some left to buy my pencils," added Amy.

"How will we give the things?" asked Meg.

"Put them on the table, and bring her in and see her open the bundles. Don't you remember how we used to do on our birthdays?" answered Jo.

"I used to be *so* frightened when it was my turn to sit in the big chair with the crown on, and see you all come marching round to give the presents, with a kiss. I liked the things and the kisses, but it was dreadful to have you sit looking at me while I opened the bundles," said Beth, who was toasting her face and the bread for tea, at the same time.

"Let Marmee think we are getting things for ourselves, and then surprise her. We must go shopping tomorrow afternoon, Meg; there is so much to do about the play for Christmas night," said Jo, marching up and down, with her hands behind her back and her nose in the air.

"I don't mean to act any more after this time; I'm getting too old for such things," observed Meg, who was as much a child as ever about "dressing-up" frolics.

"You won't stop, I know, as long as you can trail round in a white gown with your hair down, and wear gold-paper jewelry. You are the best actress we've got, and there'll be an end of everything if you quit the boards," said Jo. "We ought to rehearse tonight. Come here, Amy, and do the fainting scene, for you are as stiff as a poker in that."

"I can't help it; I never saw anyone faint, and I don't choose to make myself all black and blue, tumbling flat as you do. If I can go down easily I'll drop; if I can't, I shall fall into a chair and be graceful; I don't care if Hugo does come at me with a pistol," returned Amy, who was not gifted with dramatic power, but was chosen because she was small enough to be borne out shrieking by the villain of the piece.

"Do it this way: clasp your hands so, and stagger across the room, crying frantically, 'Roderigo! save me! save me!'" and away went Jo with a melodramatic scream which was truly thrilling.

Amy followed, but she poked her hands out stiffly before her, and jerked herself along as if she went by machinery; and her "Ow!" was more suggestive of pins being run into her than of fear and anguish. Jo gave a despairing groan, and Meg laughed outright, while Beth let her bread burn as she watched the fun, with interest.

"It's no use! Do the best you can when the time comes, and if the audience laughs, don't blame me. Come on, Meg."

Then things went smoothly, for Don Pedro defied the world in a speech of two pages without a single break; Hagar, the witch, chanted an awful incantation over her kettleful of simmering toads, with weird effect; Roderigo rent his chains asunder manfully, and Hugo died in agonies of remorse and arsenic, with a wild "Ha! ha!"

"It's the best we've had yet," said Meg, as the dead villain sat up and rubbed his elbows.

"I don't see how you can write and act such splendid things, Jo. You're a regular Shakespeare!" exclaimed Beth, who firmly believed that her sisters were gifted with wonderful genius in all things.

"Not quite," replied Jo modestly. "I do think *The Witch's Curse, an Operatic Tragedy*, is rather a nice thing; but I'd like to try *Macbeth*, if we only had a trap door for Banquo. I always wanted to do the killing part. 'Is that a dagger that I see before me?'" muttered Jo, rolling her eyes and clutching at the air, as she had seen a famous tragedian do.

"No, it's the toasting fork, with Mother's shoe on it instead of the bread. Beth's stage-struck!" cried Meg, and the rehearsal ended in a general burst of laughter.

"Glad to find you so merry, my girls," said a cheery voice at the door, and actors and audience turned to welcome a tall, motherly lady, with a "can-I-help-you" look about her which was truly delightful. She was not elegantly dressed, but a noble-looking woman, and the girls thought the gray cloak and unfashionable bonnet covered the most splendid mother in the world.

"Well, dearies, how have you got on today? There was so much to do, getting the boxes ready to go tomorrow, that I didn't come home to dinner. Has anyone called, Beth? How is your cold, Meg? Jo, you look tired to death. Come and kiss me, baby."

While making these maternal inquiries Mrs. March got her wet things off, her warm slippers on, and sitting down in the easy chair, drew Amy to her lap, preparing to enjoy the happiest hour of her busy day. The girls flew about, trying to make things comfortable, each in her own way. Meg arranged the tea table; Jo brought wood and set chairs, dropping, overturning, and clattering everything she touched; Beth trotted to and fro between parlor and kitchen, quiet and busy; while Amy gave directions to everyone, as she sat with her hands folded.

As they gathered about the table, Mrs. March said, with a particularly happy face, "I've got a treat for you after supper."

A quick, bright smile went round like a streak of sunshine. Beth clapped her hands, regardless of the biscuit she held, and Jo tossed up her napkin, crying, "A letter! a letter! Three cheers for father!"

"Yes, a nice long letter. He is well, and thinks he shall get through the cold season better than we feared. He sends all sorts of loving wishes for Christmas, and an especial message to you girls," said Mrs. March, patting her pocket as if she had got a treasure there.

"Hurry and get done! Don't stop to quirk your little finger and simper over your plate, Amy," cried Jo, choking in her tea, and dropping her bread, butter side down, on the carpet, in her haste to get at the treat.

Beth ate no more, but crept away, to sit in her shadowy corner and brood over the delight to come, till the others were ready.

"I think it was so splendid of Father to go as a chaplain when he was too old to be drafted, and not strong enough for a soldier," said Meg warmly.

"Don't I wish I could go as a drummer, a *vivan*—what's its name?—or a nurse, so I could be near him and help him," exclaimed Jo, with a groan.

"It must be very disagreeable to sleep in a tent, and eat all sorts of bad-tasting things, and drink out of a tin mug," sighed Amy.

"When will he come home, Marmee?" asked Beth, with a little quiver in her voice.

"Not for many months, dear, unless he is sick. He will stay and do his work faithfully as long as he can, and we won't ask for him back a minute sooner than he can be spared. Now come and hear the letter."

They all drew to the fire, mother in the big chair with Beth at her feet, Meg and Amy perched on either arm of the chair, and Jo leaning on the back, where no one would see any sign of emotion if the letter should happen to be touching. Very few letters were written in those hard times that were not touching, especially those which fathers sent home. In this one little was said of the hardships endured, the dangers faced, or the homesickness conquered; it was a cheerful, hopeful letter, full of lively descriptions of camp life, marches, and military news; and only at the end did the writer's heart overflow with fatherly love and longing for the little girls at home.

"Give them all my dear love and a kiss. Tell them I think of them by day, pray for them by night, and find my best comfort in their affection at all times. A year seems very long to wait before I see them, but remind them that while we wait we may all work, so that these hard days need not be wasted. I know they will remember all I said to them, that they will be loving children to you, will do their duty faithfully, fight their bosom enemies bravely, and conquer themselves so beautifully that when I come back to them I may be fonder and prouder than ever of my little women."

Everybody sniffed when they came to that part; Jo wasn't ashamed of the great tear that dropped off the end of her nose, and Amy never minded the rumpling of her curls as she hid her face on her mother's shoulder and sobbed out. "I *am* a selfish girl! but I'll truly try to be better, so he mayn't be disappointed in me by and by."

"We all will!" cried Meg. "I think too much of my looks and hate to work, but won't any more, if I can help it."

"I'll try and be what he loves to call me, a 'little woman,' and not be rough and wild; but do my duty here instead of wanting to be somewhere else," said Jo, thinking that keeping her temper at home was a much harder task than facing a rebel or two down South.

Beth said nothing, but wiped away her tears with the blue army sock, and began to knit with all her might, losing no time in doing the duty that lay nearest her, while she resolved in her quiet little soul to be all that father hoped to find her when the year brought round the happy coming home.

Mrs. March broke the silence that followed Jo's words, by saying in her cheery voice, "Do you remember how you used to play *Pilgrim's Progress* when you were little things? Nothing delighted you more than to have me tie my piece bags on your backs for burdens, give you hats and sticks and rolls of paper, and let you travel through the house from the cellar, which was the City of Destruction, up, up, to the housetop, where you had all the lovely things you could collect to make a Celestial City."

"What fun it was, especially going by the lions, fighting Apollyon,* and passing through the Valley where the hobgoblins were!" said Jo.

"I liked the place where the bundles fell off and tumbled downstairs," said Meg.

---

*Greek name for the "destroying angel." In *Pilgrim's Progress*, Apollyon confronted Christian on his journey to the Celestial City.

"My favorite part was when we came out on the flat roof where our flowers and arbors and pretty things were, and all stood and sung for joy up there in the sunshine," said Beth, smiling, as if that pleasant moment had come back to her.

"I don't remember much about it, except that I was afraid of the cellar and the dark entry, and always liked the cake and milk we had up at the top. If I wasn't too old for such things, I'd rather like to play it over again," said Amy, who began to talk of renouncing childish things at the mature age of twelve.

"We never are too old for this, my dear, because it is a play we are playing all the time in one way or another. Our burdens are here, our road is before us, and the longing for goodness and happiness is the guide that leads us through many troubles and mistakes to the peace which is a true Celestial City. Now, my little pilgrims, suppose you begin again, not in play, but in earnest, and see how far on you can get before Father comes home."

"Really, Mother? Where are our bundles?" asked Amy, who was a very literal young lady.

"Each of you told what your burden was just now, except Beth; I rather think she hasn't got any," said her mother.

"Yes, I have; mine is dishes and dusters, and envying girls with nice pianos, and being afraid of people."

Beth's bundle was such a funny one that everybody wanted to laugh; but nobody did, for it would have hurt her feelings very much.

"Let us do it," said Meg thoughtfully. "It is only another name for trying to be good, and the story may help us; for though we do want to be good, it's hard work, and we forget, and don't do our best."

"We were in the Slough of Despond tonight, and mother came and pulled us out as Help did in the book. We ought to have our roll of directions, like Christian. What shall we do about that?" asked Jo, delighted with the fancy which lent a little romance to the very dull task of doing her duty.

"Look under your pillows, Christmas morning, and you will find your guidebook," replied Mrs. March.

They talked over the new plan while old Hannah cleared the table; then out came the four little workbaskets, and the needles flew as the girls made sheets for Aunt March. It was uninteresting sewing, but tonight no one grumbled. They adopted Jo's plan of dividing the long seams into four parts, and calling the quarters Europe, Asia, Africa, and America, and in that way got on capitally, especially when they talked about the different countries as they stitched their way through them.

At nine they stopped work, and sung, as usual, before they went to bed. No one but Beth could get much music out of the old piano; but she had a way of softly touching the yellow keys, and making a pleasant accompaniment to the simple songs they sung. Meg had a voice like a flute, and she and her mother led the little choir. Amy chirped like a cricket, and Jo wandered through the airs at her own sweet will, always coming out at the wrong place with a croak or a quaver that spoilt the most pensive tune. They had always done this from the time they could lisp,

"Crinkle, crinkle, 'ittle 'tar,"

and it had become a household custom, for the mother was a born singer. The first sound in the morning was her voice, as she went about the house singing like a lark; and the last sound at night was the same cheery sound, for the girls never grew too old for that familiar lullaby.

EASTER

The Beauty of the Lily
Frances Jenkins Olcott

In this story, an Easter visitor forever changes the lives of a peasant boy and his uncle by presenting them with a mysterious, miraculous flower. "Keep it white!" says the visitor. He means, of course that we should do the same for our souls, which will bloom and flourish forever if we take proper care. The author, Frances Jenkins Olcott (1872-1963), was an American who not only wrote many children's stories but edited a number of literature anthologies.

Once upon a time, in a far-distant land, there dwelt a peasant named Ivan, and with him lived his little nephew Vasily.

Ivan was gloomy and unkempt, and his restless eyes looked out from his matted hair and beard. As for the little Vasily, he was a manly child; but though his uncle was kind enough to him in his way, he neither washed him, nor combed his hair, nor taught him anything.

The hut they lived in was very miserable. Its walls were full of holes, the furniture of its one room was broken down and dusty, and its floor unswept. The little garden was filled with stones and weeds. The neighbors passing by in the daytime turned aside their heads. But they never passed at night, for fear of Ivan.

Now it happened one Easter morning that Ivan, feeling restless, rose early and went and stood before the door of the hut. The trees were budding, the air was full of bird songs, the dew lay glittering on the grass, and a nearby brook ran leaping and gurgling along. The rays of the rising sun shone slanting from the tops of the distant hills, and seemed to touch the hut.

And as Ivan looked, he saw a young man coming swiftly and lightly from the hills, and he bore on his arm a sheaf of pure white lilies. The stranger drew near, and stopped before the hut.

"Christ is risen!" he said in flute-like tones.

"He is risen indeed!" muttered Ivan through his beard.

Then the young man took a lily from his sheaf and gave it to Ivan, saying: "Keep it white!" And, smiling, he passed on.

Wonderingly Ivan gazed at the flower in his hand. Its gold-green stem seemed to support a pure white crown—or was it a translucent cup filled with light? And as the man looked into the flower's goldfringed heart, awe stole into his soul.

Then he turned and entered the hut, saying to himself, "I will put it in water."

But when he went to lay the lily on the window sill, so that he might search for a vessel to set it in, he dared not put it down, for the sill was covered with thick dust.

He turned to the table, but its top was soiled with crumbs of moldy bread and cheese mingled with dirt. He looked about the room, and not one spot could he see where he might lay the lily without sullying its pure loveliness.

He called the little Vasily and bade him stand and hold the flower. He then searched for something to put it in. He found an empty bottle which he carried to the brook and washed and filled with sparkling water. This he placed upon the table, and in it set the lily.

Then as he looked at the begrimed hands of little Vasily he thought to himself, "When I leave the room he may touch the flower and soil it." So he took the child and washed him, and combed his yellow hair; and the little one seemed to bloom like the lily itself. And Ivan gazed on him in amazement, murmuring, "I never saw it thus before!"

From that hour a change came over Ivan. He cared tenderly for the little Vasily. He washed himself and combed his own hair. He cleaned the hut and mended its walls and furniture. He carried away the weeds and stones from the garden. He sowed flowers and planted vegetables. And the neighbors passing by no longer turned their heads aside, but stopping, talked with Ivan, and sometimes gave the little Vasily presents of clothes and toys.

As for the lily, seven days it blossomed in freshness and beauty, and gave forth a delicate fragrance; but on the eighth day, when Ivan and Vasily woke, it was gone. And though they sought it in hut and garden, they did not find it.

So Ivan and the little Vasily worked from day to day among their flowers and vegetables, and talked to their neighbors, and were happy. When the long winter nights came, Ivan read aloud about the "lilies of the field" that toil not, neither do they spin, yet Solomon in all his glory was not arrayed like them. He read of that Beloved that feedeth among the lilies, and of the Rose of Sharon and the Lily-of-the-Valley.

■

So Easter came again. And early, very early in the morning, Ivan and the little Vasily arose and dressed, and went and stood before the hut. And when the splendor of the coming day shone above the distant hills, lo! the young man came swiftly and lightly, and in his arms he bore crimson roses.

He drew near, and, stopping before the hut, said sweetly: "Christ is risen!"

"He is risen, indeed!" responded Ivan and Vasily joyously.

"How beautiful is thy Lily!" said the young man.

"Alas!" answered Ivan, "it is vanished away, and we know not whither."

"Its beauty lives in thy heart," said the young man. "It can never die!"

And he took from his arm a crimson rose and gave it to Vasily, saying:

"Keep it fresh!"

But he smiled tenderly at Ivan, and passed on.

The Apple Tree

Margery Williams Bianco

In this story, two children are convinced that Easter is a person, so they wait alongside the road for him to appear. They never see him, but they do encounter a beggar and share their meager meal with him under an old apple tree. He treats them kindly in return, and they are captivated by the tales he tells about his wanderings. Then he suddenly performs two small miracles that bring the dead to life. Could he really be Easter after all? Margery Williams Bianco (1880-1944) was an American author who wrote many popular children's stories, including The Velveteen Rabbit.

O n winter days the children would put their faces close to the windowpane and say: "If only it were spring!"

The window looked out on a little garden where in summer flowers bloomed, but now it was covered with snow. The lilac bushes stood up bare and stiff, and even the wild clematis wore a gray beard like an old man and seemed bowed down with the cold. Only the lame robin, who had stayed behind when all his friends flew southward, would come and hop near the door sill, ruffling up his feathers, to peck for crumbs, and the tracks of his feet were like tiny hands in the snow.

Then their mother would say: "Cheer up, children! The winter is nearly over. Very soon Easter will be here, and then we shall have the birds and the flowers back again!"

The little sister asked: "When will it be really spring? I want it to be spring now!"

"When Easter comes," said their mother, "then it will be really spring."

"Does Easter come only in the spring?" the brother asked.

"Only in the spring."

"And suppose Easter never came at all!"

"That can not happen," their mother answered, smiling. "Easter always comes, every year."

So day by day, from the window, the little brother and sister looked out up the road to see if Easter was coming. Nearly all the people who went by they knew by sight, neighbors who would turn their heads and wave a hand to the children as they neared the gate; very few strangers passed by on the road, and none of these looked like Easter.

"Perhaps he will come tomorrow," the brother always said.

"I think he will be dressed all in white," the little sister said, "and wear a shiny thing on his head, like the lady at the circus."

"No," said her brother. "He won't be like that at all. He will ride a big black horse, and he will have a helmet and a golden belt, and carry a sword in his hand."

"I don't want him to have a sword," the little sister said. "I'm afraid of swords!"

"That's only because you're a girl. Swords can't hurt you if you aren't afraid of them." And he began to talk about the kind of horse that Easter would ride, very proud and coal black; it would lift its feet high at every step and have silver bells on the bridle.

The days passed, and presently the snow melted. The sun shone out, and little gray and pink buds showed on the tree branches. Now the lame robin was no longer as tame as he used to be; he came less often for crumbs, and instead was always flitting about the bushes, looking for the best spot to build a nest in when his family came back.

The children could play out-of-doors now, but they always kept an eye on the road, in case Easter should pass by when they weren't looking, for it would be dreadful to have waited all these weeks and then miss seeing him. Who knew but he might ride by in the night, and not stop at the cottage at all, especially if he were late and in a hurry?

And then one morning their mother stopped in her work to look at the calendar hanging on the wall by the fireplace, and exclaimed: "Why, how quickly the days do go by! Easter will be here before we know it!"

The children looked at each other and smiled.

"You see," the brother said. "He might come any minute now! We must be very careful!"

And so they always played in the front of the house, near the garden gate, where they could watch everyone who went past.

One day it really felt like spring. The sun seemed to shine more brightly than ever before; the sky was blue and the air soft and warm. Even the grass looked greener than usual, and all the new leaves on the lilac bushes had unfolded during the night. In the long grass by the gate there were dandelions in blossom.

"Easter will surely come today!" said the brother. "Let's go a little way up the road, as far as the corner near the dead apple tree, and watch for him there."

So he took the little sister by the hand, and they went out through the gate and on to the road.

"I have saved a piece of bread in my pocket from breakfast," he told her. "So if you get hungry waiting we can sit down on the big stone by the tree and eat.

They set off, the little sister treading very carefully, for she was quite small, and where the path was stony she had to look first and see just where to put down each foot. Here and there along the edge of the road were tiny flowers, blue and white, and these the little sister wanted to stop and gather to give to Easter if they saw him. It took a long time; she gathered them quite short, with hardly any stalk, so that at every few steps they dropped from her hand and had to be picked up again. But the brother was very patient; he waited each time till she was ready to go on again, and in this way they came at last to the corner where the lane joined the high road.

It was market day in the town, and a number of people were going by on the highway, but they all looked hurried or tired or busy; there was no face among them all that seemed like the face that Easter would have, except one girl, bare-headed, who was singing as she walked. She alone turned her head to smile at the children, but before they could speak to her she had gone on her way.

Nowhere, up or down the road, could they see any one who looked at all like Easter. One man rode by on a horse, but he had no sword, and he looked very cross, so the children were afraid to step out and ask him. But presently a workman came along with a bundle tied to a stick over his shoulder, and he stopped near the bank where the children were sitting to strike a light for his pipe.

"Could you tell me, please," the brother asked him, "whether Easter has gone by yet?"

"Why, no" said the workman slowly, staring at them. "Easter hasn't gone by yet, that I'm sure! I'm just going over to spend Easter day with my sister now. Over in the town where I've been working the folks don't set much store by Easter, but it's a holiday, so, thinks I, I'll pack up a few cakes for the little ones, and here I am. They'll be looking out for me surely! I wrote a letter to my sister a week ago, telling her. Just so sure as Easter comes, I said, I'll be there!"

"Then you know what Easter's like?" asked the brother.

"That I do!" said the workman. "Back in the country, when I was a boy, all the folks round about kept Easter, and we made a great feast every year. And that's why I'm going over to my sister's now, for the sake of old times, and to fetch the children a few cakes for the holiday. I'd give you some, and gladly, but it's a big family there and times are hard, so I was able to get only one apiece, all round, but that's better than nothing. Still, I slipped an apple or two in my pocket, coming along, and maybe you'd like them instead."

He pulled two big red apples out of his pocket and gave one to each of them.

"That's better than nothing," he said again as the children thanked him. "And now I must be getting on."

"Perhaps," said the brother, "you'll meet Easter on the road, if he hasn't gone by yet. Do you think you will?"

The workman laughed as if that were a great joke.

"Why, if I don't hurry up," he said, "I surely will! For it's all of twelve miles yet to my sister's house, and I just reckoned to get there by night-fall. So good-by, and a happy Easter to you both!"

He went off up the road, whistling, and walking very fast.

"Oh, dear," sighed the little sister, "I wish Easter would come quickly! I'm so tired of waiting!"

"We'll wait a little longer," said her brother, "and then we will go back and eat our lunch by the stone under the apple tree." For he too was beginning to feel rather tired of waiting there by the roadside. "You see, if there are so many people who want to keep Easter, that must make it hard for him to get about, and then it isn't his fault that he's late. Perhaps there is someone keeping him now, this very minute, and that's why he hasn't come. Of course, if he has a horse that would make it easier."

He thought of Easter, on a big black horse, riding through the villages, perhaps this very minute, and all the people stretching out their hands to stop him, and wanting him to stay with them. And the black horse tossing his head, to set all the silver bells ringing. It would be a fine thing to travel round with Easter, to walk by his side on the road and hold his horse whenever he dismounted. But the little sister thought of home, and a bowl of bread and milk, for she was getting sleepy.

The road was empty now; for a long while no one had passed up or down. But at last, very far in the distance, they could see someone moving. Under the hot, still rays of the sun, drawing the spring moisture from the earth, the air seemed to tremble; distant objects, a line of poplar trees, the red-roofed farmhouse by the hill, even the surface of the road, blended and swam together, so that the brother, shading his eyes to gaze up the highway, could not be sure if what he saw were really a figure on a horse and the flash of gold and silver trappings, or just a cloud of dust gilded by the sunlight.

For a moment he thought he heard music, distant trumpets and the shouting of many voices, and then he knew that what he really heard was only the jingle of a sheep-bell in the pasture and the crying of rooks on the plowed field, and that what he saw was no horse and rider, but only someone on foot, coming toward him along the road. And when the figure drew quite near he saw that it was a man, dressed in shabby clothes and walking slowly, as though he had come a long way on foot and was very weary. But when he saw the children he stopped to smile at them, and his smile was friendly.

"Are you waiting for someone?" he asked. "For I saw you from a long way off, looking out up the road."

"We were waiting for someone," said the brother, "but I'm afraid he can't be coming today. We have waited so long, and I think we will go back now and eat our bread under the tree, for my sister is getting tired."

"I'm tired, too," the stranger said, "so if I may I will come with you. Look, your little sister is nearly asleep!"

He picked the little sister up in his arms as he spoke. She was hot and tired and disappointed, and just getting ready to cry, but she put her head down on the man's shoulder and clung round his neck, for he held her like a person who is used to carrying little children. So they went, all three of them, back to the turn of the road and down the lane to where the apple tree grew.

It was quite an old tree, and for many years now it had not borne any blossom. Only a few twisted leaves came on it every spring, and these soon withered and dropped. It was good to cut down for firewood, the farmer said, but the months passed and no one found the time to cut it. So it had been left standing there. The bare gnarled branches made a good enough shade in the spring, and just beneath it was a big flat stone, comfortable to sit on, and near the stone a little trickling spring of water.

They sat down, the man with his back against the tree and the boy near him, and the little sister, who had forgotten her tiredness now, sat with her thumb in her mouth and looked at them both.

"I'm sorry I've only got a little piece of bread," said the brother, rather shyly, for he thought that perhaps the man was really a beggar, he was so poorly dressed, and in that case he might be quite hungry. "If I'd known I would have brought more."

"I expect it will be enough for all of us," the man said. And when he took the slice of bread from the brother's hand it certainly did seem larger than one had thought; he broke it into three pieces, and there was quite enough for all of them, as much as they wanted to eat. And it tasted wonderfully good, the brother thought; by far the best bread his mother had ever baked, but perhaps that was because he was so hungry.

They drank from the spring, and the man showed them how to make cups out of leaves, fastened with a thorn, that would hold the water. And after that he told them stories, jolly stories about the little reed that grew down in the ditch and wanted to be an oak tree, and about the king's son who had a dream, and who threw his crown away and went out into the world and became a beggar. He seemed to be a very nice man indeed, and the children were glad they had met him.

"You must have come a very long way," said the brother presently. For he couldn't help noticing how dusty the man's feet were and that his clothes were quite worn.

"I have come a long way," the man said, "and I have still a long way to go."

"Is your home very far?"

"I have no home," he said. "Sometimes I find friends with whom I can stay for a little while, and they give me shelter. And there are others, goodhearted people, who think they want me, and ask me into their houses, but they don't really want me; they have business to look after and many things to do, and after a while they find I'm only a trouble to them, and out of place in their households, and they can't spare the time for me, and so I have to go."

"Do you never go back?" asked the brother.

"Yes, if someone dies or there is real trouble in the house and no one else to turn to, then they may remember and send for me, or they just leave the door ajar so I can come in."

"It must be a fine thing to travel all over the world," said the brother. He thought again of Easter and the tall black horse. "Wouldn't it be splendid to be a king, and then you would ride into the city and all the bells would ring and the people come out to meet you."

But the man didn't answer. Perhaps he hadn't heard, or was thinking of something else.

"Did you ever ride on a horse and have a sword?" the brother asked.

"I had a sword once," said the man, "but I gave it away."

"Weren't you sorry afterward?"

But again the man didn't answer; he was murmuring something, looking down on the earth at his feet, and the brother thought: Perhaps he really is sorry about the sword and doesn't like to speak of it. It was something one shouldn't have asked, and he didn't want to hurt the man's feelings. So he said aloud:

"Won't you tell us about some of the fine things you saw when you were traveling?" The man looked up and smiled at them, and he put his hand inside the torn lining of his coat.

"This," he said, "is the most precious thing that I have found today, and I picked it up by the roadside."

He drew out his hand carefully; something very wonderful must be there, the boy thought, a tiny carved casket, or perhaps a jewel someone had dropped. But when he spread his fingers there was only a little brown bird on his hand, quite dead and limp, with its feathers ruffled, all dusty from lying in the road. The boy was disappointed; it wasn't at all what he expected to see, but the little sister reached out her hand.

"It's a bird!" she cried. "It's a dear little bird, and I don't want it to be dead!"

She stroked it with her tiny fingers as it lay on the man's hand, and there were tears in her eyes.

"Don't cry," said the man. "See, we both love the little bird, and I am going to show you something!"

He held the little dead sparrow close to his face, while the child watched, and breathed on it; something seemed to stir between his fingers, and when he opened his hand the bird flew away. Straight up in the air it flew, spreading its wings, and as the little sister looked up at it it seemed to change. She thought it had been brown, but now it was snow-white all over, like a white dove, and it hovered a moment above them, and then was gone, far up in the blue sky, but she thought she heard it singing as it flew.

The brother stared. "Where did it go?" he cried.

"I saw it lying on your hand, and then it wasn't there!"

"It flew away," said the little sister.

"It was dead," said her brother, "and dead things can not fly."

"I tell you it flew," the little sister repeated. "It flew into the sky, and I saw it!"

And she came near and put her arms round the man's neck and kissed him. "You are a nice man," she said, "and you shall have all the flowers that I gather for Easter, for you are much nicer than Easter, and no one must ever be unkind to you, because I love you. And I want you to live with us always."

And she looked at him again, and this time she said: "I think you *are* Easter, for I see a shiny thing on your head."

But though the brother looked, he only saw the sun shining through the branches of the apple tree.

"You are a kind man," he said, "even if you aren't Easter, and some day I hope you will come again and tell us some more stories, for I like your stories very much. And when I grow up and have a sword of my own I am going to give it to you."

They went home and left the man sitting there under the apple tree. His head leaned back against the tree trunk, and his arms were outstretched, and he seemed to be sleeping, and in his open hand lay the flowers the little sister had given him. But perhaps he was only resting, for he must have been very tired still.

"I tell you he is Easter," the little sister said. "He is just like I said he would be."

"He isn't Easter," said her brother, "but he is a very nice man, and I am sorry he has to walk so far."

But the little sister pulled at his hand, standing still in the road.

"Don't you see?" she cried. "There is something shining round his head, like gold, and look—the apple tree is all in flower!"

The brother looked.

"It is only the setting sun," he said. "There is no blossom on the tree, for I looked this morning. But tomorrow we'll come back and see."

In the morning, when the children went back to look, the man had gone. But it was as the little sister had said; the apple tree that had been withered for so many years was in flower. The boughs, covered with pink-and-white blossoms, stretched out against the blue sky in blessing and their perfume filled the air all about.

It was really spring; the birds were singing and far away, as the children stood under the apple tree, they could hear the bells ringing for Easter.

Stories for Older Readers

SACRIFICE, OBEDIENCE, AND DUTY

Unzen
Shusako Endō

One of Japan's greatest literary figures, Shusako Endō (1923—) has written numerous short stories and more than half a dozen novels, including The Samurai, Silence, When I Whistle, *and* Wonderful Fool. *Here, he chronicles the troubled yet ultimately inspiring history of Christianity in his native land, and he poses the question: "How far are we willing to go in order to defend our faith?" By examining the perspectives of those who chose life or death at Unzen in the context of his own feelings, the main character of Endō's story shows us that the answer is far more complex than we might think.*

As he sat on the bus for Unzen, he drank a bottle of milk and gazed blankly at the rain-swept sea. The frosty waves washed languidly against the shore just beneath the coastal highway.

The bus had not yet left the station. The scheduled hour of departure had long since passed, but a connecting bus from Nagasaki still had not arrived, and their driver was chatting idly with the woman conductor and displaying no inclination to switch on the engine. Even so the tolerant passengers uttered no word of complaint, but merely pressed their faces against the window glass. A group of bathers from the hot springs walked by, dressed in large, thickly padded kimonos. They shielded themselves from the rain with umbrellas borrowed from their inn. The counters of the gift shops were lined with all sorts of decorative shells and souvenir bean-jellies from the local hot springs, but there were no customers around to buy their wares.

"This place reminds me of Atagawa in Izu," Suguro grumbled to himself as he snapped the cardboard top back onto the milk bottle. "What a disgusting landscape."

He had to chuckle a bit at himself for coming all the way to this humdrum spot at the western edge of Kyushu. In Tokyo he had not had the slightest notion that this village of Obama, home of many of the Christian martyrs and some of the participants in the Shimabara Rebellion, would be so commonplace a town.

From his studies of the Christian era in Japan, Suguro knew that around 1630 many of the faithful had made the climb from Obama towards Unzen, which a Jesuit of the day had called "one of the tallest mountains in Japan." The Valley of Hell high up on Unzen was an ideal place for torturing Christians. According to the records, after 1629, when the Nagasaki Magistrate Takenaka Shigetsugu hit upon the idea of abusing the Christians in this hot spring inferno, sixty or seventy prisoners a day were roped together and herded from Obama to the top of this mountain.

Now tourists strolled the streets of the village, and popular songs blared out from loudspeakers. Nothing remained to remind one of that sanguinary history. But precisely three centuries before the present month of January, on a day of misty rain, the man whose footsteps Suguro now hoped to retrace had undoubtedly climbed up this mountain from Obama.

Finally the engine started up, and the bus made its way through the village. They passed through a district of two and three story Japanese inns, where men leaned with both hands on the railings of the balconies and peered down into the bus. Even those windows which were deserted were draped with pink and white washcloths and towels. When the bus finally passed beyond the hotel district, both sides of the mountain road were lined with old stone walls and squat farmhouses with thatched roofs.

Suguro had no way of knowing whether these walls and farmhouses had existed in the Christian century. Nor could he be sure that this road was the one traveled by the Christians, the officers, and the man he was pursuing. The only certain thing was that, during their fitful stops along the path, they had looked up at this same Mount Unzen wrapped in gray mist.

He had brought a number of books with him from Tokyo, but he now regretted not including a collection of letters from Jesuits of the day who had reported on the Unzen martyrdoms to their superiors in

Rome. He had thoughtlessly tossed into his bag one book that would be of no use to him on this journey—Collado's *Christian Confessions*.

The air cooled as the bus climbed into the hills, and the passengers, peeling skins from the *mikans** they had bought at Obama, listened half-heartedly to the sing-song travelogue provided by the conductor.

"Please look over this way," she said with a waxy smile. "There are two large pine trees on top of the hill we are about to circle. It's said that at about this spot, the Christians of olden days would turn around and look longingly back at the village of Obama. These trees later became known as the Looking-Back Pines."

Collado's *Christian Confessions* was published in Rome in 1632, just five years before the outbreak of the Shimabara Rebellion. By that time the shogunate's persecution of the Christians had grown fierce, but a few Portuguese and Italian missionaries had still managed to steal into Japan from Macao or Manila. The *Christian Confessions* were printed as a practical guide to Japanese grammar for the benefit of these missionaries. But what Suguro found hard to understand was why Collado had made public the confessions of these Japanese Christians, when a Catholic priest was under no circumstances permitted to reveal the innermost secrets of the soul shared with him by members of his flock.

Yet the night he read the *Confessions*, Suguro felt as though a more responsive chord had been struck within him than with any other history of the Christian era he had encountered. Every study he had read was little more than a string of paeans to the noble acts of priests and martyrs and common believers inspired by faith. They were without exception chronicles of those who had sustained their beliefs and their testimonies no matter what sufferings or tortures they had to endure. And each time he read them, Suguro had to sigh, "There's no way I can emulate people like this."

He had been baptized as a child, along with the rest of his family. Since then he had passed through many vicissitudes and somehow managed to arrive in his forties without rejecting his religion. But that was not due to firm resolve or unshakable faith. He was more than adequately aware of his own spiritual slovenliness and pusillanimity. He was certain that an unspannable gulf separated him from the ancient

---

*citrus fruit similar to tangerines

martyrs of Nagasaki, Edo, and Unzen who had effected glorious martyrdoms. Why had they all been so indomitable?

Suguro diligently searched the Christian histories for someone like himself. But there was no one to be found. Finally he had stumbled across the *Christian Confessions* one day in a second-hand bookshop, and as he flipped indifferently through the pages of the book, he had been moved by the account of a man whose name Collado had concealed. The man had the same feeble will and tattered integrity as Suguro. Gradually he had formed in his mind an image of this man—genuflecting like a camel before the priest nearly three hundred years earlier, relishing the almost desperate experience of exposing his own filthiness to the eyes of another.

"I stayed for a long time with some heathens. I didn't want the innkeeper to realize I was a Christian, so I went with him often to the heathen temples and chanted along with them. Many times when they praised the gods and Buddha's, I sinned greatly by nodding and agreeing with them. I don't remember how many times I did that. Maybe twenty or thirty times—more than twenty, anyway.

"And when the heathens and the apostates got together to slander us Christians and blaspheme against God, I was there with them. I didn't try to stop them talking or to refute them.

"Just recently, at the Shogun's orders the Magistrate came to our fief from the capital, determined to make all the Christians here apostatize. Everyone was interrogated and pressed to reject the Christian codes, or at least to apostatize in form only. Finally, in order to save the lives of my wife and children, I told them I would abandon my beliefs."

Suguro did not know where this man had been born, or what he had looked like. He had the impression he was a samurai, but there was no way to determine who his master might have been. The man would have had no inkling that his private confession would one day be published in a foreign land, and eventually fall into the hands of one of his own countrymen again, to be read by a person like Suguro. Though he did not have a clear picture of how the man looked, Suguro had some idea of the assortment of facial expressions he would have had to employ in order to evade detection. If he had been born in that age, Suguro would have had no qualms about going along with the Buddhist laymen to worship at their temples, if that meant he would not be exposed as a Christian. When someone mocked the Christian faith, he would have lowered his eyes and tried to look unconcerned. If so ordered, he might even have written out an oath of apostasy, if that would mean saving the lives of his family as well as his own.

■

A faint ray of light tentatively penetrated the clouds that had gathered over the summit of Unzen. *Maybe it will clear up,* he thought. In summer this paved road would no doubt be choked by a stream of cars out for a drive, but now there was only the bus struggling up the mountain with intermittent groans. Groves of withered trees shivered all around. A cluster of rain-soaked bungalows huddled silently among the trees, their doors tightly shut.

"Listen, martyrdom is no more than a matter of pride."

He had had this conversation in the corner of a bar in Shinjuku. A pot of Akita salted-fish broth simmered in the center of the *sake**-stained table. Seated around the pot, Suguro's elders in the literary establishment had been discussing the hero of a novel he had recently published. The work dealt with some Christian martyrs in the 1870s. The writers at the gathering claimed that they could not swallow the motivations behind those martyrdoms the way Suguro had.

"At the very core of this desire to be a martyr you'll find pride, pure and simple."

"I'm sure pride plays a part in it. Along with the desire to become a hero, and even a touch of insanity, perhaps. But—"

Suguro fell silent and clutched his glass. It was a simple task to pinpoint elements of heroism and pride among the motives for martyrdom. But when those elements were obliterated, residual motives still remained. Those residual motives were of vital importance.

"Well, if you're going to look at it that way, you can find pride and selfishness underlying virtually every human endeavor, every single act of good faith."

In the ten years he had been writing fiction, Suguro had grown

---

*rice wine

increasingly impatient with those modern novelists who tried to single out the egotism and pride in every act of man. To Suguro's mind, such a view of humanity entailed the loss of something of consummate value, like water poured through a sieve.

The road wound its way to the summit through dead grass and barren woods. In days past, lines of human beings had struggled up this path. Both pride and madness had certainly been part of their make-up, but there must have been something more to it.

"The right wing during the war, for instance, had a certain martyr mentality. I can't help thinking there's something impure going on when people are intoxicated by something like that. But perhaps I feel that way because I experienced the war myself," one of his elders snorted as he drank down his cup of tepid *sake*. Sensing an irreconcilable misunderstanding between himself and this man, Suguro could only grin acquiescently.

Before long he caught sight of a column of white smoke rising like steam from the belly of the mountain. Though the windows of the bus were closed, he smelled a faintly sulfuric odor. Milky white crags and sand came into clear focus.

"Is that the Valley of Hell?"

"No." The conductor shook her head. "It's a little farther up."

A tiny crack in the clouds afforded a glimpse of blue sky. The bus, which up until now had panted along, grinding its gears, suddenly seemed to catch its breath and picked up speed. The road had leveled off, then begun to drop. A series of arrows tacked to the leafless trees, apparently to guide hikers, read "Valley of Hell." Just ahead was the red roof of the rest-house.

Suguro did not know whether the man mentioned in the *Confessions* had come here to the Valley of Hell. But, as if before Suguro's eyes, the image of another individual had overlapped with that of the first man and now stumbled along with his head bowed. There was a little more detailed information about this second man. His name was Kichijirō, and he first appeared in the historical records on the fifth day of December, 1631, when seven priests and Christians were tortured at the Valley of Hell. Kichijirō came here to witness the fate of the fathers who had cared for him. He had apostatized much earlier, so he had been able to blend in with the crowd of spectators. Standing on tiptoe, he had witnessed the cruel punishments which the officers inflicted on his spiritual mentors.

Father Christovao Ferreira, who later broke under torture and left a filthy smudge on the pages of Japanese Christian history, sent to his homeland a letter vividly describing the events of that day. The seven Christians arrived at Obama on the evening of December the second, and were driven up the mountain all the following day. There were several look-out huts on the slope, and that evening the seven captives were forced into one of them, their feet and hands still shackled. There they awaited the coming of dawn.

"The tortures commenced on the fifth of December in the following manner. One by one each of the seven was taken to the brink of the seething pond. There they were shown the frothy spray from the boiling water, and ordered to renounce their faith. The air was chilly and the hot water of the pond churned so furiously that, had God not sustained them, a single look would have caused them to faint away. They all shouted, 'Torture us! We will not recant!' At this response, the guards stripped the garments from the prisoners' bodies and bound their hands and feet. Four of them held down a single captive as a ladle holding about a quarter of a liter was filled with the boiling water. Three ladlesful were slowly poured over each body. One of the seven, a young girl called Maria, fainted from the excruciating pain and fell to the ground. In the space of thirty-three days, each of them was subjected to this torture a total of six times."

Suguro was the last one off when the bus came to a stop. The cold, taut mountain air blew a putrid odor into his nostrils. White steam poured onto the highway from the tree-ringed valley.

"How about a photograph? Photographs, anyone?" a young man standing beside a large camera on a tripod called out to Suguro. "I'll pay the postage wherever you want to send it."

At various spots along the road stood women proffering eggs in baskets and waving clumsily-lettered signs that read "Boiled Eggs." They too touted loudly for business.

Weaving their way among these hawkers, Suguro and the rest of the group from the bus walked towards the valley. The earth, overgrown with shrubbery, was virtually white, almost the color of flesh stripped clean of its layer of skin. The rotten-smelling steam gushed ceaselessly

from amid the trees. The narrow path stitched its way back and forth
between springs of hot, bubbling water. Some parts of the white-speck-
led pools lay as calm and flat as a wall of plaster; others eerily spewed up
slender sprays of gurgling water. Here and there on the hillocks formed
from sulfur flows stood pine trees scorched red by the heat.

The bus passengers extracted boiled eggs from their paper sacks and
stuffed them into their mouths. They moved forward like a column of
ants.

"Come and look over here. There's a dead bird."

"So there is. I suppose the gas fumes must have asphyxiated it."

All he knew for certain was that Kichijirō had been a witness to
those tortures. Why had he come? There was no way of knowing
whether he had joined the crowd of Buddhist spectators in the hope of
rescuing the priests and the faithful who were being tormented. The
only tangible piece of information he had about Kichijirō was that he
had forsworn his religion to the officers, "so that his wife and children
might live." Nevertheless, he had followed in the footsteps of those
seven Christians, walking all the way from Nagasaki to Obama, then
trudging to the top of the bitterly cold peak of Unzen.

Suguro could almost see the look on Kichijirō's face as he stood at
the back of the crowd, furtively watching his former companions with
the tremulous gaze of a dog, then lowering his eyes in humiliation. That
look was very like Suguro's own. In any case, there was no way Suguro
could stand in chains before these loathsomely bubbling pools and
make any show of courage.

A momentary flash of white lit up the entire landscape; then a fierce
eruption burst forth with the smell of noxious gas. A mother standing
near the surge quickly picked up her crouching child and retreated. A
placard reading "Dangerous Beyond This Point" was thrust firmly into
the clay. Around it the carcasses of three dead swallows were stretched
out like mummies.

This must be the spot where the Christians were tortured, he thought.
Through a crack in the misty, shifting steam, Suguro saw the black out-
lines of a cross. Covering his nose and mouth with a handkerchief and
balancing precariously near the warning sign, he peered below him. The
mottled water churned and sloshed before his eyes. The Christians
must have stood just where he was standing now when they were tor-

tured. And Kichijirō would have stayed behind, standing about where the mother and her child now stood at a cautious distance, watching the spectacle with the rest of the crowd. Inwardly, did he ask them to forgive him? Had Suguro been in his shoes, he would have had no recourse but to repeat over and over again, "Forgive me! I'm not strong enough to be a martyr like you. My heart melts just to think about this dreadful torture."

Of course, Kichijirō could justify his attitude. If he had lived in a time of religious freedom, he would never have become an apostate. He might not have qualified for sainthood, but he could have been a man who tamely maintained his faith. But to his regret, he had been born in an age of persecution, and out of fear he had tossed away his beliefs. Not everyone can become a saint or a martyr. Yet must those who do not qualify as saints be branded forever with the mark of the traitor?—Perhaps he had made such a plea to the Christians who vilified him. Yet, despite the logic of his argument, he surely suffered pangs of remorse and cursed his own faint resolve.

"The apostate endures a pain none of you can comprehend."

Over the span of three centuries this cry, like the shriek of a wounded bird, reached Suguro's ears. That single line recorded in the *Christian Confessions* cut at Suguro's chest like a sharp sword. Surely those were the words Kichijirō must have shouted to himself here at Unzen as he looked upon his tormented friends.

■

They reboarded the bus. The ride from Unzen to Shimabara took less than an hour. A fistful of blue finally appeared in the sky, but the air remained cold. The same conductor forced her usual smile and commented on the surroundings in a sing-song voice.

The seven Christians, refusing to bend to the tortures at Unzen, had been taken down the mountain to Shimabara, along the same route Suguro was now following. He could almost see them dragging their scalded legs, leaning on walking-sticks and enduring lashes from the officers.

Leaving some distance between them, Kichijirō had timorously followed behind. When the weary Christians stopped to catch their breath,

Kichijirō also halted, a safe distance behind. He hurriedly crouched down like a rabbit in the overgrowth, lest the officers suspect him, and did not rise again until the group had resumed their trek. He was like a jilted woman plodding along in pursuit of her lover.

Half-way down the mountain he had a glimpse of the dark sea. Milky clouds veiled the horizon; several wan beams of sunlight filtered through the cracks. Suguro thought how blue the ocean would appear on a clear day.

"Look—you can see a blur out there that looks like an island. Unfortunately, you can't see it very well today. This is Dangō Island, where Amakusa Shirō, the commander of the Christian forces, planned the Shimabara Rebellion with his men."

At this the passengers took a brief, apathetic glance towards the island. Before long the view of the distant sea was blocked by a forest of trees.

What must those seven Christians have felt as they looked at this ocean? They knew they would soon be executed at Shimabara. The corpses of martyrs were swiftly reduced to ashes and cast upon the seas. If that were not done, the remaining Christians would surreptitiously worship the clothing and even locks of hair from the martyrs as though they were holy objects. And so the seven, getting their first distant view of the ocean from this spot, must have realized that it would be their grave. Kichijirō too would have looked at the sea, but with a different kind of sorrow—with the knowledge that the strong ones in the world of faith were crowned with glory, while the cowards had to carry their burdens with them throughout their lives.

When the group reached Shimabara, four of them were placed in a cell barely three feet tall and only wide enough to accommodate one *tatami*.* The other three were jammed into another room equally cramped. As they awaited their punishment, they persistently encouraged one another and went on praying. There is no record of where Kichijirō stayed during this time.

The village of Shimabara was dark and silent. The bus came to a stop by a tiny wharf where the rickety ferry-boat to Amakusa was

---

*floor mat

moored forlornly. Wood chips and flotsam bobbed on the small waves that lapped at the breakwater. Among the debris floated an object that resembled a rolled-up newspaper; it was the corpse of a cat.

The town extended in a thin band along the seafront. The fences of local factories stretched far into the distance, while the odor of chemicals wafted all the way to the highway.

Suguro set out towards the reconstructed Shimabara Castle. The only signs of life he encountered along the way were a couple of high-school girls riding bicycles.

"Where is the execution ground where the Christians were killed?" he asked them.

"I didn't know there was such a place," said one of them, blushing. She turned to her friend. "Have you heard of anything like that? You don't know, do you?" Her friend shook her head.

He came to a neighborhood identified as a former samurai residence. It had stood behind the castle, where several narrow paths intersected. A crumbling mud wall wound its way between the paths. The drainage ditch was as it had been in those days. Summer *mikans* poked their heads above the mud wall, which had already blocked out the evening sun. All the buildings were old, dark and musty. They had probably been the residence of a low-ranking samurai, built at the end of the Tokugawa period. Many Christians had been executed at the Shimabara grounds, but Suguro had not come across any historical documents identifying the location of the prison.

He retraced his steps, and after a short walk came out on a street of shops where popular songs were playing. The narrow street was packed with a variety of stores, including gift shops. The water in the drainage ditch was as limpid as water from a spring.

"The execution ground? I know where that is." The owner of a tobacco shop directed Suguro to a pond just down the road. "If you go straight on past the pond, you'll come to a nursery school. The execution ground was just to the side of the school."

Though they say nothing of how he was able to do it, the records indicate that Kichijirō was allowed to visit the seven prisoners on the day before their execution. Possibly he put some money into the hands of the officers.

Kichijirō offered a meager plate of food to the prisoners, who were prostrate from their ordeal.

"Kichijirō, did you retract your oath?" one of the captives asked compassionately. He was eager to know if the apostate had finally informed the officials that he could not deny his faith. "Have you come here to see us because you have retracted?"

Kichijirō looked up at them timidly and shook his head.

"In any case, Kichijirō, we can't accept this food."

"Why not?"

"Why not?" The prisoners were mournfully silent for a moment. "Because we have already accepted the fact that we will die."

Kichijirō could only lower his eyes and say nothing. He knew that he himself could never endure the sort of agony he had witnessed at the Valley of Hell on Unzen.

Through his tears he whimpered, "If I can't suffer the same pain as you, will I be unable to enter Paradise? Will God forsake someone like me?"

He walked along the street of shops as he had been instructed and came to the pond. A floodgate blocked the overflow from the pond, and the water poured underground and into the drainage ditch in the village. Suguro read a sign declaring that the purity of the water in Shimabara village was due to the presence of this pond.

He heard the sounds of children at play. Four or five young children were tossing a ball back and forth in the nursery school playground. The setting sun shone feebly on the swings and sandbox in the yard. He walked around behind a drooping hedge of rose bushes and located the remains of the execution ground, now the only barren patch within a grove of trees.

It was a deserted plot some three hundred square yards in size, grown rank with brown weeds; pines towered over a heap of refuse. Suguro had come all the way from Tokyo to have a look at this place. Or had he made the journey out of a desire to understand better Kichijirō's emotions as he stood in this spot?

The following morning the seven prisoners were hoisted onto the unsaddled horses and dragged through the streets of Shimabara to this execution ground.

One of the witnesses to the scene has recorded the events of the day:

"After they were paraded about, they arrived at the execution ground, which was surrounded by a palisade. They were taken off their horses and made to stand in front of stakes set three meters apart. Firewood was already piled at the base of the stakes, and straw roofs soaked in sea water had been placed on top of them to prevent the flames from raging too quickly and allowing the martyrs to die with little agony. The ropes that bound them to the stakes were tied as loosely as possible, to permit them, up to the very moment of death, to twist their bodies and cry out that they would abandon their faith.

"When the officers began setting fire to the wood, a solitary man broke through the line of guards and dashed towards the stakes. He was shouting something, but I could not hear what he said over the roar of the fires. The fierce flames and smoke prevented the man from approaching the prisoners. The guards swiftly apprehended him and asked if he was a Christian. At that, the man froze in fear, and jabbering, 'I am no Christian. I have nothing to do with these people! I just lost my head in all the excitement,' he skulked away. But some in the crowd had seen him at the rear of the assemblage, his hands pressed together as he repeated over and over, 'Forgive me! Forgive me!'

"The seven victims sang a hymn until the flames enveloped their stakes. Their voices were exuberant, totally out of keeping with the cruel punishment they were even then enduring. When those voices suddenly ceased, the only sound was the dull crackling of wood. The man who had darted forward could be seen walking lifelessly away from the execution ground. Rumors spread through the crowd that he too had been a Christian."

Suguro noticed a dark patch at the very center of the execution ground. On closer inspection he discovered several charred stones half-buried beneath the black earth. Although he had no way of knowing whether these stones had been used here three hundred years before, when seven Christians had been burned at the stake, he hurriedly snatched up one of the stones and put it in his pocket. Then, his spine bent like Kichijirō's, he walked back towards the road.

⤳Faith and Reason⤳

The Blue Cross
G.K. Chesterton

Father Brown, the immortal literary character created by English journalist, novelist, and poet G.K. Chesterton (1874-1936), is a country parish priest with a cherubic face and an air of unworldly simplicity. Commonly regarded as an eccentric old bumbler, in reality he is a brilliant sleuth with an uncanny understanding of the human condition. He catches master criminals like the thief Flambeau in this story, not in order to consign them to prison, but to release them from the prison of their own sin.

Between the silver ribbon of morning and the green glittering ribbon of sea, the boat touched Harwich and let loose a swarm of folk like flies, among whom the man we must follow was by no means conspicuous—nor wished to be. There was nothing notable about him, except a slight contrast between the holiday gaiety of his clothes and the official gravity of his face. His clothes included a slight, pale gray jacket, a white waist-coat, and a silver straw hat with a gray-blue ribbon. His lean face was dark by contrast, and ended in a curt black beard that looked Spanish and suggested an Elizabethan ruff. He was smoking a cigarette with the seriousness of an idler. There was nothing about him to indicate the fact that the gray jacket covered a loaded revolver, that the white waistcoat covered a police card, or that the straw hat covered one of the most powerful intellects in Europe. For this was Valentin himself, the head of the Paris police and the most famous investigator of the world; and he was coming from Brussels to London to make the greatest arrest of the century.

Flambeau was in England. The police of three countries had tracked the great criminal at last from Ghent to Brussels, from Brussels to the Hook of Holland; and it was conjectured that he would take some advantage of the unfamiliarity and confusion of the Eucharistic Congress, then taking place in London. Probably he would travel as some minor clerk or secretary connected with it; but, of course, Valentin could not be certain; nobody could be certain about Flambeau.

It is many years now since this colossus of crime suddenly ceased keeping the world in a turmoil; and when he ceased, as they said after the death of Roland, there was a great quiet upon the earth. But in his best days (I mean, of course, his worst) Flambeau was a figure as statuesque and international as the Kaiser. Almost every morning the daily paper announced that he had escaped the consequences of one extraordinary crime by committing another. He was a Gascon of gigantic stature and bodily daring; and the wildest tales were told of his outbursts of athletic humor; how he turned the *juge d' instruction* (preliminary magistrate) upside down and stood him on his head, "to clear his mind"; how he ran down the Rue de Rivoli with a policeman under each arm. It is due to him to say that his fantastic physical strength was generally employed in such bloodless though undignified scenes; his real crimes were chiefly those of ingenious and wholesale robbery. But each of his thefts was almost a new sin, and would make a story by itself. It was he who ran the great Tyrolean Dairy Company in London, with no dairies, no cows, no carts, no milk, but with some thousand subscribers. These he served by the simple operation of moving the little milk-cans outside people's doors to the doors of his own customers. It was he who had kept up an unaccountable and close correspondence with a young lady whose whole letter-bag was intercepted, by the extraordinary trick of photographing his messages infinitesimally small upon the slides of a microscope. A sweeping simplicity, however, marked many of his experiments. It is said he once repainted all the numbers in a street in the dead of night merely to divert one traveler into a trap. It is quite certain that he invented a portable pillar-box, which he put up at corners in quiet suburbs on the chance of strangers dropping postal orders into it. Lastly, he was known to be a startling acrobat; despite his huge figure, he could leap like a grasshopper and melt into the treetops like a monkey. Hence the great Valentin, when he set out to find Flambeau, was perfectly well aware that his adventures would not end when he had found him.

But how was he to find him? On this the great Valentin's ideas were still in process of settlement.

There was one thing which Flambeau, with all his dexterity of disguise, could not cover, and that was his singular height. If Valentin's quick eye had caught a tall apple-woman, a tall grenadier, or even a tolerably tall duchess, he might have arrested them on the spot. But all along his train there was nobody that could be a disguised Flambeau, any more than a cat could be a disguised giraffe. About the people on the boat he had already satisfied himself; and the people picked up at Harwich or on the journey limited themselves with certainty to six. There was a short railway official traveling up to the terminus, three fairly short market-gardeners picked up two stations afterwards, one very short widow lady going up from a small Essex town, and a very short Roman Catholic priest going up from a small Essex village. When it came to the last case, Valentin gave it up and almost laughed. The little priest was so much the essence of those Eastern flats: he had a face as round and dull as a Norfolk dumpling; he had eyes as empty as the North Sea; he had several brown-paper parcels which he was quite incapable of collecting. The Eucharistic Congress had doubtless sucked out of their local stagnation many such creatures, blind and helpless, like moles disinterred. Valentin was a skeptic in the severe style of France, and could have no love for priests. But he could have pity for them, and this one might have provoked pity in anybody. He had a large, shabby umbrella, which constantly fell on the floor. He did not seem to know which was the right end of his return ticket. He explained with a moon-calf simplicity to everybody in the carriage that he had to be careful, because he had something made of real silver "with blue stones" in one of his brown-paper parcels. His quaint blending of Essex flatness with saintly simplicity continuously amused the Frenchman till the priest arrived (somehow) at Stratford with all his parcels, and came back for his umbrella. When he did the last, Valentin even had the good nature to warn him not to take care of the silver by telling everybody about it. But to whomever he talked, Valentin kept his eye open for someone else; he looked out steadily for anyone, rich or poor, male or female who was well up to six feet; for Flambeau was four inches above it.

He alighted at Liverpool Street, however, quite conscientiously secure that he had not missed the criminal so far. He then went to Scotland Yard to regularize his position and arrange for help in case of need; he then lit another cigarette and went for a long stroll in the streets of London. As he was walking in the streets and squares beyond Victoria, he paused suddenly and stood. It was a quaint, quiet square, very typical of London, full of an accidental stillness. The tall flat houses round looked at once prosperous and uninhabited; the square of shrubbery in the center looked as deserted as a green Pacific islet. One of the four sides was much higher than the rest, like a dais; and the line of this side was broken by one of London's admirable accidents—a restaurant that looked as if it had strayed from Soho. It was an unreasonably attractive object, with dwarf plants in pots and long, striped blinds of lemon yellow and white. It stood specially high above the street, and in the usual patchwork way of London, a flight of steps from the street ran up to meet the front door almost as a fire-escape might run up to a first-floor window. Valentin stood and smoked in front of the yellow-white blinds and considered them long.

The most incredible thing about miracles is that they happen. A few clouds in heaven do come together into the staring shape of one human eye. A tree does stand up in the landscape of a doubtful journey in the exact and elaborate shape of a note of interrogation. I have seen both these things myself within the last few days. Nelson does die in the instant of victory; and a man named Williams does quite accidentally murder a man named Williamson; it sounds like a sort of infanticide. In short, there is in life an element of elfin coincidence which people reckoning on the prosaic may perpetually miss. As it has been well expressed in the paradox of Poe, wisdom should reckon on the unforeseen.

Aristide Valentin was unfathomably French; and the French intelligence is intelligence specially and solely. He was not "a thinking machine"; for that is a brainless phrase of modern fatalism and materialism. A machine only is a machine because it cannot think. But he was a thinking man, and a plain man at the same time. All his wonderful successes, that looked like conjuring, had been gained by plodding logic, by clear and commonplace French thought. The French electrify the world not by starting any paradox, they electrify it by carrying out a truism. They carry a truism so far—as in the French Revolution. But exactly because Valentin understood reason, he understood the limits of reason. Only a man who knows nothing of motors talks of motoring without petrol; only a man who knows nothing of reason talks of reasoning without strong, undisputed first principles. Here he had no strong first principles. Flambeau had been missed at Harwich; and if he was in London at all, he might be anything from a tall tramp on Wimbledon Common to a tall toastmaster at the Hotel Metropole. In such a naked state of nescience,* Valentin had a view and a method of his own.

In such cases he reckoned on the unforeseen. In such cases, when he could not follow the train of the reasonable, he coldly and carefully followed the train of the unreasonable. Instead of going to the right places—banks, police-stations, rendezvous—he systematically went to the wrong places; knocked at every empty house, turned down every cul de sac, went up every lane blocked with rubbish, went round every crescent that led him uselessly out of the way. He defended this crazy course quite logically. He said that if one had a clue this was the worst way; but if one had no clue at all it was the best, because there was just the chance that any oddity that caught the eye of the pursuer might be the same that had caught the eye of the pursued. Somewhere a man must begin, and it had better be just where another man might stop. Something about that flight of steps up to the shop, something about the quietude and quaintness of the restaurant, roused all the detective's rare romantic fancy and made him resolve to strike at random. He went up the steps, and sitting down by the window, asked for a cup of black coffee.

It was half-way through the morning, and he had not breakfasted; the slight litter of other breakfasts stood about on the table to remind him of his hunger; and adding a poached egg to his order, he proceeded musingly to shake some white sugar into his coffee, thinking all the time about Flambeau. He remembered how Flambeau had escaped, once by a pair of nail scissors, and once by a house on fire; once by having to pay for an unstamped letter, and once by getting people to look through a telescope at a comet that might destroy the world. He thought his detective brain as good as the criminal's, which was true. But he fully realized the disadvantage. "The criminal is the creative artist; the detective only the critic," he said with a sour smile, and lifted his coffee cup to his lips slowly, and put it down very quickly. He had put salt in it.

He looked at the vessel from which the silvery powder had come; it was certainly a sugar-basin; as unmistakably meant for sugar as a champagne bottle for champagne. He wondered why they should keep salt in it. He looked to see if there were any more orthodox vessels. Yes, there were two salt-cellars quite full. Perhaps there was some specialty

---

*ignorance

in the condiment in the salt-cellars. He tasted it; it was sugar. Then he looked round at the restaurant with a refreshed air of interest, to see if there were any other traces of that singular artistic taste which puts the sugar in the salt-cellars and the salt in the sugar-basin. Except for an odd splash of some dark fluid on one of the white-papered walls, the whole place appeared neat, cheerful and ordinary. He rang the bell for the waiter.

When that official hurried up, fuzzy-haired and somewhat bleary-eyed at that early hour, the detective (who was not without an appreciation of the simpler forms of humor) asked him to taste the sugar and see if it was up to the high reputation of the hotel. The result was that the waiter yawned suddenly and woke up.

"Do you play this delicate joke on your customers every morning?" inquired Valentin. "Does changing the salt and sugar never pall on you as a jest?"

The waiter, when this irony grew clearer, stammeringly assured him that the establishment had certainly no such intention; it must be a most curious mistake. He picked up the sugar-basin and looked at it; he picked up the salt-cellar and looked at that, his face growing more and more bewildered. At last he abruptly excused himself, and hurrying away, returned in a few seconds with the proprietor. The proprietor also examined the sugar-basin and then the salt-cellar; the proprietor also looked bewildered.

Suddenly the waiter seemed to grow inarticulate with a rush of words.

"I zink," he stuttered eagerly, "I zink it is those two clergymen."

"What two clergymen?"

"The two clergymen," said the waiter, "that threw soup at the wall."

"Threw soup at the wall?" repeated Valentin, feeling sure this must be some Italian metaphor.

"Yes, yes," said the attendant excitedly, pointing at the dark splash on the white paper; "threw it over there on the wall."

Valentin looked his query at the proprietor, who came to his rescue with fuller reports.

"Yes, sir," he said, "it's quite true, though I don't suppose it has anything to do with the sugar and salt. Two clergymen came in and drank soup here very early, as soon as the shutters were taken down. They were both very quiet, respectable people; one of them paid the bill and went out; the other, who seemed a slower coach altogether, was some minutes longer getting his things together. But he went at last. Only, the instant before he stepped into the street he deliberately picked up his cup, which he had only half emptied, and threw the soup slap on the wall. I was in the back room myself, and so was the waiter; so I could only rush out in time to find the wall splashed and the shop empty. It didn't do any particular damage, but it was confounded cheek; and I tried to catch the men in the street. They were too far off though; I only noticed they went round the corner into Carstairs Street."

The detective was on his feet, hat settled and stick in hand. He had already decided that in the universal darkness of his mind he could only follow the first odd finger that pointed; and this finger was odd enough. Paying his bill and clashing the glass doors behind him, he was soon swinging round into the other street.

It was fortunate that even in such fevered moments his eye was cool and quick. Something in a shop-front went by him like a mere flash; yet he went back to look at it. The shop was a popular greengrocer and fruiterer's, an array of goods set out in the open air and plainly ticketed with their names and prices. In the two most prominent compartments were two heaps, of oranges and of nuts respectively. On the heap of nuts lay a scrap of cardboard, on which was written in bold, blue chalk, "Best tangerine oranges, two a penny." On the oranges was the equally clear and exact description, "Finest Brazil nuts, 4d. a lb." M. Valentin looked at these two placards and fancied he had met this highly subtle form of humor before, and that somewhat recently. He drew the attention of the red-faced fruiterer, who was looking rather sullenly up and down the street, to this inaccuracy in his advertisements. The fruiterer said nothing, but sharply put each card into its proper place. The detective, leaning elegantly on his walking-cane, continued to scrutinize the shop. At last he said: "Pray excuse my apparent irrelevance, my good sir, but I should like to ask you a question in experimental psychology and the association of ideas."

The red-faced shopman regarded him with an eye of menace; but he continued gaily, swinging his cane. "Why," he pursued, "why are two tickets wrongly placed in a greengrocer's shop like a shovel hat that has come to London for a holiday? Or, in case I do not make myself clear, what is the mystical association which connects the idea of nuts marked as oranges with the idea of two clergymen, one tall and the other short?"

The eyes of the tradesman stood out of his head like a snail's; he really seemed for an instant likely to fling himself upon the stranger. At last he stammered angrily: "I don't know what you 'ave to do with it, but if you're one of their friends, you can tell 'em from me that I'll knock their silly 'eads off, parsons or no parsons, if they upset my apples again."

"Indeed?" asked the detective, with great sympathy. "Did they upset your apples?"

"One of 'em did," said the heated shopman; "rolled 'em all over the street. I'd 'ave caught the fool but for havin' to pick 'em up."

"Which way did these parsons go?" asked Valentin.

"Up that second road on the left-hand side, and then across the square," said the other promptly.

"Thanks," said Valentin, and vanished like a fairy. On the other side of the second square he found a policeman, and said: "This is urgent, constable; have you seen two clergymen in shovel hats?"

The policeman began to chuckle heavily. "I 'ave, sir; and if you arst me, one of 'em was drunk. He stood in the middle of the road that bewildered that—"

"Which way did they go?" snapped Valentin.

"They took one of them yellow buses over there," answered the man; "them that go to Hampstead."

Valentin produced his official card and said very rapidly: "Call up two of your men to come with me in pursuit," and crossed the road with such contagious energy that the ponderous policeman was moved to almost agile obedience. In a minute and a half the French detective was joined on the opposite pavement by an inspector and a man in plain clothes.

"Well, sir," began the former, with smiling importance, "and what may—?"

Valentin pointed suddenly with his cane. "I'll tell you on the top of that omnibus," he said, and was darting and dodging across the tangle of the traffic. When all three sank panting on the top seats of the yellow vehicle, the inspector said: "We could go four times as quick in a taxi."

"Quite true," replied their leader placidly, "if we only had an idea of where we were going."

Well, where *are* you going?" asked the other, staring.

Valentin smoked frowningly for a few seconds; then, removing his cigarette, he said: "If you *know* what a man's doing, get in front of him; but if you want to guess what he's doing, keep behind him. Stray when he strays; stop when he stops; travel as slowly as he. Then you may see what he saw and may act as he acted. All we can do is to keep our eyes skinned for a queer thing."

"What sort of a queer thing do you mean?" asked the inspector.

"Any sort of queer thing," answered Valentin, and relapsed into obstinate silence.

The yellow omnibus crawled up the northern roads for what seemed like hours on end; the great detective would not explain further, and perhaps his assistants felt a silent and growing doubt of his errand. Perhaps, also, they felt a silent and growing desire for lunch, for the hours crept long past the normal luncheon hour, and the long roads of the North London suburbs seemed to shoot out into length after length like an infernal telescope. It was one of those journeys on which a man perpetually feels that now at last he must have come to the end of the universe, and then finds he has only come to the beginning of Tufnell Park. London died away in draggled taverns and dreary scrubs, and then was unaccountably born again in blazing high streets and blatant hotels. It was like passing through thirteen separate vulgar cities all just touching each other. But though the winter twilight was already threatening the road ahead of them, the Parisian detective still sat silent and watchful, eyeing the frontage of the streets that slid by on either side. By the time they had left Camden Town behind, the policemen were nearly asleep; at least, they gave something like a jump as Valentin leapt erect, struck a hand on each man's shoulder, and shouted to the driver to stop.

They tumbled down the steps into the road without realizing why they had been dislodged; when they looked round for enlightenment they found Valentin triumphantly pointing his finger toward a window on the left side of the road. It was a large window, forming part of the long facade of a gilt and palatial public-house; it was the part reserved for respectable dining, and labeled "Restaurant." This window, like all the rest along the frontage of the hotel, was of frosted and figured glass, but in the middle of it was a big, black smash, like a star in the ice.

"Our cue at last," cried Valentin, waving his stick; "the place with the broken window."

"What window? What cue?" asked his principal assistant. "Why, what proof is there that this has anything to do with them?"

Valentin almost broke his bamboo stick with rage.

"Proof!" he cried. "Good God! the man is looking for proof! Why, of course, the chances are twenty to one that it has *nothing* to do with them. But what else can we do? Don't you see we must either follow one wild possibility or else go home to bed?" He banged his way into the restaurant, followed by his companions, and they were soon seated at a late luncheon at a little table, and looking at the star of smashed glass from the inside. Not that it was very informative to them even then.

"Got your window broken, I see," said Valentin to the waiter, as he paid his bill.

"Yes, sir," answered the attendant, bending busily over the change, to which Valentin silently added an enormous tip. The waiter straightened himself with mild but unmistakable animation.

"Ah, yes, sir," he said. "Very odd thing, that, sir."

"Indeed? Tell us about it," said the detective with careless curiosity.

"Well, two gents in black came in," said the waiter; "two of those foreign parsons that are running about. They had a cheap and quiet little lunch, and one of them paid for it and went out. The other was just going out to join him when I looked at my change again and found he'd paid me more than three times too much. 'Here,' I says to the chap who was nearly out of the door, 'you've paid too much.' 'Oh,' he says, very cool, 'have we?' 'Yes,' I says, and picks up the bill to show him. Well, that was a knock-out."

"What do you mean?" asked his interlocutor.

"Well, I'd have sworn on seven Bibles that I'd put 4s. on that bill. But now I saw I'd put 14s., as plain as paint."

"Well?" cried Valentin, moving slowly, but with burning eyes, "and then?"

"The parson at the door he says, all serene, 'Sorry to confuse your accounts, but it'll pay for the window.' 'What window?' I says. 'The one

I'm going to break,' he says, and smashed that blessed pane with his umbrella."

All the inquirers made an exclamation; and the inspector said under his breath: "Are we after escaped lunatics?" The waiter went on with some relish for the ridiculous story:

"I was so knocked silly for a second, I couldn't do anything. The man marched out of the place and joined his friend just round the corner. Then they went so quick up Bullock Street that I couldn't catch them, though I ran round the bars to do it."

"Bullock Street," said the detective, and shot up that thoroughfare as quickly as the strange couple he pursued.

Their journey now took them through bare brick ways like tunnels; streets with few lights and even with few windows; streets that seemed built out of the blank backs of everything and everywhere. Dusk was deepening, and it was not easy even for the London policemen to guess in what exact direction they were treading. The inspector, however, was pretty certain that they would eventually strike some part of Hampstead Heath. Abruptly one bulging and gas-lit window broke the blue twilight like a bull's-eye lantern; and Valentin stopped an instant before a little garish sweetstuff shop. After an instant's hesitation he went in; he stood amid the gaudy colors of the confectionery with entire gravity and bought thirteen chocolate cigars with a certain care. He was clearly preparing an opening; but he did not need one.

An angular, elderly woman in the shop had regarded his elegant appearance with a merely automatic inquiry; but when she saw the door behind him blocked with the blue uniform of the inspector, her eyes seemed to wake up.

"Oh," she said, "if you've come about that parcel, I've sent it off already."

"Parcel!" repeated Valentin; and it was his turn to look inquiring.

"I mean the parcel the gentleman left—the clergyman gentleman."

"For goodness' sake," said Valentin, leaning forward with his first real concession of eagerness, "for Heaven's sake tell us what happened exactly."

"Well," said the woman, a little doubtfully, "the clergymen came in about half an hour ago and bought some peppermints and talked a bit, and then went off toward the Heath. But a second after, one of them runs back into the shop and says, 'Have I left a parcel?' Well, I looked everywhere and I couldn't see one; so he says, 'Never mind; but if it should turn up, please post it to this address,' and he left me the address and a shilling for my trouble. And sure enough, though I thought I'd looked everywhere, I found he'd left a brown-paper parcel, so I posted it to the place he said. I can't remember the address now; it was somewhere in Westminster. But as the thing seemed so important, I thought perhaps the police had come about it."

"So they have," said Valentin shortly. "Is Hampstead Heath near here?"

"Straight on for fifteen minutes," said the woman, "and you'll come right out on the open." Valentin sprang out of the shop and began to run. The other detectives followed him at a reluctant trot.

The street they threaded was so narrow and shut in by shadows that when they came out unexpectedly into the void common and the vast sky they were startled to find the evening still so light and clear. A perfect dome of peacock-green sank into gold amid the blackening trees and the dark violet distances. The glowing green tint was just deep enough to pick out in points in crystal one or two stars. All that was left of the daylight lay in a golden glitter across the edge of Hampstead Heath and that popular hollow which is called the Vale of Heath. The holiday makers who roam this region had not wholly dispersed: a few couples sat shapelessly on benches; and here and there a distant girl shrieked in one of the swings. The glory of heaven deepened and darkened around the sublime vulgarity of man; and standing on a slope and looking across the valley Valentin beheld the thing which he sought.

Among the black and breaking groups in that distance was one especially black which did not break—a group of two figures clerically clad. Though they seemed as small as insects, Valentin could see that one of them was smaller than the other. Though the other had a student's stoop and an inconspicuous manner, he could see that the other man was well over six feet high. He shut his teeth and went forward, whirling his stick impatiently. By the time he had substantially diminished the distance and magnified the two black figures as in a vast microscope, he had perceived something else; something which startled him, and yet which he had somehow expected. Whoever was the tall priest, there could be no doubt about the identity of the short one. It was his friend of the Harwich train, the stumpy little *curé** of Essex whom he had warned about his brown-paper parcels.

Now, so as far as this went, everything fitted in finally and rationally enough. Valentin had learned by his inquiries that morning that a Father Brown from Essex was bringing up a silver cross with sapphires, a relic of considerable value, to show some foreign priests at the congress. This undoubtedly was the "silver with blue stones"; and Father Brown undoubtedly was the little greenhorn in the train. Now there was nothing wonderful about the fact that what Valentin had found out Flambeau had also found out; Flambeau found out everything. Also there was nothing wonderful in the fact that when Flambeau heard of a sapphire cross he should try to steal it; that was the most natural thing in all natural history. And most certainly there was nothing wonderful about the fact that Flambeau should have it all his own way with such a silly sheep as the man with the umbrella and the parcels. He was the sort of man whom anybody could lead on a string to the North Pole; it was not surprising that an actor like Flambeau, dressed as another priest, could lead him to Hampstead Heath. So far the crime seemed clear enough; and while the detective pitied the priest for his helplessness, he almost despised Flambeau for condescending to so gullible a victim. But when Valentin thought of all that had happened in between, of all that had led him to his triumph, he racked his brains for the smallest rhyme or reason in it. What had the stealing of a blue-and-silver cross from a priest from Essex to do with chucking soup at wallpaper? What had it to do with calling nuts oranges, or with paying for windows first and breaking them afterwards? He had come to the end of his chase; yet somehow he had missed the middle of it. When he failed (which was seldom), he had usually grasped the clue, but nevertheless missed the criminal. Here he had grasped the criminal, but still he could not grasp the clue.

The two figures that they followed were crawling like black flies across the huge green contour of a hill. They were evidently sunk in conversation, and perhaps did not notice where they were going; but they were certainly going to the wilder and more silent heights of the

---

*priest

Heath. As their pursuers rained on them, the latter had to use the undignified attitudes of the deer-stalker, to crouch behind clumps of trees and
even to crawl prostrate in deep grass. By these ungainly ingenuities the
hunters even came close enough to the quarry to hear the murmur of
the discussion, but no word could be distinguished except the word
"reason" recurring frequently in a high and almost childish voice. Once,
over an abrupt dip of land and a dense tangle of thickets, the detectives
actually lost the two figures they were following. They did not find the
trail again for an agonizing ten minutes, and then it led round the brow
of a great dome of hill overlooking an amphitheater of rich and desolate sunset scenery. Under a tree in this commanding yet neglected spot
was an old ramshackle wooden seat. On this seat sat the two priests still
in serious speech together. The gorgeous green and gold still clung to
the darkening horizon; but the dome above was turning slowly from
peacock-green to peacock-blue, and the stars detached themselves more
and more like solid jewels. Mutely motioning to his followers, Valentin
contrived to creep up behind the big branching tree, and, standing there
in deathly silence, heard the words of the strange priests for the first
time.

After he had listened for a minute and a half, he was gripped by a
devilish doubt. Perhaps he had dragged the two English policemen to
the wastes of a nocturnal heath on an errand no saner than seeking figs
on thistles. For the two priests were talking exactly like priests, piously,
with learning and leisure, about the most aerial enigmas of theology.
The little Essex priest spoke the more simply, with his round face turned
to the strengthening stars; the other talked with his head bowed, as if
he were not even worthy to look at them. But no more innocently clerical conversation could have been heard in any white Italian cloister or
black Spanish cathedral.

The first he heard was the tail of one of Father Brown's sentences,
which ended: ". . . what they really meant in the Middle Ages by the
heavens being incorruptible."

The taller priest nodded his bowed head and said:

"Ah, yes, these modern infidels appeal to their reason; but who can
look at those millions of worlds and not feel that there may well be wonderful universes above us where reason is utterly unreasonable?"

"No," said the other priest; "reason is always reasonable, even in the last limbo, in the lost borderland of things. I know that people charge the Church with lowering reason, but it is just the other way. Alone on earth, the Church makes reason really supreme. Alone on earth, the Church affirms that God Himself is bound by reason."

The other priest raised his austere face to the spangled sky and said:

"Yet who knows if in that infinite universe—?"

"Only infinite physically," said the little priest, turning sharply in his seat, "not infinite in the sense of escaping from the laws of truth."

Valentin behind his tree was tearing his fingernails with silent fury. He seemed almost to hear the sniggers of the English detectives whom he had brought so far on a fantastic guess only to listen to the metaphysical gossip of two mild old parsons. In his impatience he lost the equally elaborate answer of the tall cleric, and when he listened again it was again Father Brown who was speaking:

"Reason and justice grip the remotest and the loneliest star. Look at those stars. Don't they look as if they were single diamonds and sapphires? Well, you can imagine any mad botany or geology you please. Think of forests of adamant with leaves of brilliants. Think the moon is a blue moon, a single elephantine sapphire. But don't fancy that all that frantic astronomy would make the smallest difference to the reason and justice of conduct. On plains of opal, under cliffs cut out of pearl, you would still find a notice board, 'Thou shalt not steal.'"

Valentin was just in the act of rising from his rigid and crouching attitude and creeping away as softly as might be, felled by the one great folly of his life. But something in the very silence of the tall priest made him stop until the latter spoke. When at last he did speak, he said simply, his head bowed and his hands on his knees:

"Well, I still think that other worlds may perhaps rise higher than our reason. The mystery of heaven is unfathomable, and I for one can only bow my head."

Then, with brow yet bent and without changing by the faintest shade his attitude or voice, he added:

"Just hand over that sapphire cross of yours, will you? We're all alone here, and I could pull you to pieces like a straw doll."

The utterly unaltered voice and attitude added a strange violence to that shocking change of speech. But the guarder of the relic only seemed to turn his head by the smallest section of the compass. He seemed still to have a somewhat foolish face turned to the stars. Perhaps he had not understood. Or, perhaps, he had understood and sat rigid with terror.

"Yes," said the tall priest, in the same low voice and in the same still posture, "yes, I am Flambeau."

Then, after a pause, he said:

"Come, will you give me that cross?"

"No," said the other, and the monosyllable had an odd sound.

Flambeau suddenly flung off all his pontifical pretensions. The great robber leaned back in his seat and laughed low but long.

"No," he cried; "you won't give it me, you proud prelate. You won't give it me, you little celibate simpleton. Shall I tell you why you won't give it me? Because I've got it already in my own breast-pocket."

The small man from Essex turned what seemed to be a dazed face in the dusk, and said, with the timid eagerness of "The Private Secretary":

"Are—are you sure?"

Flambeau yelled with delight.

"Really, you're as good as a three-act farce," he cried. "Yes, you turnip, I am quite sure. I had the sense to make a duplicate of the right parcel, and now, my friend, you've got the duplicate, and I've got the jewels. An old dodge, Father Brown—a very old dodge."

"Yes," said Father Brown, and passed his hand through his hair with the same strange vagueness of manner. "Yes, I've heard of it before."

The colossus of crime leaned over to the little rustic priest with a sort of sudden interest.

"*You* have heard of it?" he asked. "Where have *you* heard of it?"

"Well, I mustn't tell you his name, of course," said the little man simply. "He was a penitent, you know. He had lived prosperously for about twenty years entirely on duplicate brown-paper parcels. And so, you see, when I began to suspect you, I thought of this poor chap's way of doing it at once."

"Began to suspect me?" repeated the outlaw with increased intensity. "Did you really have the gumption to suspect me just because I brought you up to this bare part of the heath?"

"No, no," said Brown with an air of apology. "You see, I suspected

you when we first met. It's that little bulge up the sleeve where you people have the spiked bracelet."

"How in Tartarus," cried Flambeau, "did you ever hear of the
spiked bracelet?"

"Oh, one's little flock, you know!" said Father Brown, arching his
eyebrows rather blankly. "When I was a curate in Hartlepool, there were
three of them with spiked bracelets. So, as I suspected you from the first,
don't you see, I made sure that the cross should go safe, anyhow. I'm
afraid I watched you, you know. So at last I saw you change the parcels.
Then, don't you see, I changed them back again. And then I left the
right one behind."

"Left it behind?" repeated Flambeau, and for the first time there was
another note in his voice beside his triumph.

"Well, it was like this," said the little priest, speaking in the same
unaffected way. "I went back to that sweet-shop and asked if I'd left a
parcel, and gave them a particular address if it turned up. Well, I knew
I hadn't; but when I went away again I did. So, instead of running after
me with that valuable parcel, they have sent it flying to a friend of mine
in Westminster." Then he added rather sadly: "I learnt that, too, from a
poor fellow in Hartlepool. He used to do it with handbags he stole at
railway stations, but he's in a monastery now. Oh, one gets to know, you
know," he added, rubbing his head again with the same sort of desperate apology. "We can't help being priests. People come and tell us these
things."

Flambeau tore a brown-paper parcel out of his inner pocket and
rent it in pieces. There was nothing but paper and sticks of lead inside
it. He sprang to his feet with a gigantic gesture, and cried:

"I don't believe you. I don't believe a bumpkin like you could manage all that. I believe you've still got the stuff on you, and if you don't
give it up—why, we're all alone, and I'll take it by force!"

"No," said Father Brown simply, and stood up also; "you won't take
it by force. First, because I really haven't still got it. And, second,
because we are not alone."

Flambeau stopped in his stride forward.

"Behind that tree," said Father Brown, pointing, "are two strong
policemen and the greatest detective alive. How did they come here, do
you ask? Why, I brought them, of course! How did I do it? Why, I'll tell

you if you like! Lord bless you, we have to know twenty such things when we work among the criminal classes! Well, I wasn't sure you were a thief, and it would never do to make a scandal against one of our own clergy. So I just tested you to see if anything would make you show yourself. A man generally makes a small scene if he finds salt in his coffee; if he doesn't, he has some reason for keeping quiet. I changed the salt and sugar, and *you* kept quiet. A man generally objects if his bill is three times too big. If he pays it, he has some motive for passing unnoticed. I altered your bill, and *you* paid it."

The world seemed waiting for Flambeau to leap like a tiger. But he was held back as by a spell—he was stunned with the utmost curiosity.

"Well," went on Father Brown, with lumbering lucidity, "as you wouldn't leave any tracks for the police, of course somebody had to. At every place we went to, I took care to do something that would get us talked about for the rest of the day. I didn't do much harm—a splashed wall, spilt apples, a broken window; but I saved the cross, as the cross will always be saved. It is at Westminster by now. I rather wonder you didn't stop it with the Donkey's Whistle."

"With the what?" asked Flambeau.

"I'm glad you've never heard of it," said the priest, making a face. "It's a foul thing. I'm sure you're too good a man for a Whistler. I couldn't have countered it even with the Spots myself; I'm not strong enough in the legs."

"What on earth are you talking about?" asked the other.

"Well, I did think you'd know the Spots," said Father Brown, agreeably surprised. "Oh, you can't have gone so very wrong yet!"

"How in blazes do you know all these horrors?" cried Flambeau.

The shadow of a smile crossed the round, simple face of his clerical opponent.

"Oh, by being a celibate simpleton, I suppose," he said. "Has it never struck you that a man who does next to nothing but hear men's real sins is not likely to be wholly unaware of human evil? But, as a matter of fact, another part of my trade, too, made me sure you weren't a priest."

"What?" asked the thief, almost gaping.

"You attacked reason," said Father Brown. "It's bad theology."

And even as he turned away to collect his property, the three police-men came out from under the twilight trees.

Flambeau was an artist and a sportsman. He stepped back and swept Valentin a great bow.

"Do not bow to me, *mon ami*," said Valentin, with silver clearness. "Let us both bow to our master."

And they both stood an instant uncovered, while the little Essex priest blinked about for his umbrella.

The Hint of an Explanation

Graham Greene

Best-selling British novelist Graham Greene (1904-1991) often wrote about the tremendous power of faith, especially among the poor, the downtrodden, the weak-spir-ited and the helpless. In this story, first published in 1949, a small boy resists the temp-tation to violate the sacredness of Communion and in so doing gains "the hint of an explanation" that will profoundly affect the rest of his life.

A long train journey on a late December evening, in this new ver-sion of peace, is a dreary experience. I suppose that my fellow-traveler and I could consider ourselves lucky to have a compartment to ourselves, even though the heating apparatus was not working, even though the lights went out entirely in the frequent Pennine tunnels* and were too dim anyway for us to read our books without straining our eyes, and though there was no restaurant car to give at least a change of scene. It was when we were trying simultaneously to chew the same kind of dry bun bought at the same station buffet that my companion and I came together. Before that we had sat at opposite ends of the car-riage, both muffled to the chin in overcoats, both bent low over type we could barely make out, but as I threw the remains of my cake under the seat our eyes met, and he laid his book down.

By the time we were half-way to Bedwell Junction we had found an enormous range of subjects for discussion; starting with buns and the weather, we had gone on to politics, the government, foreign affairs, the atom bomb, and, by an inevitable progression, God. We had not, how-

*The Pennines are a range of steep hills and valleys stretching from England to Scotland.

ever, become either shrill or acid. My companion, who now sat opposite me, leaning a little forward, so that our knees nearly touched, gave such an impression of serenity that it would have been impossible to quarrel with him, however much our views differed, and differ they did profoundly.

I had soon realized I was speaking to a Catholic, to someone who believed—how do they put it—in an omnipotent and omniscient Deity, while I was what is loosely called an Agnostic. I have a certain intuition (which I do not trust, founded as it may well be on childish experiences and needs) that a God exists, and I am surprised occasionally into belief by the extraordinary coincidences that beset our path like the traps set for leopards in the jungle, but intellectually I am revolted at the whole notion of such a God Who can so abandon His creatures to the enormities of Free Will. I found myself expressing this view to my companion, who listened quietly and with respect. He made no attempt to interrupt: he showed none of the impatience or the intellectual arrogance I have grown to expect from Catholics; when the lights of a wayside station flashed across his face that had escaped hitherto the rays of the one globe working in the compartment, I caught a glimpse suddenly of—what? I stopped speaking, so strong was the impression. I was carried back ten years, to the other side of the great useless conflict, to a small town, Gisors in Normandy. I was again, for a moment, walking on the ancient battlements and looking down across the gray roofs, until my eyes for some reason lit on one gray stony "back" out of the many, where the face of a middle-aged man was pressed against a windowpane (I suppose that face has ceased to exist now, just as I believe the whole town with its medieval memories has been reduced to rubble). I remembered saying to myself with astonishment, "That man is happy—completely happy." I looked across the compartment at my fellow-traveler, but his face was already again in shadow. I said weakly, "When you think what God—if there is a God—allows. It's not merely the physical agonies, but think of the corruption, even of children. . . ."

He said, "Our view is so limited," and I was disappointed at the conventionality of his reply. He must have been aware of my disappointment (it was as though our thoughts were huddled as closely as ourselves for warmth), for he went on, "Of course there is no answer here. We catch hints. . . ." and then the train roared into another tunnel and the lights again went out. It was the longest tunnel yet; we went rocking down it, and the cold seemed to become more intense with the darkness like an icy fog (perhaps when one sense—of sight—is robbed of sensation, the others grow more sensitive). When we emerged into the mere gray of night and the globe lit up once more, I could see that my companion was leaning back on his seat.

I repeated his last word as a question, "Hints?"

"Oh, they mean very little in cold print—or cold speech," he said, shivering in his overcoat. "And they mean nothing at all to a human being other than the man who catches them. They are not scientific evidence—or evidence at all for that matter. Events that don't, somehow, turn out as they were intended—by the human actors I mean, or by the thing behind the human actors."

"The thing?"

"The word Satan is so anthropomorphic."

I had to lean forward now: I wanted to hear what he had to say. I am—I really am, God knows—open to conviction.

He said, "One's words are so crude, but I sometimes feel pity for that thing. It is so continually finding the right weapon to use against its Enemy and the weapon breaks in its own breast. It sometimes seems to me so—powerless. You said something just now about the corruption of children. It reminded me of something in my own childhood. You are the first person—except for one—that I have thought of telling it to, perhaps because you are anonymous. It's not a very long story, and in a way it's relevant."

I said, "I'd like to hear it."

"You mustn't expect too much meaning. But to me there seems to be a hint. That's all. A hint."

He went slowly on, turning his face to the pane, though he could have seen nothing real in the whirling world outside except an occasional signal lamp, a light in a window, a small country station torn backwards by our rush, picking his words with precision. He said, "When I was a child they taught me to serve at Mass. The church was a small one, for there were very few Catholics where I lived. It was a market town in East Anglia, surrounded by flat, chalky fields and ditches—so many ditches. I don't suppose there were fifty Catholics all told, and for some reason there was a tradition of hostility to us. Perhaps it went back to the burning of a Protestant martyr in the sixteenth century—there was a stone marking the place near where the meat stalls stood on Wednesdays. I was only half aware of the enmity, though I knew that my school nickname of Popey Martin had something to do with my religion, and I had heard that my father was nearly excluded from the Constitutional Club when he first came to the town.

"Every Sunday I had to dress up in my surplice and serve Mass. I hated it—I have always hated dressing up in any way (which is funny when you come to think of it), and I never ceased to be afraid of losing my place in the service and doing something which would put me to ridicule. Our services were at a different hour from the Anglican, and as our small, far-from-select band trudged out of the hideous chapel the whole of the townsfolk seemed to be on the way past to the proper church—I always thought of it as the proper church. We had to pass the parade of their eyes, indifferent, supercilious, mocking; you can't imagine how seriously religion can be taken in a small town, if only for social reasons.

"There was one man in particular; he was one of the two bakers in the town, the one my family did not patronize. I don't think any of the Catholics patronized him because he was called a free-thinker—an odd title, for, poor man, no one's thoughts were less free than his. He was hemmed in by his hatred—his hatred of us. He was very ugly to look at, with one wall-eye and a head the shape of a turnip, with the hair gone on the crown, and he was unmarried. He had no interests, apparently, but his baking and his hatred, though now that I am older I begin to see other sides to his nature—it did contain, perhaps, a certain furtive love. One would come across him suddenly sometimes on a country walk, especially if one were alone and it was Sunday. It was as if he rose from the ditches, and the smear of chalk on his clothes reminded one of the flour on his working over-alls. He would have a stick in his hand and stab at the hedges, and if his mood were very black he would call out after one strange abrupt words like a foreign tongue—I know the meaning of those words, of course, now. Once the police went to his house because of what a boy said he'd seen, but nothing came of it except that the hate shackled him closer. His name was Blacker and he terrified me.

"I think he had a particular hatred of my father—I don't know why. My father was manager of the Midland Bank, and it's possible that at

some time Blacker may have had unsatisfactory dealings with the bank;
my father was a very cautious man who suffered all his life from anxiety about money—his own and other people's. If I try and picture
Blacker now I see him walking along a narrowing path between high
windowless walls, and at the end of the path stands a small boy of ten—
me. I don't know whether it's a symbolic picture or the memory of one
of our encounters—our encounters somehow got more and more frequent. You talked just now about the corruption of children. That poor
man was preparing to revenge himself on everything he hated—my
father, the Catholics, the God whom people persisted in crediting—and
that by corrupting me. He had evolved a horrible and ingenious plan.

"I remember the first time I had a friendly word from him. I was
passing his shop as rapidly as I could when I heard his voice call out with
a kind of sly subservience as though he were an under servant. 'Master
David,' he called, 'Master David,' and I hurried on. But the next time I
passed that way he was at his door (he must have seen me coming) with
one of those curly cakes in his hand that we called Chelsea buns. I didn't
want to take it, but he made me, and then I couldn't be other than polite
when he asked me to come into his parlor behind the shop and see
something very special.

"It was a small electric railway—a rare sight in those days, and he
insisted on showing me how it worked. He made me turn the switches
and stop and start it, and he told me that I could come in any morning
and have a game with it. He used the word 'game' as though it were
something secret, and it's true that I never told my family of this invi-
tation and of how, perhaps twice a week those holidays, the desire to
control that little railway became over-powering, and looking up and
down the street to see if I were observed, I would dive into the shop."

Our larger, dirtier, adult train drove into a tunnel and the light went
out. We sat in darkness and silence, with the noise of the train blocking
our ears like wax. When we were through we didn't speak at once and
I had to prick him into continuing. "An elaborate seduction," I said.

"Don't think his plans were as simple as that," my companion said,
"or as crude. There was much more hate than love, poor man, in his
make-up. Can you hate something you don't believe in? And yet he
called himself a free-thinker. What an impossible paradox, to be free and
to be so obsessed. Day by day all through those holidays his obsession

must have grown, but he kept a grip; he bided his time. Perhaps that thing I spoke of gave him the strength and the wisdom. It was only a week from the end of the holidays that he spoke to me on what concerned him so deeply.

"I heard him behind me as I knelt on the floor, coupling two coaches. He said, 'You won't be able to do this, Master David, when school starts.' It wasn't a sentence that needed any comment from me any more than the one that followed. 'You ought to have it for your own, you ought,' but how skillfully and unemphatically he had sowed the longing, the idea of a possibility. . . . I was coming to his parlor every day now; you see, I had to cram every opportunity in before the hated term started again, and I suppose I was becoming accustomed to Blacker, to that wall-eye, that turnip head, that nauseating subservience. The Pope, you know, describes himself as 'the servant of the servants of God' and Blacker—I sometimes think that Blacker was 'the servant of the servants of . . . ,' well, let it be.

"The very next day, standing in the doorway watching me play, he began to talk to me about religion. He said, with what untruth even I recognized, how much he admired the Catholics; he wished he could believe like that, but how could a baker believe? He accented 'a baker' as one might say a biologist, and the tiny train spun round the gauge O track. He said, 'I can bake the things you eat just as well as any Catholic can,' and disappeared into his shop. I hadn't the faintest idea what he meant. Presently he emerged again, holding in his hand a little wafer. 'Here,' he said, 'eat that and tell me. . . .' When I put it in my mouth I could tell that it was made in the same way as our wafers for Communion—he had got the shape a little wrong, that was all—and I felt guilty and irrationally scared. 'Tell me,' he said, 'what's the difference?'"

"'Difference?'" I asked.

"'Isn't that just the same as you eat in church?'

"I said smugly, 'It hasn't been consecrated.'

"He said, 'Do you think, if I put the two of them under a microscope, you could tell the difference?'

"But even at ten I had the answer to that question. 'No,' I said, 'the—accidents don't change,' stumbling a little on the word 'accidents' which had suddenly conveyed to me the idea of death and wounds.

"Blacker said with sudden intensity, 'How I'd like to get one of your ones in my mouth—just to see. . . .'

"It may seem odd to you, but this was the first time that the idea of transubstantiation really lodged in my mind. I had learned it all by rote; I had grown up with the idea. The Mass was as lifeless to me as the sentences in *De Bello Gallico*;* communion a routine like drill in the schoolyard, but here suddenly I was in the presence of a man who took it seriously, as seriously as the priest whom naturally one didn't count—it was his job. I felt more scared than ever.

"He said, 'It's all nonsense, but I'd just like to have it in my mouth.'

"'You could if you were a Catholic,' I said naively.

"He gazed at me with his one good eye, like a Cyclops. He said, 'You serve at Mass, don't you? It would be easy for you to get at one of those things. I tell you what I'd do—I'd swap this electric train for one of your wafers—consecrated, mind. It's got to be consecrated.'

"'I could get you one out of the box,' I said. I think I still imagined that his interest was a baker's interest—to see how they were made.

"'Oh, no,' he said, 'I want to see what your God tastes like.'

"'I couldn't do that.'

"'Not for a whole electric train, just for yourself? You wouldn't have any trouble at home. I'd pack it up and put a label inside that your dad could see: "For my bank manager's little boy from a grateful client." He'd be pleased as punch with that.'

"Now that we are grown men it seems a trivial temptation, doesn't it? But try to think back to your own childhood. There was a whole circuit of rails there on the floor at our feet, straight rails and curved, and a little station with porters and passengers, a tunnel, a foot-bridge, a level crossing, two signals, buffers, of course—and, above all, a turntable. The tears of longing came into my eyes when I looked at the turntable. It was my favorite piece—it looked so ugly and practical and true. I said weakly, 'I wouldn't know how.'

"How carefully he had been studying the ground! He must have slipped several times into Mass at the back of the church. It would have been no good, you understand, in a little town like that, presenting himself for communion. Everybody there knew him for what he was. He said to me, 'When you've been given communion you could just put it

---

*title of a history of the Gallic Wars (58 B.C.-51 B.C.) by Julius Caesar

under your tongue a moment. He serves you and the other boy first, and I saw you once go out behind the curtain straight afterwards. You'd forgotten one of those little bottles.'

"'The cruet,' I said.

"'Pepper and salt.' He grinned at me jovially, and I—well, I looked at the little railway which I could no longer come and play with when term started. I said, 'You'd just swallow it, wouldn't you?'

"'Oh, yes,' he said. 'I'd just swallow it.'

"Somehow I didn't want to play with the train any more that day. I got up and made for the door, but he detained me, gripping my lapel. He said, 'This will be a secret between you and me. Tomorrow's Sunday. You come along here in the afternoon. Put it in an envelope and post it to me. Monday morning the train will be delivered bright and early.'

"'Not tomorrow,' I implored him.

"'I'm not interested in any other Sunday,' he said. 'It's your only chance.' He shook me gently backwards and forwards. 'It will always have to be a secret between you and me,' he said. 'Why, if anyone knew they'd take away the train and there'd be me to reckon with. I'd bleed you something awful. You know how I'm always about on Sunday walks. You can't avoid a man like me. I crop up. You wouldn't even be safe in your own house. I know ways to get into houses when people are asleep.' He pulled me into the shop after him and opened a drawer. In the drawer was an odd looking key and a cut-throat razor. He said, 'There's a master key that opens all locks and that—that's what I bleed people with.' Then he patted my cheek with his plump, floury fingers and said, 'Forget it. You and me are friends.'

"That Sunday Mass stays in my head, every detail of it, as though it had happened only a week ago. From the moment of the Confession to the moment of Consecration it had a terrible importance; only one other Mass has ever been so important to me—perhaps not even one, for this was a solitary Mass which would never happen again. It seemed as final as the last Sacrament when the priest bent down and put the wafer in my mouth where I knelt before the altar with my fellow-server.

"I suppose I had made up my mind to commit this awful act—for, you know, to us it must always seem an awful act—from the moment when I saw Blacker watching from the back of the church. He had put on his best black Sunday clothes and, as though he could never quite escape the smear of his profession, he had a dab of dried talcum on his cheek, which he had presumably applied after using that cut-throat of his. He was watching me closely all the time, and I think it was fear—fear of that terrible undefined thing called bleeding—as much as covetousness that drove me to carry out my instructions.

"My fellow-server got briskly up and, taking the paten, preceded Father Carey to the altar rail where the other communicants knelt. I had the Host lodged under my tongue: it felt like a blister. I got up and made for the curtain to get the cruet that I had purposely left in the sacristy. When I was there I looked quickly round for a hiding place and saw an old copy of the *Universe* lying on a chair. I took the Host from my mouth and inserted it between two sheets—a little damp mess of pulp. Then I thought: perhaps Father Carey has put out the paper for a particular purpose and he will find the Host before I have time to remove it, and the enormity of my act began to come home to me when I tried to imagine what punishment I should incur. Murder is sufficiently trivial to have its appropriate punishment, but for this act the mind boggled at the thought of any retribution at all. I tried to remove the Host, but it stuck clammily between the pages, and in desperation I tore out a piece of the newspaper and, screwing the whole thing up, stuck it in my trousers pocket. When I came back through the curtain carrying the cruet my eyes met Blacker's. He gave me a grin of encouragement and unhappiness—yes, I am sure, unhappiness. Was it perhaps that the poor man was all the time seeking something incorruptible?

"I can remember little more of that day. I think my mind was shocked and stunned, and I was caught up too in the family bustle of Sunday. Sunday in a provincial town is the day for relations. All the family are at home, and unfamiliar cousins and uncles are apt to arrive, packed in the back seats of other people's cars. I remember that some crowd of the kind descended on us and pushed Blacker temporarily out of the foreground of my mind. There was somebody called Aunt Lucy, with a loud hollow laugh that filled the house with mechanical merriment like the sound of recorded laughter from inside a hall of mirrors, and I had no opportunity to go out alone even if I had wished to. When six o'clock came and Aunt Lucy and the cousins departed and peace returned, it was too late to go to Blacker's, and at eight it was my own bed-time.

"I think I had half forgotten what I had in my pocket. As I emptied my pocket the little screw of newspaper brought quickly back the Mass, the priest bending over me, Blacker's grin. I laid the packet on the chair by my bed and tried to go to sleep, but I was haunted by the shadows on the wall where the curtains blew, the squeak of furniture, the rustle in the chimney, haunted by the presence of God there on the chair. The Host had always been to me—well, the Host. I knew theoretically, as I have said, what I had to believe, but suddenly, as someone whistled in the road outside, whistled secretively, knowingly, to me, I knew that this which I had beside my bed was something of infinite value—something a man would pay for with his whole peace of mind, something that was so hated one could love it as one loves an outcast or a bullied child. These are adult words, and it was a child of ten who lay scared in bed, listening to the whistle from the road, Blacker's whistle, but I think he felt fairly clearly what I am describing now. That is what I meant when I said this Thing, whatever it is, that seizes every possible weapon against God, is always, everywhere, disappointed at the moment of success. It must have felt as certain of me as Blacker did. It must have felt certain, too, of Blacker. But I wonder, if one knew what happened later to that poor man, whether one would not find again that the weapon had been turned against its own breast.

"At last I couldn't bear that whistle any more and got out of bed. I opened the curtains a little way, and there right under my window, the moonlight on his face, was Blacker. If I had stretched my hand down, his fingers reaching up could almost have touched mine. He looked up at me, flashing the one good eye, with hunger—I realize now that near-success must have developed his obsession almost to the point of madness. Desperation had driven him to the house. He whispered up at me, 'David, where is it?'

"I jerked my head back at the room. 'Give it to me,' he said. 'Quick. You shall have the train in the morning.'

"I shook my head. He said, 'I've got the bleeder here, and the key. You'd better toss it down.'

"'Go away,' I said, but I could hardly speak for fear.

"'I'll bleed you first and then I'll have it just the same.'"

"'Oh, no, you won't,' I said. I went to the chair and picked it— Him—up. There was only one place where He was safe.

"I couldn't separate the Host from the paper, so I swallowed both. The newsprint stuck like a prune skin to the back of my throat, but I rinsed it down with water from the ewer. Then I went back to the window and looked down at Blacker. He began to wheedle me. 'What have you done with it, David? What's the fuss? It's only a bit of bread,' looking so longingly and pleadingly up at me that even as a child I wondered whether he could really think that, and yet desire it so much.

"'I swallowed it,' I said.

"'Swallowed it?'

"'Yes,' I said. 'Go away.'

"Then something happened which seems to me now more terrible than his desire to corrupt or my thoughtless act: he began to weep—the tears ran lopsidedly out of the one good eye and his shoulders shook. I only saw his face for a moment before he bent his head and strode off, the bald turnip head shaking, into the dark. When I think of it now, it's almost as if I had seen that Thing weeping for its inevitable defeat. It had tried to use me as a weapon, and now I had broken in its hands and it wept its hopeless tears through one of Blacker's eyes."

The black furnaces of Bedwell Junction gathered around the line. The points switched and we were tossed from one set of rails to another. A spray of sparks, a signal light changing to red, tall chimneys jetting into the gray night sky, the fumes of steam from stationary engines—half the cold journey was over, and now remained the long wait for the slow cross-country train. I said, "It's an interesting story. I think I should have given Blacker what he wanted. I wonder what he would have done with it."

"I really believe," my companion said, "that he would first of all have put it under his microscope—before he did all the other things I expect he had planned."

"And the hints," I said. "I don't quite see what you mean by that."

"Oh, well," he said vaguely, "you know for me it was an odd beginning, that affair, when you come to think of it," but I never should have known what he meant had not his coat, when he rose to take his bag from the rack, come open and disclosed the collar of a priest.

I said, "I suppose you think you owe a lot to Blacker."

"Yes," he said, "you see, I am a very happy man."

LOVE

The Other Wise Man

Henry Van Dyke

(Adapted and abridged)

Henry van Dyke (1852-1933) was an American Presbyterian clergyman, educator, and novelist. The Other Wise Man *was one of his most popular tales. The narrator tells us about a dream in which Artaban, a member of the priestly caste of ancient Persia known as the Magi or Wise Men, sets off for Bethlehem to find the King whose coming was foretold by the stars and to present him with a gift of three precious jewels. But he stops to aid a wounded man and misses the caravan to Bethlehem. Artaban wanders for more than thirty years, until one day he enters Jerusalem and hears that the King for whom he has long been searching is about to be crucified. On his way to ransom Jesus with his one remaining jewel, he hears a cry for help from a young girl about to be sold into slavery. He is torn between fulfilling his life-long dream and helping a stranger in need, but in the end he knows that, whatever the cost, he must perform one final act of love.*

You know the story of the Three Wise Men of the East, and how they traveled from far away to offer their gifts at the manger-cradle in Bethlehem. But have you ever heard the story of the Other Wise Man, who also saw the star in its rising, and set out to follow it, yet did not arrive with his brethren in the presence of the young child Jesus? Of the great desire of this fourth pilgrim, and how it was denied, yet accomplished in the denial; of his many wanderings and the probations of his soul; of the long way of his seeking and the strange way of his finding the One whom he sought—I would tell the tale as I have heard fragments of it in the Hall of Dreams, in the palace of the Heart of Man.

In the days when Augustus Caesar was master of many kings and Herod reigned in Jerusalem, there lived in the city of Ecbatana, among the mountains of Persia, a certain man named Artaban. His house stood close to the outermost of the walls which encircled the royal treasury. From his roof he could look over the seven-fold battlements of black and white and crimson and blue and red and silver and gold, to the hill where the summer palace of the Parthian emperors glittered like a jewel in a crown.

Around the dwelling of Artaban spread a fair garden, a tangle of flowers and fruit-trees, watered by a score of streams descending from the slopes of Mount Orontes, and made musical by innumerable birds. But all color was lost in the soft and odorous darkness of the late September night, and all sounds were hushed in the deep charm of its silence, save the splashing of the water, like a voice half-sobbing and half-laughing under the shadows. High above the trees a dim glow of light shone through the curtained arches of the upper chamber, where the master of the house was holding council with his friends.

He stood by the doorway to greet his guests—a tall, dark man of about forty years, with brilliant eyes set near together under his broad brow, and firm lines graven around his fine, thin lips; the brow of a dreamer and the mouth of a soldier, a man of sensitive feeling but inflexible will—one of those who, in whatever age they may live, are born for inward conflict and a life of quest.

His robe was of pure white wool, thrown over a tunic of silk; and a white, pointed cap, with long lapels at the sides, rested on his flowing black hair. It was the dress of the ancient priesthood of the Magi, called the fire-worshippers.

"Welcome!" he said, in his low, pleasant voice, as one after another entered the room, "Welcome, Abdus; peace be with you, Rhodaspes and Tigranes, and with you my father, Abgarus. You are all welcome. This house grows bright with the joy of your presence."

There were nine of the men, differing widely in age, but alike in the richness of their dress of many-colored silks, and in the massive golden collars around their necks, marking them as Parthian nobles, and in the winged circles of gold resting upon their breasts, the sign of the followers of Zoroaster.

They took their places around a small black altar at the end of the room, where a tiny flame was burning. Artaban, standing beside it, and waving a handful of thin tamarisk branches above the fire, fed it with dry sticks of pine and fragrant oils. Then he began the ancient chant of the Yasna, and the voices of his companions joined in the hymn to Ahura-Alazda.

The fire rose with the chant, throbbing as if the flame responded to the music, until it cast a bright illumination through the whole apartment, revealing its simplicity and splendor. The floor was laid with tiles of dark blue veined with white; pilasters of twisted silver stood out against the blue walls; the clear-story of round-arched windows above them was hung with azure silk; the vaulted ceiling was a pavement of blue stones, like the body of heaven in its clearness, sown with silver stars. From the four corners of the roof hung four golden magic-wheels, called the tongues of the gods. At the eastern end, behind the altar, there were two dark-red pillars of porphyry*; above them a lintel of the same stone, on which was carved the figure of a winged archer, with his arrow set to the string and his bow drawn.

The doorway between the pillars, which opened upon the terrace of the roof, was covered with a heavy curtain of the color of a ripe pomegranate, embroidered with innumerable golden rays shooting upward from the floor. In effect the room was like a quiet, starry night, all azure and silver, flushed in the east with rosy promise of the dawn. It was, as the house of a man should be, an expression of the character and spirit of the master.

He turned to his friends when the song was ended, and invited them to be seated on the divan at the western end of the room.

"You have come tonight," said he, looking around the circle, "at my call, as the faithful scholars of Zoroaster, to renew your worship and rekindle your faith in the God of Purity, even as this fire has been rekindled on the altar. We worship not the fire, but Him of whom it is the chosen symbol, because it is the purest of all created things. It speaks to us of one who is Light and Truth. Is it not so, my father?"

"It is well said, my son," answered the venerable Abgarus. "The enlightened are never idolaters. They lift the veil of form and go in to the shrine of reality, and new light and truth are coming to them continually through the old symbols."

"Hear me, then, my father and my friends," said Artaban, "while I tell you of the new light and truth that have come to me through the most ancient of all signs. We have searched the secrets of Nature together, and studied the healing virtues of water and fire and the plants. We have read also the books of prophecy in which the future is dimly

---

*a hard, crystal-marbled Egyptian rock

foretold in words that are hard to understand. But the highest of all learning is the knowledge of the stars. To trace their course is to untangle the threads of the mystery of life from the beginning to the end. If we could follow them perfectly, nothing would be hidden from us. But is not our knowledge of them still incomplete? Are there not many stars still beyond our horizon—lights that are known only to the dwellers in the far south-land, among the spice-trees of Punt and the gold mines of Ophir?"

There was a murmur of assent among the listeners.

"The stars," said Tigranes, "are the thoughts of the Eternal. They are numberless. But the thoughts of man can be counted, like the years of his life. The wisdom of the Magi is the greatest of all wisdoms on earth, because it knows its own ignorance. And that is the secret of power. We keep men always looking and waiting for a new sunrise. But we ourselves understand that the darkness is equal to the light, and that the conflict between them will never be ended."

"That does not satisfy me," answered Artaban, "for, if the waiting must be endless, if there could be no fulfillment of it, then it would not be wisdom to look and wait. We should become like those new teachers of the Greeks, who say that there is no truth, and that the only wise men are those who spend their lives in discovering and exposing the lies that have been believed in the world. But the new sunrise will certainly appear in the appointed time. Do not our own books tell us that this will come to pass, and that men will see the brightness of a great light?"

"That is true," said the voice of Abgarus; "every faithful disciple of Zoroaster knows the prophecy of the Avesta, and carries the word in his heart. 'In that day Sosiosh the Victorious shall arise out of the number of the prophets in the east country. Around him shall shine a mighty brightness, and he shall make life everlasting, incorruptible, and immortal, and the dead shall rise again.'"

"This is a dark saying," said Tigranes, "and it may be that we shall never understand it. It is better to consider the things that are near at hand, and to increase the influence of the Magi in their own country, rather than to look for one who may be a stranger, and to whom we must resign our power."

The others seemed to approve these words. There was a silent feeling of agreement manifest among them; their looks responded with that indefinable expression which always follows when a speaker has uttered the thought that has been slumbering in the hearts of his listeners. But Artaban turned to Abgarus with a glow on his face, and said: "My father, I have kept this prophecy in the secret place of my soul. Religion without a great hope would be like an altar without a living fire. And now the flame has burned more brightly, and by the light of it I have read other words which also have come from the fountain of Truth, and speak yet more clearly of the rising of the Victorious One in his brightness."

He drew from the breast of his tunic two small rolls of fine parchment, with writing upon them, and unfolded them carefully upon his knee.

"In the years that are lost in the past, long before our fathers came into the land of Babylon, there were wise men in Chaldea, from whom the first of the Magi learned the secret of the heavens. And of these Balaam the son of Beor was one of the mightiest. Hear the words of his prophecy: 'There shall come a star out of Jacob, and a scepter shall arise out of Israel.'"

The lips of Tigranes drew downward with contempt, as he said: "Judah was a captive by the waters of Babylon, and the sons of Jacob were in bondage to our kings. The tribes of Israel are scattered through the mountains like lost sheep, and from the remnant that dwells in Judea under the yoke of Rome neither star nor scepter shall arise."

"And yet," answered Artaban, "it was the Hebrew Daniel, the mighty searcher of dreams, the counselor of kings, the wise Belteshazzar, who was most honored and beloved of our great King Cyrus. A prophet of sure things and a reader of the thoughts of the Eternal, Daniel proved himself to our people. And these are the words that he wrote." Artaban read from the second roll: "'Know, therefore, and understand that from the going forth of the commandment to restore Jerusalem, unto the Anointed One, the Prince, the time shall be seven and threescore and two weeks.'"

"But, my son," said Abgarus, doubtfully, "these are mystical numbers. Who can interpret them, or who can find the key that shall unlock their meaning?"

Artaban answered: "It has been shown to me and to my three companions among the Magi—Caspar, Melchior, and Balthazar. We have searched the ancient tablets of Chaldea and computed the time. It falls in this year. We have studied the sky, and in the spring of the year we saw two of the greatest planets draw near together in the sign of the Fish, which is the house of the Hebrews. We also saw a new star there, which shone for one night and then vanished. Now again the two great planets are meeting. This night is their conjunction. My three brothers are watching by the ancient Temple of the Seven Spheres, at Borsippa, in Babylonia, and I am watching here. If the star shines again, they will wait ten days for me at the temple, and then we will set out together for Jerusalem, to see and worship the promised one who shall be born King of Israel. I believe the sign will come. I have made ready for the journey. I have sold my possessions, and bought these three jewels—a sapphire, a ruby, and a pearl—to carry them as tribute to the King. And I ask you to go with me on the pilgrimage, that we may have joy together in finding the Prince who is worthy to be served."

But his friends looked on with strange and alien eyes. A veil of doubt and mistrust came over their faces, like a fog creeping up from the marshes to hide the hills. They glanced at each other with looks of wonder and pity, as those who have listened to incredible sayings, the story of a wild vision, or the proposal of an impossible enterprise.

At last Tigranes said: "Artaban, this is a vain dream. It comes from too much looking upon the stars and the cherishing of lofty thoughts. It would be wiser to spend the time in gathering money for the new fire-temple at Chala. No king will ever rise from the broken race of Israel, and no end will ever come to the eternal strife of light and darkness. He who looks for it is a chaser of shadows. Farewell."

And another said: "Artaban, I have no knowledge of these things, and my office as guardian of the royal treasure binds me here. The quest is not for me. But if thou must follow it, fare thee well."

And another said: "I am ill and unfit for hardship, but there is a man among my servants whom I will send with thee when thou goest, to bring me word how thou farest."

So, one by one, they left the house of Artaban. But Abgarus, the oldest and the one who loved him the best, lingered after the others had gone, and said, gravely: "My son, it may be that the light of truth is in this sign that has appeared in the skies, and then it will surely lead to the Prince and the mighty brightness. Or it may be that it is only a shadow of the light, as Tigranes has said, and then he who follows it will have a long pilgrimage and a fruitless search. But it is better to follow even the shadow of the best than to remain content with the worst. And those who would see wonderful things must often be ready to travel alone. I am too old for this journey, but my heart shall be a companion of thy pilgrimage day and night, and I shall know the end of thy quest. Go in peace."

■

Alone after all, Artaban must indeed ride wisely and well if he would keep the appointed hour with the other Magi; for the route was a hundred and fifty *parasangs*,* and fifteen was the utmost that he could travel in a day. But he knew his horse Vasda's strength, and pushed forward without anxiety, making the fixed distance every day, though he must travel late into the night, and in the morning long before sunrise.

Over many a cold and desolate pass, crawling painfully across the wind-swept shoulders of the hills; down many a black mountain-gorge, where the river roared and raced before him like a savage guide; across many a smiling vale, with terraces of yellow limestone full of vines and fruit-trees; through the oak-groves of Carine and the dark Gates of Zagros, walled in by precipices; into the ancient city of Chala, where the people of Samaria had been kept in captivity long ago; and out again by the mighty portal, riven through the encircling hills, where he saw the image of the High Priest of the Magi sculptured on the wall of rock, with hand uplifted as if to bless the centuries of pilgrims; past the entrance of the narrow defile, filled from end to end with orchards of peaches and figs, through which the river Gyndes foamed down to meet him; over the broad rice-fields, where the autumnal vapors spread their deathly mists; following along the course of the river, under tremulous shadows of poplar and tamarind, among the lower hills; and out upon the flat plain, where the road ran straight as an arrow through the stubble-fields and parched meadows; past the city of Ctesiphon, where the Parthian emperors reigned, and the vast metropolis of Seleucia which

*Persian measure of length, about three-and-a-half miles

Alexander built; across the swirling floods of Tigris and the many channels of Euphrates, flowing yellow through the corn-lands—Artaban pressed onward until he arrived, at nightfall on the tenth day, beneath the shattered walls of populous Babylon.

Vasda was almost spent, and Artaban would gladly have turned into the city to find rest and refreshment for himself and for her. But he knew that it was three hours' journey yet to the Temple of the Seven Spheres, and he must reach the place by midnight if he would find his comrades waiting. So he did not halt, but rode steadily across the stubble-fields.

A grove of date-palms made an island of gloom in the pale yellow sea. As she passed into the shadow Vasda slackened her pace, and began to pick her way more carefully. Near the farther end of the darkness an access of caution seemed to fall upon her. She scented some danger or difficulty; it was not in her heart to fly from it—only to be prepared for it, and to meet it wisely, as a good horse should do. The grove was close and silent as the tomb; not a leaf rustled, not a bird sang. She felt her steps before her delicately, carrying her head low, and sighing now and then with apprehension. At last she gave a quick breath of anxiety and dismay, and stood stock-still, quivering in every muscle, before a dark object in the shadow of the last palm-tree.

Artaban dismounted. The dim starlight revealed the form of a man lying across the road. His humble dress and the outline of his haggard face showed that he was probably one of the Hebrews who still dwelt in great numbers around the city. His pallid skin, dry and yellow as parchment, bore the mark of the deadly fever which ravaged the marsh-lands in autumn. The chill of death was in his lean hand, and, as Artaban released it, the arm fell back inertly upon the motionless breast.

He turned away with a thought of pity, leaving the body to that strange burial which the Magians deemed most fitting—the funeral of the desert, from which the kites and vultures rise on dark wings, and the beasts of prey slink furtively away. When they are gone there is only a heap of white bones on the sand. But, as he turned, a long, faint, ghostly sigh came from the man's lips. The bony fingers gripped the hem of the Magian's robe and held him fast.

Artaban's heart leaped to his throat, not with fear, but with a dumb resentment at the importunity of this blind delay. How could he stay here in the darkness to minister to a dying stranger? What claim had this unknown fragment of human life upon his compassion or his service? If he lingered but for an hour he could hardly reach Borsippa at the appointed time. His companions would think he had given up the journey. They would go without him. He would lose his quest.

But if he went on now, the man would surely die. If Artaban stayed, life might be restored. His spirit throbbed and fluttered with the urgency of the crisis. Should he risk the great reward of his faith for the sake of a single deed of charity? Should he turn aside, if only for a moment, from the following of the star, to give a cup of cold water to a poor, perishing Hebrew?

"God," he prayed, "direct me in the holy path, the way of wisdom which Thou only knowest."

Then he turned back to the sick man. Loosening the grasp of his hand, he carried him to a little mound at the foot of the palm-tree. He unbound the thick folds of the turban and opened the garment above the sunken breast. He brought water from one of the small canals near by, and moistened the sufferer's brow and mouth. He mingled a draught of one of those simple but potent remedies which he carried always in his girdle—for the Magians were physicians as well as astrologers—and poured it slowly between the colorless lips. Hour after hour he labored as only a skillful healer of disease can do. At last the man's strength returned; he sat up and looked about him.

"Who art thou?" he said, in the rude dialect of the country, "and why hast thou sought me here to bring back my life?"

"I am Artaban the Magian, of the city of Ecbatana, and I am going to Jerusalem in search of one who is to be born King of the Jews, a great Prince and Deliverer of all men. I dare not delay any longer upon my journey, for the caravan that has waited for me may depart without me. But see, here is all that I have left of bread and wine, and here is a potion of healing herbs. When thy strength is restored thou canst find the dwellings of the Hebrews among the houses of Babylon."

The Jew raised his trembling hand solemnly to heaven. "Now may the God of Abraham and Isaac and Jacob bless and prosper the journey of the merciful, and bring him in peace to his desired haven. Stay! I have nothing to give thee in return—only this: that I can tell thee where the Messiah must be sought. For our prophets have said that he should be born not in Jerusalem, but in Bethlehem of Judah. May the Lord bring thee in safety to that place, because thou hast had pity upon the sick."

Of course, Artaban missed the other Magi. When he arrived at the appointed meeting place he saw a little cairn of broken bricks, and under them a piece of papyrus. He caught it up and read: "We have waited past the midnight, and can delay no longer. We go to find the King. Follow us across the desert."

Artaban sat down upon the ground and covered his head in despair. "How can I cross the desert," said he, "with no food and a spent horse? I must return to Babylon, sell my sapphire, and buy a train of camels and provisions for the journey. I may never overtake my friends. Only God the merciful knows whether I shall not lose the sight of the King because I tarried to show mercy." There was a silence in the Hall of Dreams, where I was listening to the story of the Other Wise Man. Through this silence I saw, but very dimly, his figure passing over the dreary undulations of the desert, high upon the back of his camel, rocking steadily onward like a ship over the waves.

The land of death spread its cruel net around him. The stony waste bore no fruit but briers and thorns. The dark ledges of rock thrust themselves above the surface here and there, like the bones of perished monsters. Arid and inhospitable mountain-ranges rose before him, furrowed with dry channels of ancient torrents, white and ghastly as scars on the face of nature. Shifting hills of treacherous sand were heaped like tombs along the horizon. By day, the fierce heat pressed its intolerable burden on the quivering air. By night the jackals prowled and barked in the distance, and the lion made the black ravines echo with his hollow roaring, while a bitter, blighting chill followed the fever of the day. Through heat and cold, the Magian moved steadily onward.

Then I saw the blue waters of the Lake of Galilee, and the fertile plain of Esdraelon, and the hills of Ephraim, and the highlands of Judah. Through all these I followed the figure of Artaban moving steadily onward, until he arrived at Bethlehem. And it was the third day after the three Wise Men had come to that place and had found Mary and Joseph, with the young child, Jesus, and had laid their gifts of gold and frankincense and myrrh at his feet.

Then the Other Wise Man drew near, weary, but full of hope, bearing his gifts to offer to the King. "For now at last," he said, "I shall surely find him, though I be alone, and later than my brethren. This is the place of which the Hebrew exile told me that the prophets had spoken, and here I shall behold the rising of the great light. But I must inquire about the visit of my brethren, and to what house the star directed them, and to whom they presented their tribute."

The streets of the village seemed to be deserted, and Artaban wondered whether the men had all gone up to the hill-pastures to bring down their sheep. From the open door of a cottage he heard the sound of a woman's voice singing softly. He entered and found a young mother hushing her baby to rest. She told him of the strangers from the far East who had appeared in the village three days ago, and how they said that a star had guided them to the place where Joseph of Nazareth was lodging with his wife and her new-born child, and how they had paid reverence to the child and given him many rich gifts.

"But the travelers disappeared again," she continued, "as suddenly as they had come. We were afraid at the strangeness of their visit. We could not understand it. The man of Nazareth took the child and his mother, and fled away that same night secretly, and it was whispered that they were going to Egypt. Ever since, there has been a spell upon the village; something evil hangs over it. They say that the Roman soldiers are coming from Jerusalem to force a new tax from us, and the men have driven the flocks and herds far back among the hills, and hidden themselves to escape it."

Artaban listened to her gentle, timid speech, and the child in her arms looked up in his face and smiled, stretching out its rosy hands to grasp at the winged circle of gold on his breast. His heart warmed to the touch. It seemed like a greeting of love and trust to one who had journeyed long in loneliness and perplexity, fighting with his own doubts and fears, and following a light that was veiled in clouds.

"Why might not this child have been the promised Prince?" he asked within himself, as he touched its soft cheek. "Kings have been born ere now in lowlier houses than this, and the favorite of the stars may rise even from a cottage. But it has not seemed good to the God of wisdom to reward my search so soon and so easily. The one whom I seek has gone before me; and now I must follow the King to Egypt."

Suddenly there came the noise of a wild confusion in the streets of the village, a shrieking and wailing of women's voices, a clangor of brazen trumpets and a clashing of swords, and a desperate cry: "The soldiers! The soldiers of Herod! They are killing our children."

The young mother's face grew white with terror. She clasped her child to her bosom, and crouched motionless in the darkest corner of the room, covering him with the folds of her robe, lest he should wake and cry.

But Artaban went quickly and stood in the doorway of the house. His broad shoulders filled the portal from side to side, and the peak of his white cap all but touched the lintel.

The soldiers came hurrying down the street with their swords. At the sight of the stranger in his imposing dress they hesitated with surprise. The captain of the band approached the threshold to thrust him aside. But Artaban did not stir. His face was as calm as though he were watching the stars, and in his eyes there burned that steady radiance before which even the half-tamed hunting leopard shrinks, and the bloodhound pauses in his leap. He held the soldier silently for an instant, and then said in a low voice: "I am all alone in this place, and I am waiting to give this jewel to the prudent captain who will leave me in peace."

He showed the ruby, glistening in the hollow of his hand like a great drop of blood.

The captain was amazed at the splendor of the gem. The pupils of his eyes expanded with desire, and the hard lines of greed wrinkled around his lips. He stretched out his hand and took the ruby.

"March on!" he cried to his men, "there is no child here. The house is empty."

Artaban prayed: "God of truth, forgive my sin! I have said the thing that is not, to save the life of a child. And two of my gifts are gone. I have spent for man that which was meant for God. Shall I ever be worthy to see the face of the King?"

But the voice of the woman, weeping for joy in the shadow behind him, said very gently: "Because thou hast saved the life of my little one, may the Lord bless thee and keep thee; the Lord make His face to shine upon thee and be gracious unto thee; the Lord lift up His countenance upon thee and give thee peace."

■

Again there was a silence in the Hall of Dreams, deeper and more mysterious than the first interval, and I understood that the years of Artaban were flowing very swiftly under the stillness, and I caught only a glimpse, here and there, of the river of his life shining through the mist that concealed its course.

I saw him moving among the throngs of men in populous Egypt, seeking everywhere for traces of the household that had come down from Bethlehem, and finding them under the spreading sycamore-trees of Heliopolis, and beneath the walls of the Roman fortress of New Babylon beside the Nile traces so faint and dim that they vanished before him continually, as footprints on the wet river-sand glisten for a moment with moisture and then disappear.

I saw him again at the foot of the pyramids, which lifted their sharp points into the intense saffron glow of the sunset sky, changeless monuments of the perishable glory and the imperishable hope of man. He looked up into the face of the crouching Sphinx and vainly tried to read the meaning of the calm eyes and smiling mouth. Was it, indeed, the mockery of all effort and all aspiration, as Tigranes had said—the cruel jest of a riddle that has no answer, a search that never can succeed? Or was there a touch of pity and encouragement in that inscrutable smile— a promise that even the defeated should attain a victory, and the disappointed should discover a prize, and the ignorant should be made wise, and the blind should see, and the wandering should come into the haven at last?

I saw him again in an obscure house of Alexandria, taking counsel with a Hebrew rabbi. The venerable man, bending over the rolls of parchment on which the prophecies of Israel were written, read aloud the pathetic words which foretold the sufferings of the promised Messiah—the despised and rejected of men, the man of sorrows and acquainted with grief.

"And remember, my son," said he, fixing his eyes upon the face of Artaban, "the King whom thou seekest is not to be found in a palace, nor among the rich and powerful. If the light of the world and the glory of Israel had been appointed to come with the greatness of earthly splendor, it must have appeared long ago. The light for which the world is waiting is a new light, the glory that shall rise out of patient and

triumphant suffering. And the kingdom which is to be established forever is a new kingdom, the royalty of unconquerable love.

"I do not know how this shall come to pass, nor how the turbulent
kings and peoples of earth shall be brought to acknowledge the Messiah
and pay homage to him. But this I know. Those who seek him will do
well to look among the poor and the lowly, the sorrowful and the
oppressed."

So I saw the other Wise Man again and again, traveling from place
to place, and searching. He passed through countries where famine lay
heavy upon the land, and the poor were crying for bread. He made his
dwelling in plague-stricken cities where the sick were languishing in the
bitter companionship of helpless misery. He visited the oppressed and
the afflicted in the gloom of subterranean prisons, and the crowded
wretchedness of slave-markets, and the weary toil of galley-ships. In all
this populous and intricate world of anguish, though he found none to
worship, he found many to help. He fed the hungry, and clothed the
naked, and healed the sick, and comforted the captive; and his years
passed more swiftly than the weaver's shuttle that flashes back and forth
through the loom while the web grows and the pattern is completed.

It seemed almost as if he had forgotten his quest. But once I saw
him for a moment as he stood alone at sunrise, waiting at the gate of a
Roman prison. He had taken from a secret resting-place in his bosom
the pearl, the last of his jewels. As he looked at it, a mellower luster, a
soft and iridescent light, full of shifting gleams of azure and rose, trembled upon its surface. It seemed to have absorbed some reflection of the
lost sapphire and ruby. So the secret purpose of a noble life draws into
itself the memories of past joy and past sorrow. All that has helped it, all
that has hindered it, is transfused by a subtle magic into its very essence.
It becomes more luminous and precious the longer it is carried close to
the warmth of the beating heart.

Then, at last, while I was thinking of this pearl, and of its meaning,
I heard the end of the story of the other Wise Man.

∎

Three-and-thirty years of the life of Arbatan had passed away, and
he was still a pilgrim and a seeker after the light. His hair, once darker

than the cliffs of Zagros, was now white as the wintry snow that covered them. His eyes, that once flashed like flames of fire, were dull as embers smoldering among the ashes.

Worn and weary and ready to die, but still looking for the King, he had come for the last time to Jerusalem. He had often visited the holy city before, and had searched all its lanes and crowded hovels and black prisons without finding any trace of the family of Nazarenes who had fled from Bethlehem long ago. But now it seemed as if he must make one more effort, and something whispered in his heart that, at last, he might succeed.

It was the season of the Passover. The city was thronged with strangers. The children of Israel, scattered in far lands, had returned to the Temple for the great feast, and there had been a confusion of tongues in the narrow streets for many days.

But on this day a singular agitation was visible in the multitude. The sky was veiled with a portentous gloom. Currents of excitement seemed to flash through the crowd. A secret tide was sweeping them all one way. The clatter of sandals and the soft, thick sound of thousands of bare feet scuffing over the stones, flowed unceasingly along the street that leads to the Damascus gate.

Artaban joined a group of people from his own country, Parthian Jews who had come up to keep the Passover, and inquired of them the cause of the tumult, and where they were going.

"We are going," they answered, "to the place called Golgotha, outside the city walls, where there is to be an execution. Have you not heard what has happened? Two famous robbers are to be crucified, and with them another, called Jesus of Nazareth, a man who has done many wonderful works among the people, so that they love him greatly. But the priests and elders have said that he must die, because he gave himself out to be the Son of God. And Pilate has sent him to the cross because he said that he was the King of the Jews."

How strangely these familiar words fell upon the tired heart of Artaban! They had led him for a lifetime over land and sea. And now they came to him mysteriously, like a message of despair. The King had arisen, but he had been denied and cast out. He was about to perish. Perhaps he was already dying. Could it be the same who had been born in Bethlehem thirty-three years ago, at whose birth the star had appeared in heaven, and of whose coming the prophets had spoken?

Artaban's heart beat unsteadily with that troubled, doubtful apprehension which is the excitement of old age. But he said within himself: "The ways of God are stranger than the thoughts of men, and it may be that I shall find the King, at last, in the hands of his enemies, and shall come in time to offer my pearl for his ransom before he dies."

So the old man followed the multitude with slow and painful steps toward the Damascus gate of the city. Just beyond the entrance of the guard-house a troop of Macedonian soldiers came down the street, dragging a young girl with torn dress and disheveled hair. As the Magian paused to look at her with compassion, she broke suddenly from the hands of her tormentors, and threw herself at his feet, clasping him around the knees. She had seen his white cap and the winged circle on his breast.

"Have pity on me," she cried, "and save me, for the sake of the God of Purity! I also am a daughter of the true religion which is taught by the Magi. My father was a merchant of Parthia, but he is dead, and I am seized for his debts to be sold as a slave. Save me from worse than death!"

Artaban trembled.

It was the old conflict in his soul, which had come to him in the palm-grove of Babylon and in the cottage at Bethlehem—the conflict between the expectation of faith and the impulse of love. Twice the gift which he had consecrated to the worship of religion had been drawn to the service of humanity. This was the third trial, the ultimate probation, the final and irrevocable choice.

Was it his great opportunity, or his last temptation? He could not tell. One thing only was clear in the darkness of his mind—it was inevitable. And does not the inevitable come from God?

One thing only was sure to his divided heart—to rescue this helpless girl would be a true deed of love. And is not love the light of the soul?

He took the pearl from his bosom. Never had it seemed so luminous, so radiant, so full of tender, living luster. He laid it in the hand of the slave.

"This is thy ransom, daughter! It is the last of my treasures which I kept for the King."

While he spoke, the darkness of the sky deepened, and shuddering tremors ran through the earth, heaving convulsively like the breast of one who struggles with mighty grief.

The walls of the houses rocked to and fro. Stones were loosened and crashed into the street. Dust clouds filled the air. The soldiers fled in terror, reeling like drunken men. But Artaban and the girl whom he had ransomed crouched helpless beneath the wall of the Praetorium.*

What had he to fear? What had he to hope? He had given away the last remnant of his tribute for the King. He had parted with the last hope of finding him. The quest was over, and it had failed. But, even in that thought, accepted and embraced, there was peace. It was not resignation. It was not submission. It was something more profound and searching. He knew that all was well, because he had done the best that he could from day to day. He had been true to the light that had been given to him. He had looked for more. And if he had not found it, if a failure was all that came out of his life, doubtless that was the best that was possible. He had not seen the revelation of "life everlasting, incorruptible and immortal." But he knew that even if he could live his earthly life over again, it could not be otherwise than it had been.

One more lingering pulsation of the earthquake quivered through the ground. A heavy tile, shaken from the roof, fell and struck the old man on the temple. He lay breathless and pale, with his gray head resting on the young girl's shoulder, and the blood trickling from the wound. As she bent over him, fearing that he was dead, there came a voice through the twilight, very small and still, like music sounding from a distance, in which the notes are clear but the words are lost. The girl turned to see if someone had spoken from the window above them, but she saw no one.

Then the old man's lips began to move, as if in answer, and she heard him say in the Parthian tongue:

"Not so, my Lord! For when saw I thee and hungered and fed thee? Or thirsty, and gave thee drink? When saw I thee a stranger, and took

---

*a Roman court where prisoners' sentences were handed down

thee in? Or naked, and clothed thee? When saw I thee sick or in prison, and came unto thee? Three-and-thirty years have I looked for thee; but I have never seen thy face, nor ministered to thee, my King."

He ceased, and the sweet voice came again. And again the maid heard it, very faint and far away. But now it seemed as though she understood the words:

"Verily I say unto thee, in as much as thou hast done it unto one of the least of these my brethren, thou, hast done it unto me."

■

A calm radiance of wonder and joy lighted the pale face of Artaban like the first ray of dawn on a snowy mountain-peak. A long breath of relief exhaled gently from his lips.

His journey was ended. His treasures were accepted. The Other Wise Man had found the King.

Give What You Are Given[†]

Jan de Hartog

From The Spiral Road[*]

Dutch-born Quaker novelist Jan de Hartog (1914—) has written many plays and novels that have been made into films and translated into dozens of languages. The Spiral Road *(published in English in 1957) is set in the Dutch East Indies, where Anton Zorgdrager lies near death, overcome with malaria and near-madness. For months, the young doctor has been alone at Outpost Mamawi, which is nothing more than an abandoned railway car in a remote jungle clearing. He has been battling against "guna-guna," the black magic of the cunning and ruthless witch doctor who killed his predecessor, Dr. Ganwitz. But even more importantly, he has been waging a battle against God and refusing to face up to his own sins. Anton's mentor, Dr. Brits-Jansen, has come to rescue him, but he can do nothing. He sends for Willem Waterreus, unaware that the old Salvationist missionary has been undergoing profound doubts about his own faith. In desperation, Willem prays to God and asks what can he possibly give Anton—and God answers that he can give only what he has been given: love.*

---

[*]In some passages the full names of the characters and brief explanations about their identity have been added in order to make it clear to whom the author was referring.

*O*nly holiness, wrote Ganwitz in the diary he left behind, *will work against this black plague*. Brits-Jansen had tried everything in his portable medicine box and, bar holiness, there seemed to be only one solution left: back to civilization, with the unconscious boy on a stretcher, and deliver him into the hands of the psychiatrists in Batavia. That prospect decided him. He would override prejudice, and follow Ganwitz's advice. He sent the *prahu* [boat] with the corporal and four soldiers to Wareni, the nearest settlement, with two telegrams: one for Willem Waterreus: *Zorgdrager dying, you only hope, come soonest via Head of Service Batavia*, and one for his superior, the little runt Kramer, *Zorgdrager . . . permanent coma diagnosis . . . give Waterreus Salvation Army facilities for coming Wareni planewise if costs prohibitive rob my pension regards.*

The *prahu* left, and it seemed a relief that a decision had been made; yet then and there began the most lugubrious week of his life—alone with four terrified Madurese* and a pygmy in a haunted railway carriage in the wilderness; a ghostly hut full of secret rustlings, soft knockings, lispings, hummings and the heartbeat of distant drums, with an unconscious boy dying in trembling lamplight. Never before had he felt such enmity in the jungle; every sound seemed an explosion of hatred, every rustle, crack, squawk or snap in that stillness seemed to emanate from one gigantic living being, watching them, holding its breath, restraining itself from betraying its presence in the mounting fury of its hatred, while it circled slowly and noiselessly around the defenseless railway carriage that cowered in the shrubs. In the end even the barely breathing, unconscious boy seemed to be listening to the silent waiting enemy. It might be loneliness, boredom, anxiety about the boy; whatever it might be, he began to understand how the boy had gone *mataglap* [mad]. The tension became so unbearable that, in the end, he felt like drawing that circle in the sand, slowly, slowly, as he had watched so many natives do before leaping up, shrieking, to throw themselves upon their imaginary enemy, the jungle.

After a couple of days even the pygmy began to droop. At first, he had made tea and cooked the meal in the kitchen on the edge of the

---

*natives of the Javanese island of Madura employed by the Dutch as soldiers

418 THE CHRISTIAN'S TREASURY

clearing with apelike indifference to all supernatural goings-on. But on the second day he used the Primus in the hut; on the third he refused to leave the hut altogether, even to go to the latrine, so he found himself forced to throw him out onto the verandah like a puppy, the moment he noticed him squatting in a corner with sanctimonious eyes. The first night the Madurese slept underneath their own bivouac shelter on the edge of the creek; the second they carried their mats to the verandah; the third they joined him in the hut. The result was unexpected, as he had never believed in familiarity with the dark brother of the Equator: the concentration of their collective human intelligence in that iron box seemed to give him a sort of protection against the panting hatred of the night. They forgot the difference in their worlds and discovered their common humanity in the face of the supernatural menace of the wilderness. For had the Papuans* wandered near the camp, had their drums rolled in the caverns of the forest, they would have prepared themselves with a sigh of relief for a fight between men. But the drums hummed only rarely, and so far away that their rolling seemed a sound of the wilderness itself, a grunting stripped of humanity, part of the slow encirclement of that paralyzing, venomous hatred.

The fourth night they did not sleep. Without betraying that they were consciously doing so, they helped one another to remain awake. For all shared a prehistoric fear: that the demons of the wilderness would pounce upon them and garrote them the moment they let the light of their humanity be hooded by their closed eyelids. They started by sighing on their mats, scratching, coughing, smacking their lips, tossing and turning, slapping the bare skin of their thighs and their arms, as if to swat a mosquito. They had left the lamp burning low, a blue twilight in the night; in the heart of darkness he turned it up and let it blaze, shrill and yellow. They rolled up their mats and started to throw dice while he sat leafing through the diaries once more at the table. After half an hour, he joined them in their game; and at first he won because he cheated. Then he lost because, as his fear deepened, he became concerned that God should feel kindly disposed toward him. But the game soon lost its attraction, for every time the dice clattered and rolled the

---

*New Guinea natives; in this case they are the followers of the witchdoctor and the enemies of all at Outpost Mamawi

wilderness seemed to profit from those small noises by creeping a step nearer outside. In the end, they just sat, leaning against the wall and the table, listening with their eyes glistening in the lamplight. The harder they listened and the more silent they became, the more they heard: strange flutelike warblings wandered through the night, a huge, panting breath seemed to heave close by, as if a colossal body lay just behind the carriage, its ear to the wall. The distant drums pulsated so regularly in that silence that, at last, he realized it was his own heart. The panting behind the thin partition might be that of the dying boy, Anton Zorgdrager, whose breath came almost inaudibly, but seemed to reverberate in the stillness of their listening.

The fifth night, this strange unison into one silent family round the boy's deathbed became so strong that it brought him closer to the natives and the pygmy than he had ever felt since his arrival in the Far East. Never had he been so conscious of their common humanity as during that night. The creatures whom for thirty-five years he had submitted to auscultation and percussion, into whose gullets and recta he had peered, whom he had operated on and inspected, suddenly revealed themselves as his brothers that night, without their exchanging a word. He felt closer to them than he had ever felt to anyone; for, with everyone else, he had always remained I, Brits-Jansen; whereas with those silent Madurese and that whimpering pygmy in the railway carriage of Mamawi he suddenly found himself thinking We. He shared his cigarettes with them, and from the tacit way in which they accepted them and handed round the match with the flame, he realized that they felt the same way. The abyss of three centuries vanished during that night watch; he realized how pathetically superior he had felt to these brothers for thirty-five years, and that he was the poorer for it.

But even that feeling of unity, security, and brotherhood in the face of the menace of prehistoric evils evaporated on the sixth night as the fear grew fiercer. It grew every hour; in the end he knew: one more night like this and someone will run amok. He expected it to be the corporal, for he had stopped blinking his eyes as he sat staring at the lamp as if hypnotized. That glassy stare in a marble face was the beginning.

The seventh night he put everything ready in case of trouble: a rattan rope, a syringe with scopolamine. At four o'clock in the morning, the corporal got up, quietly, but with an odd, jerky stiffness. At the very moment that he stretched out his hand toward his *kris*, they all leaped on him. The pygmy rammed himself between his calves like a pig and tripped him over, the others pinioned arms and legs; within three seconds, his thumb slowly pressed home the piston of the syringe. They dragged the panting madman to the verandah, where he lay vomiting in the darkness, retching and groaning, for twenty minutes; then they dragged him back into the hut, where he lay, limp, on his mat, moaning softly. That night he knew: I have lost. Of course those telegrams were nonsense, of course Willem won't come and, if he does come, it will be even worse nonsense. There is nothing for it but to sail back to Manokwari tomorrow, and let the psychiatrists in Batavia take over. At sunrise, he said, calmly, *"Muatkan"*—load the boat, and discovered how intensely the Madurese had been waiting for that order. Within fifteen minutes, the *prahu* was loaded, the hut emptied; they lifted the stretcher with the boy—and at that moment, something rustled in the forest, and something black slunk through the green shadows in the crown of a tree. If the boy should ever be carried out of the hut, he would die as Ganwitz and Hugenholtz had died: his body pierced by black arrows. He gave the order to unload again. The pygmy cooked a very bad meal, and they sat down in a circle around the stretcher with the boy, waiting for the night.

But no one spoke a word, and he was overcome by a bleak loneliness, for the brothers had become enemies. He knew that they were waiting for a chance to flee and leave him alone under the spell of the *guna-guna*, alone and lost beyond hope in the haunted wilderness. Before night fell, he made them pull the *prahu* ashore, right into the center of the clearing, and after the lamp was lit and they were all gathered together in the railway carriage once more, he sat looking around innocently, but without relaxing for a second. His hands were in his pockets, and in his right-hand pocket was his gun. The boy breathed very weakly, irregularly; they were waiting for his death, and if he did not die within the next twelve hours, there would be fighting in Outpost Mamawi, a crazed outbreak of senseless slaughter, a whole community running amok.

The only one who was with him during those darkest hours, that eternity of listening and waiting, giddy with tension and thirst, was the pygmy. Stegomyia did not long for the security of the open sea, alone in a *prahu* with four mad Madurese; Stegomyia longed for the nearness of his giant friend, for the reassuring radiation of his body warmth, for the sturdy thumping of his fatherly heart underneath the triple layer of singlet, fat and ribs. Stegomyia crept, during that worst night, closer and closer to him, and for the first time he sniffed the smell of the pygmy with a sentimental nostalgia. He began to get weird thoughts, as he sat listening and waiting in the deepening night. He saw himself bargain with Saint Peter for admission of the pygmy into the hereafter. He saw them pass together through gates of gilded marzipan, with in the distance Christmas mangers full of sugar animals on cotton-wool clouds. He saw himself and Stegomyia enter the Colonial Club in The Hague, the dwarf in a miniature dinner jacket and top hat, like Coba the Chimpanzee in the children's zoo in Amsterdam. He saw himself on a raft in the Pacific with an oar for a mast and his singlet for a flag of distress, and Stegomyia fishing, with fleas as bait. He thought for the first time about the pygmy's mother, and saw her hug the mouse-small infant and feed it with a fountain-pen filler. He got so dizzy with the effort of keeping his eyes open, holding his breath to listen, feeling his buttocks go numb, sweating almost audibly in the hot teeming night, that he felt with tears of relief the bites of the first fleas received from Stegomyia in his trembling intimacy. He motioned to the pygmy to catch them; during the next half hour, he sat, his burning eyes wide open, frowning, grinning, and giggling while tiny hands crawled and scurried up and down his back, round his waist and sharp little nails bit here and there like a bird's beak. But in the end even that no longer helped to keep the sleep at bay. A couple more hours, one more hour, and he would sag aside, turn turtle in sleep, snoring, to wake up and find the Madurese gone.

As Stegomyia's flea hunting no longer had any effect, he fought his battle with sleep by standing up. He stood for hours, swaying, snorting, his head bent under the low ceiling, while the Madurese sat motionlessly waiting. When at long last the sun rose, he staggered outside, the pygmy at his heels, shuffled across the clearing toward the jetty, sat down at the end with his legs dangling over the edge and then, with the sigh of a dying bullock, he slumped on his back, asleep. He was awakened by splashing, leaped to his feet, bellowing, "*Brenti, brenti, kembali traperduli!*" and the *prahu* came sailing back obediently, its sail hanging limp in the windless air. He was trying to work out in his mind how the double-crossing b——s had managed to drag the boat into the water without waking him up, when he saw a hand wave at him. A white hand. Then a face smiled and nodded; a white face. Willem.

The arrival of the old Salvationist in Post Mamawi was unforgettable in its normalcy. He climbed ashore, said, "How are you, brother?" and shook his hand, then he looked around at the railway carriage, the flower bed, the flag and the pygmy with cheerful kindness and said, "What a charming spot."

A charming spot. It almost made him burst into tears with relief, tenderness, and nerves. Then the old man asked, "What can I do for you?"

"Nothing," he said, stupidly. "Only, I thought perhaps you could pray a bit for the boy or something. I believe he is—well—bewitched."

Willem looked at him in surprise with his white old man's eyes and said, "Fancy."

He led the way toward the hut. The Madurese, asleep on the floor, woke up with a start and the old man wished them a good morning. Then he bent over the stretcher with the boy, put his hand on his forehead, and the boy moved.

That movement, at that moment, was so uncanny, after all those days and nights of still unconsciousness on that stretcher, that everyone stood gaping at the boy as if they could not believe their eyes. The pygmy, the corporal, the soldiers, he himself, they gaped at the sleeping boy as at a miracle; Willem looked round, puzzled, and asked, "What would you like me to do?"

He put his hands on those thin shoulders and said, "That boy, Willem, has been lying in a coma for a week. I have done everything I could, but I could not bring him back to life. Yet the moment you put your hand on his forehead, he moves!"

"Oh," Willem said, "but what. . . ."

"That boy, Willem," he said, urgently, "is possessed by a devil. I have asked you to come because—because I wanted to try everything to save him, even nonsense. But now I know it is not nonsense, now I believe, I am certain that if you stay and pray for that boy, he has a chance."

"But I am not a faith healer; I. . . ."

"Willem," he said, "for thirty years I tried to save your wife Betsy and cure her leprosy, and I did not succeed. Try to save that boy for me, try for just one night, and. . . ." And then he stopped in embarrassment.

Willem knelt by the side of the stretcher. He took the hands of the boy in his, and looked at him. A dead silence fell in the hut, and everyone held his breath, waiting for the magic word. It was a long time before the word came; the old man held the hands of the boy in his and looked at the gray, cavernous face without speaking. No one moved, for he was about to speak the magic word against the *guna-guna*. But he said nothing; he only held the hands of the boy in his, and looked at him.

When the sun stood in its zenith over Mamawi, he had still said nothing.

When the shadow of the flag had crept up to the verandah, he still held those hands in his, and he had still said nothing.

When the evening mist crept out of the creek toward the hut, and the darkness came out of the forest, he still knelt beside the stretcher, the boy's hand in his, looking at the lifeless face, but the magic word had not been spoken.

When night fell and the dwarf lit the lamp, he still had not moved. He seemed to sleep, staring at the boy's face, but there was a stillness around him that burned with strength.

The Madurese were squatting around him in a circle, waiting for the word, but it did not come. It did not come when the noises of the night began to rustle in the wilderness. It did not come when the flame of the lamp began to twitch, to die. It had not come when all of them, one by one, had fallen asleep. He wanted to remain awake, to go on staring at the white old man, kneeling by that sleeping boy on the stretcher, but, like Peter, he dozed off into a strange, silver sleep and woke up in the blue of the dawn.

The first thing he saw was the empty stretcher, and he closed his eyes again with a feeling of relief; then suddenly, it penetrated to him: the stretcher was empty!

He scrambled to his feet, wide awake, ran outside; on the verandah he had to stop in his tracks so abruptly that he nearly dived down the steps. For there sat the boy, on the steps, his head in his hands, the arm of the old man round his shoulders.

The Madurese, awakened by his exit, gathered silently behind him, peering over his shoulder. He felt Stegomyia press against his knee, until he too stood still and watched. The old man seemed to whisper to the boy, while the sun broke slowly through the rolling clouds of the morning mist. Then Willem stood up, and with him the boy, who staggered away a few steps; then Willem led him back toward the verandah. The Madurese retreated, Stegomyia scurried away, he himself stepped aside with a feeling of awe and took off his helmet as they passed.

When they had vanished inside the hut he slumped in the chair, and though it collapsed with a tearing crash, though he hurled the wreckage over the balustrade, though he stared at the butterflies dancing above the thin flat smoke until his eyes smarted, he did not wake up from his dream. He had seen the truth; old Ganwitz had been right. When Willem Waterreus received the telegram, he went to Batavia at once although he did not understand a word of it. How could he be "the only hope" at a young doctor's deathbed in the wilderness? Only in Batavia, in the office of the Head of the Government Health Service, did he begin to get a notion of what it was all about. A man in shirt sleeves sat behind a table full of telephones at the foot of a chart of the archipelago, and rose to greet him as he came in. "Sorry to have bothered you, Captain," Kramer said, "but this is really Brits-Jansen's idea. Would you mind going to New Guinea?"

"Why?" he asked.

"Young Zorgdrager has gone *mataglap*, and I gather that Brits-Jansen hopes your influence may do him good. Cigar? Oh, I'm sorry, of course not. Mind if I light one?"

"No, not at all. Please go ahead. . . ."

He watched the man strike a match, blow the first smoke of his cigar at the fan that whirred overhead, and then the man said, "If I may give you some advice, without knowing the finer points of the case: I would not let myself be influenced by—how shall I say?—atmospheric conditions. Do you believe in black magic?"

He smiled, despite his uneasiness. "No," he answered, "I don't believe in black magic."

"That's what I thought," said the man, "hence my advice. The trouble with that boy is a bad conscience. If you ask me, he has collapsed in solitude under an exaggerated feeling of guilt. You believe that any sin, however grave it may be, can be forgiven, don't you?"

"Indeed," he replied, "but that doesn't exclude punishment."

"Of course. But, if you ask me, the punishment has been meted out in this case. If I were you, I'd tell that boy that this'll do—I mean: that he has sinned, been punished and mustn't try to be any wiser than Our Lord. A feeling of guilt can also be a form of spiritual pride." He must have looked astonished, for the man smiled and continued, "I don't want to poach on your preserves, sir. You are, after all, a specialist in your own field as I am in mine. But, you see, I've had this boy in front of this table several times, and during my ten years in this office I've known several like him. Son of pious parents, adolescent hatred against everything connected with Christianity, anti-conventional in sexual relationships, emotional crisis with spouse, and then: into the jungle, tail between the legs. The difficulty with those boys is that they will think of their own salvation exclusively, never forget their own souls for anyone else's. Here in the Far East, and certainly in our profession, they all reach crossroads sooner or later, where either they leave their souls to the Almighty and get on with the job, or else disintegrate morally as well as physically into jetsam of the jungle. In the case of this boy Zorgdrager, I would appreciate it if you could help him a bit for he has a good head and might become a really good doctor. Do you follow me?"

"Not quite," he answered, apologetically. "How do you think I can help him?"

"I'm sure, Captain," the man said with a hint of a smile, "that you'll discover that for yourself the moment you set eyes on your patient. I have a plane for you to Wareni. You leave in an hour's time."

He was driven to the airport, to arrive that same night in Wareni. A *prahu* took him along the coast and, during the voyage, he prayed that God would give him one, if only one, indication of what was expected of him. But what God gave him was peace and confidence, and He charged him with His power, but He did not give him the knowledge of how to use it.

At last, after a very hot journey, he arrived in a neat little settlement in the jungle where Brits-Jansen lay asleep on a jetty. He was taken into a railway carriage transformed into a dwelling and there, on a stretcher, lay the boy, unconscious, dirty, and emaciated, like the prodigal son on the threshold of his father's house. A deep compassion welled up in him for that tortured body, that cavernous face, those eyes closed in torment. It was terribly hot and stifling in the room; it made him dizzy and he did not understand exactly what Brits-Jansen told him. "Bewitched," he said excitedly. "Moved only when you touched him." For the first time since Betsy's death, he felt himself overcome by a feeling of insecurity, not doubt, not fear, but a growing unsureness, as if God had overestimated him. For he did not understand a word of it, nothing at all; Brits-Jansen said, "Pray," as if it were a kind of massage, and that made him almost angry with helplessness. In his bewilderment and his increasing feeling of insecurity, he knelt by the side of the boy and took his hands in his and asked God, "Give me an answer," but it was as if he were kneeling alone with that boy in a dark emptiness, waiting.

The boy was unconscious, and only now as he knelt beside him did he see how deeply he had sunk. He was almost unrecognizable as the frightened, perky young sinner he had left behind in that bungalow in Batavia; this was the prodigal son at his journey's end. The face was so moving in its utter loneliness that a small warmth of love and comfort seemed to radiate through his arms into that emaciated body, and then it was as if God gave the answer. "Child," said God to Willem, "I have filled you with the bounty of my love for more than sixty years. Now give me back my talent."

It was a strange answer, and he searched the boy's face to see if perhaps he could find an elucidation of the answer there. And then, perhaps because it grew cooler in the room and because his thoughts slowly came to rest, he realized that the boy was slowly sinking backward into the darkness of death; but it seemed as if the compassion penetrating to him through that darkness caused him to hesitate, as if he were groping blindly around him for the thin thread of hope that was being lowered into the mine shaft of his desolation. A prayer formed in his thoughts: "God, let him live." And with that prayer, it was as if a few drops of his own life drained out of him into that tortured body. It frightened him, for it gave him a sensation that he had not known for a long time: fear of death; as if, in exchange for those few drops of hope and life, a few drops of fear of death had flowed back into him. He sat a few moments in doubt and felt an odd animal urge to let go of the boy's hands and retire within his own prayer; but the thought that God had planted in him came back again: "For sixty years I have filled you with the bounty of my love. Now give me back my talent." Then he began to understand.

Instead of his receiving an answer for the hundred-thousandth time, he must at last provide the answer himself, the answer that God had demanded of His own Son: Here is a human being, one of the countless that are dying at this moment on earth. Are you ready to exchange your life for his? There he lies, a sinner, a weakling, a heathen. I have given you, in my loving-kindness, all the strength, all the love, and all the faith that Betsy attained after a lifetime of dreadful suffering. Now, at the summit of your state of grace; now, when you are about to eke out all you possess to as many human beings as possible for years to come; now I force you to your knees at the side of one worthless human being, and I ask: Are you ready to give it all back to me for the sake of this one? Or is the only answer that you can give to my boundless mercy an abacus, on which you calculate where you can be most useful? Answer, Willem, my child: can it be that the only thing my love has wrought within you is a feeling of being chosen, a human pride? "I have fought for that grace for forty years, I won't sacrifice myself for one black soul, I am worth more than he"? Or do you say: "Father, I under-stand none of it, but Thy will be done"?

He answered: how do I know that it is Thy will? and it seemed as if a wave of his life gushed from his body into the boy, to pull back a wave of the blackest, deepest despair in its stead.

He wanted to get up, to go outside and come to himself, for this was folly. He was giddy with heat, he was an old man, he was not well in the closeness of this hut, his life was oozing away through his arms. Why had these idiots brought him out of his colony, where hundreds were waiting for his help and his comfort, to throw him on his knees after an exhausting journey at the side of a deathbed, saying, "Pray!" as if he were a sort of juggler? But he did not get up; he remained motionless with the boy's hands in his, for somewhere a Voice whispered, "Don't ask, Willem. Answer. No sparrow falls to earth without being called by me; would an old, tired man be kneeling by the deathbed of a boy in the wilderness without being called by me?"

It was the beginning of an interminable, relentless battle between the remnants of his self-love and that Voice from eternity. For it was not a decision, it was a battle, an endless struggle between his fading life force and a mounting fear of death. It seemed as if, in those first hours of indecision, his hands were riveted to the boy's, for when night fell and he battled to get up, he remained nailed to that place of judgment beside the stretcher, by a force that overpowered him.

He became so weak and so terribly afraid at the dripping, dripping, dripping of that mysterious life force from his trembling arms into the panting body in the darkness that he prayed, moaned, implored for help, to Betsy, to all the comrades who had gone before through that dark gate of fear toward their promotion to glory. It seemed as if all the peace, all the equilibrium, all the faith and trust that he had won during his nights of nightmares in the past were taken away from him once more in a new nightmare of teeming hallucinations. All the time, two voices hammered in the background, one calling, "It's folly, imagination, you are working yourself into a frenzy for nothing, nothing at all; it is tiredness, it is the heat, it is ridiculous to squat there with still knees and numbed thighs, smarting eyes and cramped hands; get up! Go away! Put an end to that unworthy performance! Let the boy die, if die he must, pray for his soul, if you have to do something, but get up, get up, don't lower yourself any deeper into that pit full of the demons of your imagination, get up, get up, you are a Christian, not a quack, polluter of God's pure teachings, get up, get up, stop that sentimental adulteration, that vain play-acting as if you were imitating Jesus on the Cross, shame, shame on you, this is not Christianity, this is not written in the Bible, stop desecrating God's Holy Commandments in a stage performance! Get out of here; you idolator, counterfeiter of the truth! God will punish you for this betrayal, for this degradation of all that is holy, get out, you hypocrite, into the darkness, go, go!" But that other voice went on repeating: "Even if everything you can think of to justify your going away were true, for sixty years I have filled you with the bounty of my love; now give me back my talent."

Then, toward the end of the night in which he gave away everything that he had ever received, a human shape appeared in the doorway, a silhouette with tangled hair, black against the blue of the dawn. He took it to be one of the soldiers asleep in the hut, who had gone out without his having been aware of it. But, suddenly, the boy started to move. The hands he had held in his, throughout the night, suddenly began to live, tried to free themselves, and the fear that radiated from them was so terrifying that he felt he would faint if he did not get up now. He got up, the boy's hands in his; the boy rose from his stretcher, tried to tear himself away, to flee, but he pulled him gently toward the doorway, and saw that the silhouette was an old native. He said, dizzy with exhaustion, "Excuse me, please." The native drew back and he helped the boy outside, stumbling on the threshold. The native drew back, slowly, as they sat down at the edge of the verandah on the steps and stood staring at them while the boy pressed himself against him, trembling. Then the native drew slowly back, until he vanished in the darkness. There was an almost invisible blueness around them, the very first color of the dawn.

The fresh air revived him for, after sitting on those steps for a while, beside the boy, a lightness overcame him with the dawn, a lighthearted peace, a lightheaded clarity, in which there was one floating, humming thought: God is Love. Whatever might happen, however helpless he might be sitting there now, on those steps, with all his certainties scattered: God is Love. If he had sinned, God is Love. If he had obeyed, God is Love. He said it, a radiant prayer: "God is love, God is love."

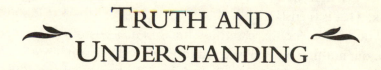

TRUTH AND UNDERSTANDING

The Three Hermits

Leo Tolstoy

One of Russia's and the world's greatest writers and philosophers, Leo Tolstoy (1828-1910), retells an old Volga legend in which a very learned and exalted leader of the church learns a humbling lesson from three eccentric but very pious hermits.

A bishop was sailing from Archangel to the Solovétsk Monastery, and on the same vessel were a number of pilgrims on their way to visit the shrines at that place. The voyage was a smooth one. The wind favorable and the weather fair. The pilgrims lay on deck, eating, or sat in groups talking to one another. The bishop, too, came on deck, and as he was pacing up and down he noticed a group of men standing near the prow and listening to a fisherman, who was pointing to the sea and telling them something. The Bishop stopped and looked in the direction in which the man was pointing. He could see nothing, however, but the sea glistening in the sunshine. He drew nearer to listen, but when the man saw him, he took off his cap and was silent. The rest of the people also took off their caps and bowed.

"Do not let me disturb you, friends," said the bishop. "I came to hear what this good man was saying."

"The fisherman was telling us about the hermits," replied one, a tradesman, rather bolder than the rest.

"What hermits?" asked the bishop, going to the side of the vessel and seating himself on a box. "Tell me about them. I should like to hear. What were you pointing at?"

"Why, that little island you can just see over there," answered the man, pointing to a spot ahead and a little to the right. "That is the island where the hermits live for the salvation of their souls."

"Where is the island?" asked the bishop. "I see nothing."

"There, in the distance, if you will please look along my hand. Do you see that little cloud? Below it, and a bit to the left, there is just a faint streak. That is the island."

The bishop looked carefully, but his unaccustomed eyes could make out nothing but the water shimmering in the sun.

"I cannot see it," he said. "But who are the hermits that live there?"

"They are holy men," answered the fisherman. "I had long heard tell of them, but never chanced to see them myself till the year before last."

And the fisherman related how once, when he was out fishing, he had been stranded at night upon that island, not knowing where he was. In the morning, as he wandered about the island, he came across an earth hut, and met an old man standing near it. Presently two others came out, and after having fed him and dried his things, they helped him mend his boat.

"And what are they like?" asked the bishop.

"One is a small man and his back is bent. He wears a priest's cassock and is very old; he must be more than a hundred, I should say. He is so old that the white of his beard is taking a greenish tinge, but he is always smiling, and his face is as bright as an angel's from heaven. The second is taller, but he also is very old. He wears a tattered peasant coat. His beard is broad, and of a yellowish gray color. He is a strong man. Before I had time to help him, he turned my boat over as if it were only a pail. He too is kindly and cheerful. The third is tall and has a beard as white as snow and reaching to his knees. He is stern, with overhanging eyebrows; and he wears nothing but a piece of matting tied round his waist."

"And did they speak to you?" asked the bishop.

"For the most part they did everything in silence and spoke but little even to one another. One of them would just give a glance, and the others would understand him. I asked the tallest whether they had lived there long. He frowned, and muttered something as if he were angry; but the oldest one took his hand and smiled, and then the tall one was quiet. The oldest one only said: 'Have mercy upon us,' and smiled."

While the fisherman was talking, the ship had drawn nearer to the island.

"There, now you can see it plainly, if your lordship will please to look," said the tradesman, pointing with his hand.

The bishop looked, and now he really saw a dark streak which was the island. Having looked at it a while, he left the prow of the vessel, and going to the stern, asked the helmsman:

"What island is that?"

"That one," replied the man, "has no name. There are many such in this sea."

"Is it true that there are hermits who live there for the salvation of their souls?"

"So it is said, your lordship, but I don't know if it's true. Fishermen say they have seen them; but of course they may only be spinning yarns."

"I should like to land on the island and see these men," said the bishop. "How could I manage it?"

"The ship cannot get close to the island," replied the helmsman, "but you might be rowed there in a boat. You had better speak to the captain."

The captain was sent for and came.

"I should like to see these hermits," said the bishop. "Could I not be rowed ashore?"

The captain tried to dissuade him.

"Of course it could be done," said he, "but we should lose much time. And if I might venture to say so to your lordship, the old men are not worth your pains. I have heard say that they are foolish old fellows, who understand nothing, and never speak a word, any more than the fish in the sea."

"I wish to see them," said the bishop, "and I will pay you for your trouble and loss of time. Please let me have a boat."

There was no help for it; so the order was given. The sailors trimmed the sails, the steersman put up the helm, and the ship's course was set for the island. A chair was placed at the prow for the bishop, and he sat there, looking ahead. The passengers all collected at the prow, and gazed at the island. Those who had the sharpest eyes could presently make out the rocks on it, and then a mud hut was seen. At last one man saw the hermits themselves. The captain brought a telescope and, after looking through it, handed it to the bishop.

"It's right enough. There are three men standing on the shore. There, a little to the right of that big rock."

The bishop took the telescope, got it into position, and he saw the three men: a tall one, a shorter one, and one very small and bent, standing on the shore and holding each other by the hand.

The captain turned to the bishop.

"The vessel can get no nearer in than this, your lordship. If you wish to go ashore, we must ask you to go in the boat, while we anchor here."

The cable was quickly let out; the anchor cast, and the sails furled. There was a jerk, and the vessel shook. Then, a boat having been lowered, the oarsmen jumped in, and the bishop descended the ladder and took his seat. The men pulled at their oars and the boat moved rapidly towards the island. When they came within a stone's throw, they saw three old men: a tall one with only a piece of matting tied round his waist, a shorter one in a tattered peasant coat, and a very old one bent with age and wearing an old cassock—all three standing hand in hand.

The oarsmen pulled in to the shore and held on with the boathook while the bishop got out.

The old men bowed to him, and he gave them his blessing, at which they bowed still lower. Then the bishop began to speak to them.

"I have heard," he said, "that you, godly men, live here saving your own souls and praying to our Lord Christ for your fellow men. I, an unworthy servant of Christ, am called, by God's mercy, to keep and teach His flock. I wished to see you, servants of God, and to do what I can to teach you, also."

The old men looked at each other smiling, but remained silent.

"Tell me," said the bishop, "what you are doing to save your souls and how you serve God on this island."

The second hermit sighed, and looked at the oldest, the very ancient one. The latter smiled, and said:

"We do not know how to serve God. We only serve and support ourselves, servant of God."

"But how do you pray to God?" asked the bishop.

"We pray in this way," replied the hermit. "Three are ye, three are we, have mercy upon us."

And when the old man said this, all three raised their eyes to heaven, and repeated:

"Three are ye, three are we, have mercy upon us!"

The bishop smiled.

"You have evidently heard something about the Holy Trinity," said he. "But you do not pray aright. You have won my affection, godly men. I see you wish to please the Lord, but you do not know how to serve Him. That is not the way to pray; but listen to me, and I will teach you. I will teach you, not a way of my own, but the way in which God in the Holy Scriptures has commanded all men to pray to Him."

And the bishop began explaining to the hermits how God had revealed Himself to men; telling them of God the Father, and God the Son, and God the Holy Ghost.

"God the Son came down on earth," said he, "to save men, and this is how He taught us all to pray. Listen, and repeat after me: 'Our Father.'"

And the first old man repeated after him, "Our Father," and the second said, "Our Father," and the third said, "Our Father."

"Which art in heaven," continued the bishop.

The first hermit repeated, "Which art in heaven," but the second blundered over the words, and the tall hermit could not say them properly. His hair had grown over his mouth so that he could not speak plainly. The very old hermit, having no teeth, also mumbled indistinctly.

The bishop repeated the words again, and the old men repeated them after him. The bishop sat down on a stone, and the old men stood before him, watching his mouth, and repeating the words as he uttered them. And all day long the bishop labored, saying a word twenty, thirty, a hundred times over, and the old men repeated it after him. They blundered, and he corrected them, and made them begin again.

The bishop did not leave off till he had taught them the whole of the Lord's Prayer so that they could not only repeat it after him, but could say it by themselves. The middle one was the first to know it, and to repeat the whole of it alone. The Bishop made him say it again and again, and at last the others could say it too.

It was getting dark and the moon was appearing over the water before the bishop rose to return to the vessel. When he took leave of the old men they all bowed down to the ground before him. He raised them, and kissed each of them, telling them to pray as he had taught them. Then he got into the boat and returned to the ship.

And as he sat in the boat and was rowed to the ship he could hear the three voices of the hermits loudly repeating the Lord's Prayer. As the boat drew near the vessel their voices could no longer be heard, but they could still be seen in the moonlight, standing as he had left them on the shore, the shortest in the middle, the tallest on the right, the middle one on the left. As soon as the bishop had reached the vessel and got on board, the anchor was weighed and the sails unfurled. The wind filled them and the ship sailed away, and the bishop took a seat in the stern and watched the island they had left. For a time he could still see the hermits, but presently they disappeared from sight, though the island was still visible. At last it too vanished, and only the sea was to be seen, rippling in the moonlight.

The pilgrims lay down to sleep, and all was quiet on deck. The bishop did not wish to sleep, but sat alone at the stern, gazing at the sea where the island was no longer visible, and thinking of the good old men. He thought how pleased they had been to learn the Lord's Prayer; and he thanked God for having sent him to teach and help such godly men.

So the bishop sat, thinking, and gazing at the sea where the island had disappeared. And the moonlight flickered before his eyes, sparkling, now here, now there, upon the waves. Suddenly he saw something white and shining, on the bright path which the moon cast across the sea. Was it a seagull, or the little gleaming sail of some small boat? The bishop fixed his eyes on it, wondering.

"It must be a boat sailing after us," thought he, "but it is overtaking us very rapidly. It was far, far away a minute ago, but now it is much nearer. It cannot be a boat, for I can see no sail; but whatever it may be, it is following us and catching us up."

And he could not make out what it was. Not a boat, nor a bird, nor a fish! It was too large for a man, and besides a man could not be out there in the midst of the sea. The bishop rose, and said to the helmsman:

"Look there, what is that, my friend? What is it?" the bishop repeated, though he could now see plainly what it was—the three hermits running upon the water, all gleaming white, their gray beards shining, and approaching the ship as quickly as though it were not moving.

The steersman looked, and let go the helm in terror.

"Oh, Lord! The hermits are running after us on the water as though it were dry land!"

The passengers, hearing him, jumped up and crowded to the stern. They saw the hermits coming along hand in hand, and the two outer ones beckoning the ship to stop. All three were gliding along upon the water without moving their feet. Before the ship could be stopped, the hermits had reached it, and raising their heads, all three as with one voice, began to say:

"We have forgotten your teaching, servant of God. As long as we kept repeating it we remembered, but when we stopped saying it for a time, a word dropped out, and now it has all gone to pieces. We can remember nothing of it. Teach us again."

The bishop crossed himself, and leaning over the ship's side, said:

"Your own prayer will reach the Lord, men of God. It is not for me to teach you. Pray for us sinners."

And the bishop bowed low before the old men; and they turned and went back across the sea. And a light shone until daybreak on the spot where they were lost to sight.

The Fire Balloons

Ray Bradbury

Ray Bradbury (1920—) is America's preeminent science fiction writer and is known for such gripping books as The Martian Chronicles *and* Fahrenheit 451. *He has also written many wonderful short stories and some, like "The Fire Balloons," blend science fiction with religion. In this story, two Episcopal priests with very different ideas about spreading the Gospel to the "heathen" discover that perhaps they are the ones with much to learn.*

Fire exploded over summer night lawns. You saw sparkling faces of uncles and aunts. Skyrockets fell up in the brown shining eyes of cousins on the porch, and the cold charred sticks thumped down in dry meadows far away.

The Very Reverend Father Joseph Daniel Peregrine opened his eyes. What a dream: He and his cousins with their fiery play at his grandfather's ancient Ohio home so many years ago!

He lay listening to the great hollow of the church, the other cells where other fathers lay. Had they, too, on the eve of the flight of the rocket *Crucifix*, lain with memories of the Fourth of July? Yes. This was like those breathless Independence dawns when you waited for the first concussion and rushed out on the dewy sidewalks, your hands full of loud miracles.

So here they were, the Episcopal fathers, in the breathing dawn before they pinwheeled off to Mars, leaving their incense through the velvet cathedral of space.

"Should we go at all?" whispered Father Peregrine. "Shouldn't we solve our own sins on Earth? Aren't we running from our lives here?"

He arose, his fleshy body, with its rich look of strawberries, milk, and steak, moving heavily.

"Or is it sloth?" he wondered. "Do I dread the journey?"

He stepped into the needle-spray shower.

"But I shall take you to Mars, body." He addressed himself. "Leaving old sins here. And on to Mars to find *new* sins?"

A delightful thought, almost. Sins no one had ever thought of.

Oh, he himself had written a little book: *The Problem of Sin on Other Worlds*, ignored as somehow not serious enough by his Episcopal brethren.

Only last night, over a final cigar, he and Father Stone had talked of it.

"On Mars sin might appear as virtue. We must guard against virtuous acts there that, later, might be found to be sins!" said Father Peregrine, beaming. "How exciting! It's been centuries since so much adventure has accompanied the prospect of being a missionary!"

"I will recognize sin," said Father Stone bluntly, "*even* on Mars."

"Oh, we priests pride ourselves on being litmus paper, changing color in sin's presence," retorted Father Peregrine, "but what if Martian chemistry is such we do not color *at all*! If there are new senses on Mars, you must admit the possibility of unrecognizable sin."

"If there is no malice aforethought, there is no sin or punishment for same—the Lord assures us that," Father Stone replied.

"On Earth, yes. But perhaps a Martian sin might inform the subconscious of its evil, telepathically, leaving the conscious mind of man free to act, seemingly without malice! What *then*?"

"What *could* there be in the way of new sins?"

Father Peregrine leaned heavily forward. "Adam *alone* did not sin. Add Eve, and you add temptation. Add a second man and you make adultery possible. With the addition of sex or people, you add sin. If men were armless they could not strangle with their hands. You would not have that particular sin of murder. Add arms, and you add the possibility of a new violence. Amoebas cannot sin because they reproduce by fission. They do not covet wives or murder each other. Add sex to amoebas, add arms and legs, and you would have murder and adultery. Add an arm or leg or person, or take away each, and you add or subtract possible evil. On Mars, what if there are five new senses, organs, invisible limbs we can't conceive of—then mightn't there be five *new sins*?"

Father Stone gasped. "I think you *enjoy* this sort of thing!"

"I keep my mind alive, Father; just alive, is all."

"Your mind's always juggling, isn't it?—mirrors, torches, plates."

"Yes. Because sometimes the Church seems like those posed circus tableaus where the curtain lifts and men, white, zinc-oxide, talcum-powder statues, freeze to represent abstract Beauty. Very wonderful. But I hope there will always be room for me to dart about among the statues, don't you, Father Stone?"

Father Stone had moved away. "I think we'd better go to bed. In a few hours we'll be jumping up to see your *new* sins, Father Peregrine."

■

The rocket stood ready for the firing.

The fathers walked from their devotions in the chilly morning, many a fine priest from New York or Chicago or Los Angeles—the Church was sending its best—walking across town to the frosty field. Walking, Father Peregrine remembered the bishop's words:

"Father Peregrine, you will captain the missionaries, with Father Stone at your side. Having chosen you for this serious task, I find my reasons deplorably obscure, Father, but your pamphlet on planetary sin did not go unread. You are a flexible man. And Mars is like that uncleaned closet we have neglected for millenniums. Sin has collected there like bric-a-brac. Mars is twice the earth's age and has had double the number of Saturday nights, liquor baths, and eye-poppings at women as naked as white seals. When we open that closet door, things will fall on us. We need a quick, flexible man—one whose mind can dodge. Anyone a little too dogmatic might break in two. I feel you'll be resilient, Father; the job is yours."

The bishop and the fathers knelt.

The blessing was said and the rocket given a little shower of holy water. Arising, the bishop addressed them:

"I know you will go with God, to prepare the Martians for the reception of His Truth. I wish you all a *thoughtful* journey."

They filed past the bishop, twenty men, robes whispering, to deliver their hands into his kind hands before passing into the cleansed projectile.

"I wonder," said Father Peregrine, at the last moment, "if Mars is hell? Only waiting for our arrival before it bursts into brimstone and fire."

"Lord, be with us," said Father Stone.

The rocket moved.

■

Coming out of space was like coming out of the most beautiful cathedral they had ever seen. Touching Mars was like touching the ordinary pavement outside the church five minutes after having *really* known your love for God.

The fathers stepped gingerly from the steaming rocket and knelt upon Martian sand while Father Peregrine gave thanks.

"Lord, we thank Thee for the journey through Thy rooms. And, Lord, we have reached a new land, so we must have new eyes. We shall hear new sounds and must need have new ears. And there will be new sins, for which we ask the gift of better and firmer and purer hearts. Amen."

They arose.

And here was Mars like a sea under which they trudged in the guise of submarine biologists, seeking life. Here the territory of hidden sin. Oh, how carefully they must all balance, like gray feathers, in this new element, afraid that walking *itself* might be sinful; or breathing, or simple fasting!

And here was the mayor of First Town come to meet them with outstretched hand. "What can I do for you, Father Peregrine?"

"We'd like to know about the Martians. For only if we know about them can we plan our church intelligently. Are they ten feet tall? We will build large doors. Are their skins blue or red or green? We must know when we put human figures in the stained glass so we may use the right skin color. Are they heavy? We will build sturdy seats for them."

"Father," said the mayor, "I don't think you should worry about the Martians. There are two races. One of them is pretty well dead. A few are in hiding. And the second race—well, they're not quite human."

"Oh?" Father Peregrine's heart quickened.

"They're round luminous globes of light, Father, living in those hills. Man or beast, who can say? But they act intelligently, I hear." The mayor shrugged. "Of course, they're not men, so I don't think you'll care—"

"On the contrary," said Father Peregrine swiftly. "Intelligent, you say?"

"There's a story. A prospector broke his leg in those hills and would have died there. The blue spheres of light came at him. When he woke, he was down on a highway and didn't know how he got there."

"Drunk," said Father Stone.

"That's the story," said the mayor. "Father Peregrine, with most of the Martians dead, and only these blue spheres, I frankly think you'd be better off in First City. Mars is opening up. It's a frontier now, like in the old days on Earth, out West, and in Alaska. Men are pouring up here. There's a couple thousand black Irish mechanics and miners and day laborers in First Town who need saving, because there're too many wicked women came with them, and too much ten-century-old Martian wine—"

Father Peregrine was gazing into the soft blue hills.

Father Stone cleared his throat. "Well, Father?"

Father Peregrine did not hear. "Spheres of blue *fire*?"

"Yes, Father."

"Ah," Father Peregrine sighed.

"Blue balloons." Father Stone shook his head. "A circus!"

Father Peregrine felt his wrists pounding. He saw the little frontier town with raw, fresh-built sin, and he saw the hills, old with the oldest and yet perhaps an even newer (to him) sin.

"Mayor, could your black Irish laborers wait one more day?"

"Sure, Father."

Father Peregrine nodded to the hills. "Then that's where we'll go."

There was a murmur from everyone.

"It would be so simple," explained Father Peregrine, "to go into town. I prefer to think that if the Lord walked here and people said, 'Here is the beaten path,' He would reply, 'Show me the weeds. I will *make* a path.'"

"But—"

"Father Stone, think how it would weigh upon us if we passed sinners by and did not extend our hands."

"But globes of fire!"

"I imagine man looked funny to other animals when he first appeared. Yet he has a soul, for all his homeliness. Until we prove otherwise, let us assume that these fiery spheres have souls."

"All right," agreed the mayor, "but you'll be back to town."

"We'll see. First, some breakfast. Then you and I, Father Stone, will walk alone into the hills. I don't want to frighten those fiery Martians with machines or crowds. Shall we have breakfast?"

The fathers ate in silence.

At nightfall Father Peregrine and Father Stone were high in the hills. They stopped and sat upon a rock to enjoy a moment of relaxation and waiting. The Martians had not as yet appeared, and they both felt vaguely disappointed.

"I wonder—" Father Peregrine mopped his face. "Do you think if we called 'Hello!' they might answer?"

"Father Peregrine, won't you ever be serious?"

"Not until the good Lord is. Oh, don't look so terribly shocked, please. The Lord is not serious. In fact, it is a little hard to know just what else He is except loving. And love has to do with humor, doesn't it? For you cannot love someone unless you put up with him, can you? And you cannot put up with someone constantly unless you can laugh at him. Isn't that true? And certainly we are ridiculous little animals wallowing in the fudge bowl, and God must love us all the more because we appeal to His humor."

"*I* never thought of God as humorous," said Father Stone.

"The Creator of the platypus, the camel, the ostrich, and man? Oh, come now!" Father Peregrine laughed.

But at this instant, from among the twilight hills, like a series of blue lamps lit to guide their way, came the Martians.

Father Stone saw them first. "Look!"

Father Peregrine turned and the laughter stopped in his mouth.

The round blue globes of fire hovered among the twinkling stars, distantly trembling.

"Monsters!" Father Stone leaped up. But Father Peregrine caught him. "Wait!"

"We should've gone to town!"

"No, listen, look!" pleaded Father Peregrine.

"I'm afraid!"

"Don't be. This is God's work!"

"The devil's!"

"No, now, quiet!" Father Peregrine gentled him, and they crouched with the soft blue light on their upturned faces as the fiery orbs drew near.

And again, Independence Night, thought Father Peregrine, tremoring. He felt like a child back in those July Fourth evenings, the sky blowing apart, breaking into powdery stars and burning sound, the concussions jingling house windows like the ice on a thousand thin ponds. The aunts, uncles, cousins crying, "Ah!" as to some celestial physician. The summer sky colors. And the Fire Balloons, lit by an indulgent grandfather, steadied in his massively tender hands. Oh, the memory of those lovely Fire Balloons, softly lighted, warmly billowed bits of tissue, like insect wings, lying like folded wasps in boxes and, last of all, after the day of riot and fury, at long last from their boxes, delicately unfolded, blue, red, white, patriotic—the Fire Balloons! He saw the dim faces of dear relatives long dead and mantled with moss as Grandfather lit the tiny candle and let the warm air breathe up to form the balloon plumply luminous in his hands, a shining vision which they held, reluctant to let it go; for, once released, it was yet another year gone from life, another Fourth, another bit of Beauty vanished. And then up, up, still up through the warm summer night constellations, the Fire Balloons had drifted, while red-white-and-blue eyes followed them, wordless, from family porches. Away into deep Illinois country, over night rivers and sleeping mansions the Fire Balloons dwindled, forever gone. . . .

Father Peregrine felt tears in his eyes. Above him the Martians, not one but a *thousand* whispering Fire Balloons, it seemed, hovered. Any moment he might find his long-dead and blessed grandfather at his elbow, staring up at Beauty.

But it was Father Stone.

"Let's go, please, Father!"

"I must speak to them." Father Peregrine rustled forward, not knowing what to say, for what had he ever said to the Fire Balloons of time past except with his mind: *You are beautiful, you are beautiful*, and that was not enough now. He could only lift his heavy arms and call upward, as he had often wished to call after the enchanted Fire Balloons, "Hello!"

But the fiery spheres only burned like images in a dark mirror. They seemed fixed, gaseous, miraculous, forever.

"We come with God," said Father Peregrine to the sky.

"Silly, silly, silly." Father Stone chewed the back of his hand. "In the name of God, Father Peregrine, stop!"

But now the phosphorescent spheres blew away into the hills. In a moment they were gone.

Father Peregrine called again, and the echo of his last cry shook the hills above. Turning, he saw an avalanche shake out dust, pause, and then, with a thunder of stone wheels, crash down the mountain upon them.

"Look what you've done!" cried Father Stone.

Father Peregrine was almost fascinated, then horrified. He turned, knowing they could run only a few feet before the rocks crushed them into ruins. He had time to whisper, *Oh, Lord*! and the rocks fell!

"Father!"

They were separated like chaff from wheat. There was a blue shimmering of globes, a shift of cold stars, a roar, and then they stood upon a ledge two hundred feet away watching the spot where their bodies should have been buried under tons of stone.

The blue light evaporated.

The two fathers clutched each other. "What happened?"

"The blue fires lifted us!"

"We ran, *that* was it!"

"No, the globes saved us."

"They couldn't!"

"They *did*."

The sky was empty. There was a feel as if a great bell had just stopped tolling. Reverberations lingered in their teeth and marrow.

"Let's get away from here. You'll have us killed."

"I haven't feared death for a good many years, Father Stone."

"We've proved nothing. Those blue lights ran off at the first cry. It's useless."

"No." Father Peregrine was suffused with a stubborn wonder. "Somehow, they saved us. That proves they have souls."

"It proves only that they *might* have saved us. Everything was confused. We might have escaped, ourselves."

"They are not animals, Father Stone. Animals do not save lives, especially of strangers. There is mercy and compassion here. Perhaps, tomorrow, we may prove more."

"Prove what? How?" Father Stone was immensely tired now; the outrage to his mind and body showed on his stiff face. "Follow them in helicopters, reading chapter and verse? They're not human. They haven't eyes or ears or bodies like ours."

"But I feel something about them," replied Father Peregrine. "I know a great revelation is at hand. They saved us. They *think*. They had a choice; let us live or die. That proves free will!"

Father Stone set to work building a fire, glaring at the sticks in his hands, choking on the gray smoke. "I myself will open a convent for nursling geese, a monastery for sainted swine, and I shall build a miniature apse in a microscope so that paramecium can attend services and tell their beads with their flagella."

"Oh, Father Stone."

"I'm sorry." Father Stone blinked redly across the fire. "But this is like blessing a crocodile before he chews you up. You're risking the entire missionary expedition. We belong in First Town, washing liquor from men's throats and perfume off their hands!"

"Can't you recognize the human in the inhuman?"

"I'd much rather recognize the inhuman in the human."

"But if I prove these things sin, know sin, know a moral life, have free will and intellect, Father Stone?"

"That will take much convincing."

The night grew rapidly cold, and they peered into the fire to find their wildest thoughts, while eating biscuits and berries, and soon they were bundled for sleep under the chiming stars. And just before turning over one last time Father Stone, who had been thinking for many minutes to find something to bother Father Peregrine about, stared into the soft pink charcoal bed and said, "No Adam and Eve on Mars. No original sin. Maybe the Martians live in a state of God's grace. Then we can go back down to town and start work on the Earthmen."

Father Peregrine reminded himself to say a little prayer for Father Stone, who got so mad and who was now being vindictive, God help him. "Yes, Father Stone, but the Martians killed some of our settlers. That's sinful. There must have been an Original Sin and a Martian Adam and Eve. We'll find them. Men are men, unfortunately, no matter what their shape, and inclined to sin."

But Father Stone was pretending sleep.

■

Father Peregrine did not shut his eyes.

Of course they couldn't let these Martians go, could they? With a compromise to their consciences, could they go back to the new colonial towns, those towns so full of sinful ways? Wasn't that the place for the fathers? Wasn't this trek into the hills merely a personal whim? Was he really thinking of God's Church, or was he quenching the thirst of a spongelike curiosity? Those blue round globes of St. Anthony's fire— how they burned in his mind! What a challenge, to find the man behind the mask, the human behind the inhuman. Wouldn't he be proud if he could say, even to his secret self, that he had converted a rolling huge pool table full of fiery spheres! What a sin of pride! Worth doing penance for! But then one did many prideful things out of Love, and he loved the Lord so much and was so happy at it that he wanted everyone else to be happy too.

The last thing he saw before sleep was the return of the blue fires, like a flight of burning angels silently singing him to his worried rest.

■

The blue round dreams were still there in the sky when Father Peregrine awoke in the early morning.

Father Stone slept like a stiff bundle, quietly. Father Peregrine watched the Martians floating and watching him. They were human— he *knew* it. But he must prove it or face a dry-mouthed, dry-eyed bishop telling him kindly to step aside.

But how to prove humanity if they hid in the high vaults of the sky? How to bring them nearer and provide answers to the many questions?

"They saved us from the avalanche."

Father Peregrine arose, moved off among the rocks, and began to climb the nearest hill until he came to a place where a cliff dropped sheerly to a floor two hundred feet below. He was choking from his vigorous climb in the frosty air. He stood, getting his breath.

"If I fell from here, it would surely kill me."

He let a pebble drop. Moments later it clicked on the rocks below.

"The Lord would never forgive me."

He tossed another pebble.

"It wouldn't be suicide, would it, if I did it out of Love . . . ?"

He lifted his gaze to the blue spheres. "But first another try." He called to them: "Hello, hello!"

The echoes tumbled upon each other, but the blue fires did not blink or move.

He talked to them for five minutes. When he stopped, he peered down and saw Father Stone, still indignantly asleep, below in the little camp.

"I must prove everything." Father Peregrine stepped to the cliff rim. "I am an old man. I am not afraid. Surely the Lord will understand that I am doing this for Him?"

He drew a deep breath. All his life swam through his eyes and he thought, In a moment shall I die? I am afraid that I love living much too much. But I love other things more.

And, thinking thus, he stepped off the cliff.

He fell.

"Fool!" he cried. He tumbled end over end. "You were wrong!" The rocks rushed up at him, and he saw himself dashed on them and sent to glory. "Why did I do this thing?" But he knew the answer, and an instant later was calm as he fell. The wind roared around him and the rocks hurtled to meet him.

And then there was a shift of stars, a glimmering of blue light, and he felt himself surrounded by blueness and suspended. A moment later he was deposited, with a gentle bump, upon the rocks, where he sat a full moment, alive, and touching himself, and looking up at those blue lights that had withdrawn instantly.

"You saved me!" he whispered. "You wouldn't let me die. You knew it was wrong."

He rushed over to Father Stone who still lay quietly asleep. "Father, Father, wake up!" He shook him and brought him round. "Father, they saved me!"

"Who saved you?" Father Stone blinked and sat up.

Father Peregrine related his experience.

"A dream, a nightmare; go back to sleep," said Father Stone irritably. "You and your circus balloons."

"But I was awake!"

"Now, now, Father, calm yourself. There now."

"You don't believe me? Have you a gun? Yes, there, let me have it."

"What are you going to do?" Father Stone handed over the small pistol they had brought along for protection against snakes or other similar and unpredictable animals.

Father Peregrine seized the pistol. "I'll prove it!"

He pointed the pistol at his own hand and fired.

"Stop!"

There was a shimmer of light, and before their eyes the bullet stood upon the air, poised an inch from his open palm. It hung for a moment, surrounded by a blue phosphorescence. Then it fell, hissing, into the dust.

Father Peregrine fired the gun three times—at his hand, at his leg, at his body. The three bullets hovered, glittering, and, like dead insects, fell at their feet.

"You see?" said Father Peregrine, letting his arm fall, and allowing the pistol to drop after the bullets. "They know. They understand. They are not animals. They think and judge and live in a moral climate. What animal would save me from myself like this? There is no animal would do that. Only another man, Father. Now, do you believe?"

Father Stone was watching the sky and the blue lights, and now, silently, he dropped to one knee and picked up the warm bullets and cupped them in his hand. He closed his hand tight.

The sun was rising behind them.

"I think we had better go down to the others and tell them of this and bring them back up here," said Father Peregrine.

By the time the sun was up, they were well on their way back to the rocket.

■

Father Peregrine drew the round circle in the center of the blackboard.

"This is Christ, the son of the Father."

He pretended not to hear the other fathers' sharp intake of breath.

"This is Christ, in all his Glory," he continued.

"It looks like a geometry problem," observed Father Stone.

"A fortunate comparison, for we deal with symbols here. Christ is no less Christ, you must admit, in being represented by a circle or a square. For centuries the cross has symbolized his love and agony . So this circle will be the Martian Christ. This is how we shall bring Him to Mars."

The fathers stirred fretfully and looked at each other.

"You, Brother Mathias, will create, in glass, a replica of this circle, a globe, filled with bright fire. It will stand upon the altar."

"A cheap magic trick," muttered Father Stone.

Father Peregrine went on patiently: "On the contrary. We are giving them God in an understandable image. If Christ had come to us on Earth as an octopus, would we have accepted him readily?" He spread his hands. "Was it then a cheap magic trick of the Lord's to bring us Christ through Jesus, in man's shape? After we bless the church we build here and sanctify its altar and this symbol, do you think Christ would refuse to inhabit the shape before us? You know in your hearts He would not refuse."

"But the body of a soulless animal!" said Brother Mathias.

"We've already gone over that, many times since we returned this morning, Brother Mathias. These creatures saved us from the avalanche. They realized that self-destruction was sinful and prevented it, time after time. Therefore we must build a church in the hills, live with them, to find their own special ways of sinning, the alien ways, and help them to discover God."

The fathers did not seem pleased at the prospect.

"Is it because they are so odd to the eye?" wondered Father Peregrine. "But what is a shape? Only a cup for the blazing soul that God provides us all. If tomorrow I found that sea lions suddenly possessed free will, intellect, knew when not to sin, knew what life was and tempered justice with mercy and life with love, then I would build an undersea cathedral. And if the sparrows should, miraculously, with God's will, gain everlasting souls tomorrow, I would freight a church with helium and take after them, for all souls, in any shape, if they have free will and are aware of their sins, will burn in hell unless given their rightful communions. I would not let a Martian sphere burn in hell, either, for it is a sphere only in mine eyes. When I close my eyes it stands before me, an intelligence, a love, a soul—and I must not deny it."

"But that glass globe you wish placed on the altar," protested Father Stone.

"Consider the Chinese," replied Father Peregrine imperturbably. "What sort of Christ do Christian Chinese worship? An oriental Christ, naturally. You've all seen oriental Nativity scenes. How is Christ dressed? In Eastern robes. Where does He walk? In Chinese settings of bamboo and misty mountain and crooked tree. His eyelids taper, His cheekbones rise. Each country, each race adds something to Our Lord. I am reminded of the Virgin of Guadalupe, to whom all Mexico pays its love. Her skin? Have you noticed the paintings of her? A dark skin, like that of her worshipers. Is this blasphemy? Not at all. It is not logical that men should accept a God, no matter how real, of another color. I often wonder why our missionaries do well in Africa, with a snow-white Christ. Perhaps because white is a sacred color, in albino, or any other form, to the African tribes. Given time, mightn't Christ darken there too? The form does not matter. Content is everything. We cannot expect these Martians to accept an alien form. We shall give them Christ in their own image."

"There's a flaw in your reasoning, Father," said Father Stone. "Won't the Martians suspect us of hypocrisy? They will realize that we don't worship a round, globular Christ, but a man with limbs and a head. How do we explain the difference?"

"By showing there is none. Christ will fill any vessel that is offered. Bodies or globes, He is there, and each will worship the same thing in a different guise. What is more, we must *believe* in this globe we give the Martians. We must believe in a shape which is meaningless to us as to form. This spheroid *will* be Christ. And we must remember that we ourselves, and the shape of our Earth Christ would be meaningless, ridiculous, a squander of material to these Martians."

Father Peregrine laid aside his chalk. "Now let us go into the hills and build our church."

■

The Fathers began to pack their equipment.

The church was not a church but an area cleared of rocks, a plateau on one of the low mountains, its soil smoothed and brushed, and an altar established whereon Brother Mathias placed the fiery globe he had constructed.

At the end of six days of work the "church" was ready.

"What shall we do with this?" Father Stone tapped an iron bell they had brought along. "What does a bell mean to *them*?"

"I imagine I brought it for our own comfort," admitted Father Peregrine. "We need a few familiarities. This church seems so little like a church. And we feel somewhat absurd here—even I; for it is something new, this business of converting the creatures of another world. I feel like a ridiculous play actor at times. And then I pray to God to lend me strength."

"Many of the fathers are unhappy. Some of them joke about all this, Father Peregrine."

"I know. We'll put this bell in a small tower for their comfort, anyway."

"What about the organ?"

"We'll play it at the first service, tomorrow."

"But, the Martians—"

"I know. But again, I suppose, for our own comfort, our own music. Later we may discover theirs."

■

They arose very early on Sunday morning and moved through the coldness like pale phantoms, rime tinkling on their habits; covered with chimes they were, shaking down showers of silver water.

"I wonder if it is Sunday here on Mars?" mused Father Peregrine, but seeing Father Stone wince, he hastened on, "It might be Tuesday or Thursday—who knows? But no matter. My idle fancy. It's Sunday to *us*. Come."

The fathers walked into the flat wide area of the "church" and knelt, shivering and blue-lipped.

Father Peregrine said a little prayer and put his cold fingers to the organ keys. The music went up like a flight of pretty birds. He touched the keys like a man moving his hands among the weeds of a wild garden, startling up great soarings of beauty into the hills.

The music calmed the air. It smelled the fresh smell of morning. The music drifted into the mountains and shook down mineral powders in a dusty rain.

The fathers waited.

"Well, Father Peregrine." Father Stone eyed the empty sky where the sun was rising, furnace-red. "I don't see our friends."

"Let me try again." Father Peregrine was perspiring.

He built an architecture of Bach, stone by exquisite stone, raising a musical cathedral so vast that its furthest chancels were in Nineveh,* its furthest dome at St. Peter's left hand. The music stayed and did not crash in ruin when it was over, but partook of a series of white clouds and was carried away among other lands.

The sky was still empty.

"They'll come!" But Father Peregrine felt the panic in his chest, very small, growing. "Let us pray. Let us ask them to come. They read minds; they *know*."

The fathers lowered themselves yet again, in rustlings and whispers. They prayed.

And to the East, out of the icy mountains of seven o'clock on Sunday morning or perhaps Thursday morning or maybe Monday morning on Mars, came the soft fiery globes.

They hovered and sank and filled the area around the shivering priests. "Thank you; oh, thank you, Lord." Father Peregrine shut his eyes tight and played the music, and when it was done he turned and gazed upon his wondrous congregation.

And a voice touched his mind, and the voice said:

"We have come for a little while."

"You may stay," said Father Peregrine.

"For a little while only," said the voice quietly. "We have come to tell you certain things. We should have spoken sooner. But we had hoped that you might go on your way if left alone."

Father Peregrine started to speak, but the voice hushed him.

"We are the Old Ones," the voice said, and it entered him like a blue gaseous flare and burned in the chambers of his head.

"We are the old Martians, who left our marble cities and went into the hills, forsaking the material life we had lived. So very long ago we became these things that we now are. Once we were men, with bodies

---

*the ancient capital of Assyria, now in modern-day Iraq

and legs and arms such as yours. The legend has it that one of us, a good man, discovered a way to free man's soul and intellect, to free him of bodily ills and melancholies, of deaths and transfigurations, of ill humors and senilities, and so we took on the look of lightning and blue fire and have lived in the winds and skies and hills forever after that, neither prideful nor arrogant, neither rich nor poor, passionate nor cold. We have lived apart from those we left behind, those other men of this world, and how we came to be has been forgotten, the process lost; but we shall never die, nor do harm. We have put away the sins of the body and live in God's grace. We covet no other property; we have no property. We do not steal, nor kill, nor lust, nor hate. We live in happiness. We cannot reproduce; we do not eat or drink or make war. All the sensualities and childishnesses and sins of the body were stripped away when our bodies were put aside. We have left sin behind, Father Peregrine, and it is burned like the leaves in the autumn, and it is gone like the soiled snow of an evil winter, and it is gone like the flowers of a red-and-yellow spring, and it is gone like the panting nights of hottest summer, and our season is temperate and our clime is rich in thought."

Father Peregrine was standing now, for the voice touched him at such a pitch that it almost shook him from his senses. It was an ecstasy and a fire washing through him.

"We wish to tell you that we appreciate your building this place for us, but we have no need of it, for each of us is a temple unto himself and needs no place wherein to cleanse himself. Forgive us for not coming to you sooner, but we are separate and apart and have talked to no one for ten thousand years, nor have we interfered in any way with the life of this planet. It has come into your mind now that we are the lilies of the field; we toil not, neither do we spin. You are right. And so we suggest that you take the parts of this temple into your own new cities and there cleanse others. For, rest assured, we are happy and at peace."

The fathers were on their knees in the vast blue light, and Father Peregrine was down, too, and they were weeping, and it did not matter that their time had been wasted; it did not matter to them at all.

The blue spheres murmured and began to rise once more, on a breath of cool air.

"May I"—cried Father Peregrine, not daring to ask, eyes closed— "may I come again, someday, that I may learn from you?"

The blue fires blazed. The air trembled.

Yes. Someday he might come again. Someday.

And then the Fire Balloons blew away and were gone, and he was like a child, on his knees, tears streaming from his eyes, crying to himself, "Come back, come back!" And at any moment Grandfather might lift him and carry him upstairs to his bedroom in a long-gone Ohio town.

They filed down out of the hills at sunset. Looking back, Father Peregrine saw the blue fires burning. No, he thought, we couldn't build a church for the likes of you. You're Beauty itself.

What church could compete with the fireworks of the pure soul?

Father Stone moved in silence beside him. And at last he spoke:

"The way I see it is there's a Truth on every planet. All parts of the Big Truth. On a certain day they'll all fit together like the pieces of jigsaw. This has been a shaking experience. I'll never doubt again, Father Peregrine. For this Truth here is as true as Earth's Truth, and they lie side by side. And we'll go on to other worlds, adding the sum of the parts of the Truth until one day the whole Total will stand before us like the light of a new day."

"That's a lot, coming from you, Father Stone."

"I'm sorry now, in a way, we're going down to the town to handle our own kind. Those blue lights now. When they settled about us, and that *voice*. . . ." Father Stone shivered.

Father Peregrine reached out to take the other's arm. They walked together.

"And you know," said Father Stone finally, fixing his eyes on Brother Mathias, who strode ahead with the glass sphere tenderly carried in his arms, that glass sphere with the blue phosphorous light glowing forever inside it, "you know, Father Peregrine, that globe there—"

"Yes?"

"It's Him. It is Him, after all."

Father Peregrine smiled, and they walked down out of the hills toward the new town.

❧LEGENDS AND HEROES❧

The Death of King Arthur[†]

Donna Fletcher Crow

From Glastonbury

American historical fiction writer Donna Crow (1941—) brings both ancient history and ancient Christianity alive in her epic novel, Glastonbury *(1992), which traces the development of Britain from Celtic to Tudor times. The famous Abbey of Glastonbury on the holy isle of Avalon, where St. Joseph of Arimethea founded the first Christian church in England, is the focal point. In this scene (in which the Celtic, Roman, and Saxon names of the period are employed), King Arthur (Arthurius) is dying of wounds suffered in a battle against his kinsman, the Saxon chieftain Cheldric and his son, Medraut (Mordred). King Arthur's battle captain, Sir Bedivere (Baudwin), the monk-historian Brother Gildas, and Queen Guinevere (Gwenhumara) take him to Glastonbury for his last rites and secret burial.*

Baudwin and Gildas lay Arthurius in the boat with his broken head in Gwenhumara's lap and, towing the canoe behind them, they set out in the coracle [leather boat] for the Isle of Avalon.

Mist rose across the marsh, and the setting sun turned all a gentle pink-tinged gray. Curlew and kestrel sang them on their way. When they reached the island, the sun had set, and no pink remained in the misted world; the Tor [high, rocky hill] was shrouded from sight, and no more birdsong could be heard, but the chant of the monks at evening prayers bade them welcome.

Arthurius was laid on a pile of softest furs in the best of the guest huts with a flickering candle to keep vigil. Through the night the holy brothers sang prayers for the High King in the Old Church, and Baudwin and Gwenhumara sat by his side.

The night was long, and yet not long enough for Gwenhumara sitting by the side of her husband-king who was there and yet was not there. Through the open window of the cell the night bird's call and the scent of earliest apple blossoms kept company with the prayers of those who watched. Gwenhumara's heart-prayer and soul-cry would not be stilled. Again and again her longing approached the throne of Heaven.

She called upon her God to grant this, her one last request. When at last through the small square opening the queen saw the Tor, gold-etched with the sun rising behind it, she knew her day had come.

Even so the end was not yet. For with the dawn the king opened his eyes as if from natural sleep and spoke in a voice weak, but clear, "Gwenhumara, my heart's light, bide you with me."

"I will, lord of my heart; always I will." She shifted closer to his cot and held his hand.

Then he turned his gaze from Gwenhumara to Caliburnus* lying close beside him as it ever had since first it was given to him on that same misted island. "Baudwin, worthy one, Caliburnus of the cut steel has felled her last foe for Britain from my hand. Take her now and make return to the Lady of the Lake for the great prize with which she gifted me. And bid her pray for the soul of Arthurius."

"My lord. . . ." Baudwin choked on his words.

"Na, na, my eques [knight]. By God's grace we have done what we set ourselves to do. And the doing was good. We have kept alive for a space the last glimmering flames of the old order. And it has been good. Perhaps on the other side of the dark that now closes over us, perhaps when men build a new order, the stories told of us will help them. And that will be good."

Baudwin protested, "But why must it be so? Why must the dark come?"

"We must go down into the dark just as the year does every twelve-month cycle at Samain [Celtic New Year]. Every year the winter dark descends, but the spring lightness follows. So will it be for Britain. It grows cold; our wintertime approaches, but the spring of new birth will follow, and after that the bright glory of summer."

None in the room could make answer, for fullness of heart. Baudwin stood uneasily, clasping Caliburnus to his chest. Arthurius spoke with a ring of his old command in his voice, "Take the sword now, Baudwin, but tell no one when I am dead. Such knowledge would be a weapon for Cheldric. Say rather that I have gone away for healing, and that I will return when Britain has need of me."

---

*Excalibur, the sword given to King Arthur by the Lady of the Lake, the Abbess Nimue

Baudwin left the room, and a few minutes later his place at Arthurius's side was taken by Brother Gildas. "I will hear him confess if he will." The look that followed the words clearly suggested that Gwenhumara leave them alone.

"I will stay by his side."

In the end, it didn't matter, for although Arthurius still breathed, he had spoken his last. The priest leaned down and placed the tiniest crumb of the bread of Christ's body on the king's tongue. "Whoever eats this bread will live forever."

"Lord, have mercy," the queen responded in a whisper.

The priest followed with a single drop of the wine of Christ's blood. "Our crucified and risen Lord has redeemed us, alleluia."

"Christ, have mercy." The response was little more than a deep breath.

Gildas then pulled the stopper from a small vial of sweet-smelling oil and poured it over the king's head. "As Christ was anointed Priest, Prophet, and King, so may you live always as a member of His body, sharing the life ever-lasting in this world and the next. In the name of the Father, and of the Son, and of the Holy Ghost, may the Lord who has freed you from sin bring you safely to His kingdom in Heaven. Glory to Him forever and ever." The priest departed before the queen's response.

"Into Your hands, Lord, I commend my spirit."

When Baudwin returned, Arthurius breathed no more. But as the eques turned to comfort the queen, he saw that she too had breathed her last. The smallest of gentle smiles was still on her lips that her prayer had been granted. "Bide with me," Arthurius had said. Faithful ever, she meant her "I will."

So the great hollowed oak that had borne Arthurius and Gwenhumara to Avalon became their coffin, like the ancient royalty of the Celtic people who at their death had been put in ships to sail to the land of Avallach.

But even in death the royal pair was not without controversy. The ever-frowning Gildas held up his hand when the body of Gwenhumara would be placed beside that of her king. "It will not do. She was accused of adultery. One so branded cannot be buried in holy ground."

Abbot Indract stepped forward. "Accused she was, but never proved."

Gildas held his position. "Sa, sa. But we cannot take such a risk. If we bury her unworthily, we will dishonor all who lie in this hallowed soil. And the shame will be on our heads."

"So let it be on my head." Indract was firm. "I will not bear the shame of having the queen torn from the king's side in death. Let God who knows all hearts judge."

Gildas gave a curt nod that was more a jerk. "So. Let her share the coffin. But let her lie at his feet, as a dishonored wife."

Indract dipped his head in assent. "So be it. And if we are wrong, God forgive us." He crossed himself that his words might have the force of prayer.

"The grave must be deep and deep. It must not be discovered by the enemies of the Britain that Arthurius lived ever to protect." Baudwin directed Brothers Logor and Breden who were turning the sod beside the old church with sharp spades.

At a depth of five feet they stopped. But Baudwin would not declare it deep enough and took the spade from a weary Logor to dig on. It was late that evening when Baudwin and Wencreth, who had taken the spade from Brother Breden, had doubled the depth of the grave and Baudwin declared it was well. The oaken coffin had been sealed and lowered with ropes and most of the shovelfuls of earth returned to their resting when Brother Benegius joined the small circle, followed by two serving boys bearing a large flat stone on which he had labored all day. The stone bore a leaden cross inscribed painstakingly by the monk's own hand, "HIC JACET SEPULTUS INCLYTUS REX ARTHURIUS IN INSULA AVALONIA."

"Here lies buried the renowned King Arthurius in the Isle of Avalonia," Indract read by the light of the wavering taper in the fading day. "It is well, my brother. . . ."

"No." Baudwin spoke sharply, then recalled himself. "Forgive me, holy Father, but the High King's orders were clear. His grave is to be unmarked."

"So it shall be." Indract nodded. "We will bury the memorial stone with him." So the stone, leaden cross facing the buried coffin, was placed in the grave and all covered with the fresh brown earth.

With the last shovelful Indract raised his hands over the grave. "If we believe that our Lord Jesus Christ died and rose again, God will bring forth with Him from the dead those also who have fallen asleep believing in Him at the last day, at the sound of the trumpet, when all shall rise."

And the brothers responded, "I will praise You, Lord, for You have rescued me. I will praise You, for You have turned my sorrow into joy."

"Glory be to the Father, and to the Son, and to the Holy Ghost, as it was in the beginning, is now, and ever shall be, world without end, amen."

As the monks turned to go, Brother Breden, youngest of their number and yet not so young anymore, said, "We are so few. Are we all that is left of Logres [spiritual Britain]? Does the flame flicker so dimly?"

Gildas stopped still and, for once unfrowning, turned to his brothers. "I would speak to you in comfort the words of our long gone-away Archbishop Merlinus Ambrosius Dubricius [Merlin] who said, 'The light was before the dark, righteousness before evil, grace before sin. God the Creator existed before Satan the destroyed. So will light outlive dark, so is righteousness stronger than evil, so will grace overcome sin.' The darkness closes over us, my brothers, but the light will shine again. And this light—the shining of Logres—will be remembered on the other side of the dark."

The brothers made their silent, brown-shadowed way up the path to the chanting of their nighttime prayers in the Old Church, leaving Baudwin alone by the grave of Arthurius High King and Gwenhumara High Queen. He sat on the evening dew-damp grass and brought from the soft golden doeskin bag on his shoulder the harp he had carried with him from Camel Hill. A night thrush sang from the overhanging branch of a flowering apple tree, and he waited until her song was finished, for the bard would not stifle his sister. Then his fingers moved across the strings. "The Summer Kingdom has gone. It could not last upon this earth. It was but a vision, a foretaste of what is to come for those who love—for those who love Him who is the King above all High Kings. His Kingdom of Summer, of peace, and of love will come for all time."

The words came out in a strange chanting to a random plucking of strings, not at all the flowing bardsong Baudwin was wont to make. Yet the words rang with conviction. They were the words he found in his heart, and he knew they were true.

"But even so the end is not yet. The evil will not triumph forever. All that you did, my Arthurius, all that you lived for, my king, will rise again. It will live for generation unto generation. It will come again and again to each age with its own truth. Truth, like light, cannot die.

"It is given unto man—even such a man as you, my Arthurius—for you were but a man—once to die. In the end, all must die. But what you lived for, lives beyond and beyond.

"The triumph will be ours."

Joan Meets the King[†]
Mark Twain (Samuel Clemens)

From The Personal Recollections of Joan of Arc

Mark Twain (1835–1910) spent twelve years researching his book on Joan of Arc, the fifteenth-century heroine of the Hundred Years War. He considered it his best work, and it was his judgment that the peasant girl who became commander of the French army against the English was indeed a saint. The narrator of the story is a fictional character, Sieur Louis de Conte, Joan's personal secretary. He is witness to her triumphs on the battlefield, her trial for witchcraft by French clerics who sympathized with the English, and her martyrdom at the stake. In the two chapters that follow, he gives an account of how she finally meets the Dauphin, heir to the throne and future King Charles VII. In the opening paragraphs several other characters are introduced: her brother Pierre and her childhood friends, Paladin and Noel Rainguesson.

We rested and otherwise refreshed ourselves two or three hours at Gien, but by that time the news was abroad that the young girl commissioned of God to deliver France was come; wherefore, such a press of people flocked to our quarters to get sight of her that it seemed best to seek a quieter place; so we pushed on and halted at a small village called Fierbois.

We were now within six leagues of the King, who was at the Castle of Chinon. Joan dictated a letter to him at once, and I wrote it. In it she said she had come a hundred and fifty leagues to bring him good news, and begged the privilege of delivering it in person. She added that although she had never seen him she would know him in any disguise and would point him out.

The two knights rode away at once with the letter. The troop slept all the afternoon, and after supper we felt pretty fresh and fine, especially our little group of young Domremians.* We had the comfortable tap-room of the village inn to ourselves, and for the first time in ten unspeakably long days were exempt from bodings and terrors and hardships and fatiguing labors. The Paladin had suddenly become his ancient self again, and was swaggering up and down, a very monument of self-complacency. Noel Rainguesson said—

"I think it is wonderful, the way he has brought us through."

"Who?" asked Joan.

"Why, the Paladin."

The Paladin seemed not to hear.

"What had he to do with it?" asked Pierre d' Arc.

"Everything. It was nothing but Joan's confidence in his discretion that enabled her to keep up her heart. She could depend on us and on herself for valor, but discretion is the winning thing in war, after all; discretion is the rarest and loftiest of qualities, and he has got more of it than any other man in France—more of it, perhaps, than any other sixty men in France."

"Now you are getting ready to make a fool of yourself, Noel Rainguesson," said the Paladin, "and you want to coil some of that long tongue of yours around your neck and stick the end of it in your ear, then you'll be the less likely to get into trouble."

"I didn't know he had more discretion than other people," said Pierre, "for discretion argues brains, and he hasn't any more brains than the rest of us, in my opinion."

"No, you are wrong there. Discretion hasn't anything to do with brains; brains are an obstruction to it, for it does not reason, it feels. Perfect discretion means absence of brains. Discretion is a quality of the heart—solely a quality of the heart; it acts upon us through feeling. We know this because if it were an intellectual quality it would only perceive a danger, for instance, where a danger exists; whereas—"

"Hear him twaddle—the d—- idiot!" muttered the Paladin.

"—whereas, it being purely a quality of the heart, and proceeding by feeling, not reason, its reach is correspondingly wider and sublimer, enabling it to perceive and avoid dangers that haven't any existence at

---

*refers to the small French village of Domremy where Joan and her friends were born

all; as for instance that night in the fog, when the Paladin took his horse's ears for hostile lances and got off and climbed a tree—"

"It's a lie! a lie without shadow of foundation, and I call upon you all to beware how you give credence to the malicious inventions of this ramshackle slander-mill that has been doing its best to destroy my character for years, and will grind up your own reputations for you, next. I got off to tighten my saddle-girth—I wish I may die in my tracks if it isn't so—and whoever wants to believe it can, and whoever don't, can let it alone."

"There, that is the way with him, you see; he never can discuss a theme temperately, but always flies off the handle and becomes disagreeable. And you notice his defect of memory. He remembers getting off his horse, but forgets all the rest, even the tree. But that is natural; he would remember getting off the horse because he was so used to doing it. He always did it when there was an alarm and the clash of arms at the front."

"Why did he choose that time for it?" asked Jean.

"I don't know. To tighten up his girth, he thinks, to climb a tree, I think; I saw him climb nine trees in a single night."

"You saw nothing of the kind! A person that can lie like that deserves no one's respect. I ask you all to answer me. Do you believe what this reptile has said?"

All seemed embarrassed, and only Pierre replied. He said, hesitatingly—

"I—well, I hardly know what to say. It is a delicate situation. It seems offensive to refuse to believe a person when he makes so direct a statement, and yet I am obliged to say, rude as it may appear, that I am not able to believe the whole of it—no, I am not able to believe that you climbed nine trees."

"There!" cried the Paladin; "now what do you think of yourself, Noel Rainguesson? How many do you believe I climbed, Pierre?"

"Only eight."

The laughter that followed inflamed the Paladin's anger to white heat, and he said—

"I bide my time—I bide my time. I will reckon with you all, I promise you that!"

"Don't get him started," Noel pleaded; "he is a perfect lion when he gets started. I saw enough to teach me that, after the third skirmish.

After it was over I saw him come out of the bushes and attack a dead man single-handed."

"It is another lie; and I give you fair warning that you are going too far. You will see me attack a live one if you are not careful."

"Meaning me, of course. This wounds me more than any number of injurious and unkind speeches could do. Ingratitude to one's bene-factor—"

"Benefactor? What do I owe you, I should like to know?"

"You owe me your life. I stood between the trees and the foe, and kept hundreds and thousands of the enemy at bay when they were thirsting for your blood. And I did not do it to display my daring, I did it because I loved you and could not live without you."

"There—you have said enough! I will not stay here to listen to these infamies. I can endure your lies, but not your love. Keep that corrup-tion for somebody with a stronger stomach than mine. And I want to say this, before I go. That you peoples' small performances might appear the better and win you the more glory, I hid my own deeds through all the march. I went always to the front, where the fighting was thickest, to be remote from you, in order that you might not see and be discouraged by the things I did to the enemy. It was my purpose to keep this a secret in my own breast, but you force me to reveal it. If you ask for my witnesses, yonder they lie, on the road we have come. I found that road mud, I paved it with corpses. I found that country sterile, I fer-tilized it with blood. Time and again I was urged to go to the rear because the command could not proceed on account of my dead. And yet you, you miscreant, accuse me of climbing trees! Pah!"

And he strode out, with a lofty air, for the recital of his imaginary deeds had already set him up again and made him feel good.

Next day we mounted and faced toward Chinon. Orleans was at our back, now, and close by, lying in the strangling grip of the English; soon, please God, we would face about and go to their relief. From Gien the news had spread to Orleans that the peasant Maid of Vaucouleurs* was on her way, divinely commissioned to raise the siege. The news made a great excitement and raised a great hope—the first breath of

---

*the town Joan made her first base of operations

hope those poor souls had breathed in five months. They sent commissioners at once to the King to beg him to consider this matter, and not throw this help lightly away. These commissioners were already at Chinon by this time

When we were half-way to Chinon we happened upon yet one more squad of enemies. They burst suddenly out of the woods, and in considerable force, too; but we were not the apprentices we were ten or twelve days before; no, we were seasoned to this kind of adventure now; our hearts did not jump into our throats and our weapons tremble in our hands. We had learned to be always in battle array, always alert, and always ready to deal with any emergency that might turn up. We were no more dismayed by the sight of those people than our commander was. Before they could form, Joan had delivered the order, "Forward!" and we were down upon them with a rush. They stood no chance; they turned tail and scattered, we ploughing through them as if they had been men of straw. That was our last ambuscade, and it was probably laid for us by that treacherous rascal the King's own minister and favorite, De la Tremouille.

We housed ourselves in an inn, and soon the town came flocking to get a glimpse of the Maid. Ah, the tedious King and his tedious people! Our two good knights came presently, their patience well wearied, and reported. They and we reverently stood—as becomes persons who are in the presence of Kings and the superiors of Kings—until Joan, troubled by this mark of homage and respect, and not content with it nor yet used to it, although we had not permitted ourselves to do otherwise since the day she prophesied that wretched traitor's death and he was straightway drowned, thus confirming many previous signs that she was indeed an ambassador commissioned of God, commanded us to sit; then the Sieur de Metz said to Joan:

"The King has got the letter, but they will not let us have speech with him."

"Who is it that forbids?"

"None forbids, but there be three or four that are nearest his person—schemers and traitors every one—that put obstructions in the way, and seek all ways, by lies and pretexts, to make delay. Chiefest of these are Georges de la Tremouille and that plotting fox the Archbishop of Rheims. While they keep the King idle and in bondage to his sports and follies, they are great and their importance grows; whereas if ever he assert himself and rise and strike for crown and country like a man, their reign is done. So they but thrive they care not if the crown go to destruction and the King with it."

"You have spoken with others besides these?"

"Not of the Court, no—the Court are the meek slaves of those reptiles, and watch their mouths and their actions, acting as they act, thinking as they think, saying as they say: wherefore they are cold to us, and turn aside and go another way when we appear. But we have spoken with the commissioners from Orleans. They said with heat: 'It is a marvel that any man in such desperate case as is the King can moon around in this torpid way, and see his all go to ruin without lifting a finger to stay the disaster. What a most strange spectacle it is! Here he is, shut up in this wee corner of the realm like a rat in a trap; his royal shelter this huge gloomy tomb of a castle, with wormy rags for upholstery and crippled furniture for use, a very house of desolation; in his treasury forty francs, and not a farthing more, God be witness! no army, nor any shadow of one; and by contrast with this hungry poverty you behold this crownless pauper and his shoals of fools and favorites tricked out in the gaudiest silks and velvets you shall find in any Court in Christendom. And look you, he knows that when our city falls—as fall it surely will except succor come swiftly—France falls: he knows that when that day comes he will be an outlaw and a fugitive, and that behind him the English flag will float unchallenged over every acre of his great heritage; he knows these things, he knows that our faithful city is fighting all solitary and alone against disease, starvation, and the sword to stay this awful calamity, yet he will not strike one blow to save her, he will not hear our prayers, he will not even look upon our faces.' That is what the commissioners said, and they are in despair."

Joan said, gently—

"It is pity, but they must not despair. The Dauphin will hear them presently. Tell them so."

She almost always called the King the Dauphin. To her mind he was not King yet, not being crowned.

"We will tell them so, and it will content them, for they believe you come from God. The Archbishop and his confederates have for a backer that veteran soldier Raoul de Gaucourt, Grand Master of the Palace, a worthy man but simply a soldier, with no head for any greater matter. He cannot make out to see how a country girl, ignorant of war, can take a sword in her small hand and win victories where the trained generals of France have looked for defeats only, for fifty years—and always found them. And so he lifts his frosty mustache and scoffs."

"When God fights it is but small matter whether the hand that bears His sword is big or little. He will perceive this in time. Is there none in that Castle of Chinon who favors us?"

"Yes, the King's mother-in-law, Yolande, Queen of Sicily, who is wise and good. She spoke with the Sieur Bertrand."

"She favors us, and she hates those others, the King's beguilers," said Bertrand. "She was full of interest, and asked a thousand questions, all of which I answered according to my ability. Then she sat thinking over these replies until I thought she was lost in a dream and would wake no more. But it was not so. At last she said, slowly, and as if she were talking to herself: "A child of seventeen—a girl—country bred—untaught—ignorant of war, the use of arms, and the conduct of battles—modest, gentle, shrinking—yet throws away her shepherd's crook and clothes herself in steel, and fights her way through a hundred and fifty leagues of hostile territory, never losing heart or hope and never showing fear, and comes—she to whom a king must be a dread and awful presence—and will stand up before such a one and say, 'Be not afraid, God has sent me to save you! Ah, whence could come a courage and conviction so sublime as this but from very God Himself!' She was silent again awhile, thinking, and making up her mind; then she said, 'And whether she comes of God or no, there is that in her heart that raises her above men—high above all men that breathe in France today—for in her is that mysterious something that puts heart into soldiers, and turns mobs of cowards into armies of fighters that forget what fear is when they are in that presence—fighters who go into battle with joy in their eyes and songs on their lips, and sweep over the field like a storm—that is the spirit that can save France, and that alone, come it whence it may! It is in her, I do truly believe, for what else could have borne up that child on that great march, and made her despise its dangers and fatigues? The King must see her face to face—and shall!' She dismissed me with those good words, and I know her promise will be kept. They will delay her all they can—those animals—but she will not fail, in the end."

"Would she were King!" said the other knight, fervently. "For there is little hope that the King himself can be stirred out of his lethargy. He is wholly without hope, and is only thinking of throwing away everything and flying to some foreign land. The commissioners say there is a spell upon him that makes him hopeless—yes, and that it is shut up in a mystery which they cannot fathom."

"I know the mystery," said Joan, with quiet confidence; "I know it, and he knows it, but no other but God. When I see him I will tell him a secret that will drive away his trouble, then he will hold up his head again."

I was miserable with curiosity to know what it was that she would tell him, but she did not say, and I did not expect she would. She was but a child, it is true; but she was not a chatterer to tell great matters and make herself important to little people; no, she was reserved, and kept things to herself, as the truly great always do.

The next day Queen Yolande got one victory over the King's keepers, for in spite of their protestations and obstructions she procured an audience for our two knights, and they made the most they could out of their opportunity. They told the King what a spotless and beautiful character Joan was, and how great and noble a spirit animated her, and they implored him to trust in her, believe in her, and have faith that she was sent to save France. They begged him to consent to see her. He was strongly moved to do this, and promised that he would not drop the matter out of his mind, but would consult with his council about it. This began to look encouraging. Two hours later there was a great stir below, and the innkeeper came flying up to say a commission of illustrious ecclesiastics was come from the King—from the King his very self, understand!—think of this vast honor to his humble little hostelry!—and he was so overcome with the glory of it that he could hardly find breath enough in his excited body to put the facts into words. They were come from the King to speak with the Maid of Vaucouleurs. Then he flew downstairs, and presently appeared again, backing into the room and bowing to the ground with every step, in front of four imposing and austere bishops and their train of servants.

Joan rose, and we all stood. The bishops took seats, and for a while no word was said, for it was their prerogative to speak first, and they wore so astonished to see what a child it was that was making such a noise in the world and degrading personages of their dignity to the base function of ambassadors to her in her plebeian tavern, that they could not find any words to say, at first. Then presently their spokesman told Joan they were aware that she had a message for the King, wherefore she was now commanded to put it into words, briefly and without waste of time or embroideries of speech.

As for me, I could hardly contain my joy—our message was to reach the King at last! And there was the same joy and pride and exultation in the faces of our knights, too, and in those of Joan's brothers. And I knew that they were all praying—as I was—that the awe which we felt in the presence of these great dignitaries, and which would have tied our tongues and locked our jaws, would not affect her in the like degree, but that she would be enabled to word her message well, and with little stumbling, and so make a favorable impression here, where it would be so valuable and so important.

Ah dear, how little we were expecting what happened then! We were aghast to hear her say what she said. She was standing in a reverent attitude, with her head down and her hands clasped in front of her; for she was always reverent toward the consecrated servants of God. When the spokesman had finished, she raised her head and set her calm eye on those faces, not any more disturbed by their state and grandeur than a princess would have been, and said, with all her ordinary simplicity and modesty of voice and manner:

"Ye will forgive me, reverend sirs, but I have no message save for the King's ear alone."

Those surprised men were dumb for a moment, and their faces flushed darkly; then the spokesman said:

"Hark ye, do you fling the King's command in his face and refuse to deliver this message of yours to his servants appointed to receive it?"

"God has appointed one to receive it, and another's commandment may not take precedence of that. I pray you let me have speech of his grace the Dauphin."

"Forbear this folly, and come at your message! Deliver it, and waste no more time about it."

"You err indeed, most reverend fathers in God, and it is not well. I am not come hither to talk, but to deliver Orleans, and lead the Dauphin to his good city of Rheims, and set the crown upon his head."

"Is that the message you send to the King?"

But Joan only said, in the simple fashion which was her wont:

"Ye will pardon me for reminding you again—but I have no message to send to anyone."

The King's messengers rose in deep anger and swept out of the place without further words, we and Joan kneeling as they passed.

Our countenances were vacant, our hearts full of a sense of disaster. Our precious opportunity was thrown away; we could not understand Joan's conduct, she who had been so wise until this fatal hour. At last the Sieur Bertrand found courage to ask her why she had let this great chance to get her message to the King go by.

"Who sent them here?" she asked.

"The King."

"Who moved the King to send them?" She waited for an answer; none came, for we began to see what was in her mind—so she answered herself: "The Dauphin's council moved him to it. Are they enemies to me and to the Dauphin's weal, or are they friends?"

"Enemies," answered the Sieur Bertrand.

"If one would have a message go sound and ungarbled, does one choose traitors and tricksters to send it by?"

I saw that we had been fools, and she wise. They saw it too, so none found anything to say. Then she went on:

"They had but small wit that contrived this trap. They thought to get my message and seem to deliver it straight, yet deftly twist it from its purpose. You know that one part of my message is but this—to move the Dauphin by argument and reasonings to give me men-at-arms and send me to the siege. If an enemy carried these in the right words, the exact words, and no word missing, yet left out the persuasions of gesture and supplicating tone and beseeching looks that inform the words and make them live, where were the value of that argument—whom could it convince? Be patient, the Dauphin will hear me presently; have no fear."

The Sieur de Metz nodded his head several times and muttered as to himself:

"She was right and wise, and we are but dull fools, when all is said."

It was just my thought; I could have said it myself; and indeed it was the thought of all there present. A sort of awe crept over us, to think how that untaught girl, taken suddenly and unprepared, was yet able to penetrate the cunning devices of a King's trained advisers and defeat them. Marveling over this, and astonished at it, we fell silent and spoke no more. We had come to know that she was great in courage, fortitude, endurance, patience, conviction, fidelity to all duties—in all things, indeed, that make a good and trusty soldier and perfect him for his post; now we were beginning to feel that maybe there were greatnesses in her brain that were even greater than these great qualities of the heart. It set us thinking.

What Joan did that day bore fruit the very day after. The King was obliged to respect the spirit of a young girl who could hold her own and stand her ground like that, and he asserted himself sufficiently to put his respect into an act instead of into polite and empty words. He moved Joan out of that poor inn, and housed her, with us her servants, in the Castle of Courdray, personally confiding her to the care of Madame de Bellier, wife of old Raoul de Gaucourt, Master of the Palace. Of course this royal attention had an immediate result: all the great lords and ladies of the Court began to flock there to see and listen to the wonderful girl-soldier that all the world was talking about, and who had answered the King's mandate with a bland refusal to obey. Joan charmed them every one with her sweetness and simplicity and unconscious eloquence, and all the best and capablest among them recognized that there was an indefinable something about her that testified that she was not made of common clay, that she was built on a grander plan than the mass of mankind, and moved on a loftier plane. These spread her fame. She always made friends and advocates that way; neither the high nor the low could come within the sound of her voice and the sight of her face and go out from her presence indifferent. Well, anything to make delay. The King's council advised him against arriving at a decision in our matter too precipitately. He arrive at a decision too precipitately! So they sent a committee of priests—always priests—into Lorraine to inquire into Joan's character and history—a matter which would consume several weeks, of course. You see how fastidious they were. It was as if people should come to put out the fire when a man's house was burning down, and they waited till they could send into another country to find out if he had always kept the Sabbath or not, before letting him try.

So the days poked along; dreary for us young people in some ways, but not in all, for we had one great anticipation in front of us; we had never seen a king, and now some day we should have that prodigious spectacle to see and to treasure in our memories all our lives; so we were on the lookout, and always eager and watching for the chance. The others were doomed to wait longer than I, as it turned out. One day great news came—the Orleans commissioners, with Yolande and our knights, had at last turned the council's position and persuaded the King to see Joan.

Joan received the immense news gratefully but without losing her head, but with us others it was otherwise; we could not eat or sleep or do any rational thing for the excitement and the glory of it. During two days our pair of noble knights were in distress and trepidation on Joan's account, for the audience was to be at night, and they were afraid that Joan would be so paralyzed by the glare of light from the long files of torches, the solemn pomps and ceremonies, the great concourse of renowned personages, the brilliant costumes, and the other splendors of the Court, that she, a simple country maid, and all unused to such things, would be overcome by these terrors and make a piteous failure.

No doubt I could have comforted them, but I was not free to speak. Would Joan be disturbed by this cheap spectacle, this tinsel show, with its small King and his butterfly dukelets?—she who had spoken face to face with the princes of heaven, the familiars of God, and seen their retinue of angels stretching back into the remoteness of the sky, myriads upon myriads, like a measureless fan of light, a glory like the glory of the sun streaming from each of those innumerable heads, the massed radiance filling the deeps of space with a blinding splendor? I thought not.

Queen Yolande wanted Joan to make the best possible impression upon the King and the Court, so she was strenuous to have her clothed in the richest stuffs, wrought upon the princeliest pattern, and set off with jewels; but in that she had to be disappointed, of course, Joan not being persuadable to it, but begging to be simply and sincerely dressed, as became a servant of God, and one sent upon a mission of a serious sort and grave political import. So then the gracious Queen imagined and contrived that simple and witching costume which I have described to you so many times, and which I cannot think of even now in my dull age without being moved just as rhythmical and exquisite music moves one; for that was music, that dress—that is what it was—music that one saw with the eyes and felt in the heart. Yes, she was a poem, she was a dream, she was a spirit when she was clothed in that.

She kept that raiment always, and wore it several times upon occasions of state, and it is preserved to this day in the Treasury of Orleans, with two of her swords, and her banner, and other things now sacred because they had belonged to her.

At the appointed time the Count of Vendôme, a great lord of the Court, came richly clothed, with his train of servants and assistants, to conduct Joan to the King, and the two knights and I went with her, being entitled to this privilege by reason of our official positions near her person.

When we entered the great audience hall, there it all was, just as I have already painted it. Here were ranks of guards in shining armor and with polished halberds [axes]; two sides of the hall were like flower-gardens for variety of color and the magnificence of the costumes; light streamed upon these masses of color from two hundred and fifty flambeaux [torches]. There was a wide free space down the middle of the hall, and at the end of it was a throne royally canopied, and upon it sat a crowned and sceptered figure nobly clothed and blazing with jewels.

It is true that Joan had been hindered and put off a good while, but now that she was admitted to an audience at last, she was received with honors granted to only the greatest personages. At the entrance door stood four heralds in a row, in splendid tabards [sleeveless coats], with long slender silver trumpets at their mouths, with square silken banners depending from them embroidered with the arms of France. As Joan and the Count passed by, these trumpets gave forth in unison one long rich note, and as we moved down the hall under the pictured and gilded vaulting, this was repeated at every fifty feet of our progress—six times in all. It made our good knights proud and happy, and they held themselves erect, and stiffened their stride, and looked fine and soldierly. They were not expecting this beautiful and honorable tribute to our little country maid

Joan walked two yards behind the Count, we three walked two

yards behind Joan. Our solemn march ended when we were as yet some eight or ten steps from the throne. The Count made a deep obeisance, pronounced Joan's name, then bowed again and moved to his place among a group of officials near the throne. I was devouring the crowned personage with all my eyes, and my heart almost stood still with awe.

The eyes of all others were fixed upon Joan in a gaze of wonder which was half worship, and which seemed to say, "How sweet—how lovely—how divine!" All lips were parted and motionless, which was a sure sign that those people, who seldom forget themselves, had forgotten themselves now, and were not conscious of anything but the one object they were gazing upon. They had the look of people who are under the enchantment of a vision.

Then they presently began to come to life again, rousing themselves out of the spell and shaking it off as one drives away little by little a clinging drowsiness or intoxication. Now they fixed their attention upon Joan with a strong new interest of another sort; they were full of curiosity to see what she would do—they having a secret and particular reason for this curiosity. So they watched. This is what they saw:

She made no obeisance, nor even any slight inclination of her head, but stood looking toward the throne in silence. That was all there was to see, at present.

I glanced up at De Metz, and was shocked at the paleness of his face. I whispered and said—

"What is it man, what is it?"

His answering whisper was so weak I could hardly catch it—

"They have taken advantage of the hint in her letter to play a trick upon her! She will err, and they will laugh at her. That is not the King that sits there."

Then I glanced at Joan. She was still gazing steadfastly toward the throne, and I had the curious fancy that even her shoulders and the back of her head expressed bewilderment. Now she turned her head slowly, and her eye wandered along the lines of standing courtiers till it fell upon a young man who was very quietly dressed; then her face lighted joyously, and she ran and threw herself at his feet, and clasped his knees, exclaiming in that soft melodious voice which was her birthright and was now charged with deep and tender feeling—

"God of his grace give you long life, O dear and gentle Dauphin!"

In his astonishment and exultation De Metz cried out—

"By the shadow of God, it is an amazing thing!" Then he mashed all the bones of my hand in his grateful grip, and added, with a proud shake at his mane, "Now, what have these painted infidels to say!"

Meantime the young person in the plain clothes was saying to Joan—

"Ah, you mistake, my child, I am not the King. There he is," and he pointed to the throne.

The knight's face clouded, and he muttered in grief and indignation—

"Ah, it is a shame to use her so. But for this lie she had gone through safe. I will go and proclaim to all the house what—"

"Stay where you are!" whispered I and the Sieur Bertrand in a breath, and made him stop in his place.

Joan did not stir from her knees, but still lifted her happy face toward the King, and said—

"No, gracious liege, you are he, and none other."

De Metz's troubles vanished away, and he said—

"Verily, she was not guessing, she *knew*. Now, how could she know? It is a miracle. I am content, and will meddle no more, for I perceive that she is equal to her occasions, having that in her head that cannot profitably be helped by the vacancy that is in mine."

This interruption of his lost me a remark or two of the other talk; however, I caught the King's next question:

"But tell me who you are, and what would you?"

"I am called Joan the Maid, and am sent to say that the King of Heaven wills that you be crowned and consecrated in your good city of Rheims, and be thereafter Lieutenant of the Lord of Heaven, who is King of France. And He willeth also that you set me at my appointed work and give me men-at-arms." After a slight pause she added, her eye lighting at the sound of her words, "For then will I raise the siege of Orleans and break the English power!"

The young monarch's amused face sobered a little when this martial speech fell upon that sick air like a breath blown from embattled camps and fields of war, and his trifling smile presently faded wholly away and disappeared. He was grave, now, and thoughtful. After a little he waved his hand lightly and all the people fell away and left those two

by themselves in a vacant space. The knights and I moved to the opposite side of the hall and stood there. We saw Joan rise at a sign, then she
and the King talked privately together.

All that host had been consumed with curiosity to see what Joan
would do. Well, they had seen, and now they were full of astonishment
to see that she had really performed that strange miracle according to
the promise in her letter; and they were fully as much astonished to find
that she was not overcome by the pomps and splendors about her, but
was even more tranquil and at her ease in holding speech with a
monarch than ever they themselves had been, with all their practice and
experience.

As for our two knights, they were inflated beyond measure with
pride in Joan, but nearly dumb, as to speech, they not being able to think
out any way to account for her managing to carry herself through this
imposing ordeal without ever a mistake or an awkwardness of any kind
to mar the grace and credit of her great performance.

The talk between Joan and the King was long and earnest, and held
in low voices. We could not hear, but we had our eyes and could note
effects; and presently we and all the house noted one effect which was
memorable and striking, and has been set down in memoirs and histories and in testimony at the Process of Rehabilitation by some who witnessed it; for all knew it was big with meaning, though none knew what
that meaning was at that time, of course. For suddenly we saw the King
shake off his indolent attitude and straighten up like a man, and at the
same time look immeasurably astonished. It was as if Joan had told him
something almost too wonderful for belief, and yet of a most uplifting
and welcome nature.

It was long before we found out the secret of this conversation, but
we know it now, and all the world knows it. That part of the talk was
like this—as one may read in all histories. The perplexed King asked
Joan for a sign. He wanted to believe in her and her mission, and that
her Voices were supernatural and endowed with knowledge hidden
from mortals, but how could he do this unless these Voices could prove
their claim in some absolutely unassailable way? It was then that Joan
said—

"I will give you a sign, and you shall no more doubt. There is a
secret trouble in your heart which you speak of to none—a doubt which

wastes away your courage, and makes you dream of throwing all away and fleeing from your realm. Within this little while you have been praying, in your own breast, that God of his grace would resolve that doubt, even if the doing of it must show you that no kingly right is lodged in you."

It was that that amazed the King, for it was as she had said: his prayer was as the secret of his own breast, and none but God could know about it. So he said:

"The sign is sufficient. I know, now, that these Voices are of God. They have said true in this matter; if they have said more, tell it me—I will believe."

"They have resolved that doubt, and I bring their very words, which are these: Thou art lawful heir to the King thy father, and true heir of France. God has spoken it. Now lift up thy head, and doubt no more, but give me men-at-arms and let me get about my work."

Telling him he was of lawful birth was what straightened him up and made a man of him for a moment, removing his doubts upon that head and convincing him of his royal right; and if any could have hanged his hindering and pestiferous council and set him free, he would have answered Joan's prayer and set her in the field. But no, those creatures were only checked, not checkmated; they could invent some more delays.

We had been made proud by the honors which had so distinguished Joan's entrance into that place—honors restricted to personages of very high rank and worth—but that pride was as nothing compared with the pride we had in the honor done her upon leaving it. For whereas those first honors were shown only to the great, these last, up to this time, had been shown only to the royal. The King himself led Joan by the hand down the great hall to the door, the glittering multitude standing and making reverence as they passed, and the silver trumpets sounding those rich notes of theirs. Then he dismissed her with gracious words, bending low over her hand and kissing it. Always—from all companies, high or low—she went forth richer in honor and esteem than when she came.

And the King did another handsome thing by Joan, for he sent us back to Courdray Castle torch-lighted and in state, under escort of his own troop—his guard of honor—the only soldiers he had; and finely equipped and bedizened they were, too, though they hadn't seen the color of their wages since they were children, as a body might say. The wonders which Joan had been performing before the King had been carried all around by this time, so the road was so packed with people who wanted to get a sight of her that we could hardly dig through; and as for talking together, we couldn't, all attempts at talk being drowned in the storm of shoutings and huzzas that broke out all along as we passed, and kept abreast of us like a wave the whole way.

❧ SIN AND REDEMPTION ❧

The Slough of Despond and The Interpreter's House
John Bunyan

From Pilgrim's Progress
(Adapted by Oliver Hunkin in Dangerous Journey*)*

In this modern adaptation of John Bunyan's Pilgrim's Progress *by English television writer Oliver Hunkin, Christian forsakes his home and family and sets out to find the Celestial City. He carries on his back the burden of his own sin, and he faces many dangers and temptations along the way. Bunyan (1628-1688), who tells the story as if it were a dream, was a poor tinker and lay preacher who was jailed six times for his religious views.* Pilgrim's Progress *was written during one 12-year period of imprisonment for preaching without a license. It was intended to instruct common folk about the Bible's teachings on sin and repentance. Though it recognizes the dark, sinful side of man, it is basically a tale of hope in which, with God's grace, his better nature triumphs.*

The Slough of Despond

As I walked through the wilderness of this world, I lighted on a certain place and laid me down to sleep; and as I slept, I dreamed a dream.

I dreamed that I saw a man, with his face turned away from his own house—a book in his hand, and a great burden on his back. I looked and saw him open the book and read therein; and, as he read, he wept and trembled; and not being able to contain himself, he broke out with a lamentable cry, saying: *"What shall I do to be saved?"*

For he lived in the City of Destruction, which he learnt from his book was doomed to be burned with fire from heaven, in which fearful overthrow both himself, and his wife and their four sons would miserably perish—unless some way of escape could be found.

So Christian (for that was his name) went home to talk to his family. And they were greatly worried, not because they believed that what he said was true, but because they thought some kind of madness had got into the poor man. And as it was drawing towards night, they hoped that sleep might settle his brains. With all haste they put him to bed.

But the night was as troublesome to him as the day; wherefore, instead of sleeping, he spent it in sighs and tears. So, when morning was come, and they asked him how he was, he told them: *"Worse! Worse!"*

He also started talking to them again, but they began to lose patience. Sometimes they would deride him: sometimes they would chide him; and sometimes they would quite neglect him.

So Christian went by himself into the fields—still reading his book and carrying his burden, and greatly distressed in his mind. He looked this way and that way, as if he would run, yet he stood still, because he couldn't tell which way to go.

Then—in the distance—he saw a man approaching. His name was Evangelist, and he asked Christian: "What are you weeping for?"

"Sir," he answered, "this book in my hand tells me to flee from the wrath to come. Also, I fear that this burden, which is upon my back, will sink me lower than the grave. Therefore, I need to get rid of it."

"If this is so," said Evangelist, "then why are you standing still?"

"Because I don't know where to go," he answered.

Then Evangelist pointed with his finger over a wide field. "Do you see yonder wicket-gate?" he asked.

"No," said Christian.

"Then do you see a shining light?"

"I think I do," said Christian.

Then said Evangelist: "Keep that light in your eye, and go in that direction. So shall you reach the gate. There, when you knock, it will be told you what to do."

So I saw in my dream that the man began to run. But he hadn't run far before his wife and children saw him running, and called after him to return. But the man put his fingers in his ears and ran on. He didn't look back but ran towards the middle of the plain.

The neighbors too came out to see him run, and as he ran, some mocked and others threatened. A couple of them were resolved to fetch him back by force; the name of the one was Obstinate, and the name of the other was Pliable. Now by this time the man had gone a good distance from them. Nevertheless, they pursued after him and overtook him.

"Neighbors, why have you come?" asked Christian.

"To persuade you to come back with us," they said.

"That can by no means be," said Christian. "You dwell in the City of Destruction. Be content, good neighbors, to go along with me."

"What!" said Obstinate, "and leave our friends and our comforts behind us?"

"Yes. For I seek an endless kingdom, which we may inhabit forever. Read of it, if you will, in my book."

"Tush!" cried Obstinate. "Away with your book. Will you go back with us or no?"

"No, not I."

Pliable so far had held his peace. But now he spoke: "If what Christian says is true, I intend to go with this good man."

"Very well, then," replied Obstinate. "I will go back to my own place. I'll be no companion to such fantastical fellows."

With that, they parted. Obstinate went back and Christian and Pliable went on over the plain, discoursing all the while.

"Tell me more, neighbor Christian," inquired Pliable, "about the place to which we're going."

"There are crowns of glory to be given us, and garments shining like the sun," Christian told him.

"That's very pleasant; and what else?"

"There shall be no more crying," said Christian. "For the Owner of the Place will wipe all the tears from our eyes."

"Well, my good companion, I'm glad to hear these things. Come on, let's hurry."

"I can't go any faster," answered Christian, "with this burden on my back."

Now I saw in my dream that, as they were hurrying along and talking, they had drawn near to a quagmire in the middle of the plain, which was called the Slough of Despond. And before they knew what was happening, they had both fallen into the bog. It was a bog where many travelers before them had been drowned. Here, therefore, they wallowed, being grievously bedaubed with the dirt. And Christian, because of the burden on his back, began to sink, first knee-deep—then waist-deep—into the loathsome scum.

"Neighbor Christian, where are you now?" asked Pliable.

"Truly, I do not know," Christian replied.

So Pliable began to be offended and angrily said to his fellow: "Is this the happiness you promised me? If we have such ill speed at our first setting out, what may we expect between this and our journey's end?"

With that, having no burden to contend with, Pliable scrambled out—on that side of the Slough which was nearest to his own house. And so he ran off home for a hot bath, leaving Christian to his fate. For his part, Christian was struggling to reach the side of the Slough nearest to the wicket-gate. Which he eventually did, but couldn't clamber out by reason of the burden on his back.

Then I beheld in my dream that a man came to him, whose name was Help, and asked him what he was doing there.

Christian answered: "Sir, I was bidden to go this way by a man called Evangelist."

"But did you not look for the stepping-stones?"

"Fear followed me so hard, that I fell in," replied Christian.

"That is the snare and hazard of this place," said Help. "It so spews out its filth that, at the changes of the weather, these steps are hardly seen. Here, give me your hand." So he gave him his hand, and drew him out, and set him on firm ground again. And Christian continued on his way towards the wicket-gate.

Although he didn't know it, worse trouble lay in store. For a certain Mr. Worldly Wiseman was now seen crossing the field to meet him. He dwelt in the town of Carnal Policy—a very great town, hard-by where Christian lived. This man then, having some inkling of him—for

Christian's departure from the City of Destruction was much noised abroad—began to question him.

"How now, good fellow, where are you going with that great burden?"

"I'm going to yonder wicket-gate. Have you a wife and children?" asked Mr. Worldly Wiseman.

"Why, yes," replied Christian. "But I am so heavily weighed down, I can't take pleasure in them anymore."

"Who counseled you to start upon this dangerous journey?"

"A man that came to me. His name, as I remember, was Evangelist."

"I thought as much," said Mr. Worldly Wiseman. "He is forever leading travelers astray. There's no more difficult road in the world than the one he's directed you to. I see, by the dirt on you, that you've already been in the Slough of Despond. But that Slough is only the beginning of your troubles. In the way you are going you are likely to encounter far worse things than this—lions, dragons, darkness, and death. This has been confirmed by many witnesses. So why should a man so carelessly risk his life, by giving heed to a stranger?"

After pausing for breath, Mr. Worldly Wiseman proceeded as follows: "Hear me—I am older than you—and I'll give you some advice. In yonder village there dwells a gentleman whose name is Legality, a very judicious man—a man of very good name. He has skill to help men off with their burdens. He has, to my knowledge, cured several who were going out of their wits because of them. His house is not a mile from this place, and if he's not at home himself his son—who's called Civility—will help you. Moreover, if you wish there are houses standing empty in the village at reasonable rates. The food is cheap and good, and you can send for your wife and family, and all live happily together."

Christian, we fear, was all too ready to listen to Mr. Worldly Wiseman and leave the straight path he was on. "Sir, which is the way to this honest man's house?" he inquired.

"Do you see yonder high hill?" asked Mr. Worldly Wiseman.

"Yes, very well."

"By that hill you must go, and the first house you come to is Mr. Legality's."

Thus did Mr. Worldly Wiseman courteously direct poor Christian down the wrong road. For what he had failed to tell him was the hill ahead was a fearsome mountain. It seemed to overhang the road so much that Christian—looking up as the clouds scudded over it—was afraid that it would fall upon his head. Worst than that, there were flashes of fire coming out of it. And Christian, because of his burden, might easily have fallen and thus early on his journey might have been burnt to death. Wherefore he did sweat and quake for fear.

At that moment, who should appear but Evangelist, coming to meet him with a severe and dreadful countenance, at the sight of which Christian began to blush with shame.

"Aren't you the man I found weeping outside the City of Destruction?" questioned Evangelist.

"Yes, dear sir, I am the man."

"Did not I direct you to the little wicket-gate?"

"Yes, dear sir" replied Christian.

"How is it then that you've so quickly turned aside?"

"I met, you see, a gentleman; and he persuaded me that I might find in the village before me a man who could take off my burden. He said, moreover, he would show me a better way—not so attended with difficulties as the way, sir, that you set me in."

Then said Evangelist: "Stand still a little."

So he stood trembling. And Evangelist said: "You have rejected the Word of God for the advice of Mr. Worldly Wiseman. But Mr. Legality cannot free you of your burden. Mr. Legality is a cheat. As for his son, Civility, notwithstanding his simpering looks, he cannot help you either." As he spoke, there was a great clap of thunder. And Christian called himself a thousand fools for listening to Mr. Worldly Wiseman.

"I am sorry I have hearkened to this man's counsel," he said, turning back with haste.

He spoke to no one on the way, nor, if anybody asked him, would he give them an answer. He went like one that was all the while treading on forbidden ground and could by no means think himself safe till he had regained the road he had abandoned.

But would he ever reach it? He wasn't at all sure. For narrow is the gate, it says in his book, and few are they who find it.

The Interpreter's House

I saw then, in my dream, that ahead of Christian, on a grassy bank, lay three men fast asleep, with fetters on their heels. They were called Simple, Sloth, and Presumption.

Christian knew that to sleep on this particular road was like sleeping in the rigging of a ship when a storm was brewing.

"Wake up!" he cried, "and I will help you off with your irons."

But they only opened one eye at him and yawned.

"I see no danger," said Simple.

"I want to go on sleeping," said Sloth.

"Every tub must stand on its own bottom," said Presumption.

Then they all three rolled over and went to sleep again.

So Christian proceeded on his way, troubled to think that men in such danger should so little esteem his kindness in waking them. And we are now to learn how wise it was of Christian to warn them. For as he drew near to the narrow wicket-gate, he saw that it was firmly closed.

And even as he reached it, he felt the wind of an arrow swish past his ear and bury itself in the woodwork. Looking round in terror, he now saw, on the opposite hill, a strong castle with a host of dark, menacing figures on the battlements.

Christian didn't dally. Over the gate was written: "KNOCK, AND IT SHALL BE OPENED UNTO YOU."

He knocked with all his might.

A second arrow narrowly missed him.

"Who's there?" asked a voice.

"A poor burdened traveler. I come from the City of Destruction, and I'm going to the Celestial City."

To his relief, the gate was quickly opened, and a hand pulled him in.

Then Christian asked the Guardian of the Gate, whose name was Goodwill: "What mean these arrows?"

To which he answered: "Yonder castle belongs to Beelzebub, the Prince of the Devils. Both he and his soldiers will shoot their darts at anyone who tries to enter here. They aim to kill you before you can reach safety. You are fortunate to be alive."

"I tremble and rejoice," said Christian.

"Why do you come alone?" asked Goodwill.

"Because none of my neighbors and none whom I encountered on the road saw the danger."

"Did none of them follow you?"

"Pliable came with me a little way, until we fell—both together—into the Slough of Despond," Christian answered. "At that he was discouraged and would not adventure further."

"Alas, poor man! Is it not worth running a few risks when the Heavenly City is your destination?" Goodwill asked.

"But I'm not one to talk," replied Christian. "I also nearly turned aside, persuaded by the arguments of Mr. Worldly Wiseman. And I don't know what would have become of me, had not Evangelist met me again when I was musing in the midst of my dumps. And truth to tell, I'm still much inconvenienced by this burden that is upon my back."

Then I saw in my dream that Christian asked him if he could not help him off with his burden.

"However hard I try," said Christian, "I don't seem able to move it."

"No man can get it off you," said Goodwill. "But keep to the straight and narrow path and it will lead you to the Place of Deliverance."

So Christian began to gird his loins, and to address himself to his journey. "How far will it be?" he asked himself, as he plodded on his way.

His next stop was the House of the Interpreter, who, Goodwill had told him, could give him useful lessons for his journey. It was a large and mysterious house, such as one visits in dreams. Its Master, in answer to his knock, asked him what he wanted.

"Sir," said Christian, "I am a man that is going to Mount Zion. And I was told that, if I called here, you would show me excellent things, which would help me."

"Come in," said the Interpreter.

First he led him into a parlor, which was full of dust, because it was never swept. So the Interpreter called for a serving-maid to sweep it. But the dust began to fly, and Christian began to choke. Never had there been such dust. He groped around blindly. Then he heard the Interpreter tell the maid: "Bring hither water, and sprinkle the room."

All at once the dust had cleared, and the maid was sweeping it up with pleasure.

"This parlor," said the Interpreter, "is the soul of man clogged with the dust of sin. But see how easily, by God's grace, it can be cleansed."

I saw, in my dream, that the Interpreter took Christian by the hand again and led him into a very dark room, where there sat a man in an iron cage. Now the man seemed very sad. He sat with his eyes looking down to the ground, and his hands folded together, and he sighed as if his heart would break.

Then said Christian: "Who is this?"

"Talk with him and see," said the Interpreter.

"What used you to be?" asked Christian.

"I was once a flourishing professor, both in my own eyes and also in the eyes of others," answered the man. "I was on my way, as I thought, to the Celestial City, and I was confident that I would get there."

"But what did you do to bring yourself to this condition?" Christian asked.

"I failed to keep watch," the man replied. "I followed the pleasures of this world, which promised me all manner of delights. But they proved to be an empty bubble. And now I am shut up in this iron cage— a man of despair, who can't get out."

No further explanations were given. No one said who put him there. But the Interpreter whispered to Christian: "Bear well in mind what you have seen."

Finally, Christian was led to a gateway like the one which he had lately entered. Beside it sat a man at a table, with a book and inkhorn before him to take the name of anyone who wished to pass through. But the gate was guarded by fierce men in armor, ready to do what hurt and mischief they could to any traveler. And though there stood a great company of people desirous of going in, they didn't dare. Then, as it were a scene upon the stage, Christian saw a valiant man approach.

"Set down my name, sir," he said. That done, he drew his sword and rushed upon the armed men, who laid upon him with deadly force. But the man, not at all discouraged, fell to cutting and hacking most resolutely. So, after he had received and given many wounds, he cut his way to safety.

"I think I know the lesson of this," said Christian triumphantly, as he resumed his journey. "My safety will depend, it seems, not on cleverness, but on simple courage."

How his burden had got on his back in the first place, and why nobody else had burdens—as happens in dreams—we are not told. But never had he been so eager as he was now to be rid of it. And that—did he but know it—was half the battle.

Now I saw in my dream that the road, from then on, was fenced on either side with a wall. The wall was named Salvation. Along this road did burdened Christian run. Or should we say, he did his best to run, so far as he could, with that load upon his back.

At the foot of a hill, he passed an open tomb. Then up again, upon a little knoll, he found himself beneath a wayside cross. And as its shadow fell across him, so suddenly the burden, slipping from his shoulders, fell from off his back. It tumbled down the hill. It tumbled into the mouth of the tomb. It was never seen again.

Christian kept feeling behind his back. He couldn't believe it. For it was very surprising to him that the simple act of gazing at the cross had set him free, and his burden of guilt was gone.

As he stood there in amazement, behold three Shining Ones appeared. The first one said: "Your soul is now swept clean of sin."

The second stripped him of his mud-stained rags and gave him bright new clothes.

The third one handed him a parchment. "Guard it carefully," he said, "and surrender it only when you have reached the gate of the Celestial City."

Great dangers lay ahead of him, but for the moment he was light as air. So Christian gave three leaps for joy, and went on singing.

> *Who would true valor see*
> *Let him come hither;*
> *One here will constant be*
> *Come wind, come weather*
> *There's no discouragement*
> *Shall make him once relent*
> *His first avowed intent*
> *To be a pilgrim.*

Brother Orchid

Richard Connell

*American short story writer Richard Connell's (1893-1949) classic tale of suspense,
"The Most Dangerous Game," has long been standard reading in most high school and
college literature courses, but he also wrote many other stories that are just as riveting,
including "Brother Orchid," which, shortly after its publication in 1938, inspired both
a Broadway play and a Hollywood motion picture. Brother Orchid, first introduced to
us as Little John Sarto, is a cynical, wise-cracking gangster who is forced to hide from
his would-be killers in a little, out-of-the-way monastery in the Michigan woods. At
first, he intends to use the monks sheltering him in a nefarious plot to regain control of
his underworld empire in Chicago, but something changes his mind.*

B̲e smart," the warden said. "Go straight."

A grin creased the leather face of Little John Sarto.

"I am goin' straight," he said. "Straight to Chi."

"I wouldn't if I were you, Sarto."

"Why not? I owned that burg once. I'll own it again."

"Things have changed in ten years."

"But not me," said Little John. "I still got what it takes to be on top."

"You didn't stay there," the warden observed.

"I got framed," Sarto said. "Imagine shovin' me on the rock on a
sissy income tax rap!"

"It was the only charge they could make stick," the warden said.
"You were always pretty slick, Sarto."

"I was, and I am," said Little John.

The warden frowned. "Now look here, Sarto. When a man has
done his time and I'm turning him loose, I'm supposed to give him
some friendly advice. I do it, though I know that in most cases it's a
farce. You'd think men who'd done a stretch here in Alcatraz ought to
have a sneaking notion that crime does not pay, but while I'm preaching my little sermon I see a faraway look in their eyes and I know they're
figuring out their next bank job or snatch."

"Don't class me with them small-time heisters and petty-larceny
yeggs," said Little John. "I'm a born big shot."

"You're apt to die the same way," said the warden dryly.

"That's okay by me," said Little John. "When I peg out I want to go
with fireworks, flowers and bands; but you'll have a beard to your knees

before they get out the last extra on Little John Sarto. I got a lot of livin' to do first: I got to wash out the taste of slum with a lakeful of champagne, and it'll take half the blondes in the Loop* to make me forget them nights in solitary. But most of all I got to be myself again, not just a number. For every order I've took here on the rock, I'm goin' to give two. I'm goin' to see guys shiver and jump when I speak. I've played mouse long enough. Watch me be a lion again."

The warden sighed. "Sarto," he said, "why don't you play it safe? Stay away from Chicago. Settle in some new part of the country. Go into business. You've got brains and a real gift for organization. You ran a big business once—"

"Million a month, net," put in Sarto.

"And you're only forty-six and full of health," the warden went on. "You can still make a fresh start."

"Using what for wampum?" asked Little John.

"You've got plenty salted away."

Sarto laughed a wry laugh.

"I got the ten bucks, and the ticket back to Chi, and this frowsy suit the prison gimme, and that's all I got," he said.

"Don't tell me you're broke!"

"Flat as a mat," said Little John. "I spent it like I made it—fast. A king's got to live like a king, ain't he? When I give a dame flowers, it was always orchids. My free-chow bill ran to a grand a week. They called me a public enemy but they treated me like a year-round Sandy Claws. . . . But I ain't worryin'. I was born broke. I got over it."

■

A prison guard came in to say that the launch was ready to take Sarto to the mainland.

"Well, goodbye, Warden," said Sarto jauntily. "If you ever get to Chi gimme a buzz. I'll throw a party for you."

"Wait a minute," said the warden. "I can't let you go till I make one

---

*downtown Chicago

last attempt to start you on the right track. I know a man who'll give you a job. He runs a big truck farm and—"

He stopped, for Sarto was shaking with hoarse laughter.

"Me a rube?" Little John got out. "Me a bodyguard to squashes? Warden, the stir-bugs has got you."

"It's a chance to make an honest living."

"Save it for some cluck that would feel right at home livin' with turnips," Sarto said. "I got other plans."

The siren on the launch gave an impatient belch.

"So long, Warden," said Little John. "I won't be seein' you."

"You're right there," the warden said.

Sarto's face darkened at the words.

"Meanin' Chi might be bad for my health?"

"I've heard rumors to that effect," replied the warden.

"I've heard 'em for years," said Little John. "They're a lotta rat spit. Plenty guys has talked about what they was goin' to do to me. I always sent flowers to their funerals—you heard about that."

He chuckled.

"A big heart of forget-me-nots with 'Sorry, Pal' in white orchids on it."

"All right, wise guy," the warden said. "Go to Chicago. The sooner you get rubbed out, the better for everybody. You're no good and you never will be."

"Atta clown," said Little John Sarto. "Always leave 'em laughin' when you say goodbye."

Laughing, he started out toward the big gray gate.

■

Deep in the woods in an out-of-the-world corner of Michigan, squat, unkempt Twin Pine Inn hides itself. It was silent that summer night, and dark save for a single window in the taproom. Behind the customerless bar, Fat Dutchy was drinking his fourth rock-and-rye.

"Stick 'em up. This is a heist."

The voice, low and with a snarl in it, came from the doorway behind him. Up went Fat Dutchy's hands.

"Easy with the rod," he whimpered. "There ain't a sawbuck in the joint."

"Not like the good old days," the voice said.

Dutchy turned his head. Little John Sarto was standing there with nothing more lethal in his hand than a big cigar. Dutchy blinked and goggled.

"Well, greaseball, do I look funny?" Sarto demanded.

"No—no—boss, you ain't changed a bit."

"I don't change," Sarto said. "Gimme a slug of bourbon."

Fat Dutchy sloshed four fingers of whisky into a glass. His hand trembled. Liquor splashed on the bar.

"What you got the jits about?" asked Sarto.

"You gimme a turn comin' in like you was a ghost or sumpin'," said Fat Dutchy. He wiped sweat from his mottled jowls with the bar rag. Sarto gulped his drink.

"Business bad, eh?"

"It ain't even bad, boss. It just ain't."

"Cheer up, big puss. You'll soon be scoffin' filly miggnons smothered with century notes," Sarto said. "I'm back."

Fat Dutchy rubbed his paunch and looked unhappily at the floor. "Things is different," he said.

Sarto banged his glass down on the bar.

"If one more lug tells me that, I'll kick his gizzard out," he said. "Now, listen. I'm holin' up here till I get my bearin's. Soon as I get things set, I'm goin' to town. But first I gotta contact some of the boys."

■

Fat Dutchy played nervously with the bar rag.

"Gimme another slug," Sarto ordered. "I got a ten-year thirst."

Fat Dutchy poured out the drink. Again his shaking hands made him spill some of it.

"Here's to me," said Sarto, and drank. "Now, listen: I want you to pass the office along to certain parties that I'm here and want to see 'em, pronto. For a starter, get in touch with Philly Powell, Ike Gelbert, Ouch O'Day, Willie the Knife, Benny Maletta, French Frank, Hop Latzo, Al Muller and that fresh kid that was so handy with a tommy gun—"

"Jack Buck?"

"Yeah. I may need a torpedo. When I fell out, he had the makin's of a good dropper. So get that phone workin', lard head—you know where they hang out."

"Sure," said Fat Dutchy. He held up his hand and ticked off names on his thick fingers.

"Ike Gelbert and Al Muller is in the jug doin' life jolts," he said. "Philly Powell and French Frank was crossed out right at this bar. Ouch O'Day throwed an ing-bing and was took to the fit house; the G-boys filled Benny Maletta with slugs and sent Willie the Knife to the hot squat; I dunno just where Hop Latzo is but I've heard talk he's at the bottom of Lake Mich in a barrel of concrete. So outa that lot there's only Jack Buck left and I don't guess you wanna see him—"

"Why not?"

"He's growed up," said Fat Dutchy. "He's the loud noise now. What rackets there is, Jack Buck's got 'em in his pocket."

"I'll whittle him down to his right size," said Sarto.

"Jack's in strong. He's waitin' for you, boss, and he ain't foolin'. The boys tell me it's worth three G's to the guy that settles you."

Sarto snorted. "Only three grand!" he said indignantly.

"That's serious sugar nowadays," said Fat Dutchy. "I'm tellin' you times is sour. Jack Buck has cornered the few grafts that still pay. He's got a mob of muzzlers that was in reform school when you was head man. You ain't nothin' to 'em but a name and a chance to earn three thousand fish."

Sarto sipped his drink. Lines of thought furrowed his face.

"I'll stay here till I figure out an angle," he announced.

"Boss," said Fat Dutchy, "I don't wanna speak outa turn, but wouldn't it be a smart play to take it on the lam for a while?"

"Where to?"

Fat Dutchy shrugged his stout shoulders.

"I wouldn't know, boss," he said. "When the heat's on—"

"Yeah, I know," cut in Sarto. "You're smoked wherever you go."

"What are you goin' to do, boss?"

"I'm goin' to hit the sheets and dream I'm out," said Little John. Dog-tired though he was, he could not get to sleep. His mind yanked him away from dreams, back to prison, to the death-house, where men were lying in the dark, as he was, trying to sleep.

"They got the bulge on me, at that," he thought. "They *know* when they're goin' to get it."

He felt like a man reading his own obituary, complete but for two facts: where and when.

He knew he was safe where he was, but not for long. They'd comb all the known hideouts. He tried to think of some friend he could trust to hide him. Name after name he considered and rejected. He had come to the ninety-sixth name and found no one he could count on when he fell asleep.

■

A light in his eyes and a voice in his ear jerked him awake.

A man was bending over him, smiling and saying:

"Wake up, dear. You'll be late for school."

He was a huge, soft-looking young man with a jovial freckled face. His suit was bottle-green and expensive. Sarto had never seen him before.

"Up, up, pets" he said, and waved at Sarto a big blue-black automatic.

A second man watched from the other side of the bed. He was younger and smaller than the first man, and his flour-white face was perfectly blank. Sarto did not know him either.

Sarto sat up in bed.

"Listen, fellas," he said, "if I get a break you get five grand."

"Got it on you, darling?" asked the freckled man.

"Nope. But I can dig it up inside a week."

"Sorry. We do a strictly cash business," the freckled man said.

"I'll make it ten grand," said Little John. He addressed the pallid man. "Wadda you say, bud? Ten G's."

The freckled man chuckled.

"He'd say 'no' if he could say anything," he said. "He doesn't hear, either. His eyes are good, though. His name is Harold, but we call him Dummy."

Sarto held his naked, flabby body very stiff and straight.

"Do your stuff," he said.

Dummy took his hand from his pocket. There was a pistol in it. The freckled man brushed the gun aside.

"We don't want to give this charming place a bad name," he explained to Sarto. "For Dutchy's sake."

"So that fat rat tipped you," said Sarto.

"Yes," said the freckled man. "For a modest fee. Come along, baby."

■

They were speeding through open farm country. The speedometer hit seventy-five. Sarto closed his mouth and his eyes.

"Praying?" asked the freckled man.

"Naw!"

"Better start, toots."

"I know nuttin' can help me."

"That's right," said the freckled man cheerfully. "Nothing but a miracle. But you might pray for your soul."

"Aw, go to hell."

They turned into a rutty, weed-grown road. As they bumped along through a tunnel of trees, suddenly, silently Little John Sarto began to pray.

"Listen! This is Little John Sarto of Chicago, Illinois, U.S.A. I know I got no right to ask any favors. I guess I got a bad rep up there. Well, I ain't goin' to try to lie away my record. Everything on the blotter is true. I don't claim I rate a break. All I say is I need one bad and I'll pay for it. I don't know how; but look me up in the big book. It ought to say that when I make a deal I never run out on it. If I'm talkin' out of turn, forget it. But I won't forget if—"

"Last stop. All out," sang out the freckled man. He halted the car by a thicket of thigh-high brush.

Sarto got out of the car. Dummy got out, too. He kept his gun against Little John's backbone.

"Goodbye, now," said the freckled man, and lit a cigarette.

Dummy marched Sarto off the road and into the thicket. Abruptly, like a spotlight, the moon came out. Dummy spun Sarto around. Sarto could see his face. It held neither hate nor pity. Dummy raised his pistol. As he brought it up on a level with Sarto's forehead, the breeze whipped a straggling branch of a wild rosebush across the back of his hand, and the thorns cut a wet, red line. For part of a second Dummy dropped his eyes to his bleeding hand. Sarto wheeled and dove into the underbrush. Dummy fired three quick shots. One missed. One raked across Sarto's skull. One seared his shoulder. He staggered, but kept plunging on. Dummy darted after him. Then the moon went out.

As Sarto floundered on he could hear Dummy crashing through the brush behind him. But Dummy could not hear his quarry. Dizzy and weak, the wounded man fought his frantic way through tar-black brush. Thorns stabbed him, briers clawed. A low branch smashed him on the nose, and he reeled and nearly went down. Bending double, he churned on. Then his head hit something hard, and he dropped, stunned for a moment. He reached out an unsteady hand and felt an ivy-covered wall. No sound of pursuit came to his ears.

Painfully he dragged himself up to the top of the wall. Not a sob of breath was left in him. He straddled the wall and clung to it. Then he fainted.

■

In the monastery of the Floratines, today was like yesterday and yesterday was like a day in the ninth century when the order was founded. Neither time nor war nor the hate of kings had changed their humble habits or their simple creed. Over the door this creed was carved: "Be poor in purse, pure in heart, kind in word and deed and beautify the lives of men with flowers."

These were the words of the Blessed Edric, their founder, and, ever since his day, Floratines in every land had lived by them, harming no one, helping man, raising flowers.

When King Henry VIII set his face against other monks, he let no hostile hand be laid on the few Floratines.

"They do much good," the monarch said, "and, in sooth, they have nothing worth the taking, these Little Brothers of the Flowers."

They kept the name, and it gave rise to a custom. When a man left the world behind to enter their ranks, he left his name, too, and took the name of a flower.

In the first light of a new day they sat in their refectory, forty-four men in snuff-hued robes, most of them growing old. Their tonsured polls* were brown from the sun, their faces serene from inner peace.

"Brother Geranium is late with the milk," observed Brother Tulip, eyeing his dry porridge.

"Perhaps the cow kicked him," suggested Brother Hollyhock.

"She wouldn't. She's fond of him," said Brother Nasturtium. "I'll go down to the dairy and see if anything has happened to him," volunteered Brother Nasturtium. But as he rose from his bench, Brother Geranium, popeyed and panting, burst into the room.

"There's a naked man lying in the petunia bed," he gasped out. "I think he's dead."

Little John Sarto thought he was dead, too, when he opened his eyes in the infirmary and saw Abbot Jonquil and Brother Nasturtium at his bedside.

"I made it," he exclaimed huskily. "I beat the rap."

"Take it easy, son," said the abbot. "You've been badly hurt."

"But I ain't in hell," said Little John. Then he added, "Or if I am what are you guys doing here?"

"You're alive and in a safe place."

Sarto stared at him.

"Say, do you know who I am?" he asked.

"No."

"You musta seen my mug in the papers."

"We don't see newspapers here," the abbot said. "And we don't ask who a man is if he needs help."

Sarto touched his bandaged head.

"How long am I in for?" he inquired.

"Until you are well and strong again."

"I got no money."

"Neither have we," said the abbot. "So that makes you one of us, doesn't it?"

"That's one for the book, mister," said Little John.

---

*partially shaved heads

"I'm Abbot Jonquil. This is Brother Nasturtium, your nurse. If you wish us to notify your friends—"

"I got no friends," grunted Little John.

"You have now," said the abbot.

"I tell you I'm broke."

"You poor fellow," said the abbot gently. "What a life you must have led!"

"I been round long enough to know you never get sumpin' for nuttin'."

"I think you have talked enough for the present," the abbot said. "Try to rest and try not to worry—about anything. You may stay here as long as you wish, as our guest."

He went to the door.

"I'll look in again this evening," the abbot said. "Meantime, if you need anything, tell Brother Nasturtium."

His sandals shuffled softly away down the stone corridor.

Sarto squinted at the bulky monk.

"Get me a slug of bourbon, Nasty," he said.

"If you don't mind, I'd rather be called Brother Nasturtium," said the other mildly.

"Whatever you say, only gimme a snort."

Brother Nasturtium brought him a glass of water.

"Try it," he said. "'Twill give you strength."

"Water?" said Sarto disdainfully.

"Look at lions and tigers," said Brother Nasturtium.

As he drank the water, Little John studied the man. He noted the dented nose, gnarled ears, lumpy knuckles and the jaw like an anvil.

"You was a fighter, wasn't you?" said Sarto.

"We don't ask questions like that," said Brother Nasturtium. "What we were, rich or poor, big or small, good or bad, does not matter here."

"That's double jake by me," said Little John. "I think I'm going to like it here."

"I hope so."

"Say, tell me sumpin', big boy. What's your graft?"

Brother Nasturtium's eyes twinkled.

"'Tis twenty years and more since I've heard such talk," he said. "We raise flowers and sell them in the city."

"There's a good gelt* in that," said Sarto. "You boys must be cuttin' up a nice profit."

"What we clear, and it isn't much, goes to the poor."

"That's a nutsy way to run a business," observed Little John.

■

He closed his eyes. Presently he said:

"How does a guy join up with this outfit?"

"It's fairly easy," Brother Nasturtium told him, "if a man wants to be a lay brother—"

"A which?"

"Lay brother. I'm one. They don't take holy orders. They have few religious duties, chiefly saying their prayers. They are not permitted to go outside the walls, and they must obey their superiors. The discipline is rather severe. Some men say it's like being in prison—"

"They do, do they?" said Little John.

"Except that there are no bars."

"That might make a slight difference," conceded Little John. "What are the other catches?"

"Before a man can take his first vow as a lay brother, he must be on probation for a year. That means—"

"I know about probation," said Little John. "Where do I sign?"

"You'll have to talk to the abbot."

"Shoo him in."

"Lay brothers do not shoo abbots."

"Then tell him I wanta proposition him."

"If you're in earnest about this," Brother Nasturtium said, "you might be choosing the name we are to call you.

"Just call me 'Lucky.'"

"It must be the name of a flower."

Little John thought a moment.

"I've picked my new tag,"he announced.

---

*money

"What is it?"

"Brother Orchid."

■

At dusk Brother Nasturtium left the sickroom to get his patient's supper.

When he had gone, Little John began to laugh. It hurt him to laugh, but he couldn't help it.

"Boy, oh, boy!" he said. "What a hideout!"

■

As he weeded the rose garden Brother Orchid sang softly:

Johnny saw Frankie a-coming,
Out the back door he did scoot.
Frankie took aim with her pistol,
And the gun went rooty-toot-toot.
He was her man—

He turned the tune deftly into "Abide with Me" as he saw Brother Nasturtium come out of the greenhouse and head toward him.

Three nights before he had taken the vows that made him a full-fledged lay brother. As he flicked a ladybug from a leaf, he reflected that it hadn't been such a tough year. The routine didn't bother him; he was used to one far more rigid; but he was not used to men like Abbot Jonquil, Brother Nasturtium, and the rest. At first he felt sure that some sly, dark purpose lay behind their kindness to him. He watched, warily, for the trap. No trap was sprung. Always they were thoughtful, patient, pleasant with him and with one another.

"Maybe I've got into a high-class whacky house," he thought. Whatever it was, he decided, it was perfect for his plans. There he could bide his time, snug and safe, ready to strike. He was old enough to know the wonders time can work. And he was wise enough to know that while Jack Buck reigned as czar he must remain in exile. If he ventured back to his old kingdom now, he might just as well go straight to the morgue and book a slab. But czars slip, and czars fall, sometimes suddenly in this violent world. He'd wait and be ready.

"Well, Brother Orchid, your roses are doing well," said Brother Nasturtium as he came up.

"Lay you three to one they bring more than your lilies," said Brother Orchid.

"It's a hundred to one they won't bring anything," said Brother Nasturtium, somberly. Brother Orchid looked up and saw that the face, usually so benign, was grave.

"What's the gag?" he asked.

"Our market is gone."

"How come?"

"They won't handle our flowers."

"Who won't?"

"The wholesalers. We don't belong to the association."*

"Why don't we join it?"

"They won't let us. Not a flower can be sold in the city that isn't grown in their own nurseries."

"I get it," said Brother Orchid. "The old chisel. Who's the wheels in this shakedown?"

"A man named Buck is behind it, I believe. So Abbot Jonquil learned when he was in town. He tried to see this Mr. Buck to plead with him not to take away our only means of livelihood. One of Buck's ruffians kicked him downstairs."

"I suppose the abbot was sucker enough to go to the coppers," said Brother Orchid.

"He did go to the police."

"What did *they* do—slug him?"

"No. They were polite enough. But they said that so far as they knew the Floral Protective Association was a legitimate business concern."

"The bulls still know the answers," said Brother Orchid. "And the D.A. said he'd like to do sumpin', but his hands is tied, because you gotta have evidence, and all the witnesses is scared to talk."

"You seem to know all about it."

---

*A common underworld tactic is to create bogus "merchants' associations" which business owners are forced to join and to which they pay protection money in the form of "dues."

"I seen movies," said Brother Orchid.

He weeded away, deep in thought.

"Have we got any jack in the old sack?" he asked suddenly.

"About four hundred dollars, the abbot told me."

"Peanuts," said Brother Orchid. "But enough for a couple of sec-ondhand choppers.* You and me could handle 'em. We'd need roscoes** for the rest of the boys. But I know an armory that's a soft touch. You and me and Geranium and Lilac could charge out tonight, hustle a hot short, and knock it off. Once we was heeled (armed) we could move in on Buck and his gorillas and—"

"Man alive, what sort of talk is that?" demanded the scandalized Brother Nasturtium.

"Forget it, pal," said Brother Orchid. "I guess this sun has made me slap-happy. What are we goin' to do?"

"Be patient and pray."

"And eat what?"

"Heaven knows."

"Yeah, and they claim it helps guys that help themselves."

"Maybe Mr. Buck will see the light."

Brother Orchid plucked up a clump of sour grass.

"Maybe this weed'll turn into an American Beauty," he said. He wrung the weed's neck and hurled it into his basket.

"That's the only way to treat weed," he said.

"But is it?" said Brother Nasturtium. "Wasn't everything put into the world for some good use, if man had the sense to find out what that use is?"

"That's a lot of words," said Brother Orchid. "Weeds is weeds."

"No," said Brother Nasturtium, as he turned away, "weeds are flow-ers out of place."

■

Hungry after their day of work, the Little Brothers of the Flowers waited in the refectory for their abbot to come in and say grace. They

---

*tommy-guns
**revolvers

tried to make light talk of events in their small world. But there was a shadow over them.

Abbot Jonquil entered, walking slowly. It came to them for the first time that he was a very old man.

"I'm afraid I have more bad news," he said. "Our funds have been taken from my safe. Of course none of us took them—"

He stopped and looked down the long table.

"Where is Brother Orchid?" he asked.

"Maybe he's in his cell, praying," said Brother Nasturtium. "Shall I fetch him?"

"Yes, please."

Brother Nasturtium came back alone. His big ruddy face was twisted with trouble.

"Maybe I was wrong about weeds," he said.

■

In his office, Thomas Jefferson Brownlow, special prosecutor of rackets, was talking to the press. The reporters liked him. He was so earnest and so green.

"Same old story, boys," he said. "All I can tell you is that men are selfish animals, and that's not news. I know Buck is back of all these new rackets. So do you. But I can't prove it in a court of law. The men who can simply will not go before the grand jury and tell their stories. They put their skins before their civic duty. I'm not blaming them. But the fact remains I can't force them to testify. They're not afraid of *me*. I wish they were. That's all today, gentlemen."

The reporters filed out. Brownlow bent morosely over the indictment of a jobless man who had stolen a peck of potatoes.

Swerling, his assistant, bustled in. He was excited.

"Chief," he said, "they're back."

"Who?"

"Those florists and laundrymen and fruit peddlers. And they're ready to talk."

"The devil you say!"

"Better grab 'em while they're hot, Chief," urged Swerling.

"But what's got into 'em?"

"You have me there."

"It doesn't matter," said Brownlow, "if they'll talk. Send 'em in and lock all the doors."

Once they started to talk Thomas Jefferson Brownlow had a hard job to stop them. The Grand Jury was back before its seats in the box had cooled off, and shortly thereafter Jack Buck and three of his top aides were passengers on a special train that would not stop till it had carried them to a station near a big, gray gate. Most of his lesser lieutenants also took trips, accompanied by large, official-looking men, who returned alone. A few escaped, some by taking to their heels, others by wriggling through loopholes in the law.

Mr. Brownlow was walking toward his office, debating whether he should run for governor or the Senate, when he bumped into Mr. Chris Poppadoppalous, emerging from the room where witnesses are paid their fees. Mr. Poppadoppalous beamed, bowed, and handed Mr. Brownlow a large box.

"Gardenias," he said. "I brink dem for you."

"Thanks," said Brownlow. "And there's one more thing you can do for me."

"Anythink," said Mr. Poppadoppalous with another bow.

"One day you boys were afraid to talk. The next day you talked. Why?"

"We were afraid not to," said Mr. Poppadoppalous.

"Afraid of me?" asked Brownlow, rather pleased.

Mr. Poppadoppalous tittered apologetically.

"Oh, no, sir," he said. "You're a nice man. You don't say, 'Talk, you Greek so-and-so, or I'll tear out your heart and eat it before your eyes.'"

"Did somebody say that to you?"

"Yes, sir. To all us boys."

"Who?"

"The little fellow," said Mr. Poppadoppalous, and bowed, and scurried away.

From his hotel window Little John Sarto looked out over the lighted city spread at his feet. Somebody knocked on his door.

"Come in," said Sarto.

The freckled young man came in. He had on a new suit, moss-green this time, and he was still jovial.

"Hello, sweetheart," he said.

"Hello, Eddie," said Sarto.

"You know why I'm here."

"Sure," said Sarto. "Have a drink?"

"Why not?" said Eddie, and poured out a drink from a bottle of bourbon on the table. Sarto took one, too.

"Nice going, boss," said Eddie, raising his glass. "We'll run this town right."

"We?"

"You will, I mean," said Eddie. "I'll be glad to work under a man with your brains. Poor Jack didn't have many. Nerve, yes. But he never looked ahead. You do. Well, what do you say, boss? Dummy and some of the boys are waiting downstairs for the answer. They're solid for you, boss. Anything you say goes."

Sarto didn't say anything. He went to the window and looked out over the city.

"Of course, things are rather ragged right now," said Eddie. "We'll have to take it slow and easy for awhile. But the boys are counting on you to work out some nice, new, juicy angles. The town's yours."

"I don't want it," said Little John.

"What do you mean?" Eddie was not jovial now.

"I got other plans."

"You can't run out on us."

"I'm walking out," said Sarto. "Right now."

"The boys won't like that."

"I'm doing what I like."

"That's always expensive," said Eddie.

"I know all about that."

Eddie shrugged his shoulders.

"Okay," he said, and sauntered out of the room.

Hurriedly, Little John Sarto began to strip off his loud, plaid suit.

■

"I'm right," said the warden to the chaplain, laying down the morning paper. "You say all men have some good in them. I say some men are all bad and nothing can change them. Take this fellow, Sarto. Last night in Chicago, as he was getting on a bus, he was filled full of lead."

"That hardly proves your point." The chaplain smiled. "Bullets are very democratic. They'll kill good men as well as bad, you know."

"There was nothing good about Sarto. Just listen to this: 'The police say Sarto plotted to return to power in the underworld. They are at a loss to explain why, at the time of his death, he was disguised as a monk.' Why, the scheming wolf! Whether there's any good whatsoever in such a man, I leave it to you to judge."

"He does sound pretty bad, I grant you," the chaplain said. "But, even so, I hate to condemn him or any man. I might be reversed by a higher Judge."

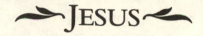

JESUS

The Crucifier Becomes a Christian[†]
Lloyd C. Douglas

From The Robe

Lloyd C. Douglas gave us many wonderful novels about religious conversion, including The Magnificent Obsession *and* The Robe, *which were made into major Hollywood films. His main characters are always hardened skeptics and atheists who refuse—at first—to believe in Christianity. They put it to every test, convinced that it will fail, and then, suddenly, they realize that it is the Truth for which they have been searching all along.*

In the first excerpt from The Robe, *the Roman officer Marcellus Gallio is ordered to crucify Jesus. He does so, and in a game of dice wins his victim's last possession—a mysterious robe that offers comfort to some and haunts others with a terrifying power. In the second excerpt, Marcellus has become a Christian and he meets the Apostle Peter, also known as the "Big Fisherman." They both feel that they have betrayed Jesus, but they resolve to carry on His mission, and they believe that He will come again.*

One of the Insula's ten companies was absent from inspection. Marcellus noticed the diminished strength of the Procurator's legion, but thought little of it. Whatever might be the nature of the business that had called out these troops so early in the day, it was of no concern to Minoa.

But when Julian, the Capernaum Commander who was taking his turn as officer of the day, glumly announced that the customary parade was canceled and that all the legionaries could return to their barracks to await further orders, Marcellus' curiosity was stirred. Returning to his quarters, he sent for Paulus, confident that this ever-active fountain of gossip could explain the mystery.

After a considerable delay, the Centurion drifted in unsteadily with flushed cheeks and bloodshot eyes. His Commander regarded him with unconcealed distaste and pointed to a chair into which the dazed and untidy Paulus eased himself gently.

"Do you know what's up?" inquired Marcellus.

"The Procurator," mumbled Paulus, "has had a bad night."

"So have you, from all appearances," observed Marcellus, frostily. "What has been going on—if it isn't a secret?"

"Pilate is in trouble." Paulus' tongue was clumsy, and he chewed out his words slowly. "He is in trouble with everybody. He is even in trouble with good old Julian, who says that if the man is a Galilean, Capernaum should have been detailed to police the trial at Herod's court."

"Would you be good enough to tell me what you are talking about?" rasped Marcellus. "What man? What trial? Begin at the beginning, and pretend I don't know anything about it."

Paulus yawned prodigiously, scrubbed his watery eyes with shaky fingers, and began to spin a long, involved yarn about last night's experiences. An imprudent carpenter from somewhere up in Galilee had been tried for disturbing the peace and inciting the people to revolt. A few days ago, he had become violent in the Temple, chasing the sacrificial animals out into the street, upsetting the money-tills, and loudly condemning the holy place as a den of robbers. "A true statement, no doubt," commented Paulus, "but not very polite."

"The fellow must be crazy," remarked Marcellus.

Paulus pursed his swollen lips judicially and shook his head.

"Something peculiar about this man," he muttered. "They arrested him last night. They've had him up before old Annas, who used to be the High Priest; and Caiaphas, the present High Priest; and Pilate—and Herod—and—"

"You seem to know a lot about it," broke in Marcellus.

Paulus grinned sheepishly.

"A few of us were seeing the holy city by moonlight," he confessed. "Shortly after midnight we ran into this mob and tagged along. It was the only entertainment to be had. We were a bit tight, sir, if you'll believe it."

"I believe it," said Marcellus. "Go on, please, with whatever you can remember."

"Well—we went to the trials. As I have said, we were not in prime condition to understand what was going on, and most of the testimony was shrieked in Aramaic. But it was clear enough that the Temple crowd and the merchants were trying to have the man put to death."

"For what happened at the Temple?"

"Yes—for that, and for going about through the country gathering up big crowds to hear him talk."

"About what?"

"A new religion. I was talking with one of Pilate's legionaries who understands the language. He said this Jesus was urging the country people to adopt a religion that doesn't have much to do with the Temple. Some of the testimony was rubbish. One fellow swore the Galilean had said that if the Temple were torn down he could put it up again in three days. Stuff like that! Of course, all they want is a conviction. Any sort of testimony is good enough."

"Where does the matter stand now?" asked Marcellus.

"I got a plenty of it at Herod's court, and came back before daybreak; dead on my feet. They had just decided to have another trial before Pilate, directly after breakfast. They are probably at the Insula now. Pilate will have to give them what they want—and"—Paulus hesitated, and then continued grimly—"what they want is a crucifixion. I heard them talking about it."

"Shall we go over?" queried Marcellus.

"I've had enough, sir, if you'll excuse me." Paulus rose with an effort and ambled uncertainly across the room. In the doorway he confronted a sentinel, garbed in the Insula uniform, who saluted stiffly.

"The Procurator's compliments," he barked, in a metallic tone.

"The ranking officers and a detachment of twenty men from the Minoa Legion will attend immediately in the Procurator's court." With another ceremonious salute, he backed out and strutted down the corridor, without waiting for a reply.

"I wonder what Pilate wants of us," reflected Marcellus, uneasily, searching the Centurion's apprehensive eyes.

"I think I can guess," growled Paulus. "Pilate doesn't confer honors on Minoa. He's going to detail us to do something too dirty and dangerous for the local troops; doesn't want his precious legion mixed up in it. The Minoa contingent will be leaving tomorrow. If any trouble results, we will be out of reach." He hitched up his belt and left the room. Marcellus stood irresolute for a moment and followed, intending to ask Paulus to order out the detachment. Through the half-open door to the Centurion's quarters, he saw him greedily gulping from an enormous cup. He strode angrily into the room.

"If I were you, Paulus," he said, sternly, "I shouldn't drink any more at present. You've already had much too much!"

"If I were you," retorted Paulus, recklessly, "I would take as much of this as I could hold!" He took a couple of uncertain steps toward Marcellus, and faced him with brazen audacity. "You're going to crucify a man today!" he muttered. "Ever see that done?"

"No." Marcellus shook his head. "I don't even know how it is done. You'll have to tell me."

Paulus carefully picked his way back to the table where the grotesquely shaped wineskin sat. Refilling the big cup, he handed it, dripping, to his Commander.

"I'll show you—when we get there," he said, huskily. "Drink that! All of it! If you don't, you'll wish you had. What we're going to do is not a job for a sober man."

Marcellus, unprotesting, took the cup and drank.

"It isn't just that the thing is sickeningly cruel," continued Paulus. "There's something strange about this man. I'd rather not have anything to do with it!"

"Afraid he'll haunt you?" Marcellus paused at the middle of the cup, and drew an unconvincing grin.

"Well—you wait—and see what you think!" murmured Paulus, wagging his head mysteriously. "The witnesses said he acted, at the

Temple, as if it were his own personal property. And that didn't sound as silly as you might think, sir. At old man Annas' house, I'm bound if he didn't act as if he owned the place. At Caiaphas' palace, everybody was on trial—but this Jesus! He was the only cool man in the crowd at the Insula. He owns that, too. Pilate felt it, I think. One of the witnesses testified that Jesus had professed to be a king. Pilate leaned forward, looked him squarely in the face, and said, 'Are you?' Mind, sir, Pilate didn't ask him, 'Did you say you were a king?' He said, 'Are you?' And he wasn't trying to be sarcastic, either."

"But that's nonsense, Paulus! Your wine-soaked imagination was playing tricks on you!" Marcellus walked across to the table and poured himself another cupful. "You get out the troops," he ordered, resolutely. "I hope you'll be able to stand straight, over at the Insula. You're definitely drunk, you know." He took another long drink, and wiped his mouth on the back of his hand. "So—what did the Galilean say to that— when Pilate asked him if he was a king?"

"Said he had a kingdom—but not in the world," muttered Paulus, with a vague, upward-spiraling gesture.

"You're worse than drunk," accused Marcellus, disgustedly. "You're losing your mind. I think you'd better go to bed. I'll report you sick."

"No—I'm not going to leave you in the lurch, Marcellus." It was the first time Paulus had ever addressed the Commander by his given name.

"You're a good fellow, Paulus," declared Marcellus, giving him his hand. He retraced his way to the wineskin. Paulus followed and took the cup from his hand.

"You have had just the right amount, sir," he advised. "I suggest that you go now. Pilate will not like it if we are tardy. He has endured abor all the annoyance he can take, for one morning's dose. I shall order out the detachment, and meet you over there."

■

With a purposely belated start, and after experiencing much difficulty in learning the way to the place of execution—an outlying field where the city's refuse was burned—Demetrius did not expect to arrive in time to witness the initial phase of the crucifixion.

Tardy as he was, he proceeded with reluctant steps; very low in spirit, weighted with a dejection he had not known since the day of his enslavement. The years had healed the chain-scars on his wrists: fair treatment at the hands of the Gallio family had done much to mend his heart: but today it seemed that the world was totally unfit for a civilized man to live in. Every human institution was loaded with lies. The courts were corrupt. Justice was not to be had. All rulers, big and little, were purchasable. Even the temples were full of deceit. You could call the roll of all the supposed reliances that laid claim to the people's respect and reverence, and there wasn't one of them that hadn't earned the bitter contempt of decent men!

Though accustomed to walk with long strides and clipped steps, Demetrius slogged along through the dirty streets with the shambling gait of a hopeless, faithless, worthless vagabond. At times his scornful thoughts almost became articulate as he passionately reviled every tribunal and judiciary, every crown and consistory [council] in the whole, wide, wicked world. Patriotism! How the poets and minstrels loved to babble about the high honor of shedding one's blood. Maybe they, too, had been bought up. Old Horace: maybe Augustus had just sent him a new coat and a cask of wine when he was inspired to write, "How sweet and glorious to die for one's country!" Nonsense! Why should any sane man think it pleasant or noble to give up his life to save the world? It wasn't fit to live in; much less die for! And it was never going to be any better. Here was this foolhardy Galilean, so thoroughly enraged over the pollution of a holy place that he had impulsively made an ineffective little gesture of protest. Doubtless nineteen out of every twenty men in this barren, beaten, beggared land would inwardly applaud this poor man's reckless courage; but, when it came to the test, these downtrodden, poverty-cursed nobodies would let this Jesus stand alone—without one friend—before the official representatives of a crooked Temple and a crooked Empire.

Loyalty? Why should any man bother himself to be loyal? Let him go out on his own, and protect himself the best he can. Why should you spend your life following at the heels of a Roman master, who alternately confided in you and humiliated you? What had you to lose, in self-respect, by abandoning this aristocrat? It wasn't hard to make one's way to Damascus.

It was a dark day for Demetrius. Even the sky was overcast with leaden, sullen clouds. The sun had shone brightly at dawn. For the past half-hour, an almost sinister gloom had been thickening.

As he neared the disreputable field, identifiable for some distance by the noisome smoke that drifted from its smoldering corruptions, he met many men walking rapidly back to the city. Most of them were well-fed, well-dressed, pompous, preoccupied; men of middle age or older, strutting along in single file, as if each had come alone. These people, surmised Demetrius, were responsible for the day's crime. It relieved him to feel that the worst of it was over. They had seen the public assassination to a successful conclusion, and were now free to return to their banks and bazaars. Some, doubtless, would go to the Temple and say their prayers.

After the last straggling group of mud hovels had been passed, the loathsome, garbage-littered field lay before him. He was amazed to see how much pollution had been conveyed to this place, for the city's streets had not shown so huge a loss of filth. A fairly clean, narrow path led toward a little knoll that seemed to have been protected. Demetrius stopped—and looked. On the green knoll, three tall crosses stood in a row. Perhaps it had been decided, as an afterthought, to execute a couple of the Galilean's friends. Could it be possible that two among them, crazed by their leader's impending torture, had attempted to defend him? Hardly: they didn't have it in them: not the ones he had seen that day on the road: not the ones he had seen this morning.

Forcing his unwilling feet, he advanced slowly to within less than a stadium of the gruesome scene. There he came to a stop. The two unidentified men were writhing on their crosses. The lonely man on the central cross was still as a statue. His head hung forward. Perhaps he was dead, or at least unconscious. Demetrius hoped so.

For a long time he stood there, contemplating this tragic sight. The hot anger that had almost suffocated him was measurably cooled now. The lonely man had thrown his life away. There was nothing to show for his audacious courage. The Temple would continue to cheat the country people who came in to offer a lamb. Herod would continue to bully and whip the poor if they inconvenienced the rich. Caiaphas would continue to condemn the blasphemies of men who didn't want the gods fetched to market. Pilate would deal out injustice—and wash his dirty hands in a silver bowl. This lonely man had paid a high price for his brief and fruitless war on wickedness. But—he had spoken: he had acted. By tomorrow, nobody would remember that he had risked everything—and lost his life—in the cause of honesty. But—perhaps a man was better off dead than in a world where such an event as this could happen. Demetrius felt very lonely too.

There was not as large a crowd as he had expected to see. There was no disorder, probably because the legionaries were scattered about among the people. It was apparent, from the negligence of the soldiers' posture, as they stood leaning on their lances, that no rioting had occurred or was anticipated.

Demetrius moved closer in and joined the outer rim of spectators. Not many of the well-to-do, who had been conspicuous at the Insula, were present. Most of the civilians were poorly dressed. Many of them were weeping. There were several women, heavily veiled and huddled in little groups, in attitudes of silent, hopeless grief. A large circle had been left unoccupied below the crosses.

Edging his way slowly forward, occasionally rising on tiptoe to search for his master, Demetrius paused beside one of the legionaries who, recognizing him with a brief nod, replied to his low-voiced inquiry. The Commander and several other officers were on the other side of the knolls at the rear of the crosses, he said.

"I brought him some water," explained Demetrius, holding up the jug. The soldier showed how many of his teeth were missing.

"That's good," he said. "He can wash his hands. They're not drinking water today. The Procurator sent out a wineskin."

"Is the man dead?" asked Demetrius.

"No—he said something awhile ago."

"What did he say? Could you hear?"

"Said he was thirsty."

"Did they give him water?"

"No—they filled a sponge with vinegar that had some sort of balm in it, and raised it to his mouth; but he wouldn't have it. I don't rightly understand what he is up there for—but he's no coward." The legionary shifted his position, pointed to the darkening sky, remarked that there was going to be a storm, and moved on through the crowd.

Demetrius did not look at the lonely man again. He edged out into the open and made a wide detour around to the other side of the knoll. Marcellus, Paulus, and four or five others here lounging in a small circle on the ground. A leather dice-cup was being shaken negligently, and passed from hand to hand. At first sight of it, Demetrius was hotly indignant. It wasn't like Marcellus to be so brutally unfeeling. A decent man would have to be very drunk indeed to exhibit such callous unconcern in this circumstance.

Now that he was here, Demetrius thought he should inquire whether there was anything he could do for his master. He slowly approached the group of preoccupied officers. After a while, Marcellus glanced up dully and beckoned to him. The others gave him a brief glance and resumed their play.

"Anything you want to tell me?" asked Marcellus, thickly.

"I brought you some water, sir."

"Very good. Put it down there. I'll have a drink presently." It was his turn to play. He shook the cup languidly and tossed out the dice.

"Your lucky day!" growled Paulus. "That finishes me." He stretched his long arms and laced his fingers behind his head. "Demetrius," he said, nodding toward a rumpled brown mantle that lay near the foot of the central cross, "hand me that coat. I want to look at it."

Demetrius picked up the garment and gave it to him. Paulus examined it with idle interest.

"Not a bad robe," he remarked, holding it up at arm's length. "Woven in the country; dyed with walnut juice. He'll not be needing it any more. I think I'll say it's mine. How about it, Tribune?"

"Why should it be yours?" asked Marcellus, indifferently. "If it's worth anything, let us toss for it." He handed Paulus the dice-cup. "High number wins. It's your turn."

There was a low mutter of thunder in the north and a savage tongue of flame leaped through the black cloud. Paulus tossed a pair of threes, and stared apprehensively at the sky.

"Not hard to beat," said Vinitius, who sat next him. He took the cup and poured out a five and a four. The cup made the circle without bettering this cast until it arrived at Marcellus.

"Double six!" he called. "Demetrius, you take care of the robe." Paulus handed up the garment.

"Shall I wait here for you, sir?" asked Demetrius.

"No—nothing you can do. Go back to the Insula. Begin packing up. We want to be off to an early start in the morning."

Marcellus looked up at the sky. "Paulus, go around and see how they are doing. There's going to be a hard storm." He rose heavily to his feet, and stood swaying. Demetrius wanted to take his arm and steady him, but felt that any solicitude would be resented. His indignation had cooled now. It was evident that Marcellus had been drinking because he couldn't bear to do this shameful work in his right mind. There was a deafening, stunning thunderclap that fairly shook the ground on which they stood. Marcellus put out a hand and steadied himself against the central cross. There was blood on his hand when he regained his balance. He wiped it off on his toga.

A fat man, expensively dressed in a black robe, waddled out of the crowd and confronted Marcellus with surly arrogance.

"Rebuke these people!" he shouted, angrily. "They are saying that the storm is a judgment on us!"

There was another gigantic crash of thunder.

"Maybe it is!" yelled Marcellus, recklessly.

The fat man waved a menacing fist.

"It is your duty to keep order here!" he shrieked.

"Do you want me to stop the storm?" demanded Marcellus.

"Stop the blasphemy. These people are crying out that this Galilean is the Son of God!"

"Maybe he *is*!" shouted Marcellus. "*You* wouldn't know!" He was fumbling with the hilt of his sword. The fat man backed away, howling that the Procurator should hear of this.

Circling the knoll, Demetrius paused for a final look at the lonely man on the central cross. He had raised his face and was gazing up into the black sky. Suddenly he burst forth with a resonant call, as if crying to a distant friend for aid.

A poorly dressed, bearded man of middle age, apparently one of the Galilean's friends from the country, rushed out of the crowd and ran down the slope weeping aloud in an abandon of grief. Demetrius grasped him by the sleeve as he stumbled past.

"What did he say?"

The man made no reply, tore himself loose, and ran on shouting his unintelligible lamentations.

Now the dying Galilean was looking down upon the crowd below him. His lips moved. His eyes surveyed the people with the same sorrow they had expressed on the road when the multitude had hailed him as their king. There was another savage burst of thunder. The darkness deepened.

Demetrius lolled up the robe and thrust it inside his tunic, pressing it tightly under his arm. The intimate touch of the garment relieved his feeling of desolation. He wondered if Marcellus might not let him keep the robe. It would be a comfort to own something that this courageous man had worn. He would cherish it as a priceless inheritance. It would have been a great experience, he felt, to have known this man; to have learned the nature of his mind. Now that there would be no opportunity to share his friendship, it would be an enduring consolation to possess his robe.

Turning about, with swimming eyes, he started down the hill. It was growing so dark now that the narrow path was indistinct. He flung a backward look over his shoulder, but the descending gloom had swallowed up the knoll.

By the time he reached the city streets, night had fallen on Jerusalem, though it was only mid-afternoon. Lights flickered in the windows. Pedestrians moved slowly, carrying torches. Frightened voices called to one another. Demetrius could not understand what they were saying, but their tone was apprehensive, as if they were wondering about the cause of this strange darkness. He wondered, too, but felt no sense of depression or alarm. The sensation of being alone and unwanted in an unfriendly world had left him. He was not lonely now. He hugged the Robe close to his side as if it contained some inexplicable remedy for heartaches.

Melas was standing in the corridor, in front of Paulus' door, when he arrived at the barracks. Demetrius was in no mood to talk, and proceeded to his master's quarters, Melas following with his torch.

"So—you went out there; eh?" said the Thracian, grimly. "How did you like it?" They entered the room and Melas applied his torch to the big stone lamps. Receiving no answer to his rough query, he asked, "What do you think this is; an eclipse?"

"I don't know," replied Demetrius. "Never heard of an eclipse lasting so long."

"Maybe it's the end of the world," said Melas, forcing an uncouth laugh.

"That will be all right with me," said Demetrius.

"Think this Jesus has had anything to do with it?" asked Melas, half in earnest.

"No," said Demetrius, "I shouldn't think so."

Melas moved closer and took Demetrius by the arm.

"Thought any more about Damascus?" he whispered.

Demetrius shook his head indifferently.

"Have you?" he asked.

"I'm going—tonight," said Melas. "The Procurator always gives a dinner to the officers on the last night. When it is over, and I have put the Centurion to bed—he'll be tight as a tambourine—I'm leaving. Better come with me. You'll wait a long time for another chance as good as this one."

"No—I'm not going," said Demetrius firmly.

"You'll not tell on me, will you?"

"Certainly not."

If you change your mind, give me a wink at the banquet." Melas sauntered toward the door. Demetrius, thinking he had gone, drew out the Robe and unfolded it under the light.

"What have you there?" queried Melas, from the doorway. "His Robe," said Demetrius, without turning.

Melas came back and regarded the blood-stained garment with silent interest.

"How do you happen to have it?" he asked, in an awed tone.

"It belongs to the Legate. The officers tossed for it. He won it."

"I shouldn't think he'd want it," remarked Melas. "I'm sure I wouldn't. It will probably bring him bad luck."

"Why *bad* luck?" demanded Demetrius. "It belonged to a brave man."

■

Marcellus came in, dazed, drunk, and thoroughly exhausted. Unbuckling his sword-belt, he handed it to Demetrius, and sank wearily into a chair.

"Get me some wine," he ordered, huskily.

Demetrius obeyed; and, on one knee, unlaced his master's dusty sandals while he drank.

"You will feel better after a cold bath, sir," he said, encouragingly.

Marcellus widened his heavy eyes with an effort and surveyed his slave with curiosity.

"Were you out there?" he asked, thickly. "Oh, yes; I remember now. You were there. You brought j—jug water."

"And brought back his Robe," prompted Demetrius.

Marcellus passed his hand awkwardly across his brow and tried to dismiss the recollection with a shuddering shrug.

"You will be going to the dinner, sir?" asked Demetrius.

"Have to," grumbled Marcellus. "Can't have off-cers laughing at us. We're tough—at Minoa. Can't have ossifers—orfficers—chortling that the sight of blood makes Minoa Legate sick."

"Quite true, sir," approved Demetrius. "A shower and a rub-down will put you in order. I have laid out fresh clothing for you."

"Very good," labored Marcellus. "Commanner Minoa never this dirty before. Wha's that?" He raked his fingers across a dark wet smudge on the skirt of his toga. "Blood!" he muttered. "Great Roman Empire does big brave deed! Wins bloody battle!" The drunken monologue trailed off into foggy incoherences. Marcellus' head sank lower and lower on his chest. Demetrius unfastened the toga, soaked a towel in cold water, and vigorously applied it to his master's puffed face and beating throat.

"Up you come, sir!" he ordered, tugging Marcellus to his feet. "One more hard battle to fight, sir. Then you can sleep it off."

Marcellus slowly pulled himself together and rested both hands heavily on his slave's shoulders while being stripped of his soiled clothing.

"I'm dirty," he mumbled to himself. "I'm dirty—outside and inside. I'm dirty—and ashamed. Unnerstand—Demetrius? I'm dirty and ashamed."

"You were only obeying orders, sir," consoled Demetrius.

"Were you out there?" Marcellus tried to focus his eyes.

"Yes, sir. A very sorry affair."

"What did you think of him?"

"Very courageous. It was too bad you had it to do, sir."

"I wouldn't do it again," declared Marcellus, truculently—"no matter who ordered it! Were you there when he called on his god to forgive us?"

"No—but I couldn't have understood his language."

"Nor I—but they told me. He looked directly at me after he had said it. I'm afraid I'm going to have a hard time forgetting that look."

Demetrius put his arm around Marcellus to steady him. It was the first time he had ever seen tears in his master's eyes.

■

The lnsula's beautiful banquet-hall had been gaily decorated for the occasion with many ensigns, banners, and huge vases of flowers. An orchestra, sequestered in an alcove, played stirring military marches. Great stone lamps on marble pillars brightly lighted the spacious room. At the head table, a little higher than the others, sat the Procurator with Marcellus and Julian on either side and the Commanders from Caesarea and Joppa flanking them. Everyone knew why Marcellus and Julian were given seats of honor. Minoa had been assigned a difficult task and Capernaum had a grievance. Pilate was glum, moody, and distraught.

The household slaves served the elaborate dinner. The officers' orderlies stood ranged against the walls, in readiness to be of aid to their masters, for the Procurator's guests—according to a long-established custom—had come here to get drunk, and not many of them had very far to go.

The representatives of Minoa were more noisy and reckless than any of the others, but it was generally conceded that much latitude should be extended in their case, for they had had a hard day. Paulus had arrived late. Melas had done what he could to straighten him up, but the Centurion was dull and dizzy—and surly. The gaiety of his table companions annoyed him. For some time he sat glumly regarding them with distaste, occasionally jerked out of his lethargy by a painful hiccup. After awhile his fellow officers took him in hand, plying him with a particularly heady wine which had the effect of whipping his jaded spirits into fresh activity. He tried to be merry; sang and shouted;

but no one could understand anything he said. Presently he upset his tall wine-cup, and laughed uproariously. Paulus was drunk.

It pleased Demetrius to observe that Marcellus was holding his own with dignity. He was having little to say, but Pilate's taciturnity easily accounted for that. Old Julian, quite sober, was eating his dinner with relish, making no effort to engage the Procurator in conversation. The other tables were growing louder and more disorderly as the evening advanced. There was much boisterous laughter; many rude practical jokes; an occasional unexplained quarrel.

The huge silver salvers, piled high with roasted meats and exotic fruits, came and went; exquisitely carved silver flagons poured rare wines into enormous silver goblets. Now and then a flushed Centurion rose from the couch on which he lounged beside his table, his servant skipping swiftly across the marble floor to assist him. After a while they would return. The officer, apparently much improved in health, would strut back to his couch and resume where he had left off. Many of the guests slept, to the chagrin of their slaves. So long as your master was able to stagger out of the room and unburden his stomach, you had no cause for humiliation; but if he went to sleep, your fellow slaves winked at you and grinned.

Demetrius stood at attention, against the wall, immediately behind his master's couch. He noted with satisfaction that Marcellus was merely toying with his food, which showed that he still had some sense left. He wished, however, that the Commander would exhibit a little more interest in the party. It would be unfortunate if anyone surmised that he was brooding over the day's events.

Presently the Procurator sat up and leaned toward Marcellus, who turned his face inquiringly. Demetrius moved a step forward and listened.

"You are not eating your dinner, Legate," observed Pilate. "Perhaps there is something else you would prefer."

"Thank you; no, sir," replied Marcellus. "I am not hungry."

"Perhaps your task, this afternoon, dulled your appetite," suggested Pilate idly.

Marcellus scowled.

"That would be a good enough reason, sir, for one's not being hungry," he retorted.

"A painful business, I'm sure," commented Pilate. "I did not enjoy my necessity to order it."

"Necessity?" Marcellus sat up and faced his host with cool impudence. "This man was not guilty of a crime, as the Procurator himself admitted."

Pilate frowned darkly at this impertinence.

"Am I to understand that the Legate of Minoa disputes the justice of the court's decision?"

"Of course," snapped Marcellus. "Justice? No one knows better than the Procurator that this Galilean was unjustly treated."

"You are forgetting yourself, Legate!" said Pilate, sternly.

"I did not initiate this conversation, sir," rejoined Marcellus, "but if my candor annoys you, we can talk about something else."

Pilate's face cleared a little.

"You have a right to your opinions, Legate Marcellus Gallio," he conceded, "though you certainly know it is unusual for a man to criticize his superior quite so freely as you have done."

"I know that, sir," nodded Marcellus, respectfully. "It is unusual to criticize one's superior. But this is an unusual case." He paused, and looked Pilate squarely in the eyes. "It was an unusual trial, an unusual decision, an unusual punishment—and the convict was an unusual man!"

"A strange person, indeed," agreed Pilate. "What did you make of him?" he asked, lowering his voice confidentially.

Marcellus shook his head.

"I don't know, sir," he replied, after an interval.

"He was a fanatic," said Pilate.

"Doubtless. So was Socrates. So was Plato."

Pilate shrugged.

"You're not implying that this Galilean was of the same timber as Socrates and Plato!"

The conversation was interrupted before Marcellus had an opportunity to reply. Paulus had risen and was shouting at him drunkenly, incoherently. Pilate scowled, as if this were a bit too much, even for a party that had lost all respect for the dignity of the Insula. Marcellus shook his head and signed to Paulus with his hand that he was quite out of order. Undeterred, Paulus staggered to the head table, leaned far across it on one unstable elbow, and muttered something that Demetrius could not hear. Marcellus tried to dissuade him, but he was obdurate and growing quarrelsome. Obviously much perplexed, the Commander turned and beckoned to Demetrius.

"Centurion Paulus wants to see that Robe," he muttered. "Bring it here."

Demetrius hesitated so long that Pilate regarded him with sour amazement.

"Go—instantly—and get it!" barked Marcellus, angrily.

Regretting that he had put his master to shame in the presence of the Procurator, Demetrius tried to atone for his reluctant obedience by moving swiftly. His heart pounded hard as he ran down the corridor to the Legate's suite. There was no accounting for the caprice of a man as drunk as Paulus. Almost anything could happen, but Paulus would have to be humored.

Folding the blood-stained, thorn-rent Robe over his arm, Demetrius returned to the banquet-hall. He felt like a traitor, assisting in the mockery of a cherished friend. Surely this Jesus deserved a better fate than to be abandoned—even in death—to the whims of a drunken soldier. Once, on the way, Demetrius came to a full stop and debated seriously whether to obey—or take the advice of Melas—and run.

Marcellus glanced at the Robe, but did not touch it.

"Take it to Centurion Paulus," he said.

Paulus, who had returned to his seat, rose unsteadily; and, holding up the Robe by its shoulders, picked his way carefully to the head table. The room grew suddenly quiet, as he stood directly before Pilate.

"Trophy!" shouted Paulus.

Pilate drew a reproachful smile and glanced toward Marcellus as if to hint that the Legate of Minoa might well advise his Centurion to mend his manners.

"Trophy!" repeated Paulus. "Minoa presents trophy to the Insula." He waved an expansive arm toward the banners that hung above the Procurator's table.

Pilate shook his head crossly and disclaimed all interest in the drunken farce with a gesture of annoyance. Undaunted by his rebuff, Paulus edged over a few steps and addressed Marcellus.

"Insula doesn't want trophy!" he prattled idiotically. "Very well! Minoa keep trophy! Legate Marcellus wear trophy back to Minoa! Put it on, Legate!"

"Please, Paulus!" begged Marcellus. "That's enough."

"Put it on!" shouted Paulus. "Here, Demetrius; hold the Robe for the Legate!" He thrust it into Demetrius' hands. Someone yelled, "Put it on!" And the rest of them took up the shout, pounding the tables with their goblets. "Put it on!"

Feeling that the short way out of the dilemma was to humor the drunken crowd, Marcellus rose and reached for the Robe. Demetrius stood clutching it in his arms, seemingly unable to release it. Marcellus was pale with anger.

"Give it to me!" he commanded, severely. All eyes were attentive, and the place grew quiet. Demetrius drew himself erect, with the Robe held tightly in his folded arms. Marcellus waited a long moment, breathing heavily. Then suddenly drawing back his arm he slapped Demetrius in the face with his open hand. It was the first time he had ever ventured to punish him.

Demetrius slowly bowed his head and handed Marcellus the Robe; then stood with slumped shoulders while his master tugged it on over the sleeves of his toga. A gale of appreciative laughter went up, and there was tumultuous applause. Marcellus did not smile. His face was drawn and haggard. The room grew still again. As a man in a dream, he fumbled woodenly with the neck of the garment, trying to pull it off his shoulder. His hands were shaking.

"Shall I help you, sir?" asked Demetrius, anxiously.

Marcellus nodded; and when Demetrius had relieved him of the Robe, he sank into his seat as if his knees had suddenly buckled under him.

"Take that out into the courtyard," he muttered, hoarsely, "and burn it!"

[But Demetrius does not burn the Robe, and it continues to torment Marcellus until he finally becomes a Christian. The story resumes here with a pilgrimage to Calvary to meet the Apostle Peter.]

Early in the afternoon, Demetrius accompanied him to edge of the disreputable field that was called Golgotha. They were quiet as they approached it. Acrid smoke curled lazily from winnows of charred refuse. In the distance a grass-covered knoll appeared as a green oasis in a desert.

"Do you remember the place, sir?" asked Demetrius, halting.

"Vaguely," murmured Marcellus. "I'm sure I couldn't have found it. Is it clear in your memory, Demetrius?"

"Quite so. I came late. I could see the crosses from here, and the crowd."

"What was I doing when you arrived?" asked Marcellus.

"You and the other officers were casting dice."

"For the Robe?"

"Yes, sir."

Neither spoke for a little while.

"I did not see the nailing, Demetrius," said Marcellus thickly. "Paulus pushed me away. I was glad enough to escape the sight. I walked to the other side of the knoll. It has been a bitter memory, I can tell you."

"Well, sir," said Demetrius, "here is the path. I shall wait you at the inn. I hope you will not be disappointed. But it seems unlikely that Simon Peter would try to keep his appointment."

"He will come, I think," predicted Marcellus. "Simon Peter is safer from arrest today than he was yesterday. Both the Insula and the Temple have tried to convince the public that the Christians have no legal or moral sanction for their beliefs. Having captured their leader, with the expectation of making a tragic example of him, they are now stunned by the discovery that their victim has walked out of prison. Neither Julian nor Herod will want to undertake an explanation of that event. They will decide that the less said or done now, in the case of the Big Fisherman, the better it will be for everybody concerned. I fully expect Simon Peter will meet me here—unless, in all the confusion, he has forgotten about it."

∎

Peter had not forgotten. Marcellus saw him coming, a long way off, marching militantly with head up and a swinging stride that betokened a confident mind. The man had leadership, reflected the admiring watcher.

As the Big Fisherman neared the grassy knoll, however, his p slowed and his shoulders slumped. He stopped and passed an unsteady hand over his massive forehead. Marcellus rose and advanced to meet him as he mounted the slight elevation with plodding feet. Peter extended his huge hand, but did not speak. They sat down on the grass near the deep pits where the crosses had stood, and for a long time they remained in silence.

At length, Peter roused from his painful meditation and stared at Marcellus with heavy eyes, which drifted back to the ground.

"I was not here that day," rumbled the deep, throaty voice. "I did not stand by him in the hour of his anguish." Peter drew a deep sigh.

Marcellus did not know what to say, or whether he was expected to say anything. The big Galilean sat ruefully studying the palms of his hands with a dejection so profound that any attempt to relieve it would have been an impertinence.

Now he regarded Marcellus with critical interest, as if noting him for the first time.

"Your Greek slave told me you were interested in the story of Jesus," he said, soberly. "And it has come to me that you were of friendly service, yesterday, when our brave Stephen was taken away. Benyosef thought he heard you profess the faith of a Christian. Is that true, Marcellus Gallio?"

"I am convinced, sir," said Marcellus, "that Jesus is divine. I believe that he is alive, and of great power. But I have much to learn about him."

"You have already gone far with your faith, my friend!" said Peter, warmly. "As a Roman, your manner of living has been quite remote from the way of life that Jesus taught. Doubtless you have done much evil, for which you should repent if you would know the fullness of his grace. But I could not ask you to repent until I had told you of the wrongs which I have done. Whatever sins you may have committed, they cannot compare to the disloyalty for which I have been forgiven. He was my dearest friend—and, on the day that he needed me, I swore that I had never known him."

Peter put his huge hands over his eyes and bowed his head. After a long moment he looked up.

"Now"—he said—"tell me how much you know about Jesus."

Marcellus did not immediately reply, and when he did so, his words were barely audible. He heard himself saying, as if someone else were speaking:

"I crucified him."

The sun was low when they rose to return to the city. In those two hours, Marcellus had heard the stirring details of a story that had come to him previously in fragments and on occasions when his mind was unprepared to appreciate them.

They had found a strange kinship in their remorse, but Peter—fired by his inspiring recollections of the Master-man—had declared it was the future that must concern them now. He had daring plans for his own activities. He was going to Caesarea—to Joppa—perhaps to Rome!

"And what will you do, Marcellus?" he asked, in a tone of challenge.

"I am going home, sir."

"To make your report to the Emperor?"

"Yes, sir."

Peter laid his big hand heavily on Marcellus' knee and earnestly studied his eyes.

"How much are you going to tell him—about Jesus?" he demanded.

"I am going to tell the Emperor that Jesus, whom we thought dead, is alive—and that he is here to establish a new kingdom."

"It will take courage to do that, my young brother! The Emperor will not like to hear that a new kingdom is coming. You may be punished for your boldness."

"Be that as it may," said Marcellus, "I shall have told him the truth."

"He will ask you how you know that Jesus lives. What will you say?"

"I shall tell him of the death of Stephanos—and the vision that he had. I am convinced that he saw Jesus!"

"Emperor Tiberius will want better proof than that."

Marcellus was silently thoughtful. It was true, as Peter had said, such testimony would have very little weight with anyone disinclined to believe. Tiberius would scoff at such evidence, as who would not? Senator Gallio would say, "You saw a dying man looking at Jesus. How do you know that is what he saw? Is this your best ground of belief that your Galilean is alive? You say he worked miracles: but you, personally, didn't see any."

"Come," said Peter, getting to his feet. "Let us go back to the city."

They strode along with very little to say, each immersed in his thoughts. Presently they were in the thick of city traffic. Peter had said he was going back to John Mark's house. Marcellus would return to the inn. Now they were passing the Temple. The sun was setting and the marble steps—throughout the day swarming with beggars—were almost deserted.

One pitiful cripple, his limbs twisted and shrunken, sat dejectedly on the lowest step, waggling his basin and hoarsely croaking for alms. Peter slowed to a stop. Marcellus had moved on, a little way, but drifted back when he observed that Peter and the beggar were talking.

"How long have you been this way, friend?" Peter was saying.

"Since my birth, sir," whined the beggar. "For God's sake—an alms!"

"I have no money," confessed Peter; then, impulsively, he went on—"but such as I have I give you!" Stretching out both hands to the bewildered cripple, he commanded, "In the name of Jesus—stand up—and walk!" Grasping his thin arms, he tugged the beggar to his feet—and he stood! Amazed—and with pathetic little whimpers—half-laughing, half-crying, he slipped his sandals along the pavement; short, uncertain, experimental steps—but he was walking. Now he was shouting!

A crowd began to gather. Men of the neighborhood who recognized the beggar were pushing in to ask excited questions. Peter took Marcellus by the arm and they moved on, walking, for some distance in silence. At length Marcellus found his voice, but it was shaky.

"Peter! How did you do that?"

"By the power of Jesus' spirit."

"But—the thing's impossible! The fellow was born crippled! He had never taken a step in his life!"

"Well—he will walk now," said Peter, solemnly.

"Tell me, Peter!" entreated Marcellus. "Did you know you had this power? Have you ever done anything like this before?"

"No—not like this," said Peter. "I am more and more conscious of his presence. He dwells in me. This power—it is not mine, Marcellus. It is his spirit."

"Perhaps he will not appear again—except in men's hearts," said Marcellus.

"Yes!" declared Peter. "He will dwell in men's hearts—and give them the power of his spirit. But—that is not all! *He will come again!*"

The Bread of Heaven

Dorothy Sayers

From The Man Born to Be King

Dorothy Sayers (1893-1957) achieved great popularity with her Lord Peter Whimsey mysteries earlier in this century, but she also wrote many important religious works. One was a cycle of plays known collectively as The Man Who Was Born to Be King. *They were broadcast on radio during World War II, and they offered a vision of faith and hope to millions of listeners. Her introduction to the plays states that Christianity has historical roots and is not just some abstract philosophy that deals in symbol and allegory. Jesus was born, did perform miracles, was crucified, and did rise from the dead. In this scene from the play,* The Bread of Heaven, *the disciples have been commanded by Jesus to travel the countryside and preach the Word. The young, naive Philip is accompanied by the older, more experienced Judas to a house in Galilee where they meet with a man named Baruch. Secretly, he is a member of the Zealots—a group of Jews dedicated to overthrowing Roman rule by violent means. Philip relates the story of a miraculous healing he performed with the help of Jesus' power, but Baruch is more interested in discovering from Judas if he can exploit that power for revolutionary ends. This scene is important not only because it sets the stage for Judas' eventual betrayal of his Master, but because it shows another dimension of his character.*

Scene I (Galilee)

THE EVANGELIST: Then Jesus called his twelve apostles together and gave them power to cast out devils and to cure diseases. And he sent them out, two by two, to preach the Kingdom of God and to heal the sick. And he said unto them:—

THE VOICE OF JESUS: Take nothing with you for your journey—no money, no food, no extra clothing—just a stick to help you along, that's all. When you come to a town or village, ask for hospitality from some decent man, and stay in his house till you leave the place. Don't gad about accepting invitations from all and sundry. If people won't take you in or listen to your teaching, shake off the dust of the place from y feet and leave it to God's judgment. And don't be afraid of anybody—God, who looks after the sparrows, will look after you. Remember, you won't be on your own: whoever receives you, receives me; and whoever receives me, receives God, who sent me.

THE EVANGELIST: And they departed, and went through the towns, preaching the gospel and healing everywhere.

BARUCH: Well, Judas, that is a wonderful story. Most interesting and impressive. You talk as well as you preach. Wife! our guest has nothing to drink.

JUDAS: No more, kind hostess, thank you.

BARUCH: One cup only. You must need it after your day's work, Philip?

PHILIP: What? I beg your pardon.

JUDAS: Philip's half asleep.

PHILIP: No, I'm quite awake.

BARUCH: He hasn't said a word all evening.

WIFE: Poor boy, he looks tired to death. A bowl of warm milk, that's what he wants, and then off to bed.

PHILIP: Thank you. I should like some milk.

WIFE: Of course you would. Here you are—drink it up like a good lad. . . . Are you sure you're feeling all right?

PHILIP: (*rousing himself*): Yes, indeed. I'm perfectly well. Please don't bother about me.

JUDAS: Philip has had rather an exciting day. He has performed his first work of healing. They brought us a poor woman, possessed with a spirit of madness—

BARUCH: You know her, my dear. Poor crazy Esther.

WIFE: Crazy Esther! And you cured her? But how marvelous! I wish I had seen that! I thought she was quite incurable.

RUCH: So did everybody.

WIFE: How did you do it? A young lad like you.

PHILIP: I don't know. I mean, I didn't do it. Jesus our Master did it.

JUDAS: Philip was only God's instrument—as we all are.

PHILIP: I suppose it was God. I know it was Jesus.

WIFE: But do tell me about it.

PHILIP: The parents brought the poor creature along and said, would we please cure her?—just like that. She looked awfully mad and miserable, and I was dreadfully sorry for them, but I hadn't an idea what to do. . . . Of course, Jesus had given us authority to heal people—but some-how I'd never thought of me doing it. I'd sort of imagined Judas doing it, and me looking on. I did try to catch your eye, Judas—but you were busy answering questions and didn't notice. . . . The parents stood and looked at me as if they expected something to happen, and I just felt an utter fool. Still, I thought I must do something—so l said a bit of a prayer and laid my hands on the woman. The minute I touched her, she went off into a kind of fit and started to struggle and shout—so I grabbed her by the shoulders. Whew!

JUDAS: Those maniacs have the strength of ten men.

BARUCH: Hers was a very powerful devil.

PHILIP: I'm pretty hefty, but it was all I could do to hold on to her. "I'm no good at this," I thought—and then it passed through my head, "Not in my own power," and I called out, "In the name of Jesus Messiah!" And all at once—you'll never believe it—

WIFE: Yes, yes—go on.

PHILIP: I felt hands close over my hands. Pressing them down. Like iron. I never dreamed that hands could be so strong. They held me, and they held the woman. I felt her shoulder bones under my fingers. . . . And then I realized that the hands were my hands. I was exerting that tremendous grip. The poor girl yelled and writhed and bit me—and I suddenly heard myself speaking, loud and quick, like somebody giving an order. . . . but it wasn't my voice at all, and I don't even know what I said.

JUDAS: You said, "Devil, be quiet and come out of her!" . . . You startled me. You spoke so like the Master.

PHILIP: It wasn't my voice. It was his.

JUDAS: When Philip spoke, the woman stopped struggling. She stood quite still and began to cry. Then she suddenly seemed to realize that there was a crowd of people staring at her. She said, "Oh, Mother, what's happened? Please take me away." She was quite gentle, and as sane as you or I.

WIFE: Well I never! Fancy that! How amazing! . . . You must have felt proud of yourself.

PHILIP: I felt absolutely done. My knees shook and the sweat poured off me, and every bone in me ached like fury. As if all my inside had been sucked out of me. . . . Judas was marvelous. He got between me and the crowd and preached a splendid sermon, while I sat on the ground and sorted myself out. . . . Judas! when the Master heals people, do you think he feels like this?

JUDAS: He could scarcely heal twenty and thirty in a day if he did. His power is native to him.

PHILIP: But it costs him something, all the same. Remember that time at Tiberias? We were pushing through a terrific crowd when he stopped dead and asked, "Who touched me?" Simon—you know his funny, rough, familiar way—Simon said, "Come, Master. We're being squashed to death in this mob, and you want to know who touched you!" But he insisted: "Somebody caught hold of me." And it turned out that a poor sick creature had snatched at the hem of his garment and been healed. When we asked him how he knew, he said, "I felt power go out of me." I didn't know what he meant, but I know now all right. . . . Yes. . . . But it's not quite the same. He felt the power go. I felt it come and go. . . . I wish I knew what to make of it.

JUDAS: It will probably come easier to you next time.

PHILIP: Yes—I'll be expecting it. I'll just keep quiet and let it happen—so that it only has to come through and not to push through, if you see what I mean. I should think it was me being so frightened that made it difficult—shouldn't you?

JUDAS: Very likely. But look here, wouldn't it be a good idea to take things quietly now? You're getting all worked up.

BARUCH: You've had a terrific experience, and you mustn't exhaust yourself, or you won't be fit for anything tomorrow. It's taken a lot out of you, you know.

PHILIP: You mean, it's time I went to bed. Yes, I expect you're right. . . . I am awfully tired. . . . Good-night, everybody. . . . And thank you very much for asking us to stay and being so kind to us.

BARUCH: You are very welcome. Wife, show our guest to his room.

JUDAS: Good-night, Philip. I'll be up in half an hour—and I want to find you asleep!

PHILIP: (*calling back*): Good-night, Judas!

BARUCH: Well, Judas Iscariot. Now that your young miracle-worker has gone to bed.

JUDAS: You think the time has come for a little political discussion. I thought you were waiting for something like that.

BARUCH: You recognized me then? I wasn't sure.

JUDAS: Oh, yes. You are Baruch the Zealot. We last met twelve months ago, when John Baptist was baptizing at the Lower Ford. You wanted to know whether he was ready to preach revolution, and whether, if he did—

BARUCH: Whether, if he did, we could count on your enthusiasm. At that time you were zealous in the cause. I have been hoping to meet you again, and when I saw you and Philip this morning, I seemed to recognize the finger of God.

JUDAS: It's safe enough to recognize the finger of God in any event. It's harder to be sure which way it's pointing. I told you then, I couldn' answer for John Baptist's intentions.

BARUCH: John the Baptist is dead. This man Jesus seems to be a different proposition.

JUDAS: Very different.

BARUCH: Tell me frankly, what is he?

JUDAS: According to the people, the Messiah of Israel. According to himself, the Messiah of Israel.

BARUCH: And according to you?

JUDAS: According to me—the Messiah of Israel; if Israel knows her own salvation.

BARUCH: Very well. Let us agree that he is the Messiah of Israel. But what sort of man is Israel's Messiah? Politician, madman, inspired prophet, religious genius? How does one handle Jesus of Nazareth?

JUDAS: He is not the sort to be handled by anybody.

BARUCH: Tush, man! Everybody has a weak point somewhere. . . . Let's stop fencing with words and put the cards on the table. . . . The man has power, that's a certainty. But unless some one handles his business for him, he'll come to a worse end than John the Baptist. The Priests and Pharisees—Heaven confound their lick-spittle, time-serving hypocrisy—will break him like a straw if he does anything to make trouble with Rome. They're only waiting for the first little slip. One word of rebellion, one hint of a national movement, one demonstration against the Emperor, and crack! down comes the trap—Church and State join hands to put an end to Israel's Messiah. And then what becomes of your salvation?

JUDAS: There is no salvation for Israel, unless—

BARUCH: Unless! Unless! I've heard that word so often. No salvation unless—you know what I say to that.

JUDAS: Go on. Say it.

BARUCH: Unless—when the moment comes, there's a popular rising, well timed, with an organization and armed force behind it. That means *our* force and *our* organization. The party is ready, as you know. All we need is a figurehead, a leader, a spell-binder to fire the imagination of the masses and make them fall in to march behind the party. . . . Brains aren't enough. You've got to appeal to the emotions—stir these peasants out of their slave mentality and give 'em something to fight and die for.

JUDAS: To die for—yes. That's the right word, Baruch. . . . I once thought as you do, that Israel should ride the royal way to triumph. But now I think we were wrong. Since I have sat at the feet of Jesus, I know why John came preaching repentance. The way to salvation is through suffering and death.

BARUCH: But I agree with you there. The people must learn to dare and suffer. But Caesar preaches another kind of salvation—prosperity, security, the world-wide peace of Rome. "Order and safety"—that is their motto. A single benevolent despotism over the whole earth—and the Lion of Judah tamed and patient, munching his ration of government fodder like a fat ox in a stall. And so they dope the masses with propaganda, while we that have heart and spirit to fight are kept quarreling among ourselves—Pharisee against Sadducee, Galilean against Samaritan, House of David against House of Herod—till we are disarmed one by one and corrupted away from within. The rot has gone far, Judas, the rot has gone far.

JUDAS: So far that it is now too late to resist. Israel must pass through the fire, and judgment must burn away her iniquity. You talk of salvation—but all the time you are trying to escape it—like a sick man shrinking from the surgeon's knife. This is the meaning of the Gospel—that all must be endured, and the cup of humiliation drunk to the very dregs. Only when we are stripped naked—when we have reached the nether-most pit of desolation—then, only then, can the white flower of happiness, the blessedness of God's salvation, blossom out of the dust of our corruption.

BARUCH: That is a Gospel of good news indeed! Is this the doctrine of your Messiah?

JUDAS: You don't understand. . . . Nobody understands him. . . . On the day that he chose out twelve of us to be his close companions, he led u up into a mountain, away from all the people. He prayed there all nigh and in the morning he called us about him and spoke to us. . . . T

mists were not yet off the hill-tops; it was cool with a little breeze, and
so quiet. There was a spring bubbling out of the rock, and he sat beside
it, and the rising sun was on his face. If only I could make you see him.
If only you could hear his voice as we heard it then, speaking about happiness, and the blessed Kingdom of God. I hear it now. . . . it will be in
my ears till I die. . . .

THE VOICE OF JESUS: . . . Listen, and I will tell you who are the happy
people whom God has blessed.

Happy are the poor, for nothing stands between them and the
Kingdom. Happy are the sorrowful, for their souls are made strong
through suffering. Happy are the humble, for they receive the whole
world as a gift. Happy are they who long for holiness as a man longs for
food, for they shall enjoy God's plenty. Happy are the merciful, for they
are mercifully judged. Happy are they who establish peace, for they
share God's very nature. Happy are the single-hearted, for they see God.

And think yourselves happy when people hate and shun you, when
they insult and revile and persecute you for the Son of Man's sake.
When that happens to you, you may laugh and dance for joy. It is a sign
that you are right with God, for all true prophets are persecuted, and
God will be your reward.

But unhappy are the rich! They have had their share of good things
already and have nothing more to look for. Unhappy are the well-fed
and self-satisfied! There is an emptiness in their souls that nothing can
fill. Unhappy are the frivolous and mocking hearts! The time will come
when they will mourn and weep and not know where to turn for comfort. And think yourselves unhappy when you are popular and
applauded by all—for only false prophets are popular.

You are the salt of the world. But if salt grows insipid and loses its
sharpness nothing can bring back its savor. It is only fit for the rubbish-
heap.

You are the light of the world. Stand up then and shine, that men
may see your well-doing and give glory to your Father in Heaven. . . .

JUDAS: . . . So he laid our burden upon us—sorrow and humility and
torment and shame, and poverty and peace of heart. God's salvation.
And we were filled with a strange happiness. Then he blessed us. And

we bathed our faces in the running stream and so came down from the mountain.

BARUCH: You make me feel as though I had been there. . . . Well, if I ever doubted the man's power, I doubt it no longer. He has done something to you that I wouldn't have believed possible. . . . I only hope, for your sake, that Jesus will give heed to his own sermons.

JUDAS: What do you mean?

BARUCH: "Only false prophets are popular." . . . If there's a popular man in Judaea today, I should say it was Jesus of Nazareth. It needs very great integrity to stand being made the idol of the people.

JUDAS: I have no fear of him. He is incorruptible.

BARUCH: So you think. And so he thinks, no doubt. But we have seen many prophets of late. They start well—then they get a following, success goes to their heads, and before you know where you are the man who was too unworldly even to earn his own living is accepting presents from rich old ladies, setting up fashionable religious cults, and creeping up the back stairs into politics.

JUDAS: You don't know Jesus.

BARUCH: He is a man. Every man has his pride—or his pet vanity. Just now it's all holy poverty and the world well lost—but on the day you see Jesus Carpenter ride into Jerusalem with palms waving and the people yelling Hosanna—remember, I told you so.

JUDAS: (*passionately*): If I thought you were right, I would kill him with my hands while he was still uncorrupted.

BARUCH: Nonsense, nonsense! These madmen of genius are made for us to use. Let him have the hosannas—but let's see to it that there's an army to march in while the going's good. Otherwise—one more opportunity for Caesar to clap down the extinguisher on what's left of Jewish liberty.

JUDAS: That is not the right way. I tell you I'll have nothing to do with

BARUCH: There's no hurry. Think it over. Sleep on it. . . . Ah, here'. wife. My dear, you are just in time to bid good-night to Judas.

WIFE: Good-night. May God's angels watch over you. Go quietly, I think your friend is asleep.

JUDAS: Good-night. Baruch, good-night. I shall not change my mind.

BARUCH: Good-night.

(*Door shut*) Well—what do you think of that pair?

WIFE: The boy is charming.

BARUCH: An honest simpleton. And Judas?

WIFE: I think he is jealous of his friend without knowing it.

BARUCH: I shouldn't wonder. Judas is a clever fool. I know where to have him, if we want to get rid of Jesus.

WIFE: Baruch—must Jesus be got rid of? Such power as his must surely be of God.

BARUCH: So is the power of fire. But it has to be harnessed. This Jesus might set the world ablaze. What a tool, what a tool he would be in the right hands! A hammer against Caiaphas—a sword in the heart of Caesar. If only we could get hold of him. . . . But I have a horrible feeling

WIFE: Yes?

BARUCH: That he may be incorruptible after all.

⮞ CHRISTMAS ⮜

The Greatest Gift
Philip Van Doren Stern

Who has not seen and enjoyed director Frank Capra's It's a Wonderful Life? *Here, you have the chance to read the original story by Philip Van Doren Stern (1900-1984) on which the Hollywood film is based. George Pratt is the main character who, with the help of his guardian angel, learns that one man's life does indeed make a difference.*

The little town straggling up the hill was bright with colored Christmas lights. But George Pratt did not see them. He was leaning over the railing of the iron bridge, staring down moodily at the black water. The current eddied and swirled like liquid glass, and occasionally a bit of ice, detached from the shore, would go gliding downstream to be swallowed up in the shadows under the bridge.

The water looked paralyzingly cold. George wondered how long a man could stay alive in it. The glassy blackness had a strange, hypnotic effect on him. He leaned still farther over the railing. . . .

"I wouldn't do that if I were you," a quiet voice beside him said.

George turned resentfully to a little man he had never seen before. He was stout, well past middle age, and his round cheeks were pink in the winter air as though they had just been shaved.

"Wouldn't do what?" George asked sullenly.

"What you were thinking of doing."

"How do you know what I was thinking?"

"Oh, we make it our business to know a lot of things," the stranger said easily.

George wondered what the man's business was. He was a most unremarkable little person, the sort you would pass in a crowd and never notice. Unless you saw his bright blue eyes, that is. You couldn't forget them, for they were the kindest, sharpest eyes you ever saw. Nothing else about him was noteworthy. He wore a moth-eaten old fur cap and a shabby overcoat that was stretched tightly across his paunchy belly. He was carrying a small black satchel. It wasn't a doctor's bag—it was too large for that and not the right shape. It was a salesman's sample kit, George decided distastefully. The fellow was probably some sort of peddler, the kind who would go around poking his sharp little nose into other people's affairs.

"Looks like snow, doesn't it?" the stranger said, glancing up appraisingly at the overcast sky. "It'll be nice to have a white Christmas. They're getting scarce these days—but so are a lot of things." He turned to face George squarely. "You all right now?"

"Of course I'm all right. What made you think I wasn't? I—"

George fell silent before the stranger's quiet gaze.

The little man shook his head. "You know you shouldn't think of such things—and on Christmas Eve of all times! You've got to consider Mary—and your mother too."

George opened his mouth to ask how this stranger could know his wife's name, but the fellow anticipated him. "Don't ask me how I know such things. It's my business to know 'em. That's why I came along this way tonight. Lucky I did too." He glanced down at the dark water and shuddered.

"Well, if you know so much about me," George said, "give me just one good reason why I should be alive."

The little man made a queer chuckling sound. "Come, come, it can't be that bad. You've got your job at the bank. And Mary and the kids. You're healthy, young, and—"

"And sick of everything!" George cried. "I'm stuck here in this mudhole for life, doing the same dull work day after day. Other men are leading exciting lives, but I—well, I'm just a small-town bank clerk that even the Army didn't want. I never did anything really useful or interesting, and it looks as if I never will. I might just as well be dead. I might better be dead. Sometimes I wish I were. In fact, I wish I'd never been born!"

The little man stood looking at him in the growing darkness.

"What was that you said?" he asked softly.

"I said I wish I'd never been born," George repeated firmly. "And I mean it too."

The stranger's pink cheeks glowed with excitement. "Why that's wonderful! You've solved everything. I was afraid you were going to give me some trouble. But now you've got the solution yourself. You wish you'd never been born. All right! Okay! You haven't!"

"What do you mean?" George growled.

"You haven't been born. Just that. You haven't been born. No one here knows you. You have no responsibilities—no job—no wife—no children. Why, you haven't even a mother. You couldn't have, of course. All your troubles are over. Your wish, I am happy to say, has been granted—officially."

"Nuts!" George snorted and turned away.

The stranger ran after him and caught him by the arm.

"You'd better take this with you," he said, holding out his satchel. "It'll open a lot of doors that might otherwise be slammed in your face."

"What doors in whose face?" George scoffed. "I know everybody in this town. And besides, I'd like to see anybody slam a door in my face."

"Yes, I know," the little man said patiently. "But take this anyway. It can't do any harm and it may help." He opened the satchel and displayed a number of brushes. "You'd be surprised how useful these brushes can be as introduction—especially the free ones. These, I mean." He hauled out a plain little hand-brush. "I'll show you how to use it." He thrust the satchel into George's reluctant hands and began: "When the lady of the house comes to the door you give her this and then talk fast. You say: "Good evening, Madam. I'm from the World Cleaning Company, and I want to present you with this handsome and useful brush absolutely free—no obligation to purchase anything at all.' After that, of course, it's a cinch. Now you try it." He forced the brush into George's hand.

George promptly dropped the brush into the satchel and fumbled with the catch, finally closing it with an angry snap. "Here," he said, and then stopped abruptly, for there was no one in sight.

The little stranger must have slipped away into the bushes growing along the river bank, George thought. He certainly wasn't going to play hide-and-seek with him. It was nearly dark and getting colder every minute. He shivered and turned up his coat collar.

The street lights had been turned on, and Christmas candles in the windows glowed softly. The little town looked remarkably cheerful. After all, the place you grew up in was the one spot on earth where you could really feel at home. George felt a sudden burst of affection even for crotchety old Hank Biddle whose house he was passing. He remembered the quarrel he had had when his car had scraped a piece of bark out of Hank's big maple tree. George looked up at the vast spread of leafless branches towering over him in the darkness. The tree must have been growing there since Indian times. He felt a sudden twinge of guilt for the damage he had done. He had never stopped to inspect the wound, for he was ordinarily afraid to have Hank catch him even looking at the tree. Now he stepped out boldly into the roadway to examine the huge trunk.

Hank must have repaired the scar or painted it over, for there was no sign of it. George struck a match and bent down to look more closely. He straightened up with an odd, sinking feeling in his stomach. There wasn't any scar. The bark was smooth and undamaged.

He remembered what the little man at the bridge had said.

It was all nonsense, of course, but the nonexistent scar bothered him.

When he reached the bank, he saw that something was wrong. The building was dark, and he knew he had turned the vault light on. He noticed, too, that someone had left the window shades up. He ran around to the front. There was a battered old sign fastened on the door. George could just make out the words:

FOR RENT OR SALE
Apply JAMES SILVA, Real Estate

Perhaps it was some boys' trick, he thought wildly. Then he saw a pile of ancient leaves and tattered newspapers in the bank's ordinarily immaculate doorway. And the windows looked as though they hadn't been washed in years. A light was still burning across the street in Jim Silva's office. George dashed over and tore the door open.

Jim looked up from his ledgerbook in surprise. "What can I do for you, young man?" he said in the polite voice he reserved for potential customers.

"The bank," George said breathlessly. "What's the matter with it?"

"The old bank building?" Jim Silva turned around and looked out of the window. "Nothing that I can see. Wouldn't like to rent or buy it, would you?"

"You mean—it's out of business?"

"For a good ten years. Went bust. Stranger 'round these parts, ain't you?"

George sagged against the wall. "I was here some time ago," he said weakly. "The bank was all right then. I even knew some of the people who worked there."

"Didn't know a feller named Marty Jenkins, did you?"

"Marty Jenkins. Why, he—" George was about to say that Marty had never worked at the bank—couldn't have, in fact, for when they had both left school they had applied for a job there and George had gotten it. But now, of course, things were different. He would have to be careful. "No, I didn't know him," he said slowly. "Not really, that is. I'd heard of him."

"Then maybe you heard how he skipped out with fifty thousand dollars. That's why the bank went broke. Pretty near ruined everybody around here." Silva was looking at him sharply. "I was hoping for a minute maybe you'd know where he is. I lost plenty in that crash myself. We'd like to get our hands on Marty Jenkins."

"Didn't he have a brother? Seems to me he had a brother named Arthur."

"Art? Oh, sure. But he's all right. He don't know where his brother went. It's had a terrible effect on him, too. Took to drink, he did. It's too bad—and hard on his wife. He married a nice girl."

George felt the sinking feeling in his stomach again. "Who did he marry?" he demanded hoarsely. Both he and Art had courted Mary.

"Girl named Mary Thatcher," Silva said cheerfully. "She lives up on the hill just this side of the church—Hey! Where are you going?"

But George had bolted out of the office. He ran past the empty bank building and turned up the hill. For a moment he thought of going straight to Mary. The house next to the church had been given them by her father as a wedding present. Naturally Art Jenkins would have gotten it if he had married Mary. George wondered whether they had children. Then he knew he couldn't face Mary—not yet anyway. He decided to visit his parents and find out more about her.

There were candles burning in the windows of the little weatherbeaten house on the side street, and a Christmas wreath was hung on the glass panel of the front door. George raised the gate latch click. A dark shape on the porch jumped up and began to growl. Then it hurled itself down the steps, barking ferociously.

"Brownie!" George shouted. "Brownie, you old fool, stop that! Don't you know me?" But the dog advanced menacingly and drove him back behind the gate. The porch light snapped on, and George's father stepped outside to call the dog off. The barking subsided to a low, angry growl.

His father held the dog by the collar while George cautiously walked past. He could see that his father did not know him. "Is the lady of the house in?" he asked.

His father waved toward the door. "Go on in," he said cordially. "I'll chain this dog up. She can be mean with strangers."

His mother, who was waiting in the hallway, obviously did not recognize him. George opened his sample kit and grabbed the first brush that came to hand. "Good evening, ma'am," he said politely. "I'm from the World Cleaning Company. We're giving out a free sample brush. I thought you might like to have one. No obligation. No obligation at all. . . ." His voice faltered.

His mother smiled at his awkwardness. "I suppose you'll want to sell me something. I'm not really sure I need any brushes."

"No ma'am. I'm not selling anything," he assured her. "The regular salesman will be around in a few days. This is just—well, just a Christmas present from the company."

"How nice," she said. "You people never gave away such good brushes before."

"This is a special offer," he said. His father entered the hall and closed the door.

"Won't you come in for a while and sit down?" his mother said. "You must be tired walking so much."

"Thank you, ma'am. I don't mind if I do." He entered the little parlor and put his bag down on the floor. The room looked different somehow, although he could not figure out why.

"I used to know this town pretty well," he said to make conversa-

"Knew some of the townspeople. I remember a girl named Mary er. She married Art Jenkins, I heard. You must know them."

ourse," his mother said. "We know Mary well."

hildren?" he asked casually.

"Two—a boy and a girl."

George sighed audibly.

"My, you must be tired," his mother said. "Perhaps I can get you a cup of tea."

"No ma'am, don't bother," he said. "I'll be having supper soon." He looked around the little parlor, trying to find out why it looked different. Over the mantelpiece hung a framed photograph which had been taken on his kid brother Harry's sixteenth birthday. He remembered how they had gone to Potter's studio to be photographed together. There was something queer about the picture. It showed only one figure—Harry's.

"That your son?" he asked.

His mother's face clouded. She nodded but said nothing.

"I think I met him, too," George said hesitantly. "His name's Harry, isn't it?"

His mother turned away, making a strange choking noise in her throat. Her husband put his arm clumsily around her shoulder. His voice, which was always mild and gentle, suddenly became harsh. "You couldn't have met him," he said. "He's been dead a long while. He was drowned the day that picture was taken."

George's mind flew back to the long ago August afternoon when he and Harry had visited Potter's studio. On their way home they had gone swimming. Harry had been seized with a cramp, he remembered. He had pulled him out of the water and had thought nothing of it. But suppose he hadn't been there!

"I'm sorry," he said miserably. "I guess I'd better go. I hope you like the brush. And I wish you both a very Merry Christmas." There, he had put his foot in it again, wishing them a Merry Christmas when they were thinking about their dead son.

Brownie tugged fiercely at her chain as George went down the porch steps and accompanied his departure with a hostile, rolling growl.

He wanted desperately now to see Mary. He wasn't sure he could stand not being recognized by her, but he had to see her.

The lights were on in the church, and the choir was making last minute preparations for Christmas vespers. The organ had been practicing "Holy Night" evening after evening until George had become thoroughly sick of it. But now the music almost tore his heart out.

He stumbled blindly up the path to his own house. The lawn was untidy, and the flower bushes he had kept carefully trimmed were neglected and badly sprouted. Art Jenkins could hardly be expected to care for such things.

When he knocked at the door there was a long silence, followed by the shout of a child. Then Mary came to the door.

At the sight of her, George's voice almost failed him. "Merry Christmas, ma'am," he managed to say at last. His hand shook as he tried to open the satchel.

When George entered the living room, unhappy as he was, he could not help noticing with a secret grin that the too-high-priced blue sofa they often had quarreled over was there. Evidently Mary had gone through the same thing with Art Jenkins and had won the argument with him too.

George got his satchel open. One of the brushes had a bright blue handle and vari-colored bristles. It was obviously a brush not intended to be given away, but George didn't care. He handed it to Mary. "This would be fine for your sofa," he said.

"My, that's a pretty brush," she exclaimed. "You're giving it away free?"

He nodded solemnly. "Special introductory offer. It's one way for the company to keep excess profits down—share them with its friends."

She stroked the sofa gently with the brush, smoothing out the velvety nap. "It is a nice brush. Thank you. I—" There was a sudden scream from the kitchen, and two small children rushed in. A little, homely-faced girl flung herself into her mother's arms, sobbing loudly as a boy of seven came running after her, snapping a toy pistol at her head. "Mommy, she won't die," he yelled. "I shot her a hunert times, but she won't die."

He looks just like Art Jenkins, George thought. Acts like him too.

The boy suddenly turned his attention to him. "Who're you?" he demanded belligerently. He pointed his pistol at George and pulled the trigger. "You're dead!" he cried. "You're dead. Why don't you fall down and die?"

There was a heavy step on the porch. The boy looked frightened and backed away. George saw Mary glance apprehensively at the door.

Art Jenkins came in. He stood for a moment in the doorway, clinging to the knob for support. His eyes were glazed, and his face was very red. "Who's this?" he demanded thickly.

"He's a brush salesman," Mary tried to explain. "He gave me this brush."

"Brush salesman!" Art sneered. "Well, tell him to get outta here. We don't want no brushes." Art hiccoughed violently and lurched across the room to the sofa where he sat down suddenly. "An'we don't want no brush salesmen neither."

George looked despairingly at Mary. Her eyes were begging him to go. Art had lifted his feet up on the sofa and was sprawling out on it, muttering unkind things about brush salesmen. George went to the door, followed by Art's son who kept snapping his pistol at him and saying: "You're dead—dead—dead!"

Perhaps the boy was right, George thought when he reached the porch. Maybe he was dead, or maybe this was all a bad dream from which he might eventually awake. He wanted to find the little man on the bridge again and try to persuade him to cancel the whole deal.

He hurried down the hill and broke into a run when he neared the river. George was relieved to see the little stranger standing on the bridge. "I've had enough," he gasped. "Get me out of this—you got me into it."

The stranger raised his eyebrows. "I got you into it! I like that! You were granted your wish. You got everything you asked for. You're the freest man on earth now. You have no ties. You can go anywhere—do anything. What more can you possibly want?"

"Change me back," George pleaded. "Change me back—please. Not just for my sake but for others too. You don't know what a mess this town is in. You don't understand. I've got to get back. They need me here."

"I understand right enough," the stranger said slowly. "I just wanted to make sure you did. You had the greatest gift of all conferred upon you—the gift of life, of being a part of this world and taking a part in it. Yet you denied that gift." As the stranger spoke, the church bell high up on the hill sounded, calling the townspeople to Christmas vespers. Then the downtown church bell started ringing.

"I've got to get back," George said desperately. "You can't cut me off like this. Why, it's murder!"

"Suicide rather, wouldn't you say?" the stranger murmured. "You brought it on yourself. However, since it's Christmas Eve—well, anyway, close your eyes and keep listening to the bells." His voice sank lower. "Keep listening to the bells. . . . "

George did as he was told. He felt a cold, wet snowdrop touch his cheek—and then another and another. When he opened his eyes, the snow was falling fast, so fast that it obscured everything around him. The little stranger could not be seen, but then neither could anything else. The snow was so thick that George had to grope for the bridge railing.

As he started toward the village, he thought he heard someone saying: "Merry Christmas," but the bells were drowning out all rival sounds, so he could not be sure.

When he reached Hank Biddle's house he stopped and walked out into the roadway, peering down anxiously at the base of the big maple tree. The scar was there, thank Heaven! He touched the tree affectionately. He'd have to do something about the wound—get a tree surgeon or something. Anyway, he'd evidently been changed back. He was himself again. Maybe it was all a dream, or perhaps he had been hypnotized by the smooth-flowing black water. He had heard of such things.

At the corner of Main and Bridge streets he almost collided with a hurrying figure. It was Jim Silva, the real estate agent.

"Hello, George," Jim said cheerfully. "Late tonight, ain't you? I should think you'd want to be home early on Christmas Eve."

George drew a long breath. "I just wanted to see if the bank is all right. I've got to make sure the vault light is on."

"Sure it's on. I saw it as I went past."

"Let's look, huh?" George said, pulling at Silva's sleeve. He wanted the assurance of a witness. He dragged the surprised real estate dealer around to the front of the bank where the light was gleaming through the falling snow. "I told you it was on," Silva said with some irritation.

"I had to make sure," George mumbled. "Thanks—and Merry Christmas!" Then he was off like a streak, running up the hill.

He was in a hurry to get home, but not in such a hurry that he couldn't stop for a moment at his parents' house, where he wrestled with Brownie until the friendly old bulldog waggled all over with delight. He grasped his startled brother's hand and wrung it frantically, wishing him an almost hysterical Merry Christmas. Then he dashed across the parlor to examine a certain photograph. He kissed his mother, joked with his father, and was out of the house a few seconds later, stumbling and slipping on the newly fallen snow as he ran on up the hill.

The church was bright with light, and the choir and the organ were going full tilt. George flung the door to his home open and called out at the top of his voice: "Mary! Where are you? Mary! Kids!"

His wife came toward him, dressed for going to church, and making gestures to silence him. "I've just put the children to bed," she protested. "Now they'll—" But not another word could she get out of her mouth, for he smothered it with kisses, and then he dragged her up to the children's room, where he violated every tenet of parental behavior by madly embracing his son and his daughter and waking them up thoroughly.

It was not until Mary got him downstairs that he began to be coherent. "I thought I'd lost you. Oh, Mary, I thought I'd lost you!"

"What's the matter, darling?" she asked in bewilderment.

He pulled her down on the sofa and kissed her again. And then, just as he was about to tell her about his queer dream, his fingers came in contact with something lying on the seat of the sofa. His voice froze.

He did not even have to pick the thing up, for he knew what it was. And he knew that it would have a blue handle and vari-colored bristles.

EASTER

Maundy Thursday
Walter Wangerin, Jr.

Although American educator and writer Walt Wangerin, Jr. (1944—) pokes some fun at our tendency as children to take things too literally, his message in this Easter story is serious: We are never too old to appreciate the mysteries of the Christian faith. In particular, when we partake of the Lord's Supper, we should always be filled with a sense of child-like awe and wonder and recall Jesus' words, "Do this in remembrance of me."

How young I was at the period of my crisis, I do not remember. Young enough to crawl beneath the pews. Short enough to stand up on the seats of pews, when the congregation arose to sing hymns, and still be hidden. Old enough to hold womanhood in awe, but much too young to tease women. Old enough to want to see Jesus. Young enough to believe that the mortal eye could see Jesus.

I wanted to see Jesus. There was the core of my crisis. I mean, see him as eyewitnesses are able to see: his robe and the rope at his waist, his square, strong hands, the sandals on his feet, his tumble of wonderful hair, and the love in his eyes, deep love in his eyes—for me!

For it seemed to me in those days that everyone else in my church must be seeing him on a regular basis and that I alone was denied the sight of my Lord. They were a contented people, confident and unconcerned. I, on the other hand, I felt like a little Cain among the Christians, from whom the dear Lord Jesus chose to hide particularly. No one seemed to tremble in the Holy House of the Lord. But I. . . .

Well, the knowledge of my peculiar exile came all in a rush one Sunday, when the preacher was preaching a mumblin' monotone of a sermon. One sentence leaped from his mouth and seized me: "We were eyewitnesses," he said. Eyewitnesses. We! I sat straight up and tuned my ear. This seemed, suddenly, the special ability of a special people to which the preacher belonged: to be eyewitnesses. Who's this we? What did they see? I glanced at my mother beside me, whose expression was not one of astonishment. Evidently, eyewitnessing was familiar stuff to her. She was one of the we. I took a fast survey of the faces behind me. Sleepy-eyed, dull-eyed, thoughtful-eyed; but no one's eyes were dazzled. None widened in wonder at what the preacher said. So then, they all belonged to the we: eyewitnesses, every one of them! "We," the preacher was saying, "have seen the majesty of Jesus. . . ."

No!

I didn't say that out loud. But I thought it very loud.

No, but I haven't! This was a stinging realization. I haven't seen Jesus! My eyes were never witnesses!

All at once the stained-glass picture of a praying Jesus wasn't enough for me. The Jesuses in my Sunday-school books were merely pictures and a kind of mockery. I did not doubt that the Lord Jesus was actually there in his house somewhere—but where?

Even before the preacher was finished preaching, I dropped to the floor and peered through a forest of ankles, front and back and side to side—seeking Jesus perhaps on his hands and knees, a Jesus crawling away from me in a robe and a rope. But I saw nothing unusual and earned nothing for my effort except the disapproval of my mother, who hauled me up by my shoulder, but who probably wouldn't understand my panic since she was one of the we.

For the rest of that service I sought in the faces around me some anxiety to match my anxious heart. But everyone sang the hymns with a mindless ease. I searched my memory for some dim moment when I might have caught a glimpse of Jesus. There was none. No, he'd never appeared to me. But he must be here, for hadn't he appeared to these others? Then why would he hide from me? Did he hate me? And where, in this temple of the Lord, would he be hiding?

Thus, my crisis.

Sunday after Sunday I looked for Jesus. I ransacked the rooms of a very large church. I acquainted myself with kitchens and closets and boiler rooms—checking for half-eaten sandwiches, a vagrant sandal, signs of the skulking Lord.

One Sunday, exactly when the preacher stood chanting the liturgy at the altar, I experienced a minor revelation. It seemed to me that the bold bass voice of the chant was not the preacher's at all, whose speaking voice was rather nasal and whining. It seemed that someone else was singing instead. For the preacher faced away from us, and the altar was as long as a man is tall, and the wooden altar (ah-ha!) was built in the shape of a monstrous coffin. Therefore, the real singer was lying inside the altar. And who else would that secret singer be—but Jesus?

I kept a shrewd eye on the altar for the rest of the service, to be sure that he didn't escape. And after the service I took my heart in my hands and crept into the chancel, crept right up to the altar, certain that the Christ was still reclining therein, waiting in his tomb, as it were, till all the people departed.

Suddenly—Ah-ha!—I popped round to the back of the altar and peered inside its hollow cavity and saw . . . not Jesus. I saw a broken chair, a very old hymnal, and dust, dust, dust as thick as the centuries of human toil and misery.

For my restless soul there was no peace. I was not suffering a crisis of faith; never once did I doubt the truth or the presence of Jesus. Mine was a crisis of love—or perhaps of knowledge. Either the Lord had decided to avoid me particularly, or else I was stupid, the only one who did not know in which room the dear Lord Jesus abided. There must be one holier than all other rooms, one room so sacred and terrible that no one mentioned it, except in whispers and elders'meetings. Not the preacher's office. Dreadful as that room was, I'd already scouted it. Not the sacristy, nor the loft for the organ pipes, nor the choir room (which smelled of human sweat). A holiest of holies, a. . . .

All at once I knew which room! My heart leaped into my throat with joy and fear at once. It was a room whose door I passed ever with a tingling hush, whose mysterious interior I had never seen. Horrified by my own bravery, but desperate to see my Jesus, I determined to venture the door of that room, and to enter.

And so it came to pass that, during a particular worship service, during a very long sermon, I claimed the privilege of children and left my mother in the pew and crept down-stairs all by myself to The Forbidden Room, the only room left where Jesus could be hiding: The Women's Rest Room.

Oh, how hot my poor face burned at my own audacity, at the danger I was daring. If the holiest place of the temple in old Jerusalem might kill an unworthy priest, how would this room of taboos receive a little boy? I swallowed and panted and sweat. But I wanted to see Jesus. I lifted my hand and I knocked.

"Jesus? Are you in there?"

No answer. None.

So I screwed my little courage together, and I sucked a breath, and I pushed on the door, and it actually opened.

"Hello? Hello? Jesus—?"

I do not remember whether that was on a Maundy Thursday. It might well have been. It should have been.

With a deep, funereal gloom I returned to my mother. With a deathly sense of finalities I took the pew beside her. I was as woeful as any disciple who heard the Lord say, "I am leaving you, and where I go you cannot come." Abandoned!

Jesus does not abide in women's rest rooms. Mirrors are there, surrounded by lights and suffused by incense. But not Jesus.

Jesus was nowhere in this church for me.

I was a most sorrowful disciple. Lord? Is it I? Did I somehow betray you that you would leave me alone in the night?

With grim, remorseful eyes I watched the service proceed. Perhaps my senses were intensified by sorrow, for I saw things as I had not seen them before. Things moved slowly, burdened by unusual weight and meaning. The preacher—far, far in the front of the church, robed in black and white was lifting bread and mumbling. Then he was lifting an enormous cup and mumbling some more mysterious words I was likely never to understand: ". . . this cup is the New Testament in my blood. . . ."

Blood. That seemed a grave word altogether.

"Do this," he was murmuring, "in remembrance of me."

Then people began to arise and to file forward. There was the deep timbre of song all around me. People were devout. Incomprehensible things were happening.

Then my mother got up. In marvelous docility, she walked forward down the aisle, away from me. My mother is a strong woman. She could haul me from the ground in one hand. This humility, then, was strange, and I stood up on the pew to watch her.

Far in the front of the church my mother diminished, almost to the size of a child. And then, to my astonishment, she did childish things: She kneeled down. She bowed her head. She let the preacher feed her! This was my mother, who knew how to make me eat! Like a little baby, she let the preacher lower the cup to her lips and give her a drink. And then she stood, and they bowed to each other; and almost, as it were, upon a cushion of air my mother floated back to me.

Oh, this was a different woman. My mighty mother seemed infinitely soft.

And when she sat beside me and lowered her head to pray, I actually smelled the difference too. She had returned in a cloud of sweetness. I tasted this exquisite scent deep in my throat, and like a puppy found myself sniffing closer and closer to my mother's face—for the odor was arising from her nostrils, from her breathing, from within her.

Suddenly she looked up to see my face just inches from hers.

"What's the matter?" she whispered, and a whole bouquet of the odor overwhelmed me.

"Mama!" I breathed in wonder. "What's that?"

She wrinkled her forehead. "What's what?" she said with frankincense.

"That," I said. I wanted to tug at her mouth. "That smell. What do I smell?"

"What I drank."

"But what is it? What's inside you?"

She began to flip for a hymn in the hymnal. "Oh, Wally," she said casually, "that's Jesus. It's Jesus inside of me."

Jesus!

My mother then joined the congregation in singing a hymn with a hundred verses. But I kept standing on the pew beside her and grinning and grinning at her profile. Jesus! I put out my hand and rested it on my mother's shoulder. She glanced up, saw that my face was exploding with grins, gave me a pat and a smile, then went back to singing.

But Jesus! She told me where Jesus was at! Not far away from me at all. Closer to me than I ever thought possible. In my mama! He never had been hiding. I'd been looking wrong. My mighty mother was his holy temple all along.

So I shocked her by throwing my arms around her neck and hugging her with the gladness of any disciple who has seen the Lord alive again.

So she hauled my little self down to the pew beside her and commanded silliness to cease, but I didn't mind. A boy can grin as silently as the sky.

■

And so it was that two commands of our Lord, delivered on Maundy Thursday, the night before he died, were twined into one for me. "Do this," he said of his Holy Supper, "in remembrance of me"— and in so doing his death and his presence would be proclaimed to all the world. My mother did it; she ate and drank; and as her faith received her Savior truly, she bore the Lord in my direction, and I met him in her.

And the second command was this: "Love one another." My mama did that too. And so there were two disciples side by side on the same pew. And one of them was grinning.

Acknowledgments

For permission to use copyright material we are indebted to the authors, literary executors, and publishers listed below (in order of appearance of the first selection by the author). Every reasonable effort has been made to trace the owners of copyrights. Our apologies to any owners whose rights we may have unwittingly infringed.

Excerpt, "I Believe," from *In Midstream: My Later Life* by Helen Keller. Copyright 1929 by Helen Keller and Crowell Publishing Company. Reprinted by permission of Doubleday, a division of Bantam Doubleday Dell Publishing Group, Inc.

"New Clothes for Old" and "They Heard the Angels Sing," from *Bedtime Stories* by Arthur S. Maxwell. Copyright 1928, 1934, 1935, 1936, 1937, 1938, 1939, 1940, 1941, 1942, 1943, 1947, 1948, 1949, 1950, 1951, 1954, 1962, 1964, 1966, 1967, 1968 by Review and Herald Publishing Association. Reprinted by permission of the publisher.

Excerpt from *Christian Letters to a Post-Christian World* and "The Bread of Heaven" from *The Man Born to Be King* by Dorothy Sayers. Reprinted by permission of David Higham Associates, London.

"The Baptism of Christ" from *The Glorious Impossible* and "O Simplicitas" by Madeleine L'Engle.

"A Prayer for Fathers," from *Who Am I God?* by Marjorie Holmes. Copyright 1970, 1971 by Marjories Holmes Mighell. Reprinted by permission of Doubleday, a division of Bantam Doubleday Dell Publishing Group, Inc.

Excerpt, "What Life Have You?" from "Choruses from 'The Rock,'" *Collected Poems, 1909-1962*, by T.S. Eliot. Copyright 1936 by Harcou